Weight Training:
A Scientific Approach

Michael H. Stone, Ph. D.

Research Director
National Strength Research Center
Department of Health, Physical Education, and Recreation
Auburn University
Auburn, Alabama

Harold S. O'Bryant, Ph. D.

Director
Kinesiology/Biomechanics Research Laboratory
Department of Health Education, Physical Education,
and Leisure Studies
Appalachian State University
Boone, North Carolina

BURGESS INTERNATIONAL GROUP INC

Edina, MN 55435/Minneapolis, MN 55435/Santa Rosa, CA 95404

Copyright © 1987, 1984 by **Bellwether Press**
ISBN 0–8087–6942–1
Printed in the United States of America.

Bellwether Press
7110 Ohms Lane
Minneapolis, Minnesota 55435

J I H G F E D C B A

To Dr. Ronald Byrd, who taught us physiology, and that the study of science should be carried out creatively and with imagination. Most of all, we thank him for helping us to deal with adversity.

Table of Contents

Preface

This edition of *Weight Training: A Scientific Approach* represents the culmination of many years of study and research. We have attempted to take a unique approach to the subject of strength-power exercise and training. We have presented current research as well as empirical data. In many cases in which answers to key questions are unknown, we offer speculation about changes in performance, physiology, and cause and effect mechanisms. We believe this approach will stimulate additional research and observations, eventually resulting in a better understanding of these important questions.

This book will be revised and updated periodically. Every effort will be made to incorporate additional research and empirical data into the appropriate chapters. Each chapter in this book stands on its own and may be read as such.

In an effort to correlate this material with various levels of expertise, we have developed a chart which specifies a level (beginning, intermediate, or advanced) for the major sections of each chapter. These guidelines immediately follow Appendix H.

We consider ourselves sports scientists; we were trained as exercise physiologists/biomechanicians. In our opinion, the most important contribution a sports scientist can make is to provide the coach-athlete with assistance in implementing sound training programs. Therefore, the purpose of this book is to provide both theoretical and practical data and concepts that will assist the coach-athlete in developing appropriate training programs.

Acknowledgments

Although many people contributed to this book, we wish to acknowledge those who made special efforts toward completing this edition:

Chip Sigmon, David Meiberg, John Rumpf, Steve Lockhart, Elmer Duncan, Kevin Kaga, Nancy Burns, Priscilla Coleman, and Rick Miller for their lifting expertise and assistance in demonstrating various exercises.

Ralph Steben and Kim Goss, as well as *Strength Training for Beauty* magazine for their generous donation of photographs.

Mike Davis, Ben Green, and the weightlifters at Louisiana State University and Auburn University for their help in understanding various aspects of weightlifting competition and training.

Danny Blessing, Rick Carter, Vaughn Christian, Don Evitt, John Garhammer, Paula Green, Guy Hornsby, Bob Johnson, Cathy Johnson, Jeff Lander, Jim McMillan, Al Miller, Barret Murphy, Pat O'Shea, Kyle Pierce, Ralph Rozenek, Lynne Stoessel, Dennis Wilson, and Jim Wright for their original and on-going efforts concerning strength training and its effects on performance and physiology.

Our wives for their patience and understanding, and for not divorcing us.

Introduction

Considering the number of people who train at health spas, participate in college weight-training classes, use weight training in athletics, or buy and use home gym equipment, weight training may well be the most popular form of physical activity in the United States. One manufacturer of home gym equipment has sold more than a million bar bell sets each year for the past several years (13). The proliferation of weight training machines and other resistive training devices would have been unimaginable only a few years ago.

The current interest in the positive effects of weight training on health and performance is primarily the result of empirical evidence derived from the painstaking trial and error experimentation of pioneer weight trainers and from objective research (12, 14). The studies and observations of Delorme and coworkers (3, 4), McMorris and Elkins (10), and McQueen (9) were the first steps among the medical and scientific community toward an understanding of the benefits of weight training in rehabilitation as well as in strength and hypertrophy gains in general. Rather than muscle boundness, evidence strongly suggests that properly applied weight training can increase speed of movement and flexibility (1, 2, 12, 14, 16). Continued research has increased our understanding of how to most efficiently gain strength, power, and muscle hypertrophy (11, 12, 14, 17); and recent studies have pointed out the health benefits of weight training (7, 8, 18).

The National Strength and Conditioning Association (NSCA) was the first professional organization that made an effort to bridge the gap between scientist, the medical profession, and coaches and athletes. The *NSCA Journal,* a peer-reviewed publication, is an excellent source of information for the scientist and coach-athlete alike. Another recent development is the establishment of the National Strength Research Center (NSRC) in the Department of Physical Education at Auburn University. The NSRC is the only institute in the western world dedicated to strength research. These two organizations, along with other individuals and interested groups, are making significant contributions toward answering basic questions concerning strength training.

Some of the current interest in resistive training stems from the renewed realization of coaches, athletes, and sports scientists that strength-power training is beneficial for athletes. Because of our society's emphasis on looking good and because of increased concern for physical fitness, interest among nonathletes also has heightened.

The benefits of weight training can be substantial to athlete and nonathlete alike. This book presents information concerning the physiological and biomechanical adaptations accompanying resistive training, reasonable methods of improving athletic performance, and methods of resistance training that can lead to improved quality of life.

Weight training (or resistive training) is a general term that is often misused. It refers to a wide range of activities that may have different goals, but that use the same basic tool (weight training) to achieve those goals (Figure 1). (Resistive training includes the use of free weights, weight stacks on machines, hydraulics, elastic bands, etc. Technically, weight-training refers to the use of free weights, weight stacks, or body weight.)

Weight Training for Body Building—Body building is a form of competition in which the goal is to create an idealized physique. The training usually involves high repetitions and the use of exercises that isolate small muscle groups. Body builders have superior muscle hypertrophy and low body fat. They often display exceptional dedication; training for high-level competition requires 3-5 hours of exercise 5-6 days per week (Figures 2 and 3).

Weight Training for General Fitness—Weight training can be used to improve various aspects of physical fitness. With properly planned training programs, weight training can be superior to other physical training regimens in promoting positive enhancement of overall physical fitness (see Chapter 3). Furthermore, weight training can be successfully integrated

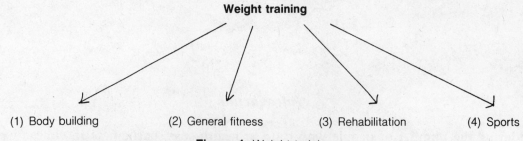

Figure 1. Weight training.

Figure 2. Bodybuilder Chip Sigmon, former Appalacian State University (ASU) student and currently ASU strength coach, pictured here after his second place finish in the 1981 Mid-America Competition.

Figure 3. At 5 ft. 10 in., bodybuilder Elaine Craig was the tallest woman in the 1984 NPC Nationals. Craig, who finished fourth, may represent a trend toward larger women doing well in bodybuilding while maintaining femininity. (Courtesy of *Strength Training for Beauty*.)

with other training modes, adding variety to training and creating a superior training program, that can be tailored to the individual.

Weight Training for Rehabilitation—Resistive training has long been used for rehabilitation from injury or surgery (3, 4, 9, 10, 14). The basic principles for the use of weight training in rehabilitation were evaluated by Delorme in 1945 (3). A variety of resistive training modes and methods are now available to assist in rehabilitation (see Chapter 3).

Weight Training for Sports—Enhancing the performance of athletes who participate in sports that require superior strength and power (weightlifting, shot putting, football, basketball, etc.) may be the most obvious benefit of weight training. As pointed out in Chapter 6, the volume, intensity, and exercise selection can be varied so that weight training can be adapted to, and result in positive performance enhancement for nearly every sport.

Although objective research has contributed to the understanding of the benefits of weight training for athletics, much of the basic knowledge of training for strength and power in athletics has resulted from the practical innovations of competitive weightlifters and powerlifters (14).

Weightlifting—Weightlifters must acquire great strength, power, agility, flexibility, and skill to successfully complete the two olympic style lifts, the snatch and the clean and jerk (See Chapter 10). The rules for weightlifting are presented in Appendix G. Besides exhibiting the physical attributes listed above, weightlifters may possess low body fat and high lean body weight as well as above average aerobic capacity (5, 15). High level weightlifters performing the olympic movements have been shown to produce the highest human power outputs ever recorded (6) (Figures 4 and 5).

Figure 4. Weightlifting, clean and jerk: Rolf Milser (82.5 kg class) performs a 200-kg (441-lb.) split jerk. (Photo by Bruce Klemens.)

Figure 5. Weightlifting, snatch: On her way to winning the 67.5 kg class at the 1985 Women's National Championships, Glenda Ford snatched this American record of 81.5 kg (179.7 lb.). A nationally ranked field athlete with best marks of 82.3 m (181+ ft.) and 23 m (50+ ft.) in the shotput, Ford's training program adheres to the principles outlined in this book. (Photo by Bruce Klemens.)

Powerlifting—Powerlifters must develop exceptional strength to compete in the squat, bench press, and deadlift. The three powerlifts are typical of the exercises used by many weight trainers and do not require as much skill as the olympic lifts. Powerlifting is one of the fastest growing sports in the world. The rules are presented in Appendix G (Figures 6 and 7).

As with weightlifters, powerlifters have high lean body weights, low body fat, and in general above average levels of physical fitness. Considering the attributes of these two groups of athletes, it is no wonder that many other sports have borrowed some of their training methods.

Summary

Weight training can be a superior method of attaining a variety of fitness and rehabilitation goals. The purpose of this book is to present the reader with reasonable information concerning weight training and its physiological and biomechanical effects.

References

1. Chui, E. F. 1964. Effects of isometric and dynamic weight-training exercises upon strength and speed of movement. *Research Quarterly* 35:246–257.

2. Clark, D. H., and F. M. Henry. 1961. Neuromotor specificity and increased speed from strength development. *Research Quarterly* 32:315–325.

3. DeLorme, T. L. 1945. Restoration of muscle power by heavy resistance exercise. *Journal of Bone and Joint Surgery* 27:645–667.

4. DeLorme, T. L., and A. L. Watkins. 1948. Techniques of progressive resistance exercise. *Archives of Physical Medicine* 29:263.

5. Fahey, T., L. Akka, and R. Rolph. 1975. Body composition and $\dot{V}O_2$ Max of exceptionally weight-trained athletes. *Journal of Applied Physiology* 39:559–561.

6. Garhammer, J. 1980. Power production by Olympic weightlifters. *Medicine and Science in Sports and Exercise* 12:54–60.

7. Johnson, C. C., M. H. Stone, A. Lopez-s, J. A. Hebert, et al. 1982. Diet and exercise in middle-aged men. *Journal of the American Dietetic Association* 81:695–701.

8. Kanakis, C., and R. C. Hickson. 1980. Left ventricular responses to a program of lower-limb strength training. *Chest* 78:618–621.

9. MacQueen, I. J. 1954. Recent advances in the technique of progressive resistance exercise. *British Medical Journal* 11:1193–1198.

10. McMorris, R. O., and E. C. Elkins. 1954. A study of production and evaluation of muscular hypertrophy. *Archives of Physical Medicine* 35:420–426.

11. O'Bryant, H. 1982. Periodization: A hypothetical training model for strength and power. Unpublished Doctoral Dissertation, Louisiana State University, Baton Rouge.

12. O'Shea, J. P. 1976. *Scientific Principles and Methods of Strength Fitness.* (2nd Edition). Reading, Massachusetts: Addison-Wesley.

13. Pilgrim, B. Executive Vice President, Diversified Products Corporation, Opelika, Alabama. Personal Communication.

14. Rasch, P. J. 1982. *Weight Training.* (4th Edition). Dubuque: Wm. C. Brown.

15. Saltin, B., and P. O. Astrand. 1967. Maximal oxygen uptake in athletes. *Journal of Applied Physiology* 23:353–358.

16. Smith, L. B., and J. D. Whitley. 1966. Influence of three different training programs on strength and speed of a limb movement. *Research Quarterly* 37:132–142.

Figure 6. Powerlifting: Doug Robertson (125 kg class), former Appalacian State University student, performing a 310-kg (688-lb.) squat in the 1983 North Carolina state meet.

Figure 7. Powerlifting: Gayle Hall, squatting 105 kg (231 lb.) on her way to placing first in the 1982 Women's California State Powerlifting Championships in the 52-kg class. (Photo by Dr. Alan Kirshner.)

17. Stone, M. H., H. O'Bryant, J. Garhammer, et al. 1982. A theoretical mode of strength training. *National Strength and Conditioning Association Journal* 4(4):36–39.

18. Stone, M. H., G. D. Wilson, D. Blessing, and R. Rozenek. (1983). Cardiovascular responses to short-term Olympic style weight-training in young men. *Canadian Journal of Applied Sports Sciences* 8:134–139.

Muscle Physiology

The interrelationships of nerve and muscle with their associated structures and function form the basis of the neuromuscular concepts presented in this chapter. Recent advances in technology have led to better instrumentation and therefore more accurate observation for the study of muscle tissue. As a result, much additional information about skeletal muscle has been obtained in the past 25 years.

Muscle Structure

A skeletal muscle consists of many thousands of single muscle cells. Unlike the typical sphere or cube-shaped cells of other tissues, a muscle cell is elongated and has many eccentrically located nuclei. The cell or *muscle fiber* is covered with a membrane called the *sarcolemma* which serves as both a covering and an insulator. Interspersed within the muscle fiber there are numerous organelles within the intercellular fluid or *sarcoplasm*. Most predominant are the *myofibrils* containing alternate protein myofilaments of *actin* and *myosin* that will be discussed in greater detail later in this chapter as related to contraction theory.

Organization of Tissues

Approximately 100 to 150 muscle fibers or cells are bound together with a connective tissue membrane, *perimysium,* to form a *fasciculus* (Figure 1–1). Several fascicles are bound together with more perimysium to form *bundles.* Located among the fascicles is an irregularly woven connective tissue called *endomysium.* Finally, many bundles are bound together with another connective tissue membrane called *epimysium* to form a whole muscle as a biceps brachii, gastrocnemius, trapezius, etc.

The intramuscular network of connective tissue is therefore present among the contractile components in the *belly* of the muscle and becomes continuous with the dense tendonous tissue at each end of the whole muscle. It is the *tendons* that attach to the outer covering of the bone, or *periosteum,* directly connecting muscles to the skeleton and thereby allowing transfer of skeletal muscle tension during contraction to exert force on the bone lever system. The tendons, having somewhat more tensile strength than muscles, provide a tough, elastic connecting structure between muscle and bone, permitting even a relatively small tendon to withstand the tension developed by a relatively large muscle. Generally, tendons located distally, or toward the end of a limb away from the body, are larger than tendons located close to the body. Such structures are by location alone more susceptible to injury (bruises, abrasions, etc.) (20, 58).

Nerve Supply

The central nervous system (CNS), or brain and spinal cord, is responsible for integration and modification of incoming stimuli, memory storage, generation of ideas, etc. However, the CNS

1

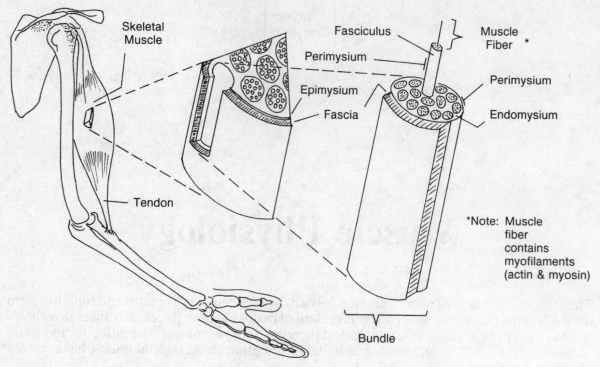

Figure 1–1. Organization of Skeletal Muscle Tissue.

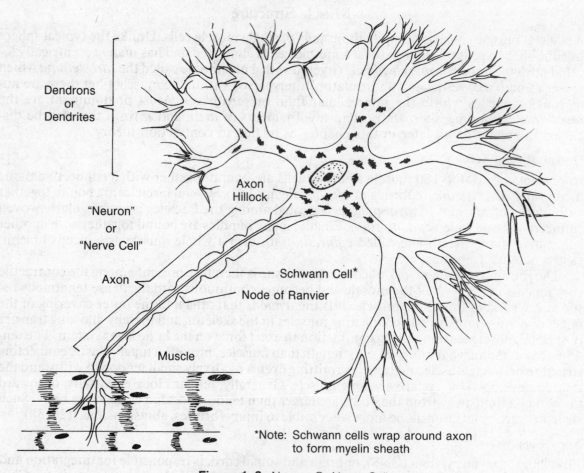

Figure 1–2. Neuron Or Nerve Cell.

initiates the electrical stimulation that ultimately results in the execution of a motor movement. This impulse is self-propagating along the length of the nerve cell or neuron that forms the basic anatomical structure of the nervous system (Figure 1–2). At rest, sodium ions (Na+), which are concentrated more heavily on the outside of the nerve membrane, cause it to be electropositive. At the same time, anions, which are located in higher concentration on the inside of the semi-permeable membrane, cause the inside of the nerve fiber to be electronegative (Figure 1–3). The *resting membrane potential* is therefore a result of the different electrical charges existing between the inside and outside of the nerve. The presence of a stimulus activates the release of *acetylcholine* (Ach) and causes the permeability of the membrane to change as the ions move to create a higher concentration of sodium (Na+) on the inside and potassium (K+) on the outside of the nerve fiber. This change in depolarization results in the generation of small bioelectrical currents called *action potentials,* which flow toward adjacent areas of the fiber and likewise along the entire length of the nerve. Such conduction of the stimulus can, in a myelinated nerve, reach speeds of 60 to 100 meters/sec (20). In this manner the *motor neurons,* via the *efferent pathway,* transmit the stimulus to initiate contraction at the site of the muscle. Muscle cells, like nerve cells, have the ability to propagate an action potential and therefore can transmit an impulse along its entire length.

Branches of the motor neuron attach by way of *myoneural junctions* and *motor endplates* (Figure 1–4) to each single muscle fiber (28). A single nerve fiber including all the muscle fibers it innervates is called a *motor unit.* Each motor unit is innervated by its own motor neuron (20), each with individualized mechanical properties and morphological characteristics (3, 8, 11, 39). The individual fibers of a motor unit may be spread over a large portion of the muscle (8). Repolarization occurs by potassium efflux. Resting membrane ion concentrations are re-established by the sodium-potassium pump after the nervous input abates (8).

Ultrastructure of Skeletal Muscle

An understanding of theoretical concepts regarding muscle contraction requires a knowledge of detailed microscopic structures within a single skeletal muscle fiber. As previously mentioned, the muscle cell is filled with sarcoplasm, chemical substances, and various organelles,

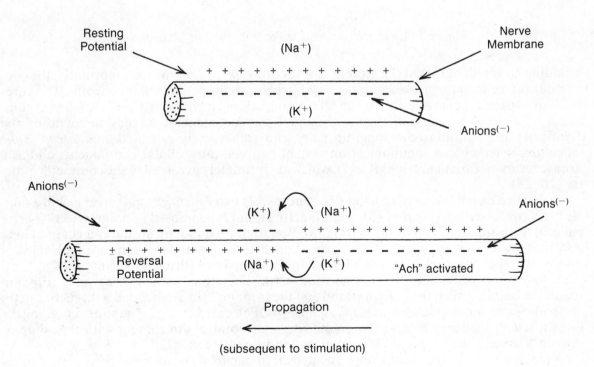

Figure 1–3. Propagation Of An Action Potential.

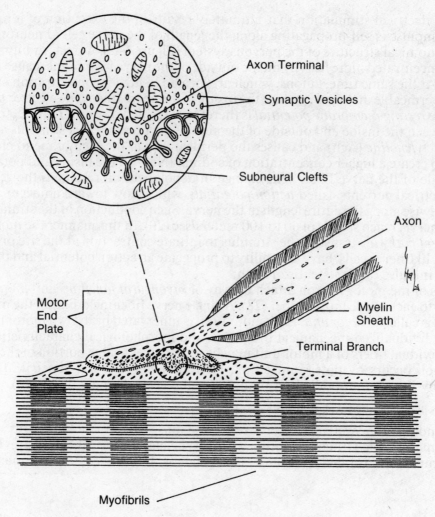

Axon Terminal

Synaptic Vesicles

Subneural Clefts

Axon

Myelin
Sheath

Terminal Branch

Motor
End
Plate

Myofibrils

Figure 1–4. Neuromuscular Junction With Related Components.

including hundreds of threadlike protein strands called *myofibrils.* Most importantly, the contractile unit, or *sarcomere,* makes up the basic structural components of the myofibril (Figures 1–5 and 1–6) and is characterized by an alternating arrangement of light and dark bands composed of *actin* and *myosin* filaments (Figure 1–7). A system of tubules surrounding the myofibrils and running both longitudinally and transversely is called the *sarcoplasmic reticulum,* it serves as a communication system between intracellular components and as a storage reservoir for calcium ions (Ca^{++}), which are intimately involved in the contractile process (20, 28).

A detailed examination of an actin filament reveals two *F-actin strands* arranged in a double helix configuration (Figure 1–8). Each F-actin strand is composed of polymerized *G-actin* molecules (thirteen per coil of the helix) (28). Bound to each F-actin strand is a chain of long thin protein molecules called *tropomyosin.* Attached to the tropomyosin are molecules of *troponin,* a tri-globed molecular complex having one portion with a high affinity for Ca^{++}, another for tropomyosin, and still another for F-actin. Therefore, in the resting state, troponin acts as the bond between the F-actin strand and the tropomyosin. Associated with each G-actin molecule is a molecule of *adenosine diphosphate* (ADP) located every 2.7 nanometers along the F-actin strand that may function as an *active site* or point of attachment with the adjacent myosin filaments when specific biochemical conditions are met (28).

Viewed with electron microscopy, the myosin filaments show up as thicker, darker structures in comparison to the actin, giving rise to the striated appearance of the alternating light

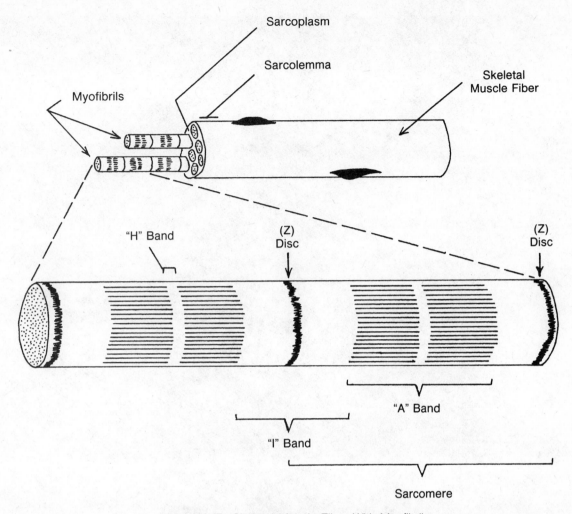

Figure 1–5. Skeletal Muscle Fiber With Myofibril.

and dark *I* and *A* bands within the myofibrils (Figures 2–5 and 2–6). A single myosin filament contains approximately 200 myosin molecules (28). Each myosin molecule consists of two peptide strands wound together to form a helix. This helix structure makes a densely woven *heavy meromyosin* portion and a less dense *light meromyosin* (Figure 1–9). Other associated structures appear as two flexible portions or "hinges" and a bi-globular "head" attached to the end of the heavy meromyosin. As the myosin molecules combine to form the myosin filament portions of the head, the heavy meromyosin protrudes to form the *cross-bridges* that lie in opposition to the adjacent actin filaments (Figure 1–10). There are 50 pairs of cross-bridges on each end of the myosin filament, each radially located so that 3 pairs occur per revolution and therefore are axially displaced 120 degrees between each cross-bridge pair (28).

Contraction Theory

Muscle contraction concepts are based largely on theoretical information deduced from tissue structures revealed through electron microscopy and the contractile characteristics of muscle dynamics. The *sliding filament* or *ratchet* theory of contraction is supported by considerable circumstantial evidence; it is discussed here in some detail as the most widely accepted explanation for skeletal muscle contraction (20, 28).

It has been postulated that the active sites on the actin filament at rest are inhibited, if not physically covered, by the troponin-tropomyosin complex. In this state the myosin cross-bridges cannot interact with these active sites. But one portion of the troponin molecule has a

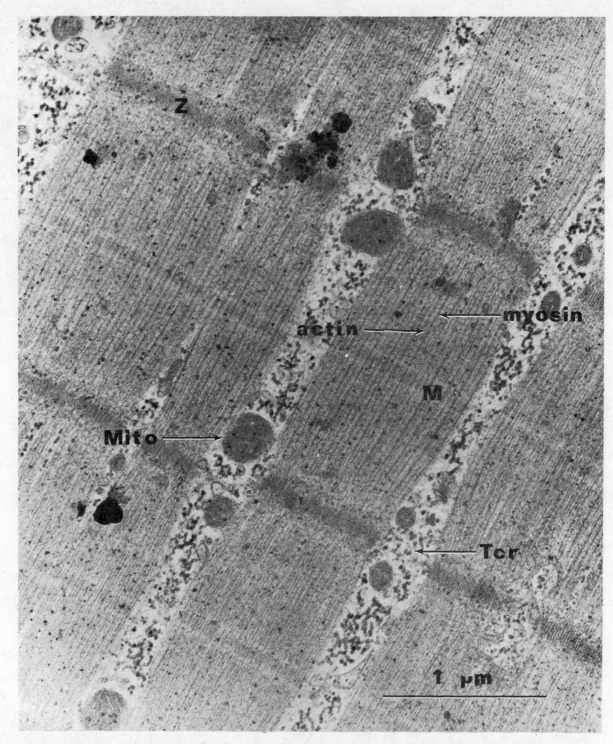

Figure 1–6. Electron Micrograph Of Longitudinally Sectioned Skeletal Muscle Tissue Showing Well Defined Actin and Myosin Filaments With (Z) Disc and Dense (M) Band Of The Myofibrils. The Mitochondria (Mito) Are Seen As Well As The Terminal Cisternae (Tcr)

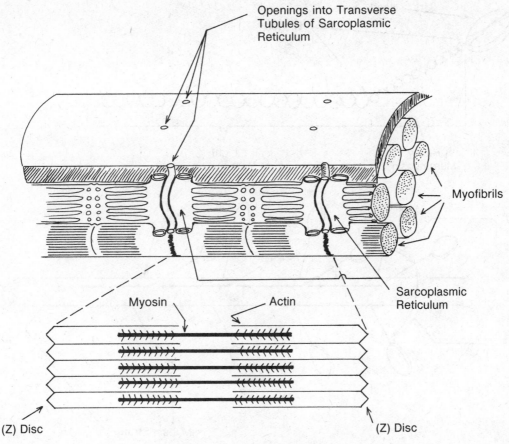

Figure 1–7. Sarcoplasmic Reticulum.

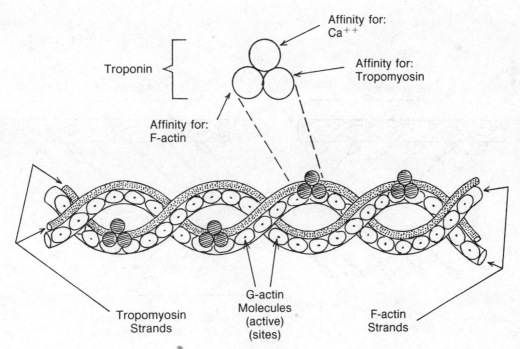

Figure 1–8. Actin Filament And Associated Structures.

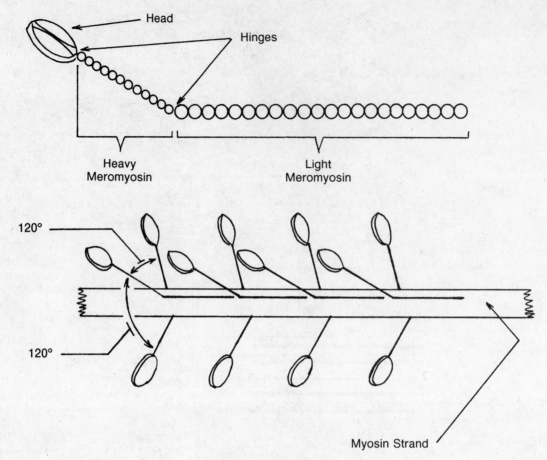

Figure 1-9. Myosin Filament.

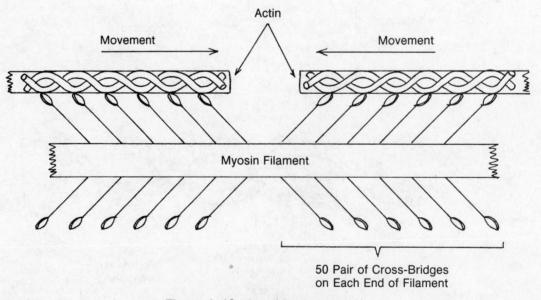

Figure 1-10. Actin-Myosin Interaction.

strong affinity for calcium ions (Ca^{++}), and during the presence of large amounts of Ca^{++} this inhibitory effect is itself inhibited. As a stimulus reaches the muscle fiber and the action potential travels over the cell membrane, large quantities of Ca^{++} are released by the sarcoplasmic reticulum into the sarcoplasm that surrounds the myofibrils. It is believed that the Ca^{++} binds with the troponin molecules, causing a confirmation change in the troponin-tropomyosin complex and subsequently exposing the active sites, therefore activating the attractive forces that permit binding between the filaments, and contraction begins (20, 28).

As contraction is initiated, it is thought that the heads of the myosin cross-bridges attach to the exposed active sites on the actin filaments and cause changes in the intramolecular forces in the head and arm of the cross-bridge. A *power stroke* occurs as these forces tilt the head toward the arm, pulling the actin filament inward (Figure 1–11). It is believed that this power stroke occurs independent of energy derived from *adenosine triphosphate* (ATP) (20, 28), although energy from ATP is thought to be necessary for this process to proceed further. A molecule of ATP binds with the cross-bridge head, causing detachment from the active site. Next, the ATP is cleaved by enzymatic action of the *ATPase* present in the heavy meromyosin. The energy released is thought to be sufficient to return the head back to the normal cocked position, once again ready for attachment to the next adjacent active site and subsequent power stroke action. These successive reactions occur to provide a continuous pulling of the actin filament. Contraction ceases as Ca^{++} is resegregated in the sarcoplasmic reticulum, and repolarization of the cell membrane occurs.

Several associated factors dealing with skeletal muscle contraction warrant further clarification:

1. Cross-bridges are thought to function independently of each other. Theoretically, the number of cross-bridges in contact with the actin filament at any given moment is directly proportional to the force generated during contraction (28).

2. Evidence indicates that large quantities of ATP are cleaved to form ADP during contraction. The amount of ATP cleaved is directly proportional to the amount of work performed by the muscle. This relationship is called the *Fenn effect* (28).

3. Greater amounts of myosin-ATPase activity cause cleaving of the ATP to proceed at a faster rate; this appears to be a primary factor contributing to the intrinsic quickness of muscle contraction (28).

4. An extensive sarcoplasmic reticulum may result in the faster transport and resegregation of Ca^{++} associated with faster contracting types of muscle tissue (28).

5. The quantity as well as the quality of skeletal muscle tissue greatly affects the force velocity relationships, as discussed in greater detail later in this chapter.

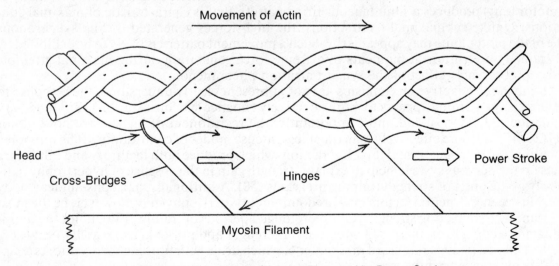

Figure 1–11. Pulling Of Actin Filament Via Power Stroke.

Dynamics of Contraction

All the muscle fibers innervated by one motor nerve are called a *motor unit* and, on the average, contain approximately 100 to 150 muscle fibers (20, 28).

In most muscles, approximately 98% of the fibers extend the entire length of the muscle with only one neuromuscular junction to each muscle fiber located near the middle of the fiber (20, 28). This allows the action potential to spread from the middle of the fiber to either end. The nature of motor unit innervation and subsequent depolarization spreading with each fiber is important because it facilitates coincident contraction (all components contracting together rather than separately) (28).

Strength Gradation

Motor unit selectivity provides us with the capability to vary the strength of muscle contraction to perform an infinite variety of movement patterns in a smooth, coordinated manner. Significance of force gradation is important for our everyday function as well as for any athletic endeavor.

When innervated by a stimulus of at least threshold level, a motor unit will contract maximally. Therefore, motor units follow the *all or none law.* Logically, the strength of a whole muscle can be near maximum when all of its motor units are stimulated (depending on pH, temperature, etc.). Conversely, a relatively weak contraction of the whole muscle will result when only a few motor units are stimulated. This manner of varying the number of motor units brought into play is called *recruitment.* Two variables associated with recruitment are the size of the individual muscle fibers and the number of muscle fibers in a single motor unit. Generally, a larger cross-sectional mass of contractile tissue will exhibit greater contractile force independent of the number of fibers (28). In addition, the number of fibers within a motor unit may vary from as many as 500 fibers to as few as 25 (20). Theoretically, if each fiber can produce 5 g of tension, the tension within a single motor unit can vary from .125 kg to 2.5 kg (Figure 1–12) (20). Force generated by a whole muscle is then a function of the **quantity** of active tissue brought into play at any one time (Figure 1–13).

Other factors affect the force generated by the whole muscle. One of these is the frequency of the stimuli to the various motor units. A single stimulus applied to a motor unit will evoke a single twitch response. If, however, a second stimulus is applied to this motor unit before it completely relaxes from the previous twitch, the tension developed by the motor unit will be greater than that generated by a single muscle twitch (20, 28). This manner of increased force production is called *summation.* At higher frequencies summation continues in the absence of any relaxation and is called *tetanus* (Figure 1–14) (20). Tetanus tension is about twice that of twitch tension in mammalian muscle.

Yet another intrinsic factor that helps determine the effective force generated by a whole muscle is the timing of the stimulus to the various motor units. The *synchronization* of many of the motor units produces a simultaneous firing pattern that is characteristic of maximal contractions. Unlike submaximal contractions, the high forces generated during synchronous firing of the motor units may appear jerky. Such a movement pattern is likely to be exhibited by well-trained powerlifters at moments of extreme force generation during maximal attempts and is an observable effect of the synchronization phenomenon.

Although the adaptive mechanisms are not at present clearly understood, the response to weight resistive training appears to more effectively enhance synchronization (28, 31, 45, 48), summation (33, 38, 59), and, most importantly, the recruitment of higher threshold motor units (29, 45, 59) more effectively than other less intense modes of conditioning. The previously mentioned *neural factors* and their interaction, which produce both facilitory and inhibitory effects on the nervous system, help to explain strength gain in the absence of hypertrophy, particularly at the onset of strength training programs (50). Additionally, at a constant lean body mass (muscle mass), neural factors may predominate. Hypertrophy may, however, be the most important factor affecting strength gain in prolonged periods of training (39), if not the dominant factor leading to an increased potential for strength and power gains overall (49, 51, 62, 63, 70). This last point is discussed in Chapter 6, which deals with training theory and its adaptation to resistance training.

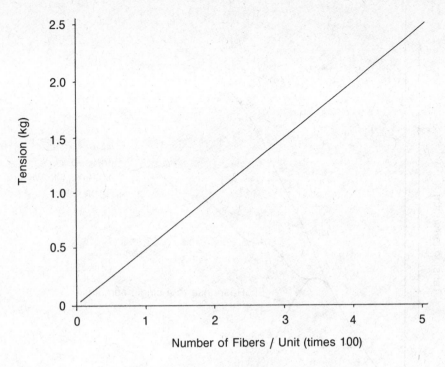

Figure 1–12. Strength of Single Motor Unit.

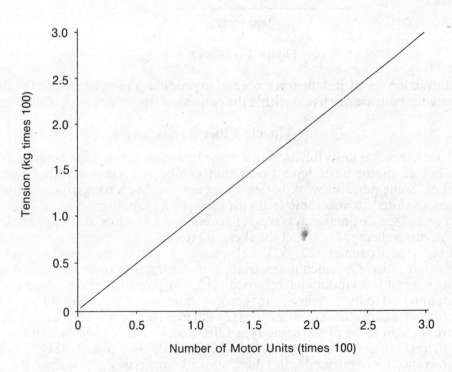

Figure 1–13. Strength Range Of Whole Muscle.

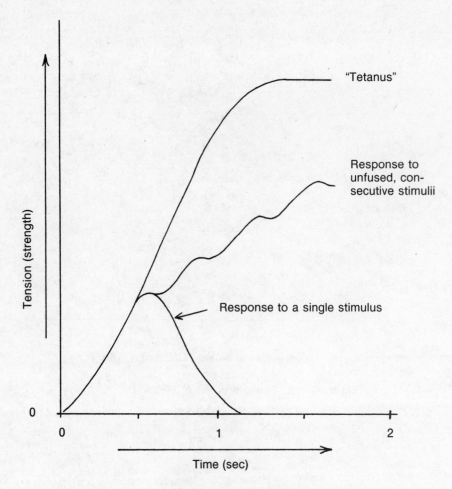

Figure 1–14. Summation.

Both contraction speed and the force needed to produce power, are related to the **quality** of contractile tissue; both are discussed within the context of fiber types in the following section.

Muscle Fiber Types

All skeletal muscle motor units function in a manner similar to what has been described previously. But not all motor units have fibers that exhibit the same metabolic or functional characteristics. Some perform work better under aerobic (with oxygen) conditions, whereas others are more suited to anaerobic (without oxygen) metabolism.

As early as 1678, a distinction was made between red and white skeletal muscle in animals (37). In 1873, researchers showed that the skeletal muscle of vertebrates as well as of man contain two fiber type extremes (27, 57). Subsequent experiments involving histochemical analyses of whole muscle revealed that variation in contraction time was linked with its contractile properties and metabolic characteristics (12, 18). Some time later, more direct study of single motor units led to the conclusion that motor units can be classified into types, each having muscle fibers that are quite homogeneous (3). All muscle fibers within any given motor unit are therefore thought to be of the same type (20). Specific fiber types are designated as *fast twitch glycolytic* (FG), *fast oxidative glycolytic* (FOG), and *slow oxidative* (SO). These terms describe their respective contractile and biochemical properties (3). Table 1–1 provides a summary of the respective characteristics of these three major muscle fiber types. Although it has been recognized that relative activity of oxidative versus glycolytic enzymes provides general indices of relative muscle unit contraction, speed, and fatigue resistance (8), the enzyme myosin-ATPase probably is the best index (2).

Table 1–1. Muscle fiber types and summary of respective characteristics.

Characteristic	Source	Fiber type		
		Fast twitch glycolytic (FG)	Fast oxidative glycolytic (FOG)	Slow Slow oxidative (SO)
Nomenclature:				
European	(8, 20, 25)	IIb	IIa	I
?	(8, 20, 25)	FF	FR	S
?	(8, 20, 25)	FT	—	ST
?	(8, 20, 25)	phasic	—	tonic
Structural:				
Mitochondria number	(13, 20, 43, 52, 71)	fewer	more	most
Mitochondria size	(13, 20, 43, 52, 71)	small	larger	largest
Cristae development	(13, 52)	less	—	most
Myofibril size	(35, 52)	small	small	large
Myofibril packing density	(35, 52)	small	small	large
Myofibril cross-sectional area	(35)	largest	small	smaller
Hypertrophy response (strength training)	(25, 52)	high	lower	lowest
Sarcoplasmic reticulum	(11, 13, 28, 52)	extensive	—	sparse
Anaerobic:				
Velocity of contraction	(20, 52)	highest	high	low
Force of contraction	(52)	highest	high	low
Velocity of relaxation	(20)	high	high	low
Myosin-ATPase activity	(2, 3)	highest	high	low
Glycolytic activity	(20, 21)	highest	high	low
Glycogen stores	(20)	high	—	high
Creatine phosphokinase (CPK)	(68)	2× more	—	—
Myokinase (MK)	(68)	2× more	—	—
Ability to resegregate Ca^{++}	(11, 13, 28, 52)	high	high	low
Cholinesterase	(28)	highest	high	low
Sulphur concentration	(72)	high	high	low
Phosphocreatine stores (PC)	(20)	high	high	low
Aerobic:				
Fatigability	(20, 21)	highest	high	low
Endurance	(20, 21)	low	high	highest
Oxidative activity	(6, 20)	low	high	mod-high
Capillization	(20, 28)	low	mod-high	high
Myoglobin	(20, 28)	low	mod-high	high
Triglyceride stores	(20)	low	—	high
Succinate dehydrogenase	(15)	low	high	highest
Neurological:				
Type motor neuron (alpha)	(8)	1	1	2
Action potential	(8)	larger	—	smaller
Neuromuscular junction	(8)	large complex	large simple	small simple
Terminal axon vesicles	(8)	high conc.	—	lower conc.
(Ach) to evoke response	(8)	more	—	less
Subneural folds	(8)	more & complex	—	less & simple
Motor end-plate area	(8)	larger	—	smaller
Receptors	(8)	20 % more		
Terminal axon length	(8)	longer	—	shorter
Mitochondria in bouton	(8)	fewer & smaller	—	more & larger
Excitatory postsynaptic potential (EPSP)	(8)	low	high	highest

Classifying Fiber Types

The current procedure for muscle fiber typing begins with a biopsy (4). Any skeletal muscle can be used as the sampling site, but the belly of the *vastus lateralis* from the outer edge of the right thigh is preferred. Muscles such as the *soleus* of the lower leg can consist of more slow twitch fibers; others, such as the *triceps* of the arm, can have more fast twitch fibers (20). The vastus lateralis may best represent an average over the entire body and is movement-specific to most sport activities.

First, all hair over the area is removed and the skin is sterilized with an antiseptic solution such as methiolate. After sterilization, the skin, subcutaneous tissue, and fascia are anesthetized with a subcutaneous injection of *xylocaine,* which deadens the pain receptors in the skin and fascia without contaminating enzymes within the biopsy sample. When the anesthetic has taken effect, a 2 mm incision is made in the skin and fascia and a *punch biopsy needle* is inserted into the muscle at a depth of approximately 1-3 cm. The needle assembly is designed to remove only a small portion of muscle tissue about the size of a match head. The portion of muscle removed will regenerate within 4 weeks or less (15). A sterile gauze is applied to the leg and an adhesive bandage is used to close the incision.

After the sample has been removed it is quick frozen with liquid nitrogen and/or other cooling agent and prepared for histochemical analysis. Cross-sectioning of the sample is done in serial sections and stained so as to determine the relative enzyme activity in the individual cells for type identification (15). The respective sizes of the cells are recorded from yet another serial section and calculations made for cross-sectional area. From these procedures the relative percentage as well as the quantity of fast versus slow twitch fibers can be determined.

Fiber Type Distribution Among Athletes

Fiber type varies from one person to another, with considerable differences existing between endurance and strength-power athletes (Table 1–2). Generally, endurance athletes have higher SO percentages whereas strength-power athletes have higher FG percentages (20). The following questions then arise: does training affect fiber type, and can such a change affect performance?

Both the distribution and functional characteristics of fiber types are, to a large degree, determined genetically (20, 42). Early researchers were convinced that no change in fiber type percentage was possible, and some indicated that this lifelong percentage was set at or shortly after birth (10, 22). Strength research generally agrees that the quantity of muscle correlates with maximal isometric strength and, likewise, a significant positive relationship exists between this value and the proportion of fast twitch muscle fibers (38). More recent evidence suggests that there is both a qualitative and a quantitative adaptation of muscle tissue in response to training. Even though fiber distribution, based on myosin-ATPase, is still thought to be governed largely by genetic factors (39, 41), high fast twitch to slow twitch area ratios found in sprinters and jumpers appear to be a result of strength training (17); similar results have been reported for weightlifters (19, 56).

The type of strength program may also be an important factor. Changes in enzyme activity following sprint strength training have been shown to cause increased creatine phosphokinase (CPK) and myokinase (MK) activity within the muscle (68). Higher demands may also be placed on faster ATP synthesis when rapid maximal contractions are repeated five to eight times with brief rest intervals (66). Consequently, a high rate of tension development should yield a higher force output. Likewise, a fast intrinsic speed of shortening in FG fibers should lead to higher force output for FG fibers at high contraction velocities (47, 66).

As one might expect, the percentage of fast twitch muscle fiber correlates positively with the force and speed of contraction (47). In addition, information illustrated in Figure 1–15 suggests that muscle fiber composition may be one factor determining the individual shape of the torque-velocity curve (28, 66). The FG/SO cross-sectional ratio may be more important in determining strength and power than simple percentages (66). Weight-training regimens characterized by more repetitions with smaller intensities affect both fast and slow fiber types

Table 1-2. Distribution of fast twitch fibers among different athletic groups (7, 14, 25, 40, 64, 67.)

Males	Approximate average FG, %
Marathoners	17.0
Swimmers	26.0
Distance runners	31.0
Speed skaters	31.5
Orienteers	32.0
Cross-country skiers	36.0
Nordic skiers	36.0
Alpine skiers	36.0
Ice hockey players	39.0
Race walkers	41.0
Canoeists	41.0
Cyclists	41.0
Body builders	44.0
Javelin throwers	50.0
Runners, 800m	52.0
Down hill skiers	52.0
Untrained subjects	54.0
Weightlifters	60.0
Shot-putters	62.0
Discus throwers	62.0
Sprinters/jumpers	63.0

Females	Approximate average FG, %
Runners, 800m	39.0
Cross-country skiers	40.5
Cyclists	49.0
Shot-putters	49.0
Discus throwers	49.0
Untrained subjects	49.0
Long and high jumpers	51.5
Javelin throwers	57.5
Sprinters	72.5

(61) and can be used effectively to enhance local muscle endurance and stimulate muscle growth (44, 46, 49, 54, 55), although such regimens do not necessarily maximize strength and power (1, 61).

Examination of world class body builders reveals more selective development of the SO fibers with less mean FG fiber area than might be expected (23, 64, 65). Muscle tissue development resulting from this high volume, low intensity training may involve increased size and number of myofibrils, enhanced protein synthesis, and addition of sarcomeres within the individual muscle fiber (16, 24). Longitudinal studies suggest, however, that strength and/ or power training may increase fast twitch fiber areas faster than slow twitch fiber areas (25, 52). Some have proposed that in such extreme hypertrophy, exercise-induced formation of new muscle fibers may even occur (26, 60, 65). The stimuli for this fiber splitting or *hyperplasia* is unknown (60). At best, the recent evidence, though mounting, is inconclusive.

Training programs sometimes used by strength-power athletes utilize fewer repetitions with near maximal loads. This high intensity, low volume approach stimulates the fast twitch fibers (61) and typically results in faster contraction speeds and hence development of higher power outputs at relative workloads (Figure 1-16) (9, 28, 69). This ability to produce higher

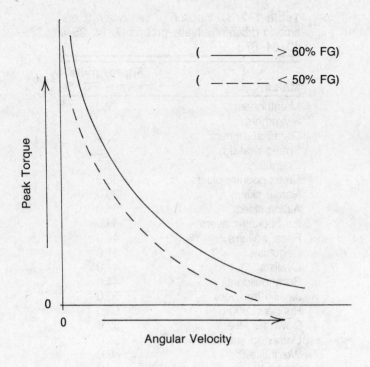

Figure 1–15. Torque Velocity Curve For Groups Of Differing Fiber Composition.

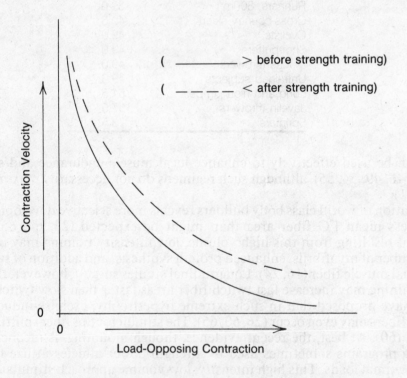

Figure 1–16. Training Induced Changes In The Force-Velocity Curve.

power outputs may be the one most important physiological determinant affecting performance and therefore success in most major sports. Likewise, few can argue against the importance of quickness and speed (in general) for most athletic endeavors.

Some people confuse *competitive fitness* with general *physical fitness.* This issue often leads to much emphasis on endurance. Consequently, many coaches and athletes integrate distance running into their strength conditioning programs as they attempt to enhance *cardiovascular* (C-V) endurance. There is substantial evidence to suggest that simultaneous endurance training that utilizes low intensity, long duration work is counterproductive to strength-power development (32, 53) (see Chapter 6). This is consistent with other findings indicating that aerobic training results in adaptations toward oxidative metabolism at the expense of fast contracting tissues (8). A recent study based largely on immuno-histological data suggests that there exists a continuum of fiber types ranging from the slowest to the fastest contracting motor units (5) and that the contractile profiles and morphological characteristics can be changed by aerobic training to more slow twitch and, conversely, by anaerobic training to more fast twitch fibers (30, 34, 36). Qualitative examination of the skeletal muscle of endurance-trained individuals reveals an ultrastructure representative of aerobic metabolism with a well-developed mitochondrial network and greater cristae surface area for oxidative enzyme storage (Figure 1–17) (52). On the other hand, the muscle of weightlifters shows an adaptation of tissue ultrastructure involving an extensive sarcoplasmic reticulum (Figure 1–18) (52), which is a benefit toward faster and more efficient Ca^{++} transport during the production of power (13, 28).

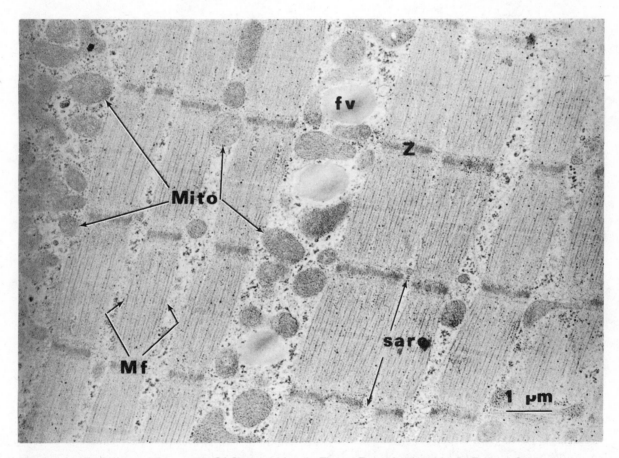

Figure 1–17. Electron Micrograph Of Skeletal Muscle Tissue From An Aerobically Trained Subject Showing Large Myofibrils (Mf), Sarcomeres (sarc), And (Z) Disc. The Mitochrondria (Mito) Are Numerous And Very Well Developed for Oxidative Metabolism. Some Fat Vacuoles (FV) Or Lipid Droplets Can Be Seen Interspersed Between The Myofibrils.

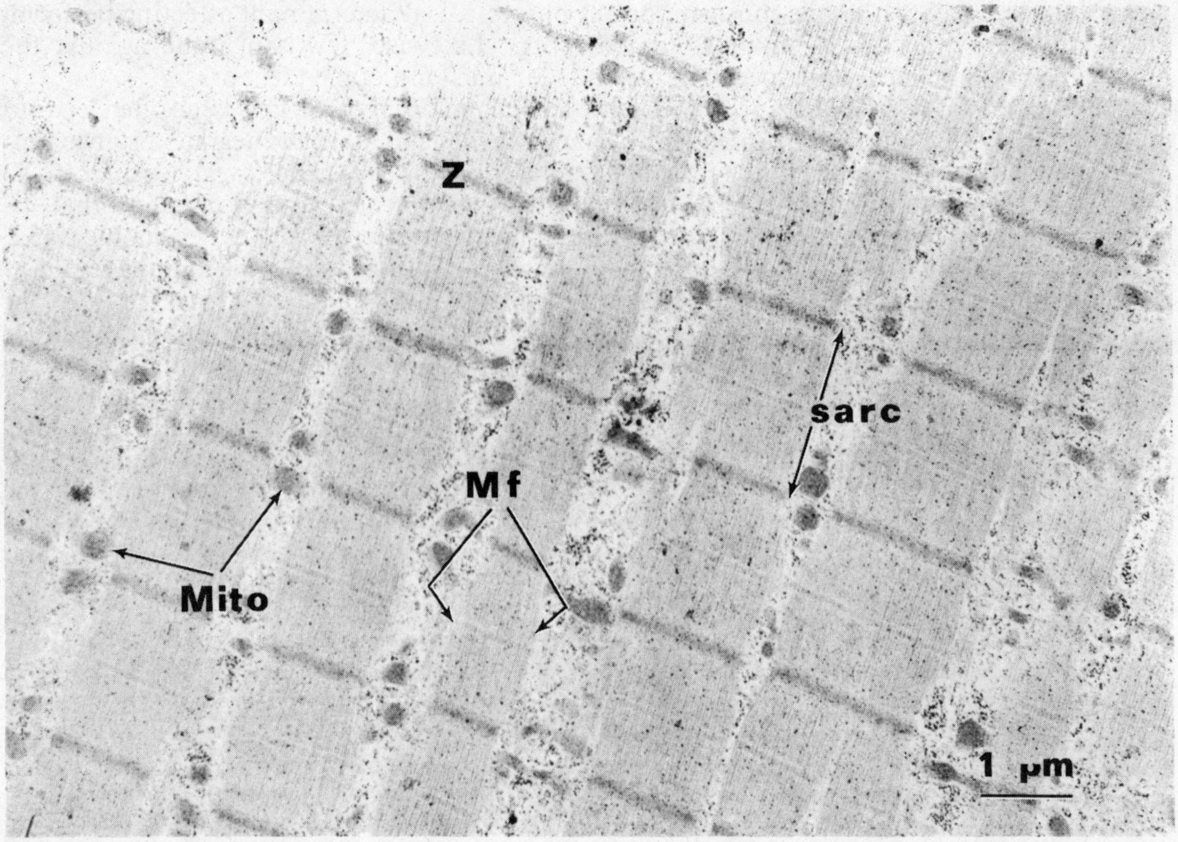

Figure 1–18. Electron Micrograph Of Skeletal Muscle Tissue From Weightlifters Showing Smaller Myofibrils (Mf), Sarcomere (sarc), (Z) Disc, And Small Mitochondria (Mito) Interspersed Among A Very Well And Regularly Developed Sarcoplasmic Reticulum To Form A Loosely Packed Myofibular Network.

Summary and Conclusions

In general, adjustments to anaerobic conditioning differ considerably from those resulting from aerobic work. Therefore, characteristic responses to aerobic and anaerobic conditioning are unique and selective to specific metabolic adaptations and are somewhat mutually exclusive. Efforts to strive for excellence in both may prove to be counterproductive. Other methods can be used to effectively enhance short-term endurance and raise anaerobic capacity. These methods are discussed in Chapter 6.

References

1. Anderson, T., and J. Kearney. 1982. Effects of three resistance training programs on muscular strength and absolute and relative endurance. *Research Quarterly* 53:1–7.

2. Barany, M. 1967. ATPase activity of myosin correlated with speed of muscle shortening. *Journal of General Physiology* 50:197–218.

3. Barnard, R. J., V. R. Edgerton, and J. B. Peter. 1970. Effect of exercise on skeletal muscle, I biochemical and histochemical properties. *Journal of Applied Physiology* 28:762–766.

4. Bergstrom, J. 1962. Muscle electrolytes in man; specimens: a study on normal subjects, kidney patients, and patients with chronic diarrhea. *Scandinavian Journal of Clinical Laboratory* (invest 14, 1, pt. 2) 68.

5. Billeter, R., H. Weber, H. Lutz, et al. 1980. Myosin types in human skeletal muscle fibers. *Histochemistry* 65:249–259.

6. Brooke, M., and K. Kaiser. 1970. Muscle fiber types: how many and what kind? *Arch. Neurol.* 23:369–379.

7. Burke, F., F. Cerny, D. Costill, and W. Fink. 1977. Characteristics of skeletal muscle in competitive cyclists. *Medicine and Science in Sports* 9:109–112.

8. Burke, R. E., and V. R. Edgerton. 1975. Motor unit properties and selective involvement in movement. In J. H. Wilmore and J. F. Keogh (Eds.). *Exercise and Sport Sciences Reviews* (vol. 3). New York: Academic Press, 31–81.

9. Caiozzo, V., J. Perrine, and R. Edgerton. 1981. Training-induced alterations of the in vivo force-velocity relationship of human muscle. *Journal of Applied Physiology* 51(3):750–753.

10. Chiakulas, J., and J. Pauly. 1965. A study of postnatal growth of skeletal muscle in the rat. *Anat. Rec.* 152:55.

11. Close, R. I. 1967. Properties of motor units in fast and slow skeletal muscles of the rat. *Journal of Physiology* 193:45–55.

12. Close, R. I. 1972. Dynamic properties of mammalian skeletal muscles. *Physiological Reviews* 52:129–197.

13. Copenhaver, W. M., D. E. Kelly, and R. L. Wood. 1978. *Bailey's Textbook of Histology* (17th edition) Baltimore: Williams & Wilkins.

14. Costill, D., J. Danials, W. Evans, et al. 1976. Skeletal muscle enzymes and fiber composition in male and female track athletes. *Journal of Applied Physiology* 40:149–154.

15. Costill, D., W. Fink, P. Van Handel, et al. 1979. *Analytical Methods for the Measurement of Human Performance* (2nd edition) Human Performance Laboratory, Ball State University, Muncie, Indiana.

16. Denny-Brown, D. 1961. Experimental studies pertaining to hypertrophy, regeneration and degeneration. *Neuromuscular Disorders* 38:147–196.

17. Edgerton, R. V. 1976. Neuromuscular adaptation to power and endurance work. *Canadian Journal of Applied Sport Science* 1:49–58.

18. Edgerton, R. V., and D. R. Simpson. 1969. The intermediate muscle fiber of rats and guinea pigs. *Journal of Histochemistry and Cytochemistry* 17:828–838.

19. Edstrom, L., and B. Ekblom. 1972. Differences in sizes of red and white muscle fibers in vastus lateralis of quadriceps femoris of normal individuals and athletes: relation to physical performance. *Scandinavian Journal of Clinical Laboratory Investigation* 30:175–181.

20. Fox, E. L., and D. K. Mathews. 1981. *The Physiological Basis of Physical Education and Athletics* (3rd edition) Philadelphia: Saunders College Publishing.

21. Garnett, R., M. O'Donovan, J. Stephen, and A. Taylor. 1978. Motor unit organization of human medial gastrocnemius. *Journal of Physiology* 287:33–43.

22. Goldspink, G. 1962. Studies on postembryonic growth and development of skeletal muscle. *Proc. Roy. Irish Acad.* 62B:135.

23. Goldspink, G. 1970. The proliferation of myofibrils during muscle fiber growth. *Journal of Cell Science* 6:593.

24. Goldspink, N. 1964. The combined effects of exercise and reduced food intake on skeletal muscle fibers. *Journal of Cell Composition and Physiology* 63:209–216.

25. Gollnick, P., R. Armstrong, C. Saubert, K. Peihl, and B. Saltin. 1972. Enzyme activity and fiber composition in skeletal muscle of untrained and trained men. *Journal of Applied Physiology* 33(3):312–319.

26. Gonyea, W. 1981. Muscle fiber splitting in trained and untrained animals. In Hutton and Miller (Eds.). *Exercise and Sport Science Reviews* (vol. 9). Philadelphia: Franklin Institute Press, 19–39.

27. Grutzner, P. 1884. Zur anatomie and physiologie der guergestreiften muskeln. *Rec. Zool. Suisse* 1:665–684.

28. Guyton, A. C. 1981. *Textbook of Medical Physiology* (6th edition). Philadelphia: W. B. Saunders Co.

29. Hakkinen, K., and P. Komi. 1982. Specificity of training-induced change in strength performance considering the integrative functions of the neuromuscular system. *World Weight Lifting.* Budapest, Hungary: International Weightlifting Federation 44–46.

30. Hakkinen, K., and P. Komi. 1983. Alterations of mechanical characteristics of human skeletal muscle during strength training. *European Journal of Applied Physiology* 50:161–172.

31. Hayes, K. C. 1978. A theory of the mechanism of muscular strength development based upon EMG evidence of motor unit synchronization. *Biomechanics of Sports and Kinanthropometry.* Miami, Florida: Symposia Specialists, Inc. 69–77.

32. Hickson, R. 1980. Interference of strength development by simultaneous training for strength and endurance. *European Journal of Applied Physiology* 45:255–263.

33. Hopper, B. 1980. Getting a grip on strength. *Swimming Technique* (August) 10–12.

34. Howald, H. 1982. Training-induced morphological and functional changes in skeletal muscle. *International Journal of Sports Medicine* 3:1–12.

35. Howells, K., T. Jordan, and J. Howells. 1978. Myofibril content of histochemical fiber types in rat skeletal muscle. *Acta Histochem. Bd.* 63:177–182.

36. Jansson, E., B. Sjodin, and P. Tesch. 1978. Changes in muscle fiber type distribution in man after physical training. *Acta Physiologica Scandinavica* 104:235–237.

37. Keul, J., E. Doll, and D. Keppler. 1972. *Energy Metabolism of Human Muscle,* Baltimore: University Park Press, 3–18.

38. Komi, P. V. 1979. Neuromuscular performance: factors influencing force and speed production. *Scandinavian Journal of Sports Science* 1:2–15.

39. Komi, P. V., and J. Karlsson. 1978. Skeletal muscle fiber types, enzyme activities and physical performance in young males and females. *Acta Physiologica Scandinavica* 103:210–218.

40. Komi, P. V., H. Rusko, J. Vos, and V. Vihko. 1977. Anaerobic performance capacity in athletes. *Acta Physiologica Scandinavica* 100:107–114.

41. Komi, P. V., J. T. Viitasalo, M. Navu, et al. 1976. Physiological and structural performance capacity: effect of heredity. *International Series on Biomechanics, Biomechanics V–A,* (vol 1A). Baltimore: University Park Press, 118–123.

42. Komi, P. V., J. T. Viitasalo, M. Havu, et al. 1977. Skeletal muscle fibers and muscle enzyme activities in monozygous and dizygous twins of both sexes. *Acta Physiologica Scandinavica* 100:385–392.

43. MacDougall, V., D. Sale, J. Moroz, et al. 1979. Mitochondrial volume density in human skeletal muscle following heavy resistance training. *Medicine and Science in Sports* 11:164–166.

44. MacQueen, I. 1954. Recent advantages in technique of progressive resistance exercise (hypertrophy and power programs in weight lifting). *British Medical Journal* 2:1193–1198.

45. Maton, B. 1976. Motor unit differentiation and integrated surface EMG in voluntary isometric contraction. *European Journal of Applied Physiology* 35:149–157.

46. McMorris, R., and E. Elkins. 1975. Study of production and evaluation of muscular hypertrophy. *Arch of Physiol. and Med. Rehab.* 35:420–426.

47. Miller, C. Fast twitch and slow twitch muscle fibers and some of their meanings to olympic weightlifters and coaches. Report of national weightlifting coaching coordinator, assistant olympic coach manager (U.S.A.).

48. Milner-Brown, H. S., R. B. Stein, and R. G. Lee. 1975. Synchronization of human motor units: possible roles of exercise and supraspinal reflexes. *Electroenceph. Clin. Neurophysiol.* 38:245–254.

49. Morehouse, L. E., and A. T. Miller. 1976. *Physiology of Exercise* (7th edition). St. Louis: C. V. Mosby Co.

50. Moritani, T., and H. A. deVries. 1979. Neural factors versus hypertrophy in the time course of muscle strength gain. *American Journal of Physical Medicine* 58:115–130.

51. O'Bryant, H. 1982. Periodization: a hypothetical training model for strength and power. Doctoral dissertation, School of Health, Physical Education, Recreation, and Dance, Louisiana State University.

52. O'Bryant, H., and M. Stone. 1982. Ultrastructure of human skeletal muscle among olympic style weight lifters. Poster presentation to Southeastern American College of Sports Medicine Convention at Virginia Tech., Blacksburg, Va., Feb. 5–6.

53. Ono, M., Miyashita, M. and T. Asami. 1976. Inhibitory effect of long distance running training on the vertical jump and other performances among aged males. *Biomechanics V–B,* Baltimore: University Park Press, 94–100.

54. O'Shea, P. 1966. Effects of selected weight training programs on the development of strength and muscular hypertrophy. *Research Quarterly* 37(1):95–102.

55. O'Shea, P. 1976. *Scientific Principles and Methods of Strength Fitness* (2nd edition). Massachusetts: Addison-Wesley.

56. Prince, F. P., R. S. Hikida, and F. C. Hagerman. 1976. Human fiber types in power lifters, distance runners, and untrained subjects. *Pflugers Archives* 363:19–26.

57. Ranvier, L. 1874. De quelques fats relatits a' l'histologie et a' la physiiologie des muscles striaes. *Arch. Physiol. Norm. Pathol.* 6:1–15.

58. Rasch, P. J., and R. K. Burke. 1974. *Kinesiology and Applied Anatomy* (5th edition). Philadelphia: Lea and Febiger.

59. Sale, D., J. MacDougall, A. Upton, and A. McComas. 1983. Effect of strength training upon motorneuron excitability in man. *Medicine and Science in Sport and Exercise* 15:57–62.

60. Salleo, A., G. Anastasi, G. LaSpala, and M. Denaro. 1980. New muscle fiber production during compensatory hypertrophy. *Medicine and Science in Sports and Exercise* 12:268–273.

61. Schmidtbleicher, D., and G. Haralambie. 1981. Changes in contractile properties of muscle after strength training in man. *European Journal of Applied Physiology* 46:221–228.

62. Stone, M. H., H. O'Bryant, and J. Garhammer. 1981. A hypothetical model for strength training. *Journal of Sports Medicine and Physical Fitness* 21:336, 342–351.

63. Stone, M. H., H. O'Bryant, J. Garhammer, et al. 1982. A theoretical model of strength training. *National Strength Coaches Association Journal* (Aug.-Sept.) 36–39.

64. Tesch, P. 1981. Muscular action and structure. *Muscle and Fitness* 42(3):38.

65. Tesch, P., and L. Larsson. 1982. Muscle hypertrophy in body builders. *European Journal of Applied Physiology* 49:301–306.

66. Thorstensson, A. 1976. Muscle strength, fiber types, and enzyme activities in man. *Acta Physiologica Scandinavica: Supplementum,* 443.

67. Thorstensson, A., L. Larsson, P. Tesch, and J. Karlsson. 1977. Muscle strength and fiber composition in athletes and sedentary men. *Medicine and Science in Sports* 9:26–30.

68. Thorstensson, A., B. Sjodin, P. Tesch, and J. Karlsson. 1977. Actomyosin ATPase, myokinase, CPK, and LDH in human fast and slow twitch muscle fibers. *Acta Physiologica Scandinavica* 99:225–229.

69. Tihanyi, J., P. Apor, and Gy. Fekete. 1982. Force-velocity-power characteristics and fiber composition in human knee extensor muscles. *European Journal of Applied Physiology* 48:331–343.

70. Ward, T., J. L. Groppel, and M. Stone. 1979. Anthropometry and performance in master and first class olympic weight lifters. *Journal of Sports Medicine and Physical Fitness* 19:205–212.

71. Watanabe, K., F. Sasaki, and M. Khan. 1978. Light and electron microscopic study of adenosine triphosphatase activity of anuran tadpole musculature. *Histochemistry* 55:293–305.

72. Wroblewski, R., G. Roomans, E. Jansson, and L. Edstrom. 1978. Electron probe x-ray microanalysis of human muscle biopsies. *Histochemistry* 55:281–292.

Bioenergetics

A basic understanding of energy production lays the foundation for understanding the metabolic basis for *specificity of exercise and training*. By understanding how energy is produced for various exercises and how the production of energy may be modified by various types of training, more efficient training programs can be designed.

Energy can be thought of as either potential or kinetic. The energy required to perform work is termed kinetic. Energy exists in various forms: nuclear, electrical, mechanical, chemical, and so on.

Metabolic processes are chemical in nature. Metabolic potential energy can be considered to be the energy stored in the chemical bonds of various molecules (i.e., proteins, carbohydrates, and fats). Kinetic energy requires the destruction of chemical bonds and the release of energy both as energy to perform work, such as muscle contraction, and as heat, which is important in maintaining body temperature (9, 25, 67, 69, 81).

The breakdown or destruction of large molecules (food → energy substrate) into smaller molecules associated with the release of energy is called *catabolism*. Constructing larger molecules from small ones can be accomplished using the energy released from catabolism. This building up process is termed *anabolism*. An example of catabolism is the breakdown of glucose to lactic acid. The construction of proteins from amino acids is an anabolic function. *Metabolism* is the term used to describe the sum total of all the catabolic and anabolic reactions occurring in living systems. Notice, in Figure 2–1, which illustrates the basic concept of metabolism, that energy derived from catabolic reactions cannot be used directly by anabolic reactions. The energy used to drive anabolic reactions is transferred via an intermediate molecule, adenosine triphosphate (ATP).

ATP allows the coupling or transfer of energy from exergonic (energy-releasing) to endergonic (energy-requiring) reactions. As such, ATP is of prime importance in muscle contraction, which is an endergonic reaction (see Chapter 1), and therefore to strength and power.

ATP contains the nitrogenous base adenine, the sugar ribose (5 carbons), and 3 phosphate groups. The hydrolysis, or removal, of 1 phosphate yields adenosine diphosphate (ADP); the hydrolysis of a second phosphate yields adenosine monophosphate (AMP). Each time a phosphate group is removed, some usable energy as well as heat is released (9, 14, 70, 74, 81). Under normal conditions the terminal phosphate group is cleaved (hydrolyzed) enzymatically to drive endergonic reactions. Thus, an important consideration is the replenishment of ATP.

The Biological Energy Systems

There are 3 basic energy systems that can help to replenish ATP. Two of these systems are anaerobic (without oxygen) and one is aerobic (with oxygen). The extent to which these energy systems are used depends on the intensity of activity. The systems are:

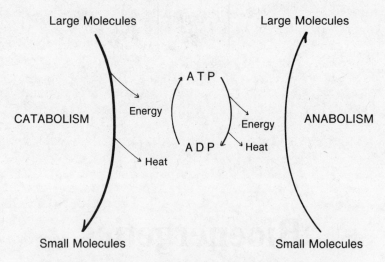

Catabolic reactions = exergonic: energy-releasing reactions.
Anabolic reactions = endergonic: energy-consuming reactions.

Figure 2–1. Metabolism.

1. ATP-CP system (and the myokinase reaction)

2. Glycolytic system

3. Oxidative system

The ATP-CP System

As ATP is used, its immediate replenishment can be accomplished through creatine phosphate (CP). Creatine phosphokinase (CPK), which is the enzyme catalyzing this reaction, is especially important in muscle contraction:

1. $$ATP \xrightarrow[\text{H}_2\text{O}]{\text{Myosin ATPase}} ADP + P_i + energy + heat$$

2. $$ADP + CP \xrightarrow{\text{CPK}} ATP + C$$

ATP and CP are stored within muscle in very small quantities. So, even though this system cannot support work for long periods, it can deliver energy very quickly.

Although often overlooked, another system that is important in high intensity work is the myokinase (or adenylate kinase) reaction (9, 67, 69):

$$2\ ADP \xrightarrow{\text{myokinase}} ATP + AMP$$

This reaction is important not only as a quick source of ATP, but also because AMP is a potent stimulator for glycolysis (9, 70).

The ATP-CP system is active at the initiation of all exercise. Along with the myokinase reaction, it is especially important in high intensity exercise such as weight training (9, 103).

The Glycolytic System

Anaerobic Glycolysis Anaerobic glycolysis uses either glucose taken from the blood or stored glycogen. It is especially important in moderately high intensity work. The enzymes responsible for glycolysis are found in the cytoplasm (sarcoplasm) of cells (9, 70) (see Figure 2–2).

The end product of anaerobic glycolysis is lactic acid (lactate). There can be several reasons for the production of lactate besides lack of oxygen or insufficient oxygen. Furthermore, a finding of a constant blood lactate level does not necessarily mean that no lactate is being produced; it may mean that production and removal are equal. Thus anaerobic glycolysis might more accurately be called fast glycolysis because energy production occurs at a rapid rate (9, 66, 70). Because of the high energy demands of fast twitch fibers, it is not surprising that these fibers contain higher concentrations and/or activities of glycolytic enzymes and enzymes for the immediate system (3, 12, 67, 84). Fast twitch fibers may also contain different isozymes than do slow twitch fibers. For example, LDH_M (muscle type) is found in higher concentrations in fast twitch fibers, whereas LDH_H (heart type) is found in higher concentrations in the heart muscle and slow twitch fibers (3, 12, 84, 111). This and other differences may allow slow twitch fibers and heart muscle to take up lactate and convert it to pyruvate, which can then be used in the Krebs cycle.

Aerobic Glycolysis   Aerobic glycolysis or slow glycolysis occurs when the activity of the mitochondria is sufficient to accept the 2 NADH produced by glycolysis (Pasteur effect) (66, 70, 81) (see Figure 2–2). During aerobic glycolysis, pyruvate enters the mitochondrial matrix via a localized carrier mechanism on the outer membrane (9, 16, 70).

Glycolytic Energy Yield   If glycolysis begins with glucose, then the following equations summarize glycolysis:

Anaerobic (fast glycolysis):
$$\text{Glucose} + 2\ P_i + 2\ ADP \longrightarrow 2\ \text{lactate} + 2\ ATP + H_2O$$
Aerobic (slow glycolysis):
$$\text{Glucose} + 2\ P_i + 2\ ADP + 2\ NAD+ \longrightarrow 2\ \text{pyruvate} + 2\ ATP + 2\ NADH + 2\ H_2O$$

Thus, the net ATP production of glycolysis beginning with one molecule of glucose is 2 ATP. If, however, glycogen is broken down into G-6-P via the enzyme phosphorylase, 3 ATP are produced (see Figure 2–2). This is because the phosphorylation using an ATP $\longrightarrow$ ADP via hexokinase is bypassed and 1 ATP is saved.

Control of Glycolysis   The primary control of glycolysis is accomplished through the phosphorylation of glucose (G-6-P) by hexokinase (9, 66, 67, 68, 69, 69, 81). The breakdown of glycogen (glycogenolysis) by phosphorylase also must be considered (9, 86, 88). The rate limiting step is:

$$\text{F-6-P} \longrightarrow \text{PFK F-1-6-DiP}$$

and is controlled by phosphofructokinase (PFK).

Glycolysis is stimulated by inorganic phosphate (Pi), ADP, and pH and is strongly stimulated by AMP (9, 68). It is inhibited by ATP, CP, citrate, and free fatty acids (FFA) (9, 45, 70).

The Oxidative (Aerobic) System

The oxidative energy system can use proteins, fats, or carbohydrates as a substrate. First we will consider carbohydrates.

If the activity of the mitochondria is high, pyruvate can be decarboxylated (lose a CO_2) to acetyl, combine with coenzyme A (COA), and enter the Krebs cycle (Figure 2–3). The NADH produced during glycolysis, and during other degradative processes such as the oxidation of fats, can enter the mitochondria via specific shuttle systems (9, 16, 64). The NADH can then be processed through the electron transport system (E.T.S.) and be used in the phosphorylation of ADP (oxidative phosphorylation) (see Figure 2–3). The complete oxidation of glucose produces approximately 38 ATP. This figure is an approximation because the shuttle systems and other factors require energy.

Triglycerides, which are stored in fat cells, can be broken down by hormone-sensitive lipase and FFA released from fat cells into the blood (9, 56, 70, 86). Free fatty acids can be taken up by muscle and used for energy. Muscle also contains small amounts of stored triglycerides and hormone-sensitive lipase and can produce an intramuscular source of FFA. This is especially important in slow twitch fibers (9, 24). In the cytoplasm (sarcoplasm) of cells, FFA are attached to COA. The FFA-COA molecule enters the mitochondria via a carnitine carrier system (9, 16, 53, 59). FFA undergoes B-oxidation, resulting in acetyl COA, which can enter the

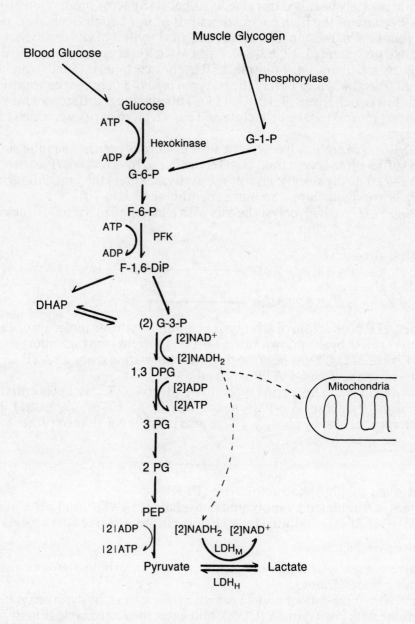

G-6-P = glucose 6 phosphate
F-6-P = fructose 6 phosphate
F-1-6-DiP = fructose 1, 6 diphosphate
DHAP = dihydroxyacetone phosphate
G-3-P = glyceraldehyde 3 phosphate
1,3 DPG = 1,3 diphosphoglycerate
3 PG = 3 phosphoglycerate

2 PG = 2 phosphoglycerate
PEP = phosphoenolpyruvate
LDH$_H$ = lactate dehydrogenase (heart type)
LDH$_M$ = lactate dehydrogenase (muscle type)
PFK = phosphofructokinase

Figure 2–2. Glycolysis.

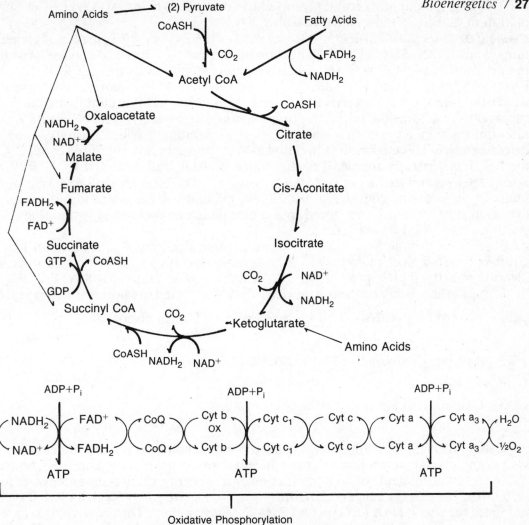

Figure 2-3. The oxidative system.

Krebs cycle, and H^+, which are carried to the electron transport system by NAD and FAD (see Figure 2–3).

Proteins can be broken down into amino acids by various catabolic processes. Skeletal muscle provides the primary store of amino acids in the body. Through transamination and deamination reactions, amino acids can be converted to their carbon skeletons, which can be converted into glucose (gluconeogenesis) (9, 70). Most carbon skeletons and amino acid residues appear as pyruvate or Krebs cycle intermediates (9, 53, 59) (see Figure 2–3). The nitrogenous waste produced by amino acid degradation is eliminated primarily through urea formation and excretion and the release of small amounts of ammonia (9, 67, 70). The elimination of nitrogenous waste products, especially ammonia, is important because they are toxic and also possibly act as fatigue products (9, 70). Recent evidence suggests that during exercise protein may be used as a substrate to a much greater extent than was previously thought (15, 40, 41, 113), which suggests that athletes may need protein above RDA values.

Energy Yield of the Oxidative Systems Under aerobic conditions 2 ATP are produced in the cytoplasm (3 ATP when starting with glycogen) for each glucose molecule. Additionally, 2 cytoplasmic NADH can be shuttled into the mitochondria. Within the mitochondria, H^+ (therefore electrons) are introduced to the electron transport system by either NADH or FADH. The oxidative phosphorylation potential (P:0) is 3 ATP for NADH and 2 ATP for

FADH (70, 81, 86). Thus, aerobic glycolysis can produce as many as 38 ATP. The complete oxidation of glucose is represented in Table 2–1.

Control of Oxidation (Aerobic System)   Regulation of the Krebs cycle is in part governed by reactions producing NADH or FADH. The ratio of oxidized to reduced coenzymes is controlled by the availability of ADP + P_i for oxidative phosphorylation in the E.T.S. If the coenzymes FAD^+ and NAD^+ are not available to accept electrons (H^+ in biological systems), the rate at which the Krebs cycle proceeds is reduced. Also, when GTP accumulates, the increase in succinyl CoA inhibits the initial reaction (oxaloacetate + acetyl CoA → citrate + CoA). The rate-limiting step in the cycle is isocitrate → $\propto$ ketoglutarate, which is catalyzed by isocitrate dehydrogenase. This enzyme is stimulated by ADP and generally inhibited by ATP. Control of the E.T.S. is relatively simple: It is stimulated by ADP and inhibited by ATP (9, 69, 70).

Relative Efficiency of Glycolysis and the Oxidative System   The efficiency of glycolysis and the oxidative system can be considered in different manners. A consideration of calories extracted relative to calories stored in a molecule is one method of estimating energy production efficiency. For example:

ATP = 7.3 Kcal·mole^{-1} 1. Anaerobic glycolysis = 2 ATP (14.6 Kcal)
Glucose = 686.0 Kcal·mole^{-1} 2. Aerobic glycolysis = 38 ATP (277.4 Kcal)
Stearate = 210.0 Kcal·mole^{-1} 3. Oxidation of stearate = 148 ATP (1080.4 Kcal)

Using the above information, a ratio of calories extracted to calories stored is as follows:

1. Anaerobic glycolysis = $\dfrac{14.6}{686.0}$ = 2.1% (3 ATP with glycogen)

2. Aerobic glycolysis = $\dfrac{277.4}{686.0}$ = 40.4%

3. Oxidation of stearate = $\dfrac{1080.4}{2100.0}$ = 51.4%

Using this method, it appears that anaerobic metabolism is not as efficient as the aerobic system and that fat metabolism is more efficient than glucose metabolism. This, however, does not consider the total rate of ATP production or free energy which is the energy free to do work (9, 69, 70). The energy change ($\triangle H$) from glucose → lactate is – 47 Kcal·mole^{-1}. If two ATP are produced the energy store ($\triangle G$) per ATP is – 7.3 Kcal·mole^{-1}. The negative sign represents energy given up, available to do work. The $\triangle H$ for the anaerobic release of 2 ATP is –11 Kcal·mole^{-1}. Thus the efficiency of anaerobic (fast) glycolysis can be assumed to be (9, 70):

$$\text{Efficiency} = \frac{2\,(-11)}{-47} = 46.8\%$$

Table 2–1. Energy conversions.

Location	Reaction	Coenzyme (electron carrier)	Theoretical ATP yield
*Cytoplasm	Glucose → Pyruvate		2
Cytoplasm	Glucose → Pyruvate	2 NAD	6
Mitochondria	Pyruvate → Acetyl CoA	2 NAD	6
Mitochondria	Isocitrate → Ketoglutarate	2 NAD	6
Mitochondria	Ketoglutarate → Succinyl CoA	2NAD	6
*Mitochondria	Succinyl CoA → Succinate	2GDP	2
Mitochondria	Succinate → Fumarate	2FAD	4
Mitochondria	Malate → Oxaloacetate	2 NAD	6
	Total		38 ATP

*Substrate level transformations.

Using this reasoning, anaerobic glycolysis and the oxidative system are in closer agreement, although the anaerobic system is somewhat less efficient (9).

Gladden and Welch (33) have presented data suggesting that, based on a constant decrease in exercise O_2 uptake and an increase in blood lactate during increased workloads, ATP synthesized by anaerobic pathways is not less efficient than aerobically synthesized ATP. This agrees with the $\triangle H$ changes above (9). But, in comparing work produced with energy expended, anaerobic efficiency (heavy work) is less than aerobic efficiency (steady state light work) (9, 33). Gladden and Welch (33) believe this result was obtained because during heavy work muscle efficiency decreases or because metabolism is not directly related to an increase in external work or both. In any case, as work moves toward high intensities it becomes less efficient.

Fuel Efficiency

Another important consideration in determining bioenergetic efficiency is the respiratory quotient (RQ). The RQ is the ratio between CO_2 produced and O_2 used during the oxidation of food (i.e., proteins, carbohydrates, or fats). RQ normally is measured with a bomb calorimeter (63). In work situations, a ventilatory ratio (R) can be created by measuring expired CO_2 and oxygen uptake (9, 30, 66). The caloric equivalents that follow were determined using this method. The method assumes that protein is not a major energy source, an assumption that will be challenged later in this chapter (9, 30, 113).

Food	Calorimetry (Kcal·g^{-1})	Biological (Kcal·g^{-1})	R	Kcal·$O_2(L)^{-1}$
Protein	5.7	4.2	0.8	4.5
Fat	9.5	9.5	0.7	4.7
Carbohydrate	4.2	4.2	1.0	5.0

Considering the R values, carbohydrates are the most efficient fuel, producing about 6.5% more energy per unit of O_2 used than fats and about 11.0% more than proteins. Thus carbohydrates are the preferred fuel (9, 81).

The R value can be used during exercise to estimate the primary substrate (food) being used for energy and to estimate the relative intensity of exercise.

Figure 2–4 shows the work intensity relationship between aerobically trained and untrained people. Notice that the R value decreases during light work and then proceeds rapidly upward as work becomes harder. The initial drop indicates a greater reliance on fats. This increased use of fats is due to two factors: the mobilization of free fatty acids (FFA) by specific hormones (9, 67, 81, 101) and the electron transport system being accelerated faster than glycolysis so that the capacity for oxidation exceeds the supply of pyruvate. Additionally, FFA inhibit PFK, the rate-limiting enzyme for glycolysis. During heavy work, as the need for a fast supply of energy increases and ADP levels increase, those processes that consume the most ADP with the least O_2 use are favored (9, 70, 81). Therefore, there is an increase in the use of anaerobic glycolysis; lactate also inhibits FFA use in the Krebs cycle (37, 41, 59). Also notice that R values may exceed 1.0, the theoretical maximum. This occurs because anaerobic glycolysis produces lactate (H^+), which increases tissue and blood lactates, lowering pH. This process overcomes the blood buffering systems (9, 70). For example:

$$\text{Buffering reaction: } CO_2 + H_2O \rightleftharpoons H_2CO_3 \rightleftharpoons HCO_3^- + H^+$$

$$\text{Heavy exercise} \rightarrow\ =\uparrow H^+$$

The production of lactate pushes this reaction to the left, causing increased CO_2 production. The excess CO_2 is blown off through the lungs during exhalation and raises the R values above 1.0 (9, 67). The importance of R values above 1.0 (as high as 1.4) is in estimating heavy and maximal efforts (9, 67).

As shown in Figure 2–4, aerobically trained people have lower R values than untrained people except at maximum efforts; this is true because of metabolic adaptations that allow trained people to use FFA more easily. These adaptations include an enhancement of oxidative enzymes and a predominance of specific isozymes (9, 67, 111). For example, LDH_H (catalyzes lactate → pyruvate) is enhanced in aerobically trained people. The importance of increased FFA use in trained people is that it spares glycogen, an important consideration in endurance activities. The sparing of glycogen is particularly important to the central nervous system, which relies primarily on carbohydrates for energy (9, 86).

Anaerobic Threshold (Onset of Blood Lactate)   The existence of an anaerobic threshold (AT) is a controversial issue. Recent evidence suggests that there are specific breakpoints in lactate accumulation as work increases (19, 21, 62, 65). The breaks in the AT are somewhat similar to the points at which intermediate and large motor units are recruited during increasing work (see Figure 5–4). The large motor units are metabolically set up for anaerobic metabolism.

Some studies suggest that training at intensities near or above the breakpoints in the AT will push the AT back (lactate accumulation occurs later). This, in effect, will allow the athlete to perform at higher percentages of max $\dot{V}O_2$ without as much lactate production (9, 21).

Furthermore, endurance performance can vary greatly among individuals even when max $\dot{V}O_2$s are equal. To some extent, endurance, especially at high intensities, may be more related to lactate production/removal and glycogen utilization than to max $\dot{V}O_2$. High volume weight training has been shown to increase high intensity work time without similar changes in max $\dot{V}O_2$ (46, 100). Speculation would suggest that some types of weight training may in some man-

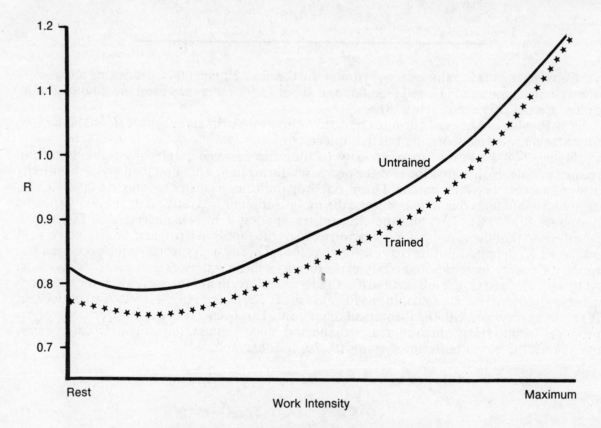

Figure 2–4. R values for aerobically untrained people.

ner modify the above factors, allowing greater endurance. A descriptive study (98) and a training study (85) suggest that weight training reduces serum lactate at submaximal loading (squatting).

Energy Production Power (Rate) and Capacity

Of importance to the exercise physiologist and the coach-athlete is how these energy systems are used. Because of the time required to gear up the other systems, the ATP-CP system is likely to be used at the initiation of most exercises to a small extent (9, 30, 67, 81). As can be logically gathered from the above discussions, the primary energy system is largely a function of the intensity of exercise (9, 25, 67, 81). Table 2–2 shows the relative contributions of the energy systems to rate and capacity for energy production. Thus, typical weight training is supported primarily through anaerobic systems.

Time is also a factor in the use of bioenergetic systems. Athletic events range from a snatch or shotput (2–3 seconds) to marathons (more than 2 hours). If a **maximum effort** is being made, the time considerations shown in Table 2–3 are reasonable.

As apparent from Tables 2–2 and 2–3, the intensity of exercise determines which primary energy systems are used. In no case, however, does any exercise or rest rely wholly on one system or another. Anaerobic and oxidative systems always contribute to a greater or lesser extent, depending on intensity (9, 25, 67, 81). This consideration is a basis of interval training.

Limiting Factors

Limiting factors for maximal performance (9, 11, 25, 45, 53, 57, 67, 71, 81) must be considered in the accumulation of fatigue from exercise and training. Table 2–4 provides examples of the various limiting factors based on depletion of energy source or substrate. Of importance to weight training is the possible effect of lactate ($\uparrow [H^+]$) in both indirectly and directly limiting contractile force (45).

Metabolic Specificity of Training

Choosing appropriate intensities and appropriate rest intervals can permit the "selection" of specific energy systems during training for specific athletic events (9, 30, 67). This is the basis of the concept of interval training (30, 67). This form of training not only helps select the appropriate energy system, but also reduces fatigue and allows more work to be accomplished at a higher intensity (9, 30, 66). Interval training is the basis for weight training.

Typical weight training has been shown to increase stores of ATP-CP and glycogen and to increase the myokinase reaction (10, 75). It **may** generally enhance anaerobic metabolism, especially considering the faster hypertrophy rates of fast twitch fibers (9, 38, 52). Aerobic training may reduce anaerobic energy production capabilities (104) (see Chapters 3 and 6). Furthermore, oxidative metabolism may be especially important in recovery from heavy anaerobic exercise (e.g., weight training) (9, 93).

Table 2–2. Rate and capacity for energy production (adapted from 9, 25, 67, 81).

System	Rate of ATP production	Capacity of ATP production
ATP-CP	1	4
Anaerobic glycolysis	2	3
Aerobic glycolysis	3	2
FFA $\rightarrow CO_2 + H_2O$	4	1

1 = Highest
2
3
4 = Lowest

Table 2–3. Bioenergetics and maximal effort duration (adapted from 9, 25, 45, 67, 75, 103).

Primary system	Duration of event
ATP-CP	0–10 sec.
ATP-CP + anaerobic glycolysis	10–30 sec.
Anaerobic glycolysis	30 sec. - 2 min.
Anaerobic glycolysis + oxidative system	2 min. - 3 min.
Oxidative system	> 3 min. and rest

Biological Energy Systems Summary

This section has presented the underlying biochemical basis for the concept of specificity of exercise and training. Fundamentally, exercise, training, and energy system selection are functions of exercise intensity, which is an important consideration in developing training programs. It also is important in developing weight-training programs with specific aims. For example, the results of circuit (and some other high volume weight-training routines) compared to high intensity, low volume programs are very different (see Chapters 6 and 7).

The Metabolic Costs of Weight Training

Weight training has become an integral part of the training programs of many athletes. Coaches and athletes recognize the important contributions that increased maximum muscular strength and power can make toward improved performance in most sports. Unfortunately, weight training programs are often implemented with little knowledge of the energy cost of weight training.

Noncircuit weight training has been criticized as providing minimal or no stimulus to improve aerobic functions or reduce body fat (79, 80). However, it should be noted that highly weight-trained athletes do possess higher than average max $\dot{V}O_2$ ($\overline{X} \simeq 55$ ml·kg^{-1}·min^{-1}) and a low percentage of body fat ($\overline{X} \simeq 10\%$) (28, 92, 96). Recent longitudinal studies using short-term noncircuit weight-training programs have produced small but significant increases in max $\dot{V}O_2$ both L·min^{-1} (47, 49, 100) and ml·kg^{-1}·min^{-1} (100), and substantial significant losses in body fat (58, 100). Furthermore, noncircuit weight training has been shown to produce positive changes in the serum lipid levels of middle age sedentary men (6, 34, 58). These studies suggest that noncircuit weight training could have a considerable metabolic turnover. If the metabolic turnover is high and/or produces a high total energy cost, this could have considerable importance in the use of weight training as part of a physical fitness program or as part of various athletic training programs. Furthermore, the addition of weight training, which produces a high total energy cost, could result in chronic fatigue and a decrease in performance (overtraining) if it is not properly integrated with other training procedures.

Table 2–4. Limiting factors by depletion (adapted from 9, 67, 81)

Type and intensity of Exercise	ATP-CP	Muscle glycogen	Liver glycogen	Fatty acids
Light (e.g., marathon)[*]	1[†]	5	4–5	2–3
Moderate (e.g., 1500m)	1–2	3	2	2
Heavy (E.g., 400m)[‡]	3	3	1	1
Very intense (e.g., shotput)	2	1	1	1
Repeated very intense (High volume weight training)[‡]	5	4–5	2–3	1–2

[*]Other limiting factors include O_2 delivery and waste removal and general wear and tear.
[†] 1 = negligible, 2 = slight, 3 = moderate, 4 = high, 5 = highest.
[‡]Other limiting factors include a decreased pH ($\uparrow$ [H$^+$]), which may interfere with muscle contraction.

Typically, anaerobic exercise produces a large O_2 debt (excess postexercise O_2 consumption), especially if an athlete uses multiple workouts each day. Many athletes use this type of extensive weight-training program at various times during their training year (e.g., shotputters, discus throwers, and powerlifters). It is commonly used by olympic weightlifters during parts of their preparation phase (100).

Oxygen Consumption ($\dot{V}O_2$) and Anaerobic Contribution to Work

Oxygen uptake is a measure of an organism's ability to function aerobically. Oxygen uptake ($\dot{V}O_2$) depends on a central (cardiac output) and a peripheral (a–$\bar{v}O_2$ diff.) factor. A rearrangement of the Fick equation describes this relationship:

$\dot{V}O_2 = c.o. \times a–\bar{v}O_2$ diff.

Therefore, max $\dot{V}O_2$ depends on the maximum values for the central and peripheral factors.

During submaximal work, $\dot{V}O_2$ increases for the first few minutes until a steady state of oxygen consumption is reached (2, 50). During this steady state, oxygen demand equals oxygen consumption. However, during the first few minutes of exercise, some of the energy cost must be supported anaerobically (106). This anaerobic support is called the *oxygen deficit* (50, 80). At the termination of exercise, $\dot{V}O_2$ remains above resting levels for a period of time that depends on the intensity and length of the exercise (see Figure 2–5). This postexercise $\dot{V}O_2$ (above resting) has been termed the *O_2 debt* (50, 80).

If the intensity of work is above the maximum $\dot{V}O_2$ one is capable of producing, then much of the work must be supported by anaerobic mechanisms. This occurrence is described in Figure 2–6. In general, as the contribution of anaerobic mechanisms supporting the exercise increases, the exercise time decreases (2, 42, 105, 107).

The O_2 Debt (Excess Postexercise Oxygen Consumption)

The O_2 debt is the amount of O_2 uptake above baseline used to restore the body to the preexercise condition (95). Early experiments suggested that the O_2 debt was largely due to the resynthesis of glycogen from lactate (80%) or the further oxidation of lactate (20%) via pyruvate and the Krebs-E.T.S. pathway (50). However Margaria et al. (77), Harvard Fatigue Laboratory, observed that the initial portion of the O_2 debt occurred without any drop in blood lactate and that a small O_2 debt could be incurred (2–3L) without any significant change in blood lactate. They went on to speculate that the O_2 debt is made up of two phases: the alactic O_2 debt and the lactic acid debt. The alactic phase was believed to represent O_2 consumption used for the restoration of ATP-CP stores and for reloading myoglobin and hemoglobin. The lactic acid O_2 debt was believed to be the O_2 used in reconverting lactate to glycogen.

Only moderate relationships have been established between the O_2 deficit and the O_2 debt (4, 44). Although the O_2 deficit may influence the size of the O_2 debt, they are not equal. Furthermore, experiments in which labeled lactate was infused into rat muscle showed that 75% of the labeled carbon appeared as CO_2 (8). This finding suggests that the major portion of lactate could be used to produce energy aerobically during recovery. A human study supporting this view showed that 10 minutes post (strenuous) exercise, no glycogen resynthesis had occurred, even though blood lactate was significantly reduced (106). Thus, only a small amount of lactate may be resynthesized to glycogen.

Increases in physiologic functioning during recovery may account for a significant and perhaps major portion of the O_2 debt. Elevated temperature stimulates metabolism and increased O_2 consumption (10). Increased respiratory muscle and heart function require increased energy supply (60). Using the above criteria to account for O_2 debt, Brooks et al. (18) have suggested that the theoretical maximum O_2 debt will not exceed 3–4L. However, O_2 debts as high as 18L have been reported (77). These large O_2 debts may be largely or partially accounted for by three factors: redistribution of electrolytes such as calcium, sodium, and potassium; tissue repair; and the effects, especially the residual effects, of the hormones (e.g., catecholamines, growth hormone, testosterone, and perhaps insulin that are released during anaerobic exercise (10, 32, 62). The possible factors affecting O_2 debt are summarized in Table 2–5.

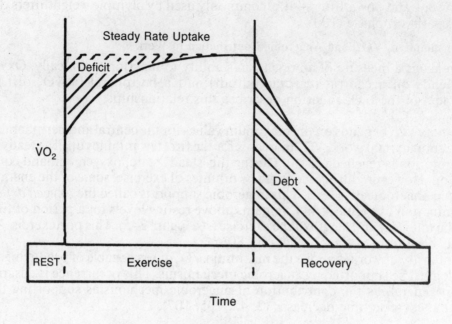

Figure 2–5. Light to moderate exercise.

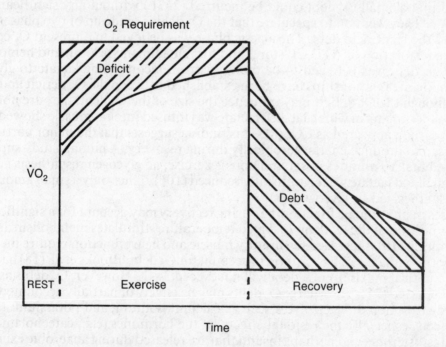

Figure 2–6. Heavy anaerobic exercise.

Table 2–5. Factors influencing O_2 debt (adapted from 8, 9, 10, 80).

1. Resynthesis of ATP.

2. Resynthesis of CP.

3. Resynthesis of glycogen from lactate (25% of lactate produced).

4. Resaturation of tissue H_2O.

5. Resaturation of venous blood.

6. Resaturation of blood in the skeletal muscle.

7. Resaturation of myoglobin.

8. Redistribution of ions within muscle and other body compartments.

9. Tissue repair.

10. Additional cardiorespiratory work.

11. Residual effects of hormone release.

12. Increased body temperature.

Recovery from Submaximal Exercise

The O_2 debt as a result of 2–3 minutes of submaximal work can be larger than the O_2 debt of longer work periods at equal intensities (107). This suggests that part of the O_2 debt may be paid back during steady state aerobic work. Support for this suggestion comes from the observation that lactate removal is increased by light to moderate aerobic recovery exercise (37).

Recovery from Intermittent Anaerobic Training

Intermittent non-steady-state work can allow a larger total workload to be accomplished; this is a basis for the concept of interval training (30, 67). Although intermittent rest periods allow more total work, stopping for rest periods also produces an increased total O_2 debt and an increased total caloric consumption as compared to nonintermittent work of a somewhat similar intensity.

O_2 Consumption and Weight Training

Considering the extensive use of weight training in physical fitness programs, rehabilitation, and athletics, surprisingly little is known concerning the energy cost of various weight-training programs.

McArdle and Foglia (79) examined the O_2 consumption and O_2 debts of a *single* set of 8 repetitions of the bench press, curl, and squat. The VO_2 and O_2 debt represented a moderate to heavy energy cost. The larger muscle mass exercise (squats) had the highest energy consumption. The total energy cost was low, as would be expected using single sets.

Circuit weight training, which entails using many small muscle mass exercises, very high repetitions, relatively light weights, and short recoveries between sets, is an attempt to increase metabolic rate during the workout period. Wilmore et al. (108) reported the average caloric expenditure per minute of a typical (universal) circuit weight- training workout to be about 9+ Kcal (male) and 6+ Kcal (female), resulting in approximately 202 (male) and 130 Kcal (female) being used in 22.5 minutes plus 12 minutes recovery. The VO_2 was less than 50% of maximum for both men and women. A recent investigation of the Nautilus Express Circuit showed similar low VO_2's, 35.9% and 38.3% of max VO_2 values for women and men, respectively (43).

Three studies have examined the energy cost of noncircuit olympic-style weight training. Laritcheva et al. (68) found that the rate of energy cost ranged from 370 to 455 Kcal per hour. They did not indicate the type of exercises used, but concluded that the total energy cost depended on the total workload (reps $\times$ weight). The total energy cost ranged from 470 Kcal in the 52 kg class to 1818 Kcal in the 110 kg class per day. They did not report the relative contribution of exercise $\dot{V}O_2$ compared to O_2 debt.

Stone et al. (99) examined the effects of various combinations of sets and reps of snatch and clean pulls on the exercise $\dot{V}O_2$ and O_2 debt. Rest between sets was held constant at 1 minute (N = 12). The average $\dot{V}O_2$ was 1.80 L·min^{-1} (range –1.40L·min^{-1} –2.45L·min^{-1}) ($\bar{x}$ = 45.2% of max $\dot{V}O_2$), producing an average caloric expenditure of 9.0 Kcal min^{-1} and a total caloric expenditure of approximately 270 Kcal for 30 minutes of exercise after and excluding 5 minutes of warmup. The observation of 10 minutes of postworkout O_2 consumption showed an additional 31.0 Kcals being used, bringing the total caloric cost to about 300 Kcals for 30 minutes of exercise. Recovery (10 minutes postworkout) was still above resting values, suggesting that the final total caloric expenditure may be quite high.

Scala (93) studied the O_2 consumption and O_2 debt of 3 weightlifters during an entire week of preparation phase training (see also 97, 100). A typical workout lasted approximately 36.5 minutes and used about 330 Kcal at a rate, not including warmup, of 9.4 Kcal·min^{-1} using the method of Wilmore et al. (108) and combining the recovery cost with the workout cost produced a rate of 10.6 Kcal·min^{-1}. Qualitatively, this represents very heavy work (9, 90). In no case was the postworkout recovery (10 minutes) complete, agreeing with Stone et al. (99). The mean caloric consumption for a week's training was approximately 4000 Kcal.

Furthermore, Scala (93) showed that during the workout the greatest O_2 consumption occurred during the rest periods between sets. The athletes were allowed to take normal rest periods. Rest $\dot{V}O_2$ averaged about 3.5 times the work $\dot{V}O_2$.

As would be expected with weightlifters, a major portion of each workout was devoted to large muscle mass, multi-segment exercises (pulls, squats, jumps, etc.). These exercises are placed first in the workout. Compared to small muscle mass exercises (presses, lat work, situps, etc.) the energy cost is considerably higher (11.5 vs. 6.8 Kcal·min^{-1}) (93). This creates about 15–30 continuous minutes of relatively high metabolic turnover, depending on how the workout is set up. These large muscle mass exercises produced a mean of 58% of the athletes' max $\dot{V}O_2$ (cycle ergometer), whereas the small muscle mass exercises represented about 40% of maximum (93).

Using timed interval squats of 60% body weight, Dohmeier et al. (23) also showed that squats (large muscle mass) can elicit training $\dot{V}O_2$'s above threshold. The timed interval squats (1 rep/4 secs) lasted for 20 minutes. These squats averaged 56% of the treadmill tested max $\dot{V}O_2$. The authors (23) concluded that this was of sufficient aerobic intensity to elicit an aerobic adaptation. This strongly agrees with the observation of Scala (93).

The above considerations concerning the metabolic consequences of various types of weight training may have important applications, especially as related to large muscle mass exercises.

Practical Considerations

Considering the total caloric cost and metabolic turnover observed in circuit weight training and high volume noncircuit weight training (91, 105), aerobic power improvements and especially reductions of fat may be possible.

Some studies suggest that exercise $\dot{V}O_2$'s as low as 45% –50% of maximum are sufficient to increase maximum aerobic power, provided they are maintained long enough (31). The incorporation of large muscle mass exercises increases the possibility of an aerobic power training effect (9, 65, 93) (see also Chapter 3). It is reasonable to assume that the large muscle mass exercises employed were to a major extent (along with the high volume) responsible for the increases in aerobic power observed by Stone et al. (100).

Several studies have noted reductions in percentage of fat and total body fat accompanying weight-training programs (6, 34, 58, 100) (see also Chapter 3). Again, it is likely that the type of exercise (large vs. small muscle mass) and the total volume of work make major contributions. The high metabolic turnover and/or total energy cost of appropriate weight training may also be sufficient to affect blood lipids in a beneficial manner. Several observations, both descriptive and longitudinal (6, 34, 55, 56, 58), suggest that high volume weight training can alter blood lipids beneficially.

The possibility of beneficial alterations in aerobic power, body fat, and other physiological parameters such as blood lipids may depend on metabolic turnover and total energy cost. Metabolic turnover, or rate of energy cost, is strongly influenced by the type of exercise used (large vs. small muscle mass) (93); total energy cost is influenced by both the type of exercise and the total volume of training. Thus, in both athletic and nonathletic settings, considerable thought should be given to extensive use of large muscle mass exercises.

The large O_2 debt produced during weight training may be reason for caution in planning training programs (93). Residual fatigue, both general and local, from heavy anaerobic exercise such as weight training can contribute to overwork (54, 93). Multi-session training such as weight training and running or weight training and sports practice at too high an intensity or volume can quickly produce overtaining and chronic fatigue.

Metabolic Costs Section Summary

Weight training can have a relatively high rate of calorie consumption and a high total caloric cost. Factors affecting energy consumption include exercise selection (large vs. small muscle mass), frequency of workouts, and loading.

Nutrition and Athletic Performance

We extend a special thanks to Ralph Rozenek, Ph.D., Health, Physical Education and Recreation, Texas Tech University for his help in preparing this section.

Of course, athletic performance is not simply determined by training alone. In the authors' opinion, one of the most overlooked and underrated aspects of athletics and performance in general is nutrition and its associated biochemistry.

Protein Metabolism

Of particular interest to coaches and athletes involved in strength/power sports is the role of protein in the diet. There is still confusion and controversy regarding the protein requirements for athletes undergoing heavy physical training. Part of the problem can be attributed to inadequacies in the experimental design of scientific studies, a lack of understanding of all aspects of protein metabolism, and individual differences. This section reviews briefly some of the major aspects of protein metabolism and requirements with respect to strength/power activities.

Protein makes up between 9% and 15% of total dietary calories for most people in the United States. Proteins are found in all cells of the body and have a function in body growth; body maintenance and repair; synthesis of enzymes, hemoglobin, myoglobin, and antibodies; and production of energy. Requirements for energy take priority over tissue building, so protein can be used as an energy source if the amounts of carbohydrates and fats in the diet are inadequate (51). A prime example of this use occurs in starvation, during which large amounts of body protein (e.g., skeletal muscle) are used to meet energy requirements. An important function of skeletal muscle is to serve as a reservoir for protein (94). Muscle protein is in a constant state of turnover. The amount of muscle protein is determined by the balance between protein anabolism and catabolism (7).

When dietary protein beyond the body's requirements is ingested, it can be converted to fat. Some people wrongly believe that excess protein in the diet is excreted in the urine so you can eat all you want. In reality, it is a metabolic byproduct of protein metabolism (e.g., urea) that is excreted.

Composition of Proteins

Proteins are composed of basic units known as amino acids. A key feature in the structure of amino acids is the nitrogen molecule. The nitrogen is essential for the formation of peptide bonds. Amino acids are linked in a particular manner, via the peptide bonds, to form proteins that perform specific functions. In discussing protein requirements, we are really referring to the requirement for amino acids. Free amino acids exist only in small quantities in the foods we eat. They are found as a mixture in proteins that must be broken down before the amino acids can be made available.

Table 2–6. Essential and nonessential amino acids.

Essential amino acids	Nonessential amino acids
Leucine	Glycine
Isoleucine	Alanine
Valine	Aspartic acid
Threonine	Glutamic acid
Lysine	Serine
Methionine	Cystine
Phenylalanine	Tyrosine
Tryptophan	Arginine
Histidine	Proline
	Hydroxyproline
	Glutamine
	Asparagine

Of the approximately 22 amino acids used in the synthesis of protein, nine are considered to be essential in adults (83), (Table 2–6). These amino acids cannot be manufactured in the body; they must be supplied in the diet. The remaining nonessential amino acids can be synthesized within the body from other substances as long as there is an adequate source of nitrogen. Dietary proteins that supply all of the amino acids needed for the formation of tissue protein are considered to have high biological value (nitrogen retained/nitrogen absorbed) and are known as complete proteins. These proteins are generally of animal origin: meat, dairy products, eggs, and fish. Proteins that lack any one of the essential amino acids are incomplete and are considered to have lower biological value (83). Proteins of this nature are generally of plant origin and include nuts, grains, legumes, and seeds.

If an essential amino acid is missing from the diet, protein synthesis is impaired and the other amino acids are not used for protein synthesis. As a result, there is an increased excretion of nitrogen. A negative nitrogen balance occurs when nitrogen excretion is greater than intake, indicating a loss of body protein. When nitrogen intake is greater than excretion, the body is in a state of positive nitrogen balance, which indicates protein anabolism. A negative nitrogen balance can occur even if only one essential amino acid is missing from the diet. A negative balance can also occur if the proportions of essential amino acids are out of balance. Two incomplete proteins that lack different amino acids can provide a complete protein when both are eaten together. This is known as mutual supplementation and has important implications in relation to vegetarian diets. The timing of meals also is important if protein synthesis is to proceed efficiently. All of the essential amino acids must be present within a 2-hour period (1). Eating two different incomplete proteins at different meals will not result in mutual supplementation. Furthermore, physical activity immediately after a meal will tend to diminish the absorption of amino acids from the intestinal tract.

The Food and Agriculture Organization/World Health Organization has established guidelines for the estimated essential amino acid patterns in the diet. An important factor in establishing the requirement for protein is protein quality. Many food products claim to have high proportions of protein, but the source and quality of the protein must be questioned. Variety in the diet insures that protein requirements, along with the requirements for other essential nutrients, are met.

Digestion of Proteins

The digestion of dietary proteins begins in the mouth, where mechanical breakdown of large food particles occurs. The smaller particles are further broken down in the stomach by the actions of the enzyme pepsin and hydrochloric acid. No absorption of protein or amino acids occurs in the stomachs of adults. A host of digestive enzymes are released from the pancreas into the small intestine, resulting in the breakdown of the peptide bonds to form small peptides and amino acids. These small peptides (di or tri peptides) are absorbed by the mucosal cells, broken down to amino acids, and released into the blood. From 95% to 97% of all amino acids are absorbed in the small intestine; little protein is found in the large intestine under normal circumstances.

There are several structurally related groups of amino acids, and each has its own transport system to facilitate absorption along the small intestine. There is competition among amino acids of the same group for transport sites (5). For example, the branch chain amino acids leucine, isoleucine, and valine compete for the same transport sites. Too much of one of these amino acids will decrease the absorption of the others. Some protein supplements contain unbalanced mixtures of amino acids, which can inhibit absorption. Predigested proteins may present a problem by flooding available transport sites. In addition, any enzymes or peptide hormones that are taken orally are rendered ineffective by digestion and absorption. Protein obtained from the food we eat apparently has the best amino acid combinations. The time involved in the digestive process allows for gradual absorption of amino acids and small peptides.

Once absorbed from the small intestine, the amino acids travel to the liver via the portal circulation. They can take several routes (Figure 2–7), depending on the particular needs of the body.

Control of Protein Metabolism

Various hormones within the body affect the amount of protein synthesis and breakdown that takes place (35, 102) (Table 2–7). These hormones have metabolic and physiologic effects throughout the body. They affect not only protein metabolism, but also carbohydrate, lipid, and water metabolism, as well as growth, behavior, and numerous other functions.

The recommended dietary allowance (RDA) for protein in adults is 0.8 g of protein/kilogram of body weight/day (83). Included in the RDA is a margin of safety that takes into account individual differences in protein metabolism; variations in the biological value of protein; nitrogen losses via urine, feces, and sweat; and physical activity. According to the RDA, there is no need for additional protein in the diet with physical activity due to the built-in margin of safety. The recommendation does state, however, that caloric intake must be adequate. It is assumed that as caloric expenditure increases with the demands of training, so do food consumption and caloric intake. Protein intake would then increase in proportion. This may not always be true, especially when a person switches into different phases of a training program. The body requires some time to readjust energy intake and output (2, 86).

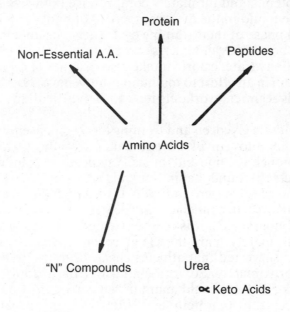

Figure 2–7. Fate of amino acids.

Table 2–7. Influence of hormones on protein.

Hormone	Synthesis	Degradation	Net effect on protein synthesis
Insulin	I*	D	I
Growth hormone	I	D	I
Androgens	I	D	I
Thyroid hormone			
Low	I	D	I
High	NC	II	D
Glucocorticoids	D	I	D†

*I = increase, D = decrease, NC = no change.
†An exception may be the myocardium where glucocorticoids may stimulate hypertrophy.

Some recent evidence suggests that protein is used to a greater extent during exercise than has previously been thought (2, 16, 17, 29, 68, 72, 113). Among the findings are the following: increased excretion of urea nitrogen in sweat and urine following endurance exercise (17), increased n-methylhistidine excretion following both endurance and weightlifting exercise (22), increased branch chain amino acids in blood and increased leucine oxidation following endurance exercise (26, 29, 72, 73), and development of sports anemia following endurance exercise (112). Another finding indicates that 5% –15% of energy for long-term exercise may be derived from protein (26, 87), which suggests increased gluconeogenesis. An increase in protein utilization may demand an increase in the requirement. It is possible that athletes may have different protein requirements depending on the nature of their activity. For example, increases in muscle size and enzymes, which are associated with anaerobic metabolism, are found in athletes who undergo strength-training programs, whereas increases in the number of mitochondria and aerobic enzymes are found in athletes who endurance train (9, 25, 67).

Another consideration is the fat and carbohydrate content of the diet (20, 71). During heavy periods of strength training (e.g., multiple sets with high repetitions) large amounts of muscle glycogen and possibly liver glycogen may be lost. If muscle glycogen is not replaced with an adequate intake of carbohydrates, then the intensity of the workouts could diminish because glycogen is the preferred energy source, and muscle protein could be used as an energy source in order to maintain adequate blood glucose levels for functioning of the central nervous system. Loss of muscle protein could ultimately compromise both size and strength. An example of this situation can be found in the dietary practices of body builders preparing for competition. During the initial phase of their training cycle they consume large quantities of food while increasing both lean body mass and fat. As competition approaches, their diet shifts to one of very little fat and carbohydrate; caloric intake also declines. Although the diet contains a large proportion of protein in an effort to maintain muscle mass, both muscle mass and fat content decrease. Under this regimen, workouts tend to feel difficult (51) and individuals tend to become irritable.

The relationship between muscle glycogen and training has been observed by Costill et al. (18) (Figure 2–8). Although the study involved endurance training (2 hours/day), many strength workouts are of high enough volume and intensity to produce similar results (91, 93). Over a 3-day period Costill et al. (18) found that individuals on a low (40%) carbohydrate diet could not adequately replace muscle glycogen. Individuals on a high (70%) carbohydrate diet could maintain muscle glycogen levels to a much greater degree. Since replacing muscle glycogen requires some time (12–48 hours) (13), it is reasonable and important to introduce easy training days. Doing so may ultimately spare muscle glycogen.

Some researchers (10) have suggested that athletes engaged in heavy resistance training programs should consume approximately 2.0+ protein/kg BW/day. Gontzea et al. (39, 40) showed that eating 1.5 protein/kg BW/day could maintain a positive nitrogen balance through several weeks of training. Subjects on 1.0 protein/kg BW/day were in a negative nitrogen balance during the same period. In these studies, the individuals on the 1.0 g protein/kg BW/day diet slowly returned to zero balance after 20 days, indicating that the body can adapt to differ-

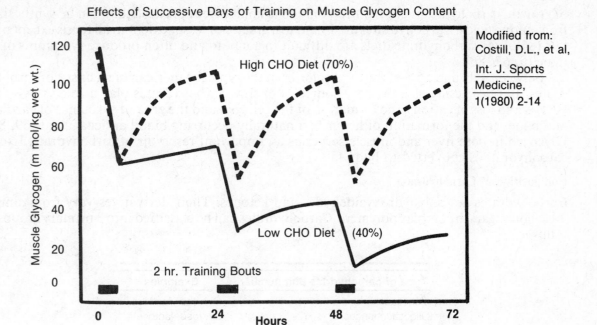

Effects of Successive Days of Training on Muscle Glycogen Content

Modified from: Costill, D.L., et al, Int. J. Sports Medicine, 1(1980) 2-14

High CHO Diet (70%)

Low CHO Diet (40%)

2 hr. Training Bouts

Muscle Glycogen (m mol/kg wet wt.)

Hours

Figure 2–8. Effects of successive days of training on muscle glycogen content (modified from 18).

ent levels of protein intake. It may, however, be necessary during the initial phases of training to increase protein intake, since factors affecting training at the beginning of a training program may influence the final outcome (39, 40, 68).

Laritcheva et al. (68) found that during periods of light training weightlifters could maintain a positive nitrogen balance on a diet that included 1.3–1.8 g protein/kg/day. During times of heavy training, 2.2–2.6 g protein/kg BW/day were necessary to maintain a positive balance. Similar results were observed by Celewjawa et al. among Polish weightlifters in hard training (15).

For a healthy individual, there appears to be little chance of harm from eating excess protein. Once the requirement has been met, the amino acids enter the metabolic pathways for fat and carbohydrate and are either used for energy or stored as fat. Observations of high level athletes who typically have high protein diets have shown that these individuals are also capable of maintaining a low percentage of body fat (27, 96). The metabolism of protein does require more water. Whereas only 50 g of water are needed to metabolize 100 Kcal of fat or carbohydrate, 350 g of water are needed to metabolize 100 Kcal of protein. Increased protein intake may affect calcium and zinc requirements (76) because there is an increased excretion of the two with high protein intakes. Many sources of protein, including meats, poultry, and fish, are low in calcium, so even modest increases in dietary protein unaccompanied by an increase in Ca^{++} may result in a loss of calcium from the body.

Nutrition Summary

Although there is still some confusion and controversy surrounding the protein requirements for athletes, increasing evidence suggests the need for increased protein, particularly during the early phases of a training program. To insure adequate protein quality and quantity, athletes should eat a wide variety of foods. A varied diet also insures adequate intake of the other insures essential nutrients. To spare protein, carbohydrate content of an athlete's diet may need to be increased, whereas the proportion of energy coming from fats can be reduced.

Carbohydrate Metabolism

As discussed above, carbohydrates are the preferred metabolic fuel. They are especially important for activities like weight training that involve high intensity exercise and training. In terms of growth, carbohydrates are required only to a small extent because they can be synthesized from amino acids. Carbohydrates are found to a greater or lesser extent in all foods except pure fats (86). Low carbohydrate diets are difficult to adapt to and often produce symptoms of fatigue (9, 67, 86).

Between 45% and 55% of the total calories in the typical American diet consist of carbohydrates. Besides acting as a primary source of energy, carbohydrates play a role in avoiding ketosis and loss of cations, the formation of the cell coat and the ground substance of cartilage and bone, and the formation of heparin, a naturally occurring blood anticoagulant (69, 86). Glycogen in both liver and muscle serves as an important reservoir of carbohydrate. Excess carbohydrate is converted to body fat.

Composition of Carbohydrates

Carbohydrates are polyhydroxyaldehydes and ketones. Their derivatives vary from simple 3-carbon sugars to complex polymers. Carbohydrates can be classified into 3 primary groups as follows:

Type of carbohydrate	Unit number	Examples
Monosaccharides	(1 unit)	Glucose, fructose
Oligosaccharides[*]	(2–10 units)	Sucrose, lactose
Polysaccharides	(> 10 units)	Starches, glycogen

[*]**Most prominent of the carbohydrates.**

Monosaccharides range from 3 carbon units (trioses) to heptoses (7 carbon units). Oligosaccharides are made up of mixtures of monosaccharides; sucrose (table sugar), for example, is a combination of glucose and fructose bound by a glycosidic linkage (69, 86). Homopolysaccharides are complex polymers containing only one type of monosaccharide; glycogen, for example, contains only glucose. Heteropolysaccharides contain mixtures of various monosaccharides (86). The most common polysaccharides found in the diet are starches (amylose and amylopectin).

Digestion of Carbohydrates

Certain polysaccharides such as cellulose, are nondigestible; others, such as raffinose, are partially digestible. Starches and most oligosaccharides and glucose polymers are totally digestible.

Digestion of carbohydrates begins with mastication (chewing). Amylase, an enzyme found in saliva, can break down starch to maltose (two molecules of glucose bound by a β-glycosidic bond), provided there is sufficient time between chewing and swallowing. In the stomach, carbohydrates are further broken down by amylase to monosaccharides at an optimum pH of 6.6–6.8. Further digestion of carbohydrates takes place in the small intestine. Disaccharides require small intestinal surface enzymes for conversion to monosaccharides; polysaccharides depend on additional pancreatic amylase for degradation. Absorption occurs in the small intestine, primarily in the duodenum. Because of a selective active transport system for galactose and glucose (and derivatives), some hexoses are absorbed faster than others (86). Fructose, mannose, and sorbital are absorbed by diffusion (84). After absorption, carbohydrates enter the bloodstream and can be taken up by the liver or other tissues (9, 39, 86).

Control of Carbohydrate Metabolism

As mentioned above, liver or muscle glycogen is the primary storage form of carbohydrates. To understand how muscles can maintain sufficient carbohydrate energy substrates for work, a brief discussion of carbohydrate synthesis and breakdown is in order.

Carbohydrate synthesis, in the form of glycogen, is primarily a function of two enzymes, glycogen synthetase, which is responsible for glycogen buildup, and phosphorylase, which is responsible for glycogen breakdown (9, 67, 70) (see Figure 2–11).

Two other important enzymes are hexokinase (found in muscle and other cells) and glucokinase (found only in the liver). These enzymes are responsible for phosphorylating glucose (9, 67, 70):

$$\text{ATP} + \text{glucose} \xrightarrow[\text{Mg}^{++}]{\text{Hexokinase}} \text{ADP} + \text{G-6-P}$$

In muscle and in the liver, this reaction is necessary for converting glucose to glycogen; in muscle and other cells, it is also a crucial first step for entry into glycolysis (9, 67, 70). Because of the effect of specific needs and because of the action of hormones such as insulin, glucokinase becomes more active as blood glucose levels increase. This augments the ability of the liver to take up blood glucose and convert it to glycogen (9, 67, 70). When blood glucose falls, the activity of glucokinase falls (9, 67, 70).

Hormones have profound effects on carbohydrate metabolism. Table 2–8 lists the basic effects of specific hormones on various metabolic processes related to carbohydrates.

Effects of Weight Training on Carbohydrate Metabolism

Increasing the intensity of exercise must be supported by increasing the contribution of anaerobic metabolism (see section on the relative efficiency of glycolysis and the oxidative system). The application of this concept to weight training is in relation to moderate to high volume work, especially when an athlete is using large muscle masses. Several studies **suggest** that weight-training exercise of this type can decrease glycogen levels (46, 91, 93, 109). Decreased glycogen levels are associated with fatigue (8, 9, 45, 57), reduced muscle contractile force (45, 48), and perhaps increased gluconeogenesis (9, 26, 71, 87, 113). Chronically reduced glycogen levels lead to overtraining.

One of the most important aspects of training is increased muscle glycogen. Intermittent anaerobic training can increase muscle glycogen (75) and **may** be one of the important adaptations associated with preparation phase training (see Chapter 6). Adopting a diet with increased carbohydrates may be advantageous before or during heavy phases of weight training (78, 113).

Need for Carbohydrates

Maintaining high glycogen levels, is important for both endurance and anaerobic activities. In strength-power sports, high glycogen levels reduce fatigue and gluconeogenesis and help maintain high levels of strength. Unfortunately, many strength-power athletes do not eat adequate amounts of carbohydrate because they believe carbohydrates add fat. Although excessive carbohydrates can add fat, they are the primary fuel for many strength-power training programs. From 50% to 55% of the calories consumed by athletes in such programs should be in the form of carbohydrates, especially complex carbohydrates (25, 86).

Carbohydrate Metabolism Summary

Carbohydrates are the preferred fuel, especially for high intensity work. Lack of carbohydrates in the diet or excessive training can chronically lower muscle glycogen, which may lead to overtraining. On a caloric basis, the diet of an athlete should consist of 50%–55% carbohydrates.

Table 2–8. Effects of hormones on carbohydrate metabolism.

Metabolic process	Hormone (+)	Hormone (−)
Cellular glucose uptake	Insulin	Glucogen
Blood glucose	Glucagon	Insulin
Glycolysis	Insulin, epinephrine	Glucagon, growth hormone
Glycogen synthesis	Insulin	Epinephrine
Liver glycogenolysis[*]	Glucagon, epinephrine	Insulin
Liver gluconeogenesis[†]	Glucagon, epinephrine, cortisol	Insulin
Increased blood glucose	Glucagon, cortisol	Insulin

[*]Glycogenolysis = breakdown of glycogen.
[†]Gluconeogenesis = production of glucose from carbohydrate and noncarbohydrate precursors (i.e., amino acids from muscle and other tissues through the action of cortisol, etc.).

Lipid Metabolism

Lipids (fats) are nonpolar substances that can be extracted from biological material with fat solvents (ether, chloroform, acetone, etc.). Although fats are important for many biological processes, they also are associated with a variety of diseases, especially cardiovascular diseases (CVD).

Fats constitute between 20% and 40% of the total dietary calories consumed in the United States. Fats, which are found in all cells, are a source of energy, and they play a role in the structure of cell membranes and in the synthesis of cholesterol and associated steroid hormones. Fat cells and intramuscular lipid-containing vacuoles are the main stores of fat (9, 70, 86). Excessive fat intake results in increased stored fat. Lipids can be divided into three basic categories (86) as follows:

Class	Lipid example	Example, site of use
Simple lipids	Fatty acids, neutral fats	Energy production
Compound lipids	Phospholipids, lipoproteins	Cell membranes
Derived lipids	Sterols	Hormones

Digestion of Lipids

The digestion of lipids is a complex physiological process that begins with mastication (chewing). Little digestion occurs in the stomach, where digestion can be slowed by the action of acid and pepsin, which break up fat emulsions, resulting in large globules of fat (69, 86). Although the stomach contains gastric lipase, this enzyme is ineffective for releasing FFA of 10 carbons or more. In the small intestine several hormones (e.g., enterogasterone, etc.) slow gastric motility, which increases the time required for digestion and absorption (86). In the duodenum, several pancreatic enzymes (such as glycerol esterhydrolase and cholesterol esterase) complete the breakdown of lipids, including triglycerides and cholesterol esters. This final digestion is accomplished in the presence of bile acids ($\downarrow$ pH). Digestion results in the formation of micelles, which contain some bile salts, glycerol, and fatty acids (70, 86). Absorption occurs by diffusion into the intestinal mucosa cells. Short and medium chain fatty acids pass through into the portal vein and are transported directly to the liver. Glycerol and fatty acids are converted to triglycerides in the mucosa cell and, along with cholesterol, form chylomicrons (lipoproteins) that are transported to the lymphatic system and are eventually emptied into the blood via the thoracic duct. Some very low density lipoproteins (VLDL) also can be formed in the mucosa cell and enter the lymphatic system (see Figure 2–9).

Fate of Lipids

Chylomicrons and some other lipids are taken up by the liver, where they are broken down and converted into other lipids and bile salts. Lipoproteins are created in the liver and released into the blood (86). Lipoproteins contain various amounts of triglycerides, phospholipids, cholesterol, and a protein coat. The protein serves mostly to make the lipids more water soluble and protect them from being hydrolized (69, 86) (see Table 2–9).

Lipids from lipoproteins released from the liver may be taken up by cells in a step catalyzed by the enzyme lipoprotein lipase (LPL). In fat cells, fatty acids are converted and stored as triglycerides; this process also occurs to a small degree in muscle and other tissues (9, 24, 53, 59). Within tissues, hormone-sensitive lipase (HSL) breaks down triglycerides to FFA and glycerol. The FFA from fat cells are released into the blood and can be taken up and used for energy. Muscle HSL breaks down stored triglycerides and makes them available for oxidation in the mitochondria (9, 53, 70) (see Figure 2–10).

Blood lipids, besides being used as energy sources, are also important in atherosclerosis development. Total cholesterol, the lipoprotein VLDL, and especially LDL, are associated with increased risk for CVD. Thus, low LDL:HDL or TC:HDL-C are advantageous in reducing CVD risk (24, 89).

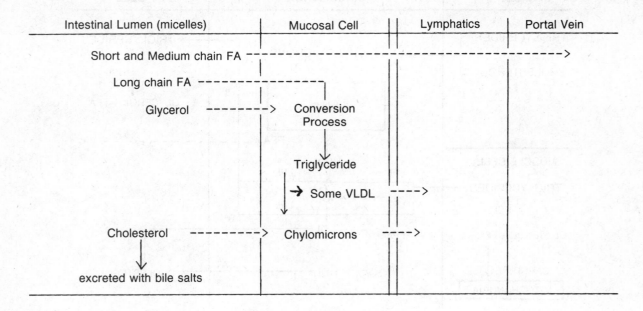

Figure 2–9. Lipid absorption.

As shown in Figure 2–10, the liver releases VLDL, some LDL, and HDL precursors into the blood; LPL removes the TG, helps to break it down, and allows FFA to enter the cell for storage or oxidation. The removal of TG from VLDL leaves a remnant, the intermediate density lipoprotein (IDL). Most of the IDL is degraded in the liver and removed as bile salts (24, 36). Some of the IDL has additional TG removed and is converted to LDL (24, 36). LDL is a major cholesterol carrier (9, 24, 86) that binds to receptors in various tissues, including liver, muscle, and arteries (9, 24, 36). In this manner, cholesterol can be deposited in these tissues (9, 24, 36). This may be a major step in the formation of atherosclerotic plaques (24, 36).

Recent research suggests that if liver cholesterol levels increase, then the number of receptors for IDL and LDL decreases. This means that more IDL will be converted to LDL (i.e., there will be increased CVD risk). HDL does not have the atherosclerotic effect of LDL; in a sense, it "scavenges" cholesterol via the enzyme lecithin cholesterol acetyl transferase (36).

Table 2–9. The lipoproteins* (9, 24, 84).

Type	Protein	TG	PL	Cholesterol and cholesterol esters
Chylomicrons†	2	83	7	8
VLDL‡	9	30	18	20
LDL	21	11	22	50
HDL#	40	8	22	20

Above the table: **Lipoprotein composition (% of total)**

*Soluble lipoproteins; structural lipoproteins (e.g., cell membranes) also exist.
†Formed in the intestinal lumen.
‡Some formed in the intestinal lumen.
#Primarily formed in the blood by the action of lecithin cholesterol acetyl transferase.
VLDL—very low density lipoproteins
LDL—low density lipoproteins
HDL—high density lipoproteins
TG—triglycerides
PL—phospholipids

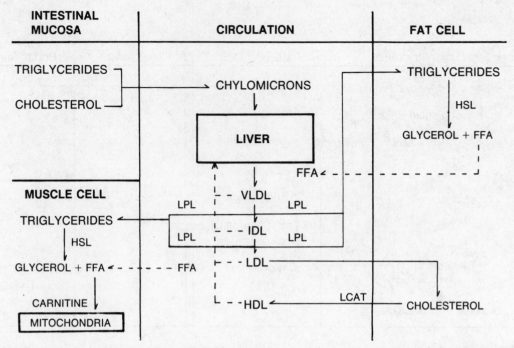

FFA—free fatty acids, VLDL—very low density lipoproteins, IDL—intermediate density lipoproteins, LDL—low density lipoproteins, HDL—high density lipoproteins, LPL—lipoprotein lipase, HSL—hormone–sensitive lipase, LCAT—lecithin cholesterol acetyl transferase.

Figure 2–10. Triglyceride–lipoprotein metabolism.

Effects of Hormones and Lipid Metabolism

As with proteins and carbohydrates, hormones can have profound effects on lipid metabolism. Table 2–10 lists the effects of specific hormones on specific aspects of lipid metabolism.

The Effects of Weight Training on Lipid Metabolism

Mobilization of FFA is an important effect supporting aerobic training (9, 24, 67). Considering the metabolic adaptations occurring from aerobic training (2, 9, 38, 47), the beneficial effects on serum lipids (increased HDL, decreased LDL, decreased LDL:HDL, and decreased TC:HDL-C) are not surprising.

It is unlikely that typical low volume weight-training exercise mobilizes FFA even moderately. However, a recent descriptive study (56) and several longitudinal studies (6, 34, 58) have shown that high volume weight training can produce beneficial alterations in serum lipids similar to what happens in aerobic work. How this occurs is unknown. It may be related to the high levels of aerobic metabolism that occur between sets and during recovery (93), it may be simple loss of body fat, or it may be a complex biochemical process. Hurley et al. (55) have suggested that hepatic triglyceride lipase may modulate HDL levels. In any case, high volume weight training can alter blood lipids beneficially (see also Chapter 3).

Table 2–10. Effect of hormones on lipid metabolism (9, 24, 32, 99).

Metabolic process	Hormone (+)	Hormone (−)
Triglyceride synthesis	Insulin	Epinephrine
Lipolysis	Cortisol	Insulin
	Epinephrine	
	Growth hormone	
	Thyroxine	
	Glucagon	

Lipid Metabolism

Lipids function in a wide range of physiological and metabolic activities including structural and energy reactions. Abnormal blood lipids are related to cardiovascular disease. Weight training can beneficially alter lipid profiles.

Hormonal Control of Energy Metabolism

The mobilization and release of substrate required for the energy systems is to a large extent the result of hormonal actions. The summary tables 2–7, 2–8, 2–9, and 2–10 list the fundamental actions these hormones have on physiological and metabolic functions related to aerobic or anerobic exercise.

The initiation of substrate mobilization for use in energy production is a function of hormones such as epinephrine. Specific epinephrine receptors on cell membranes initiate a series of actions known as the *cascade effect*. This effect is illustrated in Figure 2–11 (9, 70).

The series of events depicted in Figure 2–11 is responsible for the mobilization and release of FFA by fat cells, the release of glucose by the liver, and the intramuscular breakdown of triglycerides and glycogen for use in energy production. Notice that the intramuscular release of calcium ions stimulates glycogen breakdown. This is most important during intense muscular effort.

Effects of Weight Training on Hormone Levels

The effects of aerobic exercise and training on hormone levels have been reviewed elsewhere (32, 101). Aerobic and anaerobic exercise, including weight-training exercise, produce different effects (9, 61). Hormones, even when acutely released as in exercise, may have longlasting and profound effects (9, 32, 70, 101). The general responses of various hormones to exercise are shown in Table 2–11 (9, 32, 67, 101).

Weight-training exercise increases insulin, growth hormone, and perhaps testosterone—all anabolic hormones (67). Intense aerobic exercise has similar effects on growth hormone and testosterone (61), but there are marked differences in muscle mass. Speculation suggests that insulin, hormone interaction, or increased cell sensitivity to these hormones may be partially responsible for muscle hypertrophy. Furthermore, the markedly higher catecholamine release that occurs with heavy anaerobic activity like weight training points to higher sympatho-adrenal and emotional stress (61).

The training effects of aerobic or anaerobic exercise are largely unknown. In general, resting levels of hormones are unaffected by training (aerobic or anaerobic) (32, 101). But exercise-induced release, metabolic clearance, or cell sensitivity may change with training (9, 32, 101). It is difficult to determine what effect increased hormone turnover or increased cell sensitivity may have on normal responses to exercise, training, energy metabolism, or

Table 2–11. Hormone response to exercise[*].

Hormone	Light (≤ 62.5% max $\dot{V}O_2$) aerobic exercise	Intense aerobic exercise	Anaerobic exercise
Cortisol	No change or decrease	Increase	Increase
Catacholamines	Increase	Increase	Large increase
Insulin	Decrease	Decrease	Increase(?)
Glucagon	Increase	Increase	Unknown
Testosterone	Small increase (?)	Increase	Increase
Estradiol	Increase (?)	Increase (?)	Increase (?)
Growth hormone	Increase	Increase	Increase
Thyroxidine	No change	No change	No change (?)

[*]Some hormone responses also depend on the duration of exercise.

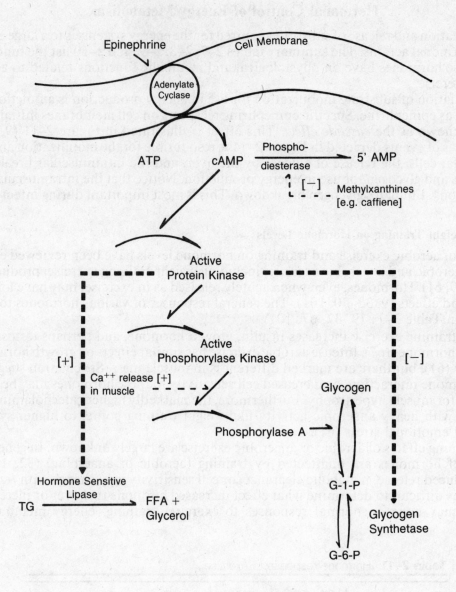

Figure 2–11. The cascade effect.

anabolic-catabolic processes. Empirically, if one considers the muscle hypertrophy and strength of the weightlifter or the endurance of the marathon runner, it is logical to believe that hormones contribute to these profound physiological and performance effects. Two recent studies that have important implications for health suggest that weight training has beneficial effects on glucose tolerance and increases insulin sensitivity. The reasons for these effects are unclear, but may be related to increased muscle mass (82, 110).

Hormonal Control Summary

Hormones produce profound physiological and metabolic effects, even when acutely released. Aerobic and anaerobic exercise and training can produce different, even opposite, effects.

Summary

Weight training exercise relies primarily on anaerobic energy systems. Energy cost considerations suggest a higher total caloric cost than previously thought, especially during high volume training that emphasizes large muscle mass exercises. Nutritional considerations suggest an increase in dietary protein and perhaps in carbohydrates, plus a reduction in fats. Finally, weight training can cause beneficial alterations in blood lipids, and may benefically alter glucose tolerance and increase insulin sensitivity. These beneficial alterations are likely to reduce the risk for cardiovascular and other degenerative diseases.

References

1. Alfin-Slater, R., et. al. 1973. *Nutrition for Today,* Wm. C. Brown, Co., Pub.

2. Astrand, P. O., and K. Rodahl. 1970. *Textbook of Work Physiology* (2nd ed.). New York: McGraw-Hill.

3. Barnard, R. J., V. R. Edgerton, T. Furakawa, and J. B. Peter. 1971. Histochemical, biochemical and contractile properties of red, white, and intermediate fibers. *American Journal of Physiology* 220:410–441.

4. Berg, W. E. 1947. Individual differences in respiratory gas exchange during recovery from moderate exercise. *American Journal of Physiology* 149:507–530.

5. Bleich, H. L., et al. 1971. Protein digestions and absorption. *New England Journal of Medicine* 300(12):659–663.

6. Blessing, D. 1983. Performance, body composition, heart rate, blood lipids and hormonal effects of short-term jogging and weight training in middle-aged sedentary men. Doctoral dissertation, Louisiana State University.

7. Booth, F. W., et al. 1982. Influence of muscle use on protein synthesis and degradation. *Exercise and Sport Science Reviews.* 10:27–48.

8. Brooks, G. A., K. E. Brauner, R. G. Cassens. 1973. Glycogen synthesis and metabolism of lactic acid after exercise. *American Journal oⱼ Physiology* 224:1162–1186.

9. Brooks, G. A., and T. D. Fahey. 1984. *Exercise Physiology: Human Bioenergetics and its Applications.* New York: John Wiley & Sons.

10. Brooks, G. A., K. J. Hittelman, J. A. Faulkner, and R. E. Beyer. 1971. Temperature, skeletal muscle mitochondrial functions and oxygen debt. *American Journal of Physiology* 220:1053–1068.

11. Brouha, L., and E. Radford. 1960. The cardiovascular system in muscular activity. In W. Johnson (Ed.). *Science and Medicine of Exercise and Sports.* New York: McGraw-Hill.

12. Burke, R. E., and V. R. Edgerton. 1975. Motor unit properties and selective involvement in movement. In J. Wilmore and J. Drough (Eds.). *Exercise and Sports Science Reviews* 3:31–81.

13. Buskirk, E. R. 1981. Some nutritional considerations in the conditioning of athletes. *Annual Review of Nutrition* 1:319–350.

14. Cain, D. F., and R. E. Davies. 1962. Breakdown of adenosine triphosphate during a single contraction of working muscle. *Biochemistry and Biophysics Research Communication* 8:361–466.

15. Celewjawa, I., and M. Homa. 1970. Food intake, nitrogen and energy balance in Polish weightlifters during training camp. *Nutrition and Metabolism* 12:259–274.

16. Chappell, J. B. 1968. Systems used for the transport of substances into mitochondria. *British Medical Bulletin* 24:150–157.

17. Consolazio, F. C., et al. 1975. Protein metabolism during intensive physical training in the young adult. *Nutrition Reviews International* 11(3):231–236.

18. Costill, D. L., et al. 1980. Nutrition for endurance sport: carbohydrate and fluid balance. *International Journal of Sports Medicine* 1:2–14.

19. Coyle, E. F., A. R. Coggan, M. K. Hemmart, and T. J. Walters. 1984. Glycogen usage performance relative to lactate threshold. (Abstract). *Medicine and Science in Sports and Exercise* 16:120.

20. Davie, M., et al. 1982. Effect of high and low carbohydrate diets on nitrogen balance during calorie restriction in obese subjects. *International Journal of Obesity* 6:457–462.

21. Davis, J. A., M. H. Frank, B. J. Whipp, and K. Wasserman. 1979. Anaerobic threshold alterations caused by endurance training in middle-aged men. *Journal of Applied Physiology* 46:1039–1046.

22. Dohm, G. L., et al. 1982. Increased excretion of urea and N-methylhistidine by rats and humans after a bout of exercise. *Journal of Applied Physiology* 3:27–33.

23. Dohmeier, T. E., P. A. Farrel, C. Foster, and M. Greenisen. 1984. Metabolic response to submaximal and maximal timed interval squats. *Medicine and Science in Sports and Exercise* 16:126.

24. DuFax, B., G. Assmann, and W. Hollman. 1982. Plasma lipoproteins and physical activity: A review. *International Journal of Sports Medicine* 3:123–136.

25. Edington, D. E., and V. R. Edgerton. 1976. *The Biology of Physical Activity.* New York: Houghton Mifflin Publ.

26. Evans, W. J., et al. 1983. Protein metabolism and endurance exercise. *Physician and Sports Medicine* 11(7):63–72.

27. Fahey, T., L. Akka, and R. Rolph. 1975. Body composition and $\dot{V}O_2$ max of exceptionally weight-trained athletes. *Journal of Applied Physiology* 39:559–561.

28. FAO/WHO (Food and Agriculture Organization/World Health Organization). 1973. Energy and Protein Requirements, Report of a joint FAO/WHO ad hoc Expert Committee, WHO Tech. Rept. Ser. No. 522; FAO Nutrition Meetings Rept. Ser. 52, WHO, Geneva.

29. Felig, P., et al. 1971. Amino acid metabolism in exercising man. *Journal of Clinical Investigation* 50:2703–2714.

30. Fox, E. L., and D. K. Mathews. 1981. *The Physiological Basis of Physical Education and Athletics.* (3rd ed.) Philadelphia: W. B. Saunders.

31. Gaesser, G. A., and R. G. Rich. 1984. Effects of high and low-intensity training on aerobic capacity and blood lipids. *Medicine and Science in Sports and Exercise* 16:269–274.

32. Galbo, J. 1981. Endocrinology and metabolism in exercise. *International Journal of Sports Medicine* 2:203–211.

33. Gladden, L. B., and H. G. Welch. 1978. Efficiency of anaerobic work. *Journal of Applied Physiology* 44:564–570.

34. Goldberg, L., D. L. Elliot, R. Schutz, and F. M. Kloster. 1984. Modification of lipid and lipoprotein levels by resistive exercise. *Journal of the American Medical Association* 252:504–506.

35. Goldberg, R. L. 1980. *Hormonal Regulation of Protein Degradation and Synthesis in Skeletal Muscle.* Fed. Proc., 39:31–36.

36. Goldstein, J., T. Kita, and M. Brown. 1983. Defective lipoprotein receptors and atherosclerosis. *New England Journal of Medicine* 309: 288-292.

37. Gollnick, P. D., and L. Hermansen. 1975. Biochemical adaptations to exercise: Anaerobic metabolism. *Exercise and Sports Sciences Reviews* 1:1–13.

38. Gollnick, P. D., and B. Saltin. 1982. Significance of skeletal muscle oxidative enzyme enhancement with endurance training. *Clinica Physiology* 2:1–12.

39. Gontzea, I., et al. 1974. The influence of muscular activity on nitrogen balance and on the need of man for proteins. *Nutrition Reports International* 10(1):35–43.

40. Gontzea, I., et al. 1975. The influence of adaptation to physical efforts on nitrogen balance in man. *Nutrition Reports International* 11(3):231–236.

41. Green, H. J., M. E. Houston, J. A. Thomson, et al. 1979. Metabolic consequences of supra maximal armwork performed during prolonged submaximal leg work. *Journal of Applied Physiology* 46:249–255.

42. Hadmann, R. 1957. The available glycogen in man and the connection between rate of oxygen intake and carbohydrate usage. *Acta Physiologica Scandinavica* 40:305–330.

43. Hempel, L. A., and C. L. Well. 1983. Oxygen utilization during performance of 20-minute Nautilus express circuit. *Medicine and Science in Sports and Exercise* 15:169.

44. Henry, F. M. 1957. Aerobic oxygen consumption and alactic debt in muscular work. *Journal of Applied Physiology* 3:427–450.

45. Hermanson, L. 1981. Effect of metabolic changes on force generation in skeletal muscle during maximal exercise. *Human Muscle Fatigue.* London: Pittman Medical.

46. Hickson, J. F., J. H. Wilmore, S. H. Constable, and M. J. Buono. 1982. Characterization of standardized weight training exercise. (Abstract). *Medicine and Science in Sports and Exercise* 14:169.

47. Hickson, R. C. 1980. Interference of strength development by simultaneously training for strength and endurance. *European Journal of Applied Physiology* 215:255–263.

48. Hickson, R. C., W. W. Heusner, and W. D. Van Huss. 1976. Skeletal muscle enzyme alterations after sprint and endurance training.

49. Hickson, R. C., M. A. Rosenkoetter, and M. M. Brown. 1980. Strength training effects on aerobic power and short-term endurance. *Medicine and Science in Sports and Exercise* 12:336–339.

50. Hill, A. V. 1924. Muscular exercise, lactic acid and the supply and utilization of oxygen. *Proceedings of the Royal Society of London* (*Biology*) 96:438 (as cited in McArdle, Katch and Katch).

51. Horton, E. S. 1982. Effects of low energy diets on work performance. *American Journal of Clinical Nutrition* 35:1228–1233.

52. Houston, M. E., and J. A. Thomson. 1977. The response of endurance-adapted adults to intense anaerobic training. *European Journal of Applied Physiology* 36:207–213.

53. Hultsmann, W. C. 1979. On the regulation of the supply of substrates for muscular activity. *Bibliothica Nutrition Dictatica* 27:11–15.

54. Hunter, G. R., and J. P. McCarthy. 1983. Pressor responses associated with high-intensity anaerobic training. *Physician and Sports Medicine* 11:151–162.

55. Hurley, B. F., J. M. Hagerg, D. R. Seals, et al. 1984. Hepatic triglyceride lipase modulates high density lipoprotein cholesterol levels in weightlifters and runners. (Abstract). *Clinical Research* 32:398a.

56. Hurley, B. F., D. R. Seals, J. M. Hagberg, et al. 1984. Strength training and lipoprotein lipid profiles: Increased HDL-cholesterol in body builders vs. powerlifters and effects of androgen use. *Journal of the American Medical Association* 252:507–513.

57. Jacobs, I., P. Kaiser, and P. Tesch. 1981. Muscle strength and fatigue after selective glycogen depletion in human skeletal muscle fibers. *European Journal of Applied Physiology* 46:47–53.

58. Johnson, C. C., H. M. Stone, A. Lopez-s, et al. 1982. Diet and exercise in middle-aged men. *Journal of the American Dietary Association* 81:695–701.

59. Jones, N. L., J. F. Heigenhauser, A. Kuksis, et al. 1980. Fat metabolism in heavy exercise. *Clinical Science* 59:469–478.

60. Karlsson, J. 1971. Lactate and phosphagen concentrations in working muscle of man. *Acta Physiologica Scandinavica Supplementum* 358–365.

61. Kindermann, W., A. Schnabel, W. M. Schmitt, et al. 1982. Catecholamines, growth hormone, cortisol, insulin, and sex hormones in anaerobic and aerobic exercise. *European Journal of Applied Physiology* 49:389–399.

62. Kindermann, W., G. Simon, and J. Jeul. 1979. The significance of the aerobic-anaerobic transition for the determination of work load intensities during endurance training. *European Journal of Applied Physiology* 42:25–34.

63. Kleiber, M. 1950. Calorimetric measurements. (In F. Uber, Ed.) *Biophysical Research Methods.* New York: Interscience Publishers.

64. Klingerberg, M. 1970. Metabolite transport in mitochondria: An example for intracellular membrane function. *Essays in Biochemistry* 6:119–159.

65. Komi, P. V., A. Ito, B. Sjodin, and J. Karlsson. 1981. Lactate breaking point and biomechanics of running. (Abstract). *Medicine and Science in Sports and Exercise* 13:114.

66. Krebs, H. A. 1972. The Pasteur effect and the relation between respiration and fermentation. *Essays in Biochemistry* 8:2–34.

67. Lamb, D. R. 1984. *Physiology of Exercise: Responses and Adaptations.* New York: MacMillan.

68. Laritcheva, K. A., N. I. Valovaya, V. I. Shubin, and P. V. Smirnov. 1978. Study of energy expenditure and protein needs of top weight lifters. (In J. Parizkova and V. A. Rogozkin, Eds.). *Nutrition, Physical Fitness and Health.* International Series on Sports Sciences, Vol. 7. Baltimore: University Park Press.

69. Lehninger, A. L. 1973. *Bioenergetics.* New York: W. A. Banjamin.

70. Lehninger, A. L. 1975. *Biochemistry.* (2nd ed.). New York: Worth Publishers.

71. Lemon, P. W. R., et al. 1980. Effect of initial glycogen levels on protein catabolism during exercise. *Journal of Applied Physiology* 48(4):624–629.

72. Lemon, P. W. R., et al. 1981. Effects of exercise on protein and amino acid metabolism. *Medicine and Science in Sports and Exercise* 13(3):141–149.

73. Lemon, P. W. R., et al. 1982. In vivo leucine oxidation at rest and during two intensities of exercise. *Journal of Applied Physiology* 53(4):947–954.

74. Lipmann, F. 1941. Metabolic generation and utilization of phosphate bond energy. *Advances in Enzymology* 1:99–162.

75. MacDougall, J. D., G. R. Ward, D. G. Sale, and J. R. Sutton. Biochemical adaptations of human skeletal muscle to heavy resistance training and immobilization. *Journal of Applied Physiology* 43:700–703.

76. Mahalko, J. R., et al. 1983. Effect of a moderate increase in dietary protein on the retention and excretion of Ca, Cu, Fe, Mg, P, and Zn by adult males. *American Journal of Clinical Nutrition* 37:8–14.

77. Margaria, R., H. T. Edwards, and D. B. Dill. 1933. The possible mechanism of contracting and paying the oxygen debt and the role of lactic acid in muscular contraction. *American Journal of Physiology* 106:687–714.

78. Maughan, R. J., and D. C. Poole, 1981. The effects of a glycogen-loading regimen on the capacity to perform aerobic exercise. *European Journal of Applied Physiology* 46:211–219.

79. McArdle, W. D., and G. F. Foglia. 1969. Energy cost and cardiorespiratory stress of isometric and weight training exercises. *Journal of Sports Medicine and Physical Fitness* 9:23–30.

80. McArdle, W. D., F. I. Katch, and V. L. Katch. 1981. *Exercise Physiology.* Philadelphia: Lea & Febiger.

81. McGilvery, R. W. 1975. *Biochemical Concepts.* Philadelphia: W. B. Saunders Co.

82. Miller, W. J., W. M. Sherman, and J. L. Ivy. 1984. Effect of strength training on glucose tolerance and post-glucose insulin response. *Medicine and Science in Sport and Exercise* 16:539–543.

83. National Academy of Sciences. 1980. *Recommended Dietary Allowances.* 9th Ed., 39–54.

84. Opie, L. H., and E. A. Newsholme. 1967. The activities of fructose 1, 6-diphosphate, phosphofructokinase, and phosphoenolpyruvate carboxykinase in white and red muscle. *Biochemical Journal* 103:391–399.

85. Pierce, K. 1986. The effects of weight training on plasma cortisol, lactate, heart rate, anxiety and perceived exertion. Unpublished doctoral dissertation, Auburn University.

86. Pike, R. L., and Brown, M. 1975. *Nutrition*: *An Integrated Approach.* (2nd ed.). New York: John Wiley & Sons.

87. Rennie, M. H., et al. 1980. Protein and amino acid turnover during and after exercise. *Biochemical Society Transactions* 8:499–504.

88. Richter, E. A., H. Galbo, and N. J. Christensen. 1981. Control of exercise-induced muscular glycogenolysis by adrenal medullary hormones in rats. *Journal of Applied Physiology* 50:21–26.

89. Rifkind, B. M., and P. Segal. 1984. Lipid research clinics program reference values for hyperlipidemia and hypolipidemia. *Journal of the American Medical Association* 250:1869–1872.

90. Robinson, D. 1974. Physiology of muscular exercise. In V. B. Montcastle (Ed.) *Medical Physiology.* Vol. 2, 13th ed. St. Louis: C. B. Mosby.

91. Rozenek, R. 1984. The effects of an acute bout of resistance exercise and self-administered anabolic steroids on plasma levels of LH, androgen, ACTH, cortisol, lactate, and psychological factors in athletes. Doctoral dissertation, Auburn University.

92. Saltin, B., and P. O. Astrand. 1967. Maximal oxygen uptake in athletes. *Journal of Applied Physiology* 23:353–358.

93. Scala, D. 1984. Oxygen uptake, oxygen debt and energy cost of high volume non-circuit Olympic style weight-training. Master's Thesis, Auburn University.

94. Sparge, E., et al. 1979. Metabolic functions of skeletal muscles of man, mammals, birds, and fishes: A review. *Journal of the Royal Society of Medicine* 72:921–925.

95. Stainsby, W. M., and J. K. Barclay. 1970. Exercise metabolism: O_2 deficit, steady level O_2 uptake and O_2 uptake in recovery. *Medicine and Science in Sports* 2:177–195.

96. Stone, M. H., D. Carter, D. P. Smith, and T. Ward. 1979. Olympic weightlifting: Physiological characteristics of the athletes. (In J. Terands, Ed.) *Science in Weightlifting.* Delmar, California: Academic Publishers, 45–53.

97. Stone, M. H., H. O'Bryant, J. Garhammer, et al. 1982. A theoretical model of strength training. *National Strength and Conditioning Association Journal* 4(4):36–39.

98. Stone, M. H., K. Pierce, R. Godsen, et al. 1985. Heart rate and lactate response in trained and untrained young males during resistive exercise. (Abstract). *Conference Abstracts, SEACSM Meeting.*

99. Stone, M. H., T. Ward, D. P. Smith, and M. Rush. 1979. Olympic weightlifting: Metabolic consequences of a workout. (In J. Terands, Ed.). *Science in Weightlifting.* Del Mar, California: Academic Publishers, 54–67.

100. Stone, M. H., G. D. Wilson, D. Blessing, and R. Rozenek. 1983. Cardiovascular responses to short-term Olympic style weight training in young men. *Canadian Journal of Applied Sports Science* 8:134–139.

101. Terjung, R. 1979. Endocrine response to exercise. (In R. S. Hutton & D. F. Miller, Eds.). *Exercise and Sports Sciences Reviews* 7:153–180.

102. Tischler, M. E. 1981. Hormonal regulation of protein degradation in skeletal and cardiac muscle. *Life Sciences* 28:2569–2576.

103. Thorstensson, P. 1976. Muscle strength, fibre types and enzymes in man. *Acta Physiologica Scandinavica* (supplementum) 443.

104. Vihko, V., A. Salmons, and J. Rontumaki. 1978. Oxidative and lysomal capacity in skeletal muscle of mice after endurance training of different intensities. *Acta Psychologica Scandinavica* 104:74–81.

105. Wells, J., B. Balke, and D. Van Fossan. 1957. Lactic acid accumulation during work. A suggested standardization of work classification. *Journal of Applied Physiology* 10:51–55.

106. Weltman, A., and U. L. Katch. 1977. Min-by-min respiratory exchange and oxygen uptake kinetics during steady-state exercise in subjects of high and low max VO_2. *Research Quarterly* 47:490–501.

107. Whipp, B. J., C. Scard, and K. Wasserman. 1970. O_2 deficit-O_2 debt relationship and efficiency of aerobic work. *Journal of Applied Physiology* 28:452–458.

108. Wilmore, J. H., R. B. Parr, P. Ward, et al. 1978. Energy cost of circuit weight training. *Medicine and Science in Sports* 10:75–78.

109. Wright, J. E., J. F. Patton, J. A. Vogel, et al. 1982. Aerobic power and body composition after 10 weeks of circuit weight training using various work: rest ratios. *Medicine and Science in Sports and Exercise* 14:170.

110. Yki-Jarvinen, H., V. A. Koivisto, M. R. Taskinen, and E. A. Nikkila. 1984. Glucose tolerance, plasma lipoproteins and tissue lipoprotein lipase activities in body builders. *European Journal of Applied Physiology* 53:253–259.

111. York, J., L. B. Oscai, and D. G. Penny. 1974. Alterations in skeletal muscle lactate dehydrogenase isozymes following exercise training. *Biochemistry and Biophysics Research Communication* 61:1387–1393.

112. Yoshimura, H., et al. 1980. Anemia during hard physical training (sports anemia) and its causal mechanism with special reference to protein nutrition. *World Review of Nutrition and Diet* 35:1–86. 1980.

113. Young, V. R., and B. Torun. 1981. Physical activity: Impact on protein and amino acid metabolism and implications for nutritional requirements. *Progress in Clinical and Biological Research* 77:57–83.

The Importance of Weight Training as a Lifetime Physical Activity

Many adults who live in the United States are physically unfit; many of these individuals also suffer from high levels of emotional stress. In our culture, low levels of fitness are the result of relatively sedentary lifestyles that begin in childhood and continue throughout life. Comparisons done in the 1950s and 1960s vividly pointed out that European children are more fit than U.S. children (1, 2, 67). Unfortunately, this pattern of inactive children growing into sedentary, physically unfit, basically unhealthy adults, is still the norm (32, 64). It has become apparent that fitness level and health status are intimately related.

From another perspective, one's physical fitness is obviously related to how one performs athletic and other work tasks. Performance fitness attributes include those factors that allow the athlete or physical laborer to perform with power, strength, endurance, agility, skill, etc. (7, 32). An excellent example of the enhancement of these attributes is represented by the Olympic decathlon champion.

Physical fitness can be assessed in terms of health fitness or performance fitness. Both types of fitness rely on the same components; differences are largely determined by the level to which individual components are developed or emphasized. For example, a weightlifter might be rather average in some components of physical fitness, but would be much above other athletes in maximum strength and power levels. On the other hand, a nonathlete, who doesn't need the great strength and power of a weightlifter, still derives health benefits from developing that aspect of fitness.

The basic components of physical fitness are cardiovascular fitness; strength, with the subcomponents of power and muscular endurance; flexibility; and body composition. The relative health and performance benefits of these components are discussed briefly in the sections that follow. The purpose of this chapter is not to compare training methods but to present evidence about the possible positive effects of resistive training on the components of physical fitness. This information is especially relevant today because of the large and increasing segment of the population that regularly engages in weight training and other forms of resistive training (10, 112).

Cardiovascular Fitness

Cardiovascular disease (CVD) is the leading cause of death in the United States. A large body of scientific evidence now suggests that regular physical activity can improve cardiovascular fitness in a manner that may reduce the likelihood of developing CVD. Appropriate training can produce lowered heart rates (99), more efficient coronary and peripheral circulation (82, 99, 111), stabilized or decreased blood pressure (11, 74, 99), positive effects on serum lipids (92, 139), more efficient pulmonary function (74), and a generally improved cardiovascular-respiratory system. Additionally, appropriate physical training can reduce the debilitating effects of CVD by increasing cardiovascular function.

From a performance standpoint, increased cardiovascular fitness exerts its greatest influence by increasing physical working capacity and reducing fatigue (7, 30, 71). An example is the great endurance of the marathon runner. The cardiovascular system functions to deliver oxygen, nutrients, hormones, and other substances to the body and to assist in removing wastes (7, 32). The oxygen delivered is related to the body's ability to produce energy (i.e., aerobic power). Many of the body's waste products—lactate, for example—have been associated with fatigue. With proper training, oxygen delivery and waste removal can be made more efficient and can accompany an increase in aerobic power (max $\dot{V}O_2$). These effects will, for many activities, allow work or athletic performance to be carried out closer to an individual's maximum ability and/or for increased periods of time. Improvement in cardiovascular fitness is related to the use of large muscle mass exercises and to the volume and intensity of training (4,7).

Effects of Weight Training on Cardiovascular Fitness and CVD Risk Factors

The studies of Paffenbarger and associates (94, 95) suggested that longshoremen whose work involved the greatest energy demands had fewer incidences of CVD and a lower mortality rate. Most of the work that longshoremen do is similar to weight training. Although many studies have suggested that aerobic training can positively affect various factors associated with physical fitness and CVD risk (20, 48, 139), weight training is generally believed to have limited value in modifying risk for CVD. This belief partially stems from research using **typical** weight-training programs that indicate a minimal effect on maximum aerobic power (31, 85). However, equating aerobic power with CVD risk is overly simplistic at best (10, 45, 46). It is becoming increasingly clear that the study of CVD risk is a multifactorial problem. This section briefly reviews the effects of resistive training on various parameters associated with cardiovascular fitness and CVD risk.

Heart Rate

Training-induced bradycardia (< 60 beats/min) is generally viewed as a positive result (60, 98). Descriptive studies of highly weight-trained athletes show them to have lower than average resting heart rates (68, 83, 105, 132). Several short-term resistive-training studies have shown significant decreases in resting heart rate (60, 69, 70, 117), heart rate during submaximal work (10, 46, 112), and recovery heart rate (69, 112). The reason for this apparent weight-training-induced bradycardia is unknown. It may, however, be related to an increased parasympathetic/sympathetic input ratio (29, 41). Bradycardia resulting from weight training is likely to be accompanied by an increased stroke volume due to a longer diastole (increased venous return), but it may not reflect a large increase in chamber size (15, 60).

Central Effects

Effects of training on intact human heart are difficult to assess. Roentenography and echocardiography have both been used to assess changes in wall thickness and chamber volume in humans. The usefulness of these methods is limited, however (96, 122).

Using roentenographic techniques, Abramyan and Dzhuganyon (3) found that weightlifters have somewhat larger left ventricular volumes, both in absolute and relative terms, than nonathletes, although not as large as those of endurance-trained athletes. Furthermore, evidence from this study suggested that heart volume depended on total training volume and the number of years the athlete had trained. Strength-power athletes were described as having medium-sized "athletic hearts."

Descriptive echocardiographic studies of strength-trained athletes indicate increased left ventricular mass (15, 83), increased left ventricular wall thickness (83, 96), increased septum thickness, and an increased septum-to-free-wall ratio (80). Furthermore, increased left ventricular mass and wall thickness have been shown to be significant even when body weight and body surface area are considered (15, 36). Chamber size shows small or no increase above control values (60, 80, 83, 96), in contrast to the large chambers observed in endurance-trained athletes (83, 96).

These descriptive studies suggest that the endurance-trained heart may be an adaptation to increased preload. On the other hand, the strength-trained heart may have adapted to handle the increased afterload (and perhaps a decreased preload due to the drop in venous return that may occur with some forms of weight-training exercises).

Longitudinal studies are few and generally limited in scope. Ricci et al. (101), using low volumes and only upper body resistive training, observed an increase in left ventricular mass after 8 weeks of training in young men. Periodic weighted running and exercises described as the push and pull coupled with extremely low volumes and intensities (i.e., small loading) over 18 weeks produced an increase in left ventricular wall thickness (109). Neither of these studies reported significant functional changes. However, Kanakis and Hickson (60) demonstrated both increased left ventricular wall thickness and increased mass accompanied by functional changes (e.g., decreased heart rate and increases in left ventricular performance). This study (60) used a higher volume of training—5×5 RM (repetitions maximum), and extensive large muscle mass exercises (e.g., squats, deadlifts); subjects trained 5 days per week. Using boys who were 11.9 years old, Servidio et al. (107) found that 8 weeks of 3-days-per-week weightlifting training produced an increased left ventricular end diastolic volume (echocardiography) and an increased calculated stroke volume.

Longitudinal animal studies have produced similar results. Jaweed et al. (57), using rats trained to climb up an incline with weights attached to their tails, produced an increased heart weight and left ventricular hypertrophy. More recently, Muntz et al. (84) implanted radioopaque markers in the left ventricular wall of 11 cats. Wall thickness was monitored monthly using cineflurography for 9 months. The cats were trained to perform isometric work (weights had to be lifted and then held using the foreleg to obtain food). Isometric work was performed several times a day and was calculated as force (weight held) $\times$ total time. A 32.5% increase in wall thickness was observed after 6 months. Furthermore, the increases in wall thickness were strongly correlated with both total and daily isometric work. Further evaluations upon sacrifice indicated that, compared to control animals, the trained group had significantly larger heart-to-body weight ratios, larger left and right ventricular weight-to-body weight ratios, and larger atrial weight-to-body weight ratios, plus all chambers exhibited enlargement. When hearts were not normalized for body weight, the same conclusions were reached. Additionally, histological quantification of myocardial fiber diameter showed significantly larger mean values (19.7 ± 0.8 μm) as compared to controls (13.4 ± 0.9 μm). These changes in the myocardium were accompanied by a decreased resting heart rate (39). In general, the longitudinal studies support the descriptive studies.

The extent to which these changes affect stroke volume and cardiac output is largely unknown. Certainly it is logical to assume that thicker—and thus stronger—myocardial walls would function to support stroke volume during high afterload exercise since this is a reason for the adaptation.

Evidence for a positive effect on stroke volume and cardiac output has been **suggested** by the observation, in weight-trained young men, of an increase in fractional shortening of the left ventricle, bradycardia, and a trend toward a larger left ventricular diastolic internal dimension (60). Two studies using echocardiography have shown increased calculated resting stroke volume. Fleck and Tesch (36) found a larger left ventricular end diastolic volume (LVEDV) and stroke volume in young adult bodybuilders, powerlifters, and weightlifters who had attained a high skill level. Servidio et al. (107) found an increased stroke volume after 8 weeks of training (3 days/week) in 12-year-old males.

Perhaps the most compelling evidence for a positive effect on stroke volume (and perhaps ejection fraction) and cardiac output comes from studies of young spontaneously hypertensive rats (75). By using propranolol and methylscopalamine, cardiac autonomic nerve blockade and myocardial response to blood-borne catacholamines were achieved. Afterload was manipulated by an adjustable snare around the thoracic aorta. The results of these experiments suggest that at any physiological level of afterload, the spontaneously hypertensive rats showed a consistently higher stroke volume. Furthermore, these studies strongly indicated that the improved strength and performance of the left ventricle of the hypertensive rats was directly related to increased wall thickness.

Speculation based on the above human and animal evidence would **suggest** that myocardial hypertrophy resulting from resistive training results in positive myocardial adaptations such as strengthened myocardium and increased stroke volume both at rest and during exercise, especially exercise resulting in high afterloads. This conclusion, of course, assumes that the hearts of hypertensive rats are reasonable models for resistive-trained human hearts.

Blood Pressure

Both systolic and diastolic blood pressure increase during isometric exercises (8, 25). The extent of the increase depends on the intensity of contraction (33, 88), the length of time the contraction is held (33, 88), the amount of muscle mass (33, 88), and perhaps, the percentage of fast twitch fibers involved (97). Although weight training is not isometric exercise, many forms have a high isometric component. There is little doubt that weight-training exercises cause increases in blood pressure (37, 134). Recently, McDougall et al. (77) presented evidence, using bodybuilders, that weight-training exercises to exhaustion produce blood pressures on the order of 400 mm Hg/300 mm Hg, especially when using large muscle masses. Freedson et al. (40), however, found that blood pressures may reach somewhat lower levels (about 240/155) using free weights and hydraulic bench-pressing for 10 repetitions at 50% of maximum isometric strength. Fleck and Dean (37) used one-arm dumbell presses and leg extensions with one leg to exhaustion with 90%, 80%, 70% and 50% of 1RM to investigate weight-training effects on blood pressure. Using 3 groups—controls, novice trainers, and bodybuilders—they (37) found that peak blood pressures (occurring at exhaustion) were about 230/150, whereas average blood pressures for all arm and leg sets were about 180/140. Furthermore, they found that the bodybuilders had lower blood pressures, both peak and average, than the other two groups.

Three factors relevant to blood pressure response to weight-training exercise should be considered. First, although peak blood pressure responses reach high levels, especially at exhaustion, they are not unlike responses to other **high intensity exercises** (i.e., cycle ergometry) (6, 9, 28). These peak blood pressures occur intermittently; it is not known whether high peak blood pressures lasting a few seconds produce more cardiovascular stress than maintaining a moderately high blood pressure for long periods, as could occur with exercise like bicycling. Second, the highest blood pressures occur at or near exhaustion or during maximum lifts. Thus, attention to modifications in training such as reducing or eliminating sets to exhaustion and reducing the number of maximal attempts may be useful. Third, one of the adaptations to weight training appears to be reducing exercise blood pressure, a beneficial effect. Given the blood pressure responses observed during many forms of weight-training exercises, caution should be observed in individuals with CVD. This does not mean that weight training should be eliminated (130).

The training effects of regular resistive exercise are also controversial. It is a common misconception that resistive training is directly responsible for the hypertension seen among some strength-power athletes. More likely explanations include essential hypertension, overtraining (55, 103), the use of androgens (137), or perhaps gaining large amounts of body mass (131).

Isometric training has been shown to lower resting systolic blood pressure in hypertensive humans and animals (13, 66). Again, although weight training is not isometric work in the strictest sense, it may include a large isometric component, thus similar decreases may be observed in weight trainers. A study of hypertensive adolescent boys showed a trend toward resting systolic blood pressure reduction following weight training (35). Stone et al. (118) found significant decreases in resting systolic but no change in diastolic pressures after 8 weeks of olympic-style weight training in young men. Goldberg et al. (46), using young adult men and women, observed decreases in both systolic and diastolic pressures at rest and during treadmill work in which subjects carried handheld weights; these observations were made after 16 weeks of weight training. Similar changes were found in a followup study (44).

Hagberg et al. (49) found significant decreases in systolic blood pressure after 5 months of weight training in borderline hypertensive adolescents. This study also showed that the weight training produced somewhat greater reductions in blood pressure than a jogging program. The weight training produced a reduced peripheral resistance. Apparently, then, weight training can have a beneficial effect on blood pressure. Although lean body mass has been positively correlated with systolic blood pressure (131), it appears that weight training can produce positive blood pressure changes concomitant with increases in lean body mass (46, 118).

Myocardial $\dot{V}O_2$

The double product (HR × SBP) is an estimate of myocardial work, which is proportional to myocardial $\dot{V}O_2$ (65, 86). Three studies have considered the effects of resistive training on the double product. In a cross-sectional study using age-matched bodybuilders and controls, Colliander and Tesch (19) found lower double products during arm ergometry at 150W and 200W in bodybuilders compared to controls. Stone et al. (118) observed a significant reduction in resting double product in young men after 8 weeks of olympic-style preparation weight training. A significant reduction in the double product during treadmill walking (up a 10° incline at 1.7 miles/hour) while holding handheld weights (2.9 kg and 7.2 kg) was found in men and women after a 16-week resistive-training program (46). These observations suggest that the hearts of the weight trainers may have become more efficient.

Again, speculation suggests one possible reason for the decrease in myocardial work accompanying the adaptations to resistive training. A simple approach to Laplace's law allows use of the following formula:

$$T = \frac{PR}{Wt}$$

Where: T = Myocardial wall tension
P = Pressure
R = Chamber radius
Wt = Wall thickness

If resistive training increases ventricular wall thickness with little change in chamber size, as seems to be the case (60, 96), then tension at a given afterload (workload) will be reduced. Wall tension is proportional to myocardial work (141). Therefore, a reduction in tension may be simultaneously accompanied by a decreased myocardial $\dot{V}O_2$.

Aerobic Power (Max $\dot{V}O_2$)

With the exception of circuit training (43, 138), resistive training has not generally been regarded as beneficial in effecting increases in max $\dot{V}O_2$. Noncircuit weight-training studies have observed either no change (31, 85) or small increases (4%) in max $\dot{V}O_2$ (L·min^{-1}) (52,53). The max $\dot{V}O_2$ of high caliber olympic-style weightlifters ($\bar{X} \simeq m^1 \cdot min^{-1} \cdot kg^{-1}$) has been reported to be above that of nonathletes (30, 105, 114). Stone et al. (118), using college-age males and a preparation (high volume) phase olympic-style weight-training program, found moderate increases in both absolute (9%) and relative (8%) terms during an 8-week study. This training program was accompanied by a considerable increase in short-term endurance as measured by cycle ergometer work to exhaustion, this finding is discussed later.

Studies of circuit weight training indicate that moderate increases in aerobic power can occur in relatively short periods of time (43, 138). These studies used high repetitions (20–30) and rest periods ranging from less than 30 seconds up to 2 minutes. Although circuit weight training is primarily anaerobic in nature (138), the high repetitions and short rest periods are used to engage aerobic metabolism as much as possible. However, in the study by Stone et al. (118), the repetitions (5–10 per set) were lower and the rest periods (3.5–3.9 minutes) were higher. These researchers used multiple training sessions on some days, and they used large muscle mass exercises (i.e., squats, pulls, weighted jumping) extensively. The greatest change in max $\dot{V}O_2$ occurred during the highest volume of training. One common factor associated with circuit weight training and the training used by Stone et al. (118) is the high total volume of work. Although highly anaerobic, the total workload must be considered. The same arguments can be made concerning the effect of the workload of aerobic training on max $\dot{V}O_2$ (4).

The mechanism by which weight training, especially noncircuit weight training, can increase max $\dot{V}O_2$ is unclear. Again, we must rely on speculation for possible answers.

The first possibility is that there might be a true aerobic training effect. Various resistive training modes and methods have shown oxygen consumption during training to range from 38% to 60% of max $\dot{V}O_2$ (51, 106, 135). Studies determining the minimum aerobic power training threshold have shown increases with as low as 45% of max $\dot{V}O_2$ in untrained subjects (3 days/week) (42). Most studies, however, suggest somewhat higher threshold values (50%–60%) (4). Therefore, some weight training protocols (i.e., circuit training and olympic weight-training preparation) may increase max $\dot{V}O_2$ because they reach the minimal threshold value.

The second possibility also involves oxygen uptake ($\dot{V}O_2$), which is the result of the interaction of central and peripheral factors ($\dot{V}O_2 = HR \times SV \times a-\bar{v}O_2$ diff). Max $\dot{V}O_2$ would encompass the maximum values for these factors. Aerobic training has been shown to cause significant increases in both factors (50, 102). But studies of highly weight-trained athletes have shown that they possess average or below average concentrations or activities of aerobic enzymes and mitochondrial numbers and sizes and that they have high percentages of fast twitch fibers (21, 26, 76, 90, 98, 123). Typical weight training causes cellular adaptations that result in increased myofibrillar/mitochondrial and cytoplasmic/mitochondrial ratios (76). Additionally, one recent study suggests that skeletal muscle capillary density may decrease with weight training (123). This evidence suggests that resistive training is not likely to enhance the peripheral factor (a–$\bar{v}O_2$ diff). Because the enhancement of the peripheral factor seems generally unlikely, a possible explanation for the increased max $\dot{V}O_2$ seen in some highly weight-trained athletes and in the Stone et al. study (118), centers around a positive central effect (i.e., increased cardiac output at maximum levels).

The third possibility is based on the fact that many researchers, especially those using weight training and weight-trained athletes, used a cycle ergometer to induce increases in work (i.e., $\dot{V}O_2$) (30, 53, 105, 118). Cycle ergometer work may be limited by maximum strength levels (53). It could be possible that increases in maximum hip and leg strength would allow a "truer" expression of max $\dot{V}O_2$.

Serum Lipids

One of the most important risk factors related to CVD is serum lipid levels. Descriptive studies of young adult male weight trainers have revealed no differences in blood lipid profiles between weight trainers and sedentary controls (18, 34). Neither of these studies reported training volumes or intensities, nor did they describe the type of exercises performed (large versus small muscle mass). Additionally, there were no appropriate controls for androgen use, which is common among weight trainers, powerlifters, and weightlifters (137) and which depresses HDL-cholesterol (56, 136). Descriptive studies of bodybuilders (high volume training) suggest beneficial lipid alterations (56, 142); these studies controlled for androgen use.

Longitudinal studies of the effects of resistive training on serum lipids have been more promising. Johnson et al. (59), using middle-aged men, were the first to show significant decreases in total cholesterol, accompanied by a significant decrease in the total cholesterol/HDL-cholesterol ratio, with no change in triglycerides, over a 12-week period. In a similar study, Blessing (10), using middle-aged men and comparing weight training to a jogging program, found the increases in HDL-cholesterol and increases in the total cholesterol/HDL-cholesterol ratio to be similar in the two experimental groups over 12 weeks. In both of these studies (10, 59), the greatest changes in serum lipids occurred during the highest volume of training. Using young men and women who were weight-trained for 16 weeks, Goldberg et al. (45) found significant decreases in total cholesterol, total cholesterol/HDL-cholesterol, and LDL cholesterol/HDL-cholesterol ratios, and nearly significant increases in HDL-cholesterol. Similar beneficial alterations in serum lipids have been reported by Ullrich et al. (129) in young men after 8 weeks of weight training. These studies (10, 45, 59) present evidence suggesting that changes in body weight (although body composition changed favorably) and diet were not factors in the serum lipid changes. It appears that resistive training may produce positive changes in serum lipids, perhaps with the total volume of training again playing an important role.

Glucose Tolerance

Another risk factor is glucose tolerance, which is significant in CVD and diabetes. Studies of bodybuilders (142), who typically use a high volume of training, and a longitudinal study (81) suggest that weight training may beneficially alter glucose tolerance and insulin sensitivity. The mechanism of these effects may be related to body composition alterations as a result of training.

Strength

Strength is the ability to produce force. The importance of strength is often underestimated, in terms of both health and performance. Stronger muscles protect the joints they cross. Strength training, besides increasing maximum skeletal muscle force output, may also increase the maximum strength of tendons and ligaments (17, 133). This strengthening effect may reduce the possibility of strains, sprains, and other injuries that often accompany physical activity. One important example is lower back injury or pain, which costs Americans millions of dollars each year. Along with increased flexibility, strengthening the abdominal and lower back muscles and supporting structures can alleviate much of this problem. Stronger maximum strength of the musculature may reduce the relative stress imposed by daily life and physical activities. This reduction may include reduced injury potential not only of the skeletal musculature, but also of other organ systems such as the cardiovascular system. This becomes most apparent during heavy lifting tasks.

The ability to produce force is important to performance for a number of reasons. First, in simply overcoming resistances, as in weightlifting, gymnastics, football, or moving boxes or furniture, the importance of strength becomes apparent. The stronger person has an advantage in lifting and moving various objects, including himself. The advantages of increased maximum strength extend beyond simple lifting tasks, however; they are considered briefly in the following sections.

Muscular Endurance

The ability to perform work when using moderate to heavy loads is usually termed muscular endurance (93). Muscular endurance is **strongly** related to anaerobic capacity. Although cardiovascular factors may contribute to muscular endurance (118), more important factors associated with its improvement appear to be increases in ATP-CP and glycogen stores, myokinase activity, and especially maximum strength. These are the factors comprising anaerobic capacity (26, 62, 71, 118).

As with strength, the importance of muscular endurance is often underestimated. In absolute terms, a stronger person has a distinct advantage in tasks requiring muscular endurance (27). An example of the benefits of increased muscular endurance in everyday work tasks would be that of a longshoreman lifting heavy boxes from the floor to a shelf. A stronger workman would fatigue less rapidly because he would be performing at a lower percentage of his maximum strength (27, 93). From an athletic standpoint, evidence increasingly suggests that high levels of muscular endurance contribute to the outcome of various sports contests (58, 116, 118).

Capen (16) was among the first researchers to investigate the effects of weight training on endurance factors. He found that weight-trained (low volume) and endurance-trained young males produced similar (6.3% vs. 6.2%) increases in endurance (300-yard run) after 10 weeks of training. He concluded that weight training was as effective in increasing cardio-respiratory endurance as endurance training. However, the 300-yard run depends more on muscular endurance and other factors than it depends on cardiorespiratory factors. Swegan (121), using a cycle ergometer at a fixed workload, found that weight-trained (low volume) young men significantly increased their time to exhaustion. Nagle and Irwin (85) divided college-age males into two groups. One group performed 2 × 5RM, the other group performed 1 set of 15RM and one set of 12RM maximum. Both groups performed the same 13 exercises 3 days per week. Steady state work was induced by using a fixed workrate (cycle ergometer) of 10,026 foot-pounds per minute. Endurance was measured by timing an increase in heart rate from 168 to 180 beats per minute. It was concluded that weight training (using 5–15 repetitions per set) did not produce a significant increase in endurance, although it did produce trends that may have represented an actual training effect. Note, however, that neither of the experimental groups in this study used training programs that could be considered high volume or high loading. This is especially true considering the multiple sessions per day, increased emphasis on large muscle mass, multiple joint exercises, and the more than 3 training sessions per week used by many of today's athletes and weight trainers in general. Although these studies (16, 85, 121) suggest increases in endurance time (using very different methods of measurement), none could be considered typical of modern methods of training (88, 93, 116, 118).

Recently, Hickson, Rosenkoetter, and Brown (53), using a relatively high volume and training load, found small increases in max $\dot{V}O_2$ (L·min^{-1}) but large increases in time to exhaustion on both a cycle ergometer and a treadmill. Using very high volumes and loading, Stone et al. (118) observed moderate gains in max $\dot{V}O_2$ but large gains in time to exhaustion on a cycle ergometer. Both of these studies (53, 118) used increasing workloads to exhaustion, which means that the subjects not only increased endurance time, but also increased the final workload before exhaustion. Although both studies found small to moderate increases in max $\dot{V}O_2$, the authors concluded that other factors, including gains in anaerobic capacity, were more important in explaining increases in endurance.

More practical measures of absolute muscular endurance include tests to exhaustion of the exercise-trained. For example, O'Bryant (88) found that weight training using the squat over 12 weeks increased the number of repetitions of the squat at an absolute (fixed submaximum weight at pre- and post-test) weight. Similar increases in short-term or muscular endurance have been observed with a variety of different weight-training exercises (5, 93, 108).

As previously stated, these increases in muscular endurance primarily rely on anaerobic capacity. Factors associated with anaerobic capacity include increased storage of substrates and increases in maximum strength. Increases of ATP-CP, glycogen, and the myokinase reaction have all been observed after weight training (78, 124). Most likely, strength is a key factor. As each motor unit becomes stronger with resistive training, fewer motor units would be needed to perform at a given submaximal workload, thus creating a greater motor unit reserve (71, 79). Furthermore, it is possible that strength training may allow an increased ability to raise motor neuron excitability during voluntary effort (104). This can be considered an increased volitional drive of motor neurons after training (104) and may also be related to increases in absolute muscular endurance.

Continuing to work in the face of fatigue is important in most performance tasks, especially in many types of sports training, athletic events, and physically demanding tasks such as rowing or longshoremen work. Aerobic training has been advocated as a method to increase short-term endurance even for highly anaerobic, strength-power oriented sports such as weightlifting (63). However, considerable evidence (52, 91, 119) strongly indicates that aerobic training reduces the ability of strength-power athletes to perform. The above studies suggest that weight training (and probably other forms of interval training) can increase short-term high intensity endurance without a concomitant loss of performance.

Anaerobic Power

In many sports, power is the most important determinant of who wins (21, 23, 11). Power—the rate at which work is performed—can be expressed as:

$$P = \frac{\text{Work}}{\text{Time}} \text{ or Force (strength)} \times \text{Velocity}$$

An increase in power allows the athlete to perform at higher workrates. As with muscular endurance, an increase in maximum power allows an athlete to work at a smaller percentage of maximum and thus endure longer at lower work rates. The same arguments apply to daily work tasks.

The expression of strength in specific movement patterns can be termed technique or skill. Increasing the velocity and force with which muscles contract in specific patterns can lead to more powerful and superior performance (58, 113, 115) (see Chapter 5). The speed with which a skill is carried out is related to power output (P = FxV); it can be simply expressed in terms of Newton's second law:

$$F = ma$$

Where: F =Muscular force
m =Mass of the object to which force is applied
a =The acceleration of the object as a result of the force

By increasing force, velocity of movement may be enhanced. Therefore, it is possible to increase speed of movement through a general strengthening of the appropriate muscles, making movements faster through appropriate strength-speed training (e.g., power snatches, power cleans) and speed training (e.g., bounding, sprinting). Also, movements can be made more efficient through practice.

Agility or maneuverability is the ability to rapidly change the direction of the body or its parts (58). Agility is strongly related to strength and power (58). Many people lack enough strength to effectively control body inertia, especially if their limbs or body are loaded (i.e., they are wearing athletic equipment or carrying packages or boxes). A 100-kilogram football running back needs great leg and hip strength and power to stop, change direction quickly, and avoid tacklers. The contribution of power is most important because in its absence, the body cannot be accelerated or projected in any direction rapidly (58, 113, 114). Agility may be enhanced by increasing muscular strength and power and by specific agility training.

Typically, stronger people produce greater maximum power outputs (22, 23). Increased power may also have positive effects on speed and agility (22, 23, 113). Several studies that used the vertical jump and the Lewis formula for vertical jump power and a stair climbing test for power have shown that significant increases in power and velocity of movement accompany increases in strength of the leg and hip extensors (88, 113, 116, 120). Thus, increasing maximum strength through resistive training can increase power output and general performance considerably.

Flexibility

The range of motion about a joint is termed flexibility. Flexibility should not be confused with joint laxity. Range of motion is related to both injury prevention and performance.

Considering injury, increased flexibility has the most obvious positive effect in contact sports (58, 133). A severe blow to an inflexible joint can result in torn muscle or connective tissue. Overtraining (overwork) injuries such as tendinitis are commonly seen among athletes and laborers. Considerable empirical evidence suggests that both contact and overtraining injuries can be reduced in number and severity by enhancing flexibility.

Various movements and positions required in sport and job performance are related to both dynamic and static flexibility (71, 133). If poor technique is established because of poor flexibility, performance suffers. Furthermore, poor technique increases injury potential (133).

A descriptive study of olympic weightlifters found them to be second only to gymnasts in a composite score of several flexibility tests (58). Observations and reviews of longitudinal studies (39, 58, 93, 100) indicate that weight training generally enhances flexibility. (Care should be taken in using full range of motion movements, not emphasizing partial movements, and in training muscles on both sides of the joint.) Increasing flexibility can decrease the injury potential and increase performance.

Body Composition

The amount of lean body mass and percentage of fat determines body composition. Obesity (excess fat content) too often accompanies the sedentary American lifestyle. As is the case with other physical fitness characteristics, being obese often gets its start in childhood. Obese children generally become obese adults.

Body composition has important relationships to cardiovascular fitness, strength, and flexibility (7, 32, 87). Obesity can reduce mechanical and metabolic efficiency (32, 87). Not only is it more difficult for an obese person to move, but also, for any given amount of external work, such a person has to expend more energy due to inefficiency (12, 82). The greater demand for energy places more stress (work) on the cardiovascular system. Additionally, obese people tend to have higher levels of cholesterol and lower HDL-cholesterol, and they generally run a greater risk of developing or suffering from CVD, diabetis mellitus, kidney disease, and degenerative arthritis (7, 32, 87).

Positive changes in body composition can be advantageous to both performance and health. Descriptive studies of highly weight-trained athletes show that they possess higher than average lean body mass and lower than average percentages of fat and total fat (14, 30, 110, 114). Studies of the caloric cost of circuit weight training (135) and the training of olympic weightlifters (72, 106) have shown the mean caloric cost to be about 9–10 kcal·min⁻¹. Thus, the metabolic turnover is certainly high enough to alter body composition. Furthermore, Scala (106) has shown that the caloric cost of large muscle mass exercises (squats, pulling movements, weighted jumps, etc.) to be nearly twice that of small muscle mass exercises (bench press, lateral raises, situps, etc.): 11.5 vs. 6.8 Kcals·min⁻¹. Therefore, it is likely that body composition can be affected and controlled more readily using large rather than small muscle mass exercises.

Several longitudinal studies have shown significant increases in lean body mass and a loss of percentage of fat and total fat. These studies have used young men (45, 88, 118), middle-aged men (10, 59), and young women (14, 45). Again, the key seems to be the total volume of training.

Volume and Intensity Considerations

The volume of weight training is equal to the total workload. The total workload is directly proportional to the total caloric cost of training. The volume of weight training is estimated by the total number of repetitions performed (73). Intensity is the power output of training; it is proportional to the rate at which energy is used. Intensity is estimated by the average weight lifted (73). Some physiological variables such as aerobic power, blood lipids, and body composition appear to be more affected by volume of training (10, 59, 118), whereas performance variables such as strength, power, and perhaps muscular endurance are more affected by the intensity of training, especially by proper variation in volume and intensity (89, 115, 116, 140). Therefore, enhancement of a particular physical fitness component or group of components may require emphasis on either volume or intensity (see Chapter 7).

Psychological Considerations

In a recent review, Folkins and Sime (38) suggested that physical training appears to assist people in coping with both physical and psychological stress and, in general, promotes well-being. Part of this improvement in well-being probably is generated by improvements in various physical fitness components. It is also possible that much of the improvement results from general changes in perceived self-image and somatotype (physique) (127).

Resistive training can improve various components of physical fitness body characteristics and mental and emotional well-being. (126, 128). Although few studies are available in this area, recent research has suggested positive psychological and emotional benefits as a result of increasing strength and resistive training. Tucker (126) used 142 randomly selected young men to assess the relationship between muscular strength and measures of mental health. Using a sum of the 1RM bench press and squat, this study showed that strong individuals were significantly more satisfied with their body parts and processes, less emotionally labile and anxious, more outgoing, and generally more confident and satisfied with themselves than their weaker counterparts (125). In a longitudinal followup study, similar conclusions were reached using weight training over a 16-week period (i.e., increases in strength increased various self-concept factors) (128). Furthermore, Dishman and Gettman (24) found that 20 weeks of weight training significantly increased the "psychic vigor and self esteem of males." Similar beneficial alterations in mental and emotional factors have been observed in high school women as a result of weight training (54). Thus, it appears that weight training can result in positive changes in self concept and emotional fitness.

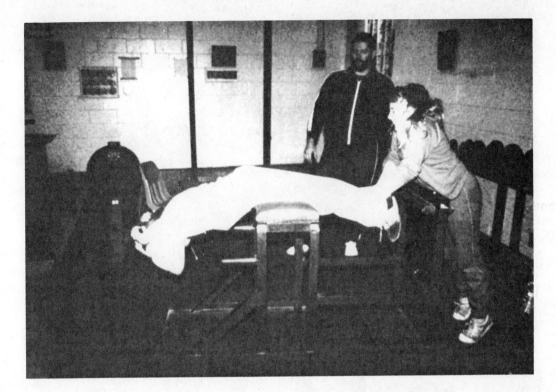

a.

b.

Figure 3–1. Nine- and eleven-year-old children using free weights during a workout. a: Hyperextensions using a roman chair sit-up bench. b: Double knee bend squats. Learning proper methods and techniques early lays the groundwork for lifetime training.

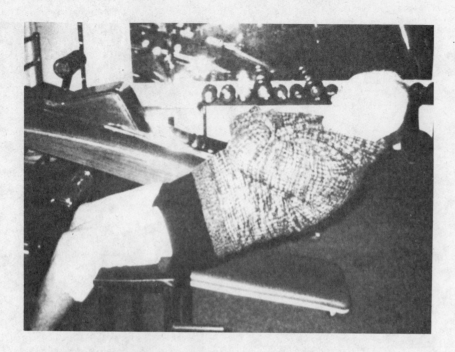

Figure 3–2. Seventy-eight-year-old Sam Barnes of Montgomery, Alabama, has worked out regularly with weights since the eighth grade and still performs a vigorous workout that includes a 100-kg squat with sets of 10, a bench press with 60 kg, and roman chair sit-ups.

Summary

Evidence indicates that resistive training can enhance both physical and emotional fitness, which may allow greater satisfaction and enjoyment in daily as well as athletic activities. Resistive-training-induced benefits in performance and health may, in the final analysis, be related to an increase in the quality of life.

References

1. *AAHPER Youth Fitness Test Manual.* 1961. Washington, D.C.: American Alliance for Health, Physical Education and Recreation.

2. *AAHPER Youth Fitness Test Manual.* 1965. Washington, D.C.: American Alliance for Health, Physical Education and Recreation.

3. Abraman, K. A., and R. A. Dzhuganyan. 1969. Athlete heart measurements. *Theory and Practice of Physical Culture* 12:27–29.

4. American College of Sports Medicine. 1978. Position statement on the recommended quantity and quality of exercise for developing and maintaining fitness in healthy adults. *Medicine and Science in Sports* 10(3):vii–x.

5. Andersen, T., and J. T. Kearny. 1982. Effects of three resistance training programs on muscular strength and absolute and relative endurance. *Research Quarterly* 53:1–7.

6. Astrand, P. O., B. Ekblom, R. Messin, et al. 1965. Intra-arterial blood pressure during exercise with different muscle groups. *Journal of Applied Physiology* 20:253–256.

7. Astrand, P. O., and K. Rodahl. 1970. *Textbook of Work Physiology.* New York: McGraw-Hill.

8. Bartels, R. L., E. L. Fox, R. W. Bowers, et al. 1967. Effects of isometric work on heart rate blood pressure and net oxygen cost. *Research Quarterly* 39:437–442.

9. Bevegard, B. S. 1963. Circulation studies in well trained athletes at rest and during heavy exercise, with special reference to stroke volume and the influence of body position. *Acta Physiologica Scandinavica* 57:26–50.

10. Blessing, D. 1983. Performance, body composition, heart rate, blood lipids and hormonal effects of short-term jogging and weight training in middle-age sedentary men. Doctoral dissertation, Louisiana State University.

11. Boyer, J. L., and F. W. Kasch. 1970. Exercise therapy in hypertensive men. *Journal of the American Medical Association* 211:1668–1671.

12. Bray, G. A. 1983. The energetics of obesity. *Medicine and Science in Sports and Exercise* 15:32–40.

13. Brosseau, D. A., T. G. Bedford, M. S. Sturek, et al. 1981. Blood pressure changes in rats performing different exercise programs (Abstract). *Medicine and Science in Sports and Exercise* 13:76.

14. Brown, C., and J. H. Wilmore. 1974. The effects of maximal resistance training on the strength and body composition of women athletes. *Medicine and Science in Sports* 6:174–177.

15. Brown, S., R. Byrd, MD. J. Singhe, et al. 1983. Echocardiographic characteristics of competitive and recreational weightlifters. *Journal of Cardiology and Ultrasonography* 2:98–104.

16. Capen, E. K. 1950. The effect of systematic weight training on power, strength and endurance. *Research Quarterly* 31:83–93.

17. Clancy, W. G. 1983. Knee ligamentous injury in sports: The past, present and future. *Medicine and Science in Sports and Exercise* 15:9–14.

18. Clarkson, P. M., R. Niwterminster, M. Fillyon, et al. 1981. High density lipoprotein cholesterol in young adult weightlifters, runners and untrained subjects. *Human Biology* 53:251–257.

19. Colliander, E. B., and P. A. Tesch. 1985. Long-term effect of heavy resistance training on rest and exercise blood pressure (Abstract). *Medicine and Science in Sports and Exercise* 17:184.

20. Cooper, K. H., M. L. Pollock, R. P. Martin, et al. 1976. Physical fitness level vs. selected coronary risk factors. *Journal of the American Medical Association* 236:166–169.

21. Costill, D. L., J. Daniels, W. Evans, et al. 1976. Skeletal muscle enzymes and fiber composition in male and female track athletes. *Journal of Applied Physiology* 4:149–154.

22. Costill, D. L., S. J. Miller, W. C. Myers, et al. 1968. Relationship among selected tests of explosive strength and power. *Research Quarterly* 39:785–787.

23. Crieland, J. M., and F. Pirnay. 1981. Anaerobic and aerobic power of top athletes. *European Journal of Applied Physiology* 47:295–300.

24. Dishman, R. K., and L. R. Gettman. 1981. Psychological vigor and self-perceptives of increased strength (Abstract). *Medicine and Science in Sports and Exercise* 13:73–74.

25. Donald, K. W., A. R. Lind, G. W. McNicol, et al. 1967. Cardiovascular responses to sustained (static) contractions. *Circulation Research* 20:115–132.

26. Edgerton, V. R. 1976. Neuromuscular adaptation to power and endurance work. *Canadian Journal of Applied Sports Science* 1:49–58.

27. Edington, D. W., and V. R. Edgerton. 1976. *The Biology of Physical Activity.* Boston: Houghton Mifflin.

28. Ekbolm, B., P. O. Astrand, B. Saltin, et al. 1968. Effect of training on circulatory response to exercise. *Journal of Applied Physiology* 24:518–528.

29. Ekbolm, B., E. Kolbum, and J. Soltysiak. 1973. Physical training, bradycardia and autonomic nervous system. *Scandinavian Journal of Clinical Investigation* 32:251–256.

30. Fahey, T., L. Akka, and R. Rolph. 1975. Body composition and $\dot{V}O_2$ max of exceptionally weight-trained athletes. *Journal of Applied Physiology* 39:559–561.

31. Fahey, T. D., and C. H. Brown. 1973. The effects of an anaerobic steroid on the strength, body composition and endurance of college males when accompanied by a weight training program. *Medicine and Science in Sports* 5:272–276.

32. Falls, H. B. 1980. Modern concepts of physical fitness. *Journal of Physical Education and Recreation* April:25–27.

33. Fardy, P. S. 1981. Isometric exercise and the cardiovascular system. *The Physician and Sports Medicine* 9:43–56.

34. Farrel, P. A., M. G. Maksud, M. L. Pollock, et al. 1982. A comparison of plasma cholesterol, triglycerides and high density lipoprotein-cholesterol in speed skaters, weightlifters and non-athletes. *European Journal of Applied Physiology* 48:77–82.

35. Fixler, E. D., and W. P. Laird. 1979. Acute hemodynamic responses of hypertensive adolescents to strenuous weightlifting (Abstract). *Medicine and Science in Sports* 11:78.

36. Fleck, S. 1985. Personal Communication and Presentation at the NSCA National Convention, Dallas.

37. Fleck, S. J., and L. S. Dean. 1985. Influence of weight-training experience on blood pressure response to exercise (Abstract). *Medicine and Science in Sports and Exercise* 17:185.

38. Folkins, C. H., and W. E. Sime. 1981. Physical fitness training and mental health. *American Journal of Psychology* 36:373–389.

39. Fox, E. L. 1984. *Sports Physiology* (2nd edition). Philadelphia: W. B. Saunders.

40. Freedson, P., B. Chang, F. Katch, et al. 1984. Intra-arterial blood pressure during free weight and hydraulic resistive exercise (Abstract). *Medicine and Science in Sports* 16:131.

41. Frick, M., R. Elovasko, and T. Somer. 1967. The mechanism of bradycardia evoked by physical training. *Cardiologia* 51:46–54.

42. Gaesser, G. A., and R. G. Rich. 1983. Time course of changes in VO$_2$ max and blood lipids during 18 weeks of high and low intensity exercise training (Abstract). *Medicine and Science in Sports and Exercise* 15:100.

43. Gettman, L. R., and M. L. Pollock. 1981. Circuit weight training: A critical review of its physiological benefits. *The Physician and Sports Medicine* 9:45–57.

44. Goldberg, L. 1985. Personal communication.

45. Goldberg, L., D. L. Elliot, R. Schutz, et al. 1984. Modifications of lipid and lipoprotein levels by resistive exercise. *Journal of the American Medical Association* 252:504–506.

46. Goldberg, L. E., R. Schutz, and F. Kloster. 1983. Improvement in cardiovascular response to exercise after weight training (Abstract). *Clinical Research* 31:9A.

47. Gonyea, W. J. 1984. Personal communication.

48. Gorman, J. F. 1978. A review of physical activity and serum lipids. *American Corrective Therapy Journal* Nov-Dec:183–189.

49. Hagberg, J. M., A. A. Ehsoni, D. Goldring, et al. 1984. Effect of weight training on blood pressure and hemodynamics in hypertensive adolescents. *Journal of Pediatrics* 104:147–151.

50. Harrison, M. H., G. A. Brown, and L. A. Cochrone. 1980. Maximal oxygen uptake: Its measurement, application and limitations. *Aviation Space and Environmental Medicine* 5:1123–1127.

51. Hempel, L. S., and C. I. Wells. 1983. Oxygen utilization during performance of the 20-minute Nautilus express circuit (Abstract). *Medicine and Science in Sports and Exercise* 15:169.

52. Hickson, R. C. 1980. Interference of strength development by simultaneously training for strength and endurance. *European Journal of Applied Physiology* 215:255–263.

53. Hickson, R. C., M. A. Rosenkoetter, and M. M. Brown. 1980. Strength training effects on aerobic power and short-term endurance. *Medicine and Science in Sports and Exercise* 12:336–339.

54. Holloway, J. B. 1985. Self-efficacy and training for strength in adolescent girls. Master's thesis, University of Southern California.

55. Hunter, G. R., and J. P. McCarthy. 1982. Pressor response associated with high-intensity anaerobic training. *The Physician and Sports Medicine* 11:151–152.

56. Hurley, B. B., D. R. Seals, J. M. Hagberg, A. C. Goldberg, et al. 1984. High density lipoprotein cholesterol in bodybuilders v powerlifters (negative effects of androgen use). *Journal of the American Medical Association* 252:507–513.

57. Jaweed, M. M., G. J. Herbison, J. F. Ditunno, et al. 1974. Heart weight of rats in different exercises. *Archives of Physical Medicine and Rehabilitation* 55:539–544.

58. Jensen, C. R., and A. G. Fisher. 1979. *Scientific Basis of Athletic Conditioning.* Philadelphia: Lea & Febiger.

59. Johnson, C. C., M. H. Stone, A. Lopez-S, et al. 1982. Diet and exercise in middle-aged men. *Journal of the American Dietary Association* 81:695–701.

60. Kanakis, C., and R. C. Hickson. 1980. Left ventricular responses to a program of lower limb strength training. *Chest* 78:618–621.

61. Kannel, W. B., P. Sorlic, and P. McNamara. The relationship of physical activity to risk of coronary heart disease: The Framingham study. In Larson, O. A., and R. O. Malmborg (eds.). 1971. *Coronary Heart Disease and Physical Fitness.* Baltimore: University Park Press.

62. Karlsson, J., B. Sjodin, I. Jacobs, et al. 1981. Relevance of muscle fibre type to fatigue in short intense and prolonged exercise in man. *Human Muscle Fatigue: Physiological Mechanisms.* London: Pitman Medical (Ciba Foundation Symposium) 82:59–74.

63. Keul, J. 1975. The relationship between circulation and metabolism during exercise. *Medicine and Science in Sports and Exercise* 5:209–219.

64. Kirshenbaum, J., and R. Sullivan. 1983. Hold on there, America. *Sports Illustrated* Feb. 61–74.

65. Kitamura, K., C. R. Jorgensen, F. L. Gobel, et al. 1979. Hemodynamic correlates of myocardial oxygen consumption during upright exercise. *Journal of Applied Physiology* 32:516–522.

66. Kiveloff, B., and O. Huber. 1971. Isometric exercise in hypertension. *Journal of the American Geriatric Society* 19:1006–1012.

67. Kraus, H., and B. Prudden. 1954. Minimum muscular fitness in school children. *Research Quarterly* 25:178–188.

68. Krestovinikov, A. N. 1953. *Physiologic der Korperubugen.* Berlin: VEB-Verlag Volk and Gesundheit.

69. Kusinitz, I., and C. W. Keeny. 1958. Effects of progressive weight training on health and physical fitness of adolescent boys. *Research Quarterly* 29:294–301.

70. Laird, W. P., D. E. Fixler, and C. D. Swanbom. 1979. Cardiovascular effects of weight training in hypertensive adolescents (Abstract). *Medicine and Science in Sports* 11:78.

71. Lamb, D. R. 1984. *Physiology of Exercise* (2nd edition). New York: MacMillan.

72. Laritcheva, K. A., N. I. Yalovaya, V. I. Shubin, et al. Study of energy expenditure and protein needs of top weightlifters. In Parizova, J., and V. A. Rogozin (eds.). 1978. *Nutrition, Physical Fitness and Health.* Baltimore: University Park Press.

73. Lear, J. 1980. *Weightlifting.* Wakefield, West Yorkshire: EP Sports Ltd.

74. Leith, D. E., and M. Bradley. 1976. Ventilatory muscle strength and endurance training. *Journal of Applied Physiology* 41:508–516.

75. Lundin, S., P. Friberg, and M. Hallback-Nordlander. 1982. Left ventricular hypertrophy improves cardiac performance in spontaneously hypertensive rats. *Acta Physiologica Scandinavica* 114:321–328.

76. MacDougall, J. D., D. G. Sale, J. R. Moroz, et al. 1978. Mitochondrial volume density in human skeletal muscle following heavy resistance training. *Medicine and Science in Sports* 11:164–166.

77. MacDougall, D., D. Tuxen, D. Sale, et al. 1983. Direct measurement of arterial blood pressure during heavy resistance training (Abstract). *Medicine and Science in Sports* 15:158.

78. MacDougall, J. D., G. R. Ward, D. G. Sale, et al. 1977. Biochemical adaptations of human skeletal muscle to heavy resistive training and immobilization. *Journal of Applied Physiology* 43:700–703.

79. McCloy, C. H. 1948. Endurance. *The Physical Educator* 5:9–23.

80. Menapace, F. J., W. J. Hammer, T. F. Ritzer, et al. 1982. Left ventricular size in competitive weightlifters: An echocardiographic study. *Medicine and Science in Sports and Exercise* 14:72–75.

81. Miller, W. J., W. M. Sherman, and J. L. Ivey. 1984. Effect of strength training on glucose tolerance and post-glucose insulin responses. *Medicine and Science in Sports and Exercise* 16:538–543.

82. Montoye, H. J., H. L. Metzner, J. B. Keller, et al. 1972. Habitual physical activity and blood pressure. *Medicine and Science in Sports* 4:175–181.

83. Morganroth, J., B. J. Maron, W. L. Henry, et al. 1975. Comparative left ventricular dimensions in trained athletes. *Annals of Internal Medicine* 82:521–524.

84. Muntz, K. H., W. J. Gonyea, and J. H. Mitchell. 1981. Cardiac hypertrophy in response to an isometric training program in the cat. *Circulation Research* 49:1092–1101.

85. Nagle, F., and I. Irwin. 1960. Effects of two systems of weight training on circulorespiratory endurance and related physiological factors. *Research Quarterly* 31:607–615.

86. Nelson, R. R., F. L. Gobel, C. R. Jorgensen, et al. 1974. Hemodynamic predictors of myocardial oxygen consumption during static and dynamic exercise. *Circulation* 50:1179–1188.

87. Novak, L. P., R. E. Hyatt, and J. F. Alexander. 1968. Body composition and physiologic functions of athletes. *Journal of the American Medical Association* 205:764–770.

88. Nutter, D. O., R. C. Schlout, and J. W. Hurst. 1972. Isometric exercise and the cardiovascular system. *Modern Concerns in Cardiovascular Disease* 41:11–15.

89. O'Bryant, H. S. 1982. Periodization: A hypothetical training model for strength and power. Doctoral dissertation, Louisiana State University.

90. O'Bryant, H. S., M. H. Stone. 1982. Ultrastructure of human skeletal muscle among olympic style weightlifters (Abstract). Southeastern American College of Sports Medicine meeting, Blacksburg, Va.

91. Ono, M., M. Miyashita, and T. Asami. 1976. Inhibitory effect of long distance running training on the vertical jump and other performances among aged males. *Biomechanics V-B.* Baltimore: University Park Press.

92. Oscai, L. B., J. A. Patterson, D. C. Bogard, et al. 1972. Normalization of serum triglycerides and lipoprotein electrophorectic patterns by exercise. *American Journal of Cardiology* 30:775–780.

93. O'Shea, J. P. 1976. *Scientific Principles and Methods of Strength Fitness* (2nd edition). Reading, Massachusetts: Addison-Wesley.

94. Paffenbarger, R. S., and W. E. Hale. 1975. Work activity and coronary heart mortality. *New England Journal of Medicine* 292:545–550.

95. Paffenbarger, R. S., M. E. Laughlin, A. S. Gima, et al. 1970. Work activity of long shoremen as related to death from coronary heart disease and stroke. *New England Journal of Medicine* 282:1109–1114.

96. Peronnet, F., R. J. Ferguson, H. Perrault, et al. 1981. Echocardiography and the athletes, heart. *The Physician and Sports Medicine* 9(5):103–112.

97. Petrofsky, J. S., C. A. Phillips, M. N. Sanka, et al. 1981. Muscle fiber recruitment and blood pressure response to isometric exercise. *Journal of Applied Physiology* 50:32–37.

98. Prince, F. P., R. S. Hikida, and F. C. Hagerman. 1976. Human muscle fiber types in powerlifters, distance runners, and untrained subjects. *Pflugers Archives* 363:19–26.

99. Raab, W. 1960. Metabolic protection and reconditioning of the heart muscle through habitual physical exercise. *Annals of Internal Medicine* 53:87–105.

100. Rasch, P. J. 1979. *Weight Training* (3rd edition). Dubuque, Iowa: Wm. C. Brown.

101. Ricci, G., D. Lajoie, R. Petitclerc, et al. 1982. Left ventricular size following endurance, sprint and strength training. *Medicine and Science in Sports and Exercise* 14:344–347.

102. Rowell, L. B. 1975. Human cardiovascular adjustments to exercise and thermal stress. *Physiological Reviews* 54:75–159.

103. Ryan, A. J. (Moderator). 1983. Overtraining in athletes (a roundtable). *The Physician and Sports Medicine* 11:92–110.

104. Sale, D. G., J. D. MacDougall, A. R. M. Upton, et al. 1983. Effects of strength training upon motoneuron excitability in man. *Medicine and Science in Sports and Exercise* 15:57–62.

105. Saltin, B., and P. O. Astrand. 1967. Maximal oxygen uptake in athletes. *Journal of Applied Physiology* 23:353–358.

106. Scala, D. 1984. VO_2, oxygen debt and energy cost of high volume non-circuit olympic style weight training. Master's thesis, Auburn University.

107. Servidio, F. J., R. L. Bartels, R. L. Hamlin, et al. 1985. The effects of weight training, using Olympic style lifts, on various physiological variables in pre-pubescent boys (Abstract). *Medicine and Science in Sports and Exercise* 17:288.

108. Shaver, L. G. 1976. Maximum dynamic strength, relative dynamic endurance and their relationship. *Research Quarterly* 42:460–465.

109. Snoeckx, L. H. E. H., H. F. M. Abeling, J. A. C. Lambreghts, et al. 1982. Echocardiographic dimensions in athletes in relation to their training programs. *Medicine and Science in Sports and Exercise* 14:428–434.

110. Spitler, D. L., F. J. Dias, S. M. Horvath, et al. 1980. Body composition and maximal aerobic capacity of bodybuilders. *Journal of Sports Medicine and Physical Fitness* 20:181–188.

111. Stevenson, J. A., V. Felcki, P. Rechnitzer, et al. 1964. Effect of exercise on coronary tree size in the rat. *Circulation Research* 15:265–269.

112. Stone, M. H., R. Byrd, D. Carter, et al. 1982. Physiological effects of short-term resistive training on middle-age sedentary men. *National Strength and Conditioning Association Journal* 4(5):16–20.

113. Stone, M. H., R. Byrd, J. Tew, et al. 1980. Relationship between anaerobic power and olympic weightlifting performance. *Journal of Sports Medicine and Physical Fitness* 20:99–102.

114. Stone, M. H., P. Carter, D. P. Smith, et al. 1979. Olympic weightlifting: Physiological characteristics of the athletes. In J. Terauds (Ed.). *Science in Weightlifting.* Del Mar, California: Academic Publishers. pp. 54–67.

115. Stone, M. H., and J. Garhammer. 1981. Some thoughts on strength and power (the Nautilus controversy). *National Strength and Conditioning Association Journal* 3(5):24–47.

116. Stone, M. H., H. O'Bryant, J. Garhammer, et al. 1982. A theoretical model of strength training. *National Strength and Conditioning Association Journal* 4(4):36–39.

117. Stone, M. H., J. K. Nelson, S. Nader, et al. 1983. Short-term weight training effects on resting and recovery heart rates. *Athletic Training* 18:69–71.

118. Stone, M. H., G. D. Wilson, D. Blessing, et al. 1983. Cardiovascular responses to short-term olympic style weight training in young men. *Canadian Journal of Applied Sports Sciences* 8:134–139.

119. Stone, M. H., D. Wilson, R. Rozenek, et al. 1984. Anaerobic capacity. *National Strength and Conditioning Association Journal* 5(6):40–65.

120. Stowers, T., J. McMillan, D. Scala, et al. 1983. The short-term effects of three different strength-power training methods. *National Strength and Conditioning Association Journal* 5(3):24–27.

121. Swegan, D. B. 1957. The comparisons of static contraction with standard weight training in effect on certain movement speeds and endurances. Doctoral dissertation, Pennsylvania State University.

122. Teicholz, L. E., T. L. Kreulin, M. V. Herman, et al. 1976. Problems in echocardiographic volume determinations: Echocardiographic-angiographic correlations in the presence of asynergy. *American Journal of Cardiology* 37:7–11.

123. Tesch, P.A., A. Thorsson, and P. Kaiser. 1984. Muscle capillary supply and fiber type characteristics in weight and power lifters. *Journal of Applied Physiology* 56:35–38.

124. Thorstensson, A. 1976. Muscle strength, fibre types, and enzymes in man. *Acta Physiologica Scandinavica* supplementum 443.

125. Tucker, L. A. 1982. Weight training experience and psychological well being. *Perceptual and Motor Skills* 55:553–554.

126. Tucker, L. A. 1983. Muscular strength and mental health. *Journal of Personality Sociology and Psychology* 45:1355–1360.

127. Tucker, L. A. 1983. Self concept: A function of self-perceived somatotype. *Journal of Psychology* 113:123–133.

128. Tucker, L. A. 1983. Effect of weight training on self concept: A profile of those influenced most. *Research Quarterly* 54:389–397.

129. Ullrich, I., C. Reid, and R. Yeater. 1985. Weight training increases HDL-cholesterol. *Medicine and Science in Sports and Exercise* 17:275.

130. Vander, L. B., B. Franklin, D. Wrisley, and M. Rubentire. 1985. Electrocardiographic (ECG) and hemodynamic responses to Nautilus training (NT) in cardiac patients: Comparisons to maximal exercise testing (GXT Max) (Abstract). *Medicine and Science in Sports and Exercise* 17:199.

131. Viitasalo, J. T., P. Komi, and J. J. Kornonen. 1979. Muscle strength and body composition as determinants of blood pressure in young men. *European Journal of Applied Physiology* 42:165–173.

132. Vorobeyev, A. N. 1978. *Weightlifting.* Budapest: International Weightlifting Federation (translated from Russian by W. Jeffrey Brice).

133. Wathen, D. (Moderator). 1983. Prevention of athletic injuries through strength training and conditioning: A round table discussion. *National Strength and Conditioning Association Journal* 5(2):14 –19.

134. Wescott, W., and B. Howeff. 1983. Blood pressure responses during weight-training exercise. *National Strength and Conditioning Association Journal* 5(1):67–71.

135. Wilmore, J. H., R. B. Parr, P. Ward, et al. 1978. Energy cost of circuit weight training. *Medicine in Science and Sports* 10:75–78.

136. Wilson, J. D., and J. E. Griffin. 1980. The use and misuse of androgens. *Metabolism* 29:1278–1295.

137. Wright, J. E. 1978. *Anabolic steroids and sports.* Natick, Massachusetts: Sports Science Consultants.

138. Wright, J. E., J. F. Patton, J. A. Vogel, et al. 1983. Anaerobic power and body composition after 10 weeks of circuit weight training using various work: rest ratios (Abstract). *Medicine in Science and Sports and Exercise* 14:170.

139. Wood, P., W. Haskell, H. Klein, et al. 1976. The distribution of plasma lipoproteins in middle-aged male runners. *Metabolism* 25:1249–1257.

140. Yessis, M. 1981. The key to strength development: Variety. *National Strength and Conditioning Association Journal* 3:32–34.

141. Yin, F. C. P. 1981. Ventricular wall stress. *Circulation Research* 49:829–842.

142. Yki-Jarvinen, H., V. A. Koivisto, M-R. Taskinen, and E. H. Nikkila. 1984. Glucose tolerance, plasma lipoproteins and tissue lipoprotein lipase activities in bodybuilders. *European Journal of Applied Physiology* 53:253–259.

The Biomechanics of Lifting

The application of biomechanical concepts to human movement is becoming increasingly important in our continued efforts to stretch the limits of human performance. Weight-resistive training is a type of exercise in which the proper application of forces in the correct sequence and direction is essential to the goals of the activity: the stimulation of desired muscle groups, the simulation of movement patterns, and the safety of the performer.

Movement Terminology

The descriptions of joint motion and muscle action provided here are pertinent to the discussion of the various muscle-movement applications of weight-resistive exercise.

Joint Motion

Flexion: Decrease in the angle of a joint, bringing the anterior or posterior surfaces closer together (e.g. arm curl).
Extension: Opposite of flexion (e.g., tricep extension).
Hyperextension: Continuation of movement past normal extension (e.g., back hyperextension).
Abduction: Moving a body segment laterally away from the body (e.g., lateral raise).
Adduction: Reverse of abduction; lateral movement of a segment toward the center line of the body (e.g., lat pull).
Pronation: Rotating palm of hand downward; inward rotation of radio-ulnar joint.
Supination: Opposite of pronation; outward rotation, placing palm upward.
Plantar Flexion: Flexion at ankle, pointing toes away from the body; also called ankle extension (e.g., heel raise).
Dorsi Flexion: Opposite of plantar flexion; pulling toes toward the body; also called ankle flexion (e.g., achilles stretch).
Inversion: Turning the sole inward, resulting in a toe-in position of the foot.
Eversion: Opposite of inversion; turning the sole outward.
Rotation: Movement inward or outward along the long axis of the body segment, or right and left twisting of the trunk and head.
Elevation: Upward movement of the shoulder girdle (scapula), as often results from a continuation of arm abduction or flexion.
Depression: Opposite of elevation; downward movement of scapula.

Muscle Action

Agonist: A muscle contracting concentrically for resultant joint action (e.g., biceps in arm curl).

74

Antagonist: A muscle whose contraction tends to produce joint action opposite from that of the agonist (e.g., triceps in arm curl).

Prime Mover: A muscle primarily responsible for causing a joint action (e.g., triceps brachii in elbow extension).

Assistant Mover: A muscle that aids the prime mover to effect a specific joint action; secondary mover (e.g., gastrocnemius in knee flexion).

Emergency Muscle: An assistant mover called into play only when maximal amounts of force are needed (e.g., long head of biceps brachii in maximal abduction of shoulder joint) (34).

Stabilizer: A muscle that anchors, steadies, or supports a segment (bone or body part) so that other muscles can function better; typically contracts statically (aids in guiding or balancing movements while lifting free weight).

Neutralizer: A muscle contracting to prevent an undesired action of another contracting muscle; may counteract one joint action of a multijoint muscle (e.g., quadriceps in propulsive phase of squat counteracts gastrocnemius flexing knee while the hamstrings negate hip flexion of the quadriceps).

Muscle Dynamics

Muscles are machines that chemically convert stored energy (see Chapters 1 and 2) into mechanical work. Similarities existing among all types of muscle tissue are: the ability to develop tension and maintain muscle tone, the ability to respond to the same kind of stimuli, the ability to produce an action potential subsequent to stimulation, the ability to atrophy (get smaller) from inadequate use or lack of circulation and to hypertrophy (get larger) in response to increased work.

There are marked differences between the three types of contractile tissues present in the human body. *Smooth muscle* is involuntary and forms the walls of the viscera in the stomach and bladder as well as the tubes found in the circulatory, digestive, respiratory, and reproductive systems. Myocardium or *cardiac muscle* exhibits the characteristic of functional syncytium, in which the whole tissue acts electrically as though it were a single cell (34). Striated or *skeletal muscle* makes up approximately 40% to 45% of the normal adult's body weight. This voluntary system includes about 434 individual muscles, of which only approximately 75 pair (see Figures 4–1 and 4–2) actually maintain posture and control movement of the body (34). It is skeletal muscle as related to weight-resistive training that will be of major concern and that therefore will be addressed in the following discussion.

Attachment and Arrangement of Fibers

When a muscle shortens, it tends to cause movement at one or more attachment points. In general, attachment for force application to the moving bone (or lever) is called the *insertion*. The distance from the insertion to the joint (axis of rotation) is the force arm of this bone-muscle lever system. As one bone moves, another usually anchors and serves as the muscle's *origin* of attachment. Frequently, the bone that serves as the lever in one movement is stationary in another (e.g., sit-ups versus leg raises), causing the origin and insertion to be reversed. To avoid confusion, it is clearer to call the end nearer the center of the body the origin, and the end farther away the insertion.

The human body is more specialized for speed than for strength, since the bone-lever system provides a mechanical arrangement that utilizes relatively large forces for rapid movement of long lever arms (discussed in greater detail in subsequent sections of this chapter). The internal configuration of skeletal muscles also bears an important relation to the force and distance generated from contraction. Two main types of muscle structure exist, fusiform and penniform, with variations for each type. *Fusiform* muscles have parallel fibers that run longitudinally (the length of the muscle). In general, the fibers of *penniform* muscles are arranged diagonally to the direction of pull. Some variations for each type and examples are listed in Figure 4–3. Typically, fusiform muscles, which are long and slender, can shorten through a greater distance but have the disadvantage of inherent weakness. Conversely, the structural design of penniform muscles, which make up 75% of the skeletal muscles in the

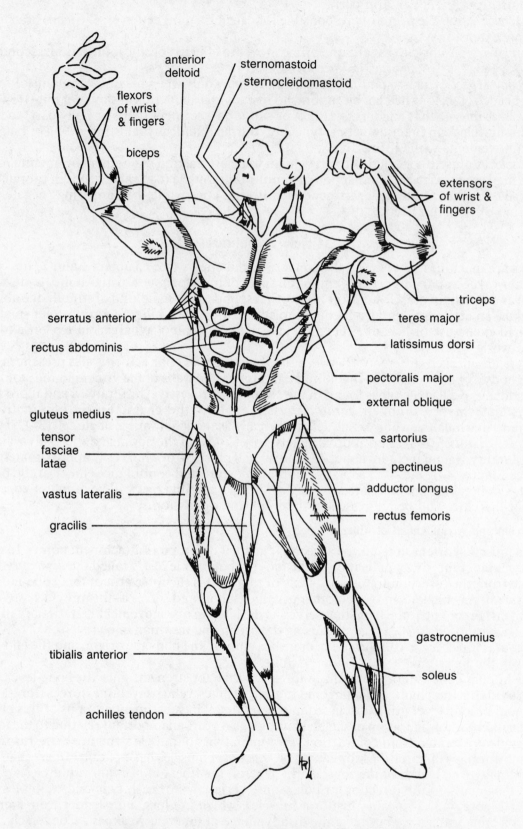

Figure 4-1. Anterior View of Some Major Skeletal Muscles.

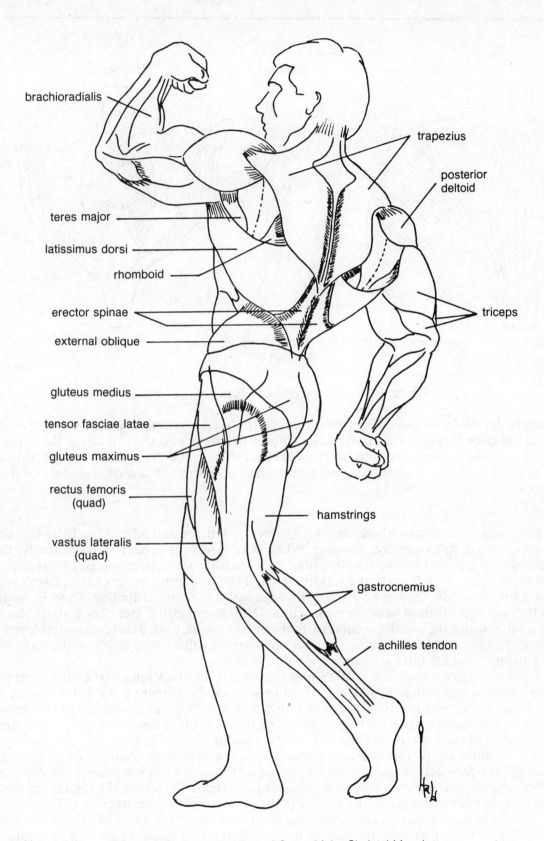

brachioradialis

trapezius

posterior
deltoid

teres major

latissimus dorsi

rhomboid

erector spinae

external oblique

triceps

gluteus medius

tensor fasciae latae

gluteus maximus

rectus femoris
(quad)

hamstrings

vastus lateralis
(quad)

gastrocnemius

achilles tendon

Figure 4–2. Posterior View of Some Major Skeletal Muscles.

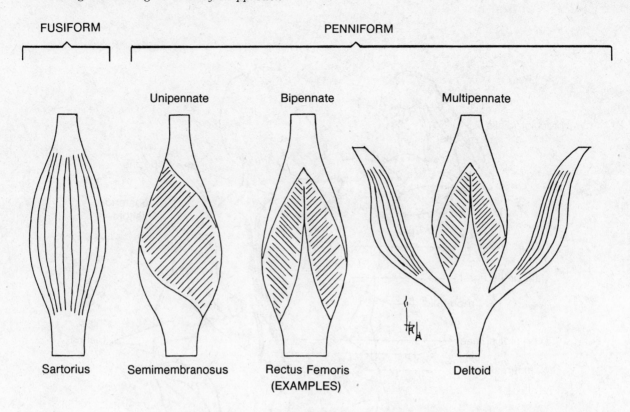

Figure 4–3. Variations In Muscle Fiber Configuration.

human body, allows for more fibers to be brought into play, resulting in greater strength of contraction exerted through a proportionally shorter distance, and thus reducing the range of movement (34). Fortunately, most musculoskeletal levers need the greater strength afforded by the penniform arrangement and suffer no apparent detriment as a consequence of shortened range of motion (34).

Muscle Action

Simplistically, muscle can only do two things: develop tension and relax. Muscle tension does not always result in movement, however. When muscle force is equal to but not greater than the resistance, a static or *isometric* (meaning same length) contraction results. In this case, no movement occurs even though energy is liberated. By strict definition, mechanical work is not accomplished because there is no distance through which the force is applied. There is, however, a thermal equivalent of work for such action. During isometrics, great amounts of heat are produced in which 0.324 calorie equals 1 foot-pound of work (34). The tension developed by skeletal muscle during an isometric contraction is partially due to the length of the sarcomere (see Chapter 1 on the ultrastructure of skeletal muscle).

A single isolated muscle fiber will exhibit maximal isometric strength when the sarcomere is at a length of approximately 2.0 to 2.2 microns (14, 19, 21) (Figure 4–4). At this length, the actin filaments are in a position for optimal interaction with the cross-bridges of the myosin. At shorter sarcomere lengths the isometric contraction falls off as the opposing actin filaments overlap, thus obscuring cross-bridge interaction, and the Z disc abuts against the ends of the myosin. To allow any further shortening, the myosin filament must accomodate by folding or spiraling (21). Similarly, at sarcomere lengths greater than 2.2 microns, fewer myosin cross-bridges interact with the actin and the tension also decreases. Therefore, the greater number of cross-bridges pulling the actin, the greater is the strength of the contraction (21).

The isometric contraction characteristics of whole muscle are much like those of a single muscle fiber except that they are demonstrated differently. Intact, whole muscle displays a tension-length curve similar to that shown in Figure 4–5; maximal isometric tension occurs at

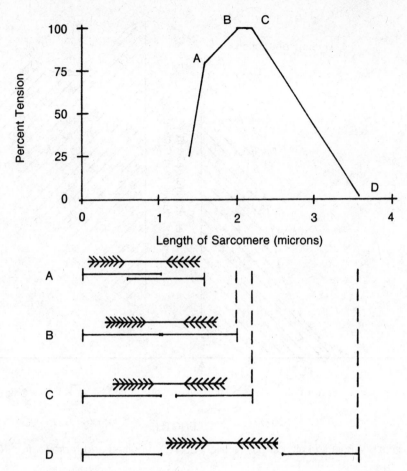

Figure 4-4. Isolated Muscle Fiber Tension to Sarcomere Length. (modified and redrawn from Gordon et al, 1966)

slightly greater than the muscle's normal resting length (14). Likewise, a large amount of *resting tension* develops before contraction if the muscle is stretched prior to contraction. Such tension is thought to result from the elastic properties of the connective tissue and other elastic components within the intact muscle. Nevertheless, the increase in isometric tension during contraction (active tension) is precipitously reduced as the muscle is stretched still farther beyond its normal resting length (21).

A word of caution: this isometric tension-length curve may not accurately reflect the effect of neurological components on dynamic movement. A neural reflex action may occur simultaneously with the pure elastic phenomenon to contribute a greater total potentiation of whole muscle force and speed production after prestretching (24). This point is discussed later in this chapter.

A *concentric* contraction is said to occur when the muscle develops enough tension to overcome the resistance, resulting in movement in the direction of the net force. Muscles operate in pairs, on opposite sides of a joint, so as one muscle (agonist) shortens, the other (antagonist) lengthens. Many times a controlled lengthening of the muscle (active tension) helps coordinate the movement. What is called *eccentric* contraction results since less net tension exists in the muscle than the resistance exerted; thus, the resistance overcomes the muscle force and the muscle lengthens. Eccentric contractions are to some extent inherent in most weight-resistive exercise. For example, the downward phases of the bench press generally require active tension in the triceps and shoulder girdle adductors. If these muscles were simply relaxed, gravity would sufficiently energize the movement, causing downward acceleration of the weight. Left unresisted, this acceleration would result in force to the chest on impact sufficient to cause serious injury.

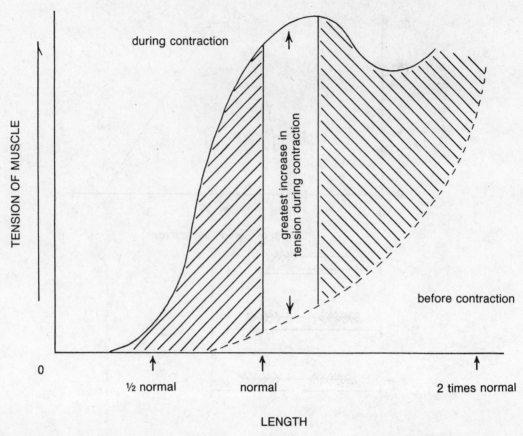

Figure 4–5. Intact, Whole Muscle Length-Tension Curve. (modified and redrawn from Guyton, 1981)

Opposing muscles also prevent injury by decelerating movement during the follow-through of ballistic movements (throwing, kicking, etc.), in which the unresisted momentum of the moving limb could potentially rotate the joint beyond the normal limits of motion. In addition, strength as well as elasticity of the antagonistic muscle groups affect posture as well as performance. Nonconstrictive flexibility in opposing muscles is likely to result in lessened myototic stimulation and therefore less drag of antagonists on agonists when maximal forces are being applied in extreme range of motion positions (34). Furthermore, disproportionate strength in two opposing antagonists can cause the segments upon which they act to deviate from their normal position and can be cause for one type of postural defect (34). Therefore, it is important during the implementation of strength programs that **sufficient attention be paid to exercises that condition muscles on both sides of the joint** in an effort to promote functional strength and prevent injury (see Chapter 7).

Figure 4–6 illustrates the relationship of both eccentric and concentric contraction speed associated with the force of contraction. In eccentric contraction, the maximum force increases to a certain point as the velocity of contraction is increased (1, 23, 27). The fact that muscle can produce a greater force output during eccentric than concentric contraction has possible application for strength training (1, 23, 29) (see Chapter 7). The force-velocity relationship represents the intrinsic mechanical characteristics of both isolated and single muscle function (see Figure 1–14, Chapter 1). This also holds true for multijoint activities involving several body segments. Figure 4–7 illustrates the force-velocity and power-velocity generated from a force platform during the propulsive phase (concentric) of vertical jumping under different weighted loads (5). Two important consequences emerge in this sequence of events: the greatest power output occurs when the force and speeds are approximately one-third maximum, and there exists an *electromechanical delay* (EMD) or time lag between the onset of an action potential and the generation of tension in the muscle. EMD includes time for excitation-contraction coupling (see Chapter 1) and the lengthening of the *series elastic components*

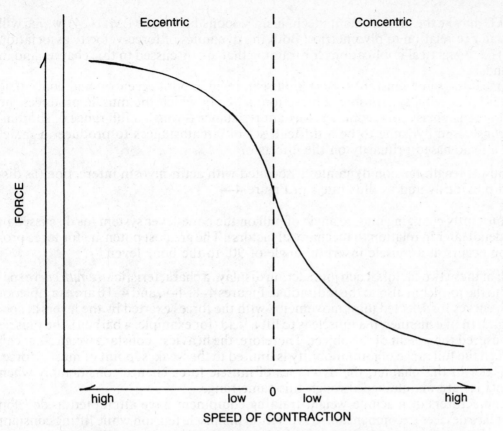

Figure 4–6. Force-Velocity Curve of Eccentric and Concentric Contraction.
(modified and redrawn from Komi, 1979)

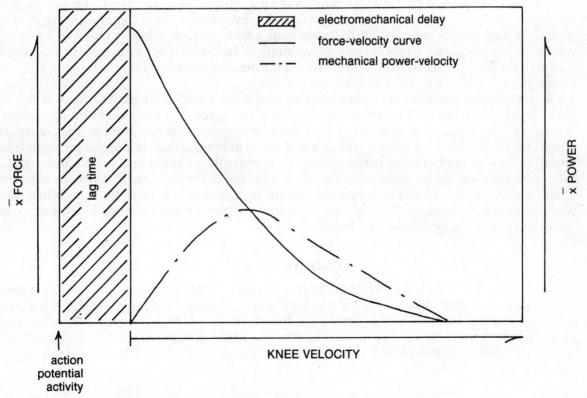

Figure 4–7. Force-,Power-Velocity Curve During Vertical Jump.

(SEC). The SEC may be the predominant mechanism responsible for the EMD (24), which will be discussed later in relation to plyometrics. Both the dynamics of force-velocity association and the EMD have practical implications for training that are discussed in this chapter and in Chapters 1 and 7.

Isotonic (meaning same tension) contractions can include both eccentric and concentric movements (34). Literally, an isotonic contraction is one in which the muscle produces the same amount of tension as it overcomes a constant resistance through a full range of shortening. This is considered by some to be a difficult set of circumstances to produce in intact muscle, with a logic based primarily on the effects of:

- The muscle length-tension dynamics associated with actin-myosin interaction (as discussed previously and as illustrated in Figure 4–4.

- The constantly changing muscle angle of pull on the bone-lever system (as discussed in more detail later in relation to mechanical factors). The greatest potential for force production occurs at a muscle insertion angle of 90° to the bone lever.

As a result of these two factors, each joint action displays a characteristic *strength curve* specific not only to the joint, but also to the individual. Figures 4–8, 4–9, and 4–10 are examples of some strength curves for selected joint movements with the forces exerted by the levers at specific joint angles. In like manner, if a muscle is to lift a load (for example, a barbell), the muscle tension must exceed the weight of the object. Therefore, the heaviest, constant weight that can be lifted through the full range of joint mobility is limited to the weakest point of muscle force. As discussed later in this chapter, the dynamics of muscle force change considerably when maximal velocities are maintained through this same range.

Some manufacturers of machine weight-training equipment have attempted to develop *variable resistance* devices to compensate for variation in muscle tension while lifting constant loads under constant velocities. Many use a variable lever or offset cam (see Figure 4–11) in an attempt to approximate the strength-curves inherently produced by the muscle-bone lever system, to purportedly maximize muscle tension throughout the full range of joint motion. Theoretically, this offset cam is supposed to vary the ratio of moments (see leverage concepts, presented later in this chapter) to accomodate the resistance so that the muscle effort is no greater at the *sticking point* (point in movement where greatest effort is made to lift a free weight) than at any other point in the range of motion. In theory, the muscle can be maximally stimulated through this accomodating effect and thereby better develop strength. This last point is subject to question; it is addressed in Chapter 5.

Other types of machines are *isokinetic* (meaning same speed) devices that use constant velocity friction mechanisms in an attempt to keep the speed of muscle shortening constant throughout the range of movement. These machines operate on the premise that muscular power, which is a function of both strength and speed of contraction, is a major factor in rehabilitation as well as in athletic performance. Consequently, proponents of these devices also claim that they require constant muscular effort over the entire movement range. In most machines currently in use however, only concentric contractions are possible, which may be a disadvantage in simulating sport-specific movement patterns while training. Machine devices are discussed in greater detail in Chapter 5.

Body Mechanics

The human body is a system of weights and levers with muscles as devices for producing force. Likewise, movements of an individual are governed by certain physical laws and principles of body mechanics or *biomechanics.* Understanding the nature of biomechanical principles and their correct use with respect to exercise can result in less wasted energy and therefore more effective movement. Consequently, poor mechanics in exercise are less efficient and may lead to strain and possible injury.

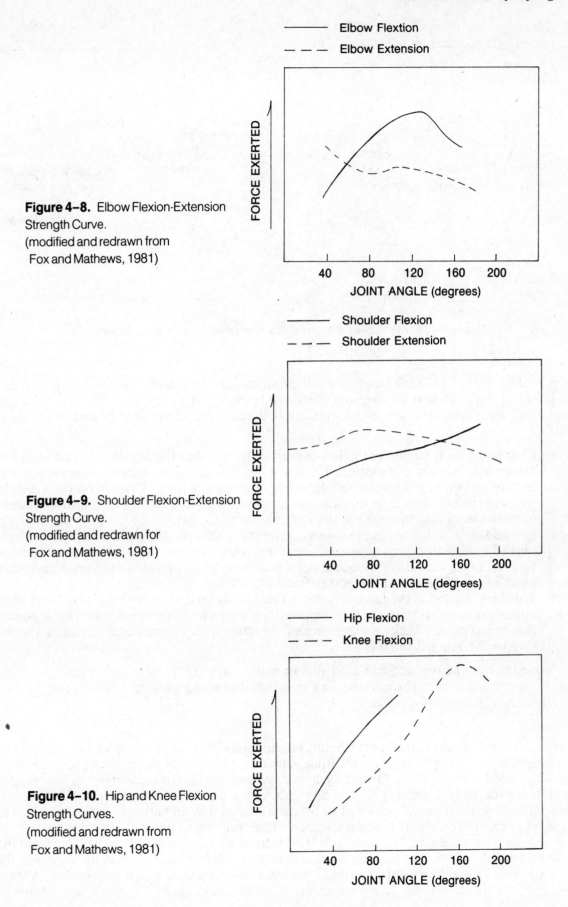

Figure 4–8. Elbow Flexion-Extension Strength Curve. (modified and redrawn from Fox and Mathews, 1981)

Figure 4–9. Shoulder Flexion-Extension Strength Curve. (modified and redrawn for Fox and Mathews, 1981)

Figure 4–10. Hip and Knee Flexion Strength Curves. (modified and redrawn from Fox and Mathews, 1981)

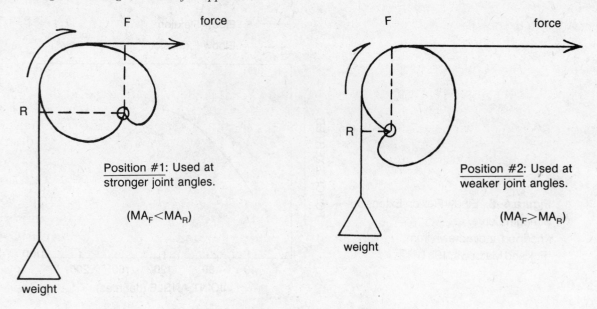

Figure 4–11. Mechanical Accomodation by Variable Resistance Device.

Laws of Motion

Between 1642 and 1727, Isaac Newton laid the foundation of modern dynamics (34). To Newton goes the credit of first discovering the three laws of rest and movement (3). Although theoretical, these laws express the relationships between forces (interactions) and their effects (34).

- **First law:** This is known as the law of *inertia*. It describes the resistance of an object to any change in its state of motion. The law states in linear terms that an object at rest will tend to remain at rest until acted upon by some outside force. Once in motion, the object will tend to remain in motion and to travel in a straight line with uniform speed unless acted on again by some net external force (3, 34).
- **Second law:** Also known as the law of *acceleration,* this law deals with the factors affecting the acceleration of an object. In linear terms it states that when a body is acted upon by a net force, the resulting acceleration is directly proportional to the mass and takes place in the direction of the acting force (3).
- **Third law:** Stated as the law of *reaction,* this law states that for every action there is an opposite and equal reaction, thus emphasizing that when a force is applied to an object, that object pushes back on the source of the effort with a force equal to and in opposition to the original force (3).

These laws can be restated and modified in many ways, both linear and angular, that are specific to the movement patterns existing in weight-training and weightlifting. They are referred to throughout this chapter.

Leverage

A brief overview of levers may prove helpful in understanding the principles of leverage and their application to weight-resistive training. A lever is a device for transmitting force and can be a helpful aid in doing work. Generally, a lever system consists of some rigid mass or implement (bone or body segment) that rotates about an axis (skeletal or mechanical joint) perpendicular to the plane of motion. The rotation is caused by an unbalanced force applied to the lever in an effort to overcome a resistance. Other important parts of a lever are the force arm and the resistance arm. The force arm (FA) is the distance measured on the lever from the point of force application to the axis of rotation; the resistance arm (RA) is the length of the lever measured from the axis of rotation to the center of weight-mass of the resistance. A lever with a greater resistance arm than force arm (RA>FA) is said to favor speed at the expense of strength. Conversely, a lever with a greater force arm than resistance arm (FA>RA) favors strength over speed.

Levers are classified into three categories, depending on the relationship between the axis (A), the force (f), and the resistance (R) (Figure 4–12).

- **First class lever:** When the axis of rotation is located between the application of force and the resistance, the system is called a first class lever. This type of lever can favor strength when the FA is longer than the RA and speed when the RA is longer than the FA. A *heel rise* exercise exhibits the use of such a lever while flexing the ankle during concentric contraction of the gastrocnemius muscle (30) (Figure 4–13).
- **Second class lever:** If the resistance (R) lies between the axis (A) and the application of force (f), the conditions are met for second class leverage. A second class lever always favors strength over speed of movement because the FA is always longer than the RA. Some weight machine devices make use of this lever system, as shown in Figure 4–14.
- **Third class lever:** When the force (f) is applied between the axis (A) and the resistance (R), a third class lever exists. A third class lever always favors speed at the expense of

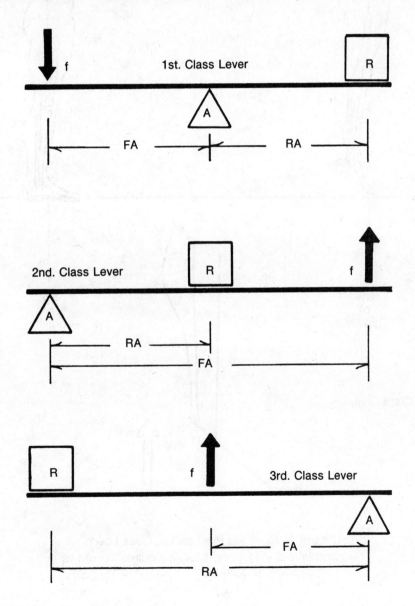

Figure 4–12. Classification of Levers.

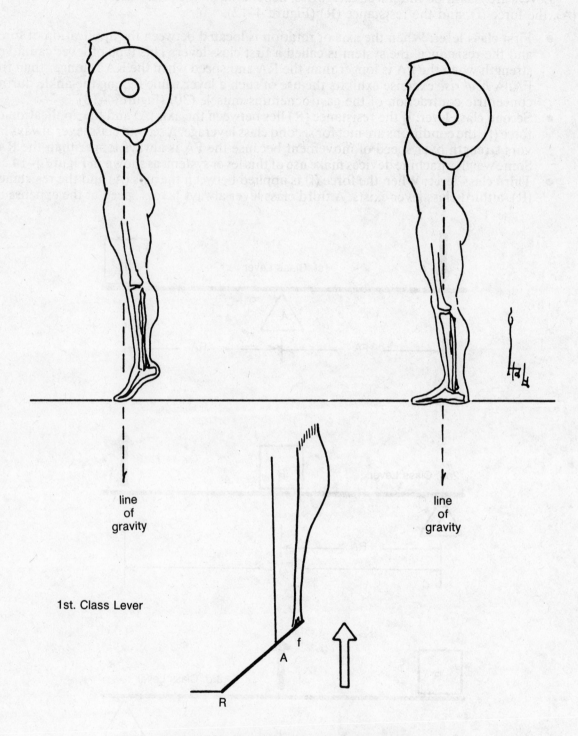

line
of
gravity

line
of
gravity

1st. Class Lever

Figure 4–13. "Heel Rise" as 1st. Class Lever.
(Arguments may exist using a slight modification of this
example as a 2nd class lever system)

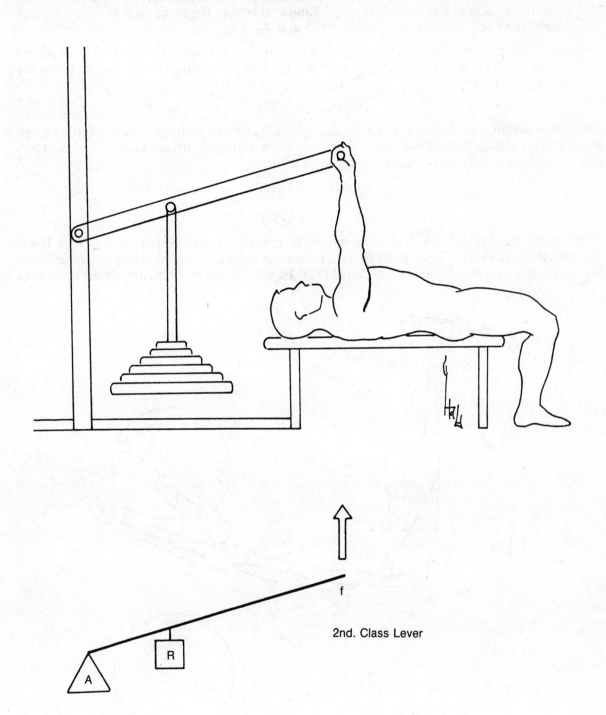

Figure 4–14. Bench Press Device as 2nd. Class Lever.

strength because the RA is always longer than the FA. The majority of bone-muscle levers in the human body are third class. Among these are the biceps brachii while flexing the elbow (i.e., arm curl) (Figures 4–15 and 4–18a).

A relationship exists between the various lever components regardless of classification and is described by the following: force (f) times the force arm (FA) equals resistance (R) times the resistance arm (RA) (32).

$$[f \times FA = R \times RA]$$

This relationship is sometimes called the *law of levers* and can be helpful in resolving forces, particularly in static states of motion. If any three of the four elements are known, the unknown can be determined by rearranging the formula so that:

$$[f = (R \times RA)/FA]$$
$$\text{or}$$
$$[R = (f \times FA)/RA]$$

In many mechanical as well as bone-muscle lever systems, however, a simple FA or RA is inadequate, and *moment arms* must be used instead. A moment arm must be perpendicular to the line of action with which it is associated (32). Therefore, the moment arm of the resistance

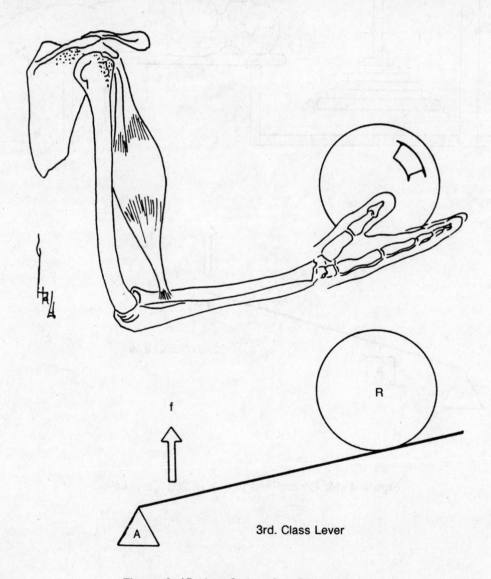

f

R

A

3rd. Class Lever

Figure 4–15. Arm Curl as 3rd. Class Lever.

(MA_R) is the distance measured from the axis of rotation of the lever perpendicular to the line of resistance (pull of gravity in most weight-resistive exercises). Likewise, the moment arm of the force (MA_F) is the distance measured from the axis of rotation of the lever perpendicular to the line of force (direction of muscle pull in bone-muscle levers). Consequently, the law of levers is slightly modified and the relationship among the lever elements in equilibrium can be best described as follows:

$$[f \times MA_F = R \times MA_R]$$

The moment arms replace FA and RA as more accurate determinants of leverage and can also be used to evaluate the mechanical advantage for producing force. As mentioned earlier, when FA>RA the lever favors strength. Therefore, the ratio of MA_F to MA_R will yield an index that can express the mechanical advantage for force production:

$$[MA_F / MA_R]$$

The larger the number the greater is the mechanical advantage favoring force. A small number indicates speed production at the expense of force. For example, because of third-class leverage and the ratio of the moments, a lateral raise held at only 80° elevation with just a 10-pound dumbbell will require approximately 300 pounds of tension in the deltoid muscle (34).

How can this knowledge about leverage be applied to advantage while lifting weight? Increasing the MA_F would help. This does occur as the muscle pull angle approaches 90° to the moving bone lever, requiring less force to move the same resistance at the same speed. Some suggest that this might also occur as a result of muscle hypertrophy in which increases in total muscle girth and/or connective tissue may increase the MA_F.

Nevertheless, more immediate results can be achieved by shortening the MA_R. This can be done by **keeping the resistance close to the body.** This principle can be applied to most any lift in which weight is pulled from the floor or from a rack (power cleans, clean pulls, dead lift, etc.). A common mistake of the novice is to allow the bar to drift far away from the body as the weight rises upward from the knees, thus slowing the velocity of the bar and achieving less work with more effort. Interestingly, the MA_R naturally shortens at the shoulder girdle as a result of contraction of the muscles that form the *rotator cuff,* thus pulling the proximal head of the humerus tighter into the joint cavity. This action, coupled with adduction of the scapula, shortens the MA_R when lifting with the arms. This makes a strong case for strengthening the muscles of the shoulder girdle in preparation for supportive or suspending movements of the upper body, for strength in the arm alone may not result in this effective modification of leverage.

In addition, note that increasing the mechanical advantage for force production is not always compatible with the objectives of training. If such a change in mechanics causes underloads on specific muscle groups (as is true of many methods of cheating), exercise may prove nonproductive toward the development of strength. Modifications in leverage may, however, be desirable if stress can be shifted from inherently weak or vulnerable areas of the body (such as the lower back) while still maintaining the integrity of the exercise.

Work

Mechanical work (W) is a function of the force (f) exerted on an object and the distance (d) through which it is displaced (Figure 4–16):

$$[W = f \times d]$$

If, however, the force is not in the same direction as the displacement, the component of force (f cos θ) in the direction of the displacement must be used to determine the work done (26) (Figure 4–17):

$$[W = f \cos \theta \times d]$$

Therefore, **for the most efficient use of force, the displacement should be along the same line and in the opposite direction to the resisting force of the object.** For example, there are many multijoint movement patterns that require weight to be lifted from the floor in front of the body. One such lift is a *clean pull* (Figure 4–16). This pattern also exists in many day-to-day activities as well as in job-related tasks. A common mistake is to lift the weight too far out in front

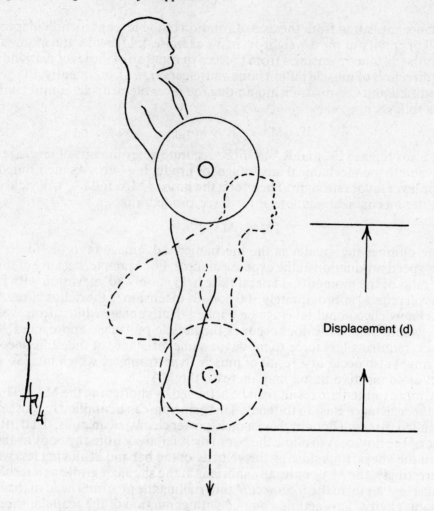

Displacement (d)

Figure 4–16. Force Exerted in Same Direction as Displacement.

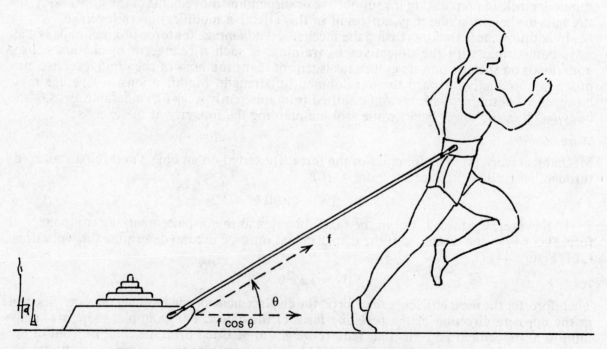

Figure 4–17. Force Exerted in Different Direction as Displacement.

of and away from the body, thus violating the previous principle. This mistake results in wasted effort and less effective movement. In addition, it often places too much stress on the small muscles of the lower back (erector spinae) and the hip extensors (hamstrings), increasing the chance of injury in these more susceptible areas.

Other lifts may isolate single muscle groups and produce segmental forces perpendicular to *lever arms* (r) (Figure 4–18a). These resultant forces produce turning motions or *torques* about axes (32). Torque (T) is a function of the muscle force (f) and the moment of force (r) (34):

$$[T = fr]$$

In Figure 4–18b, the perpendicular distance (r) from the axis of rotation (E) to the line of action (L) can be calculated by multiplying the force arm length (EI) times the sin of the muscle angle to the moving bone (b):

$$[r = EI \times \sin 57°]$$
$$= 2.5 \text{ in.} \times .83867$$
$$= 2.0967 \text{ in.}$$

Torque (T) can then be calculated by multiplying the muscle force (f) times the perpendicular distance (r) from the axis of rotation to the line of action:

$$[T = fr]$$
$$= 1000 \text{ lb.} \times 2.0967 \text{ in.}$$
$$= 2096.7 \text{ in.-lb.}$$
$$= 2096 / 12 \text{ (convert to ft.-lb.)}$$
$$= 175 \text{ ft.-lb.}$$

The perpendicular distance (r) from the axis of rotation to the line of action is dependent on the angle of muscle insertion to the moving bone. **Since the human body moves by a series of rotations, each having a different muscle insertion angle, the torque is constantly changing.** Note the example in Figure 4–18c, in which the muscle insertion angle θ c is now 112°. Applying the same procedure as before, we find a completely different torque (T):

$$[r = EI \times \sin 112°]$$
$$= 2.5 \text{ in.} \times .92719$$
$$= 2.318 \text{ in.}$$

$$[T = fr]$$
$$= 1000 \text{ lb.} \times 2.318 \text{ in.}$$
$$= 2318 \text{ in.-lb.}$$
$$= 2318 / 12 \text{ (convert to ft.-lb.)}$$
$$= 193 \text{ ft.-lb.}$$

In this last instance the same muscle force produces a higher torque. **The greatest potential for a muscle to produce torque occurs at a theoretical muscle insertion angle of 90°,** which has a sin of 1.000, indicating that the moment of force (r) and the force arm (EI) are equal. This change in torque due to variation in muscle-bone angles is related to the *strength curve* exhibited by intact muscle, which was discussed earlier in this chapter.

Since work is a function of force and distance, distal displacement of a lever is a function of both angular displacement and the length of the lever arm; torque is the product of the force and the length of the moment arm. Work (W), then, is equal to force (f) times the angular displacement (φ) (26):

$$[W = T\phi]$$

Work also can be done as an object is accelerated. According to Newton's second law, force causes acceleration of an object. In this case, resistance is the mass, or property of inertia (26). Force (f) is therefore a function of the mass (m) and the acceleration (a):

$$[f = ma]$$

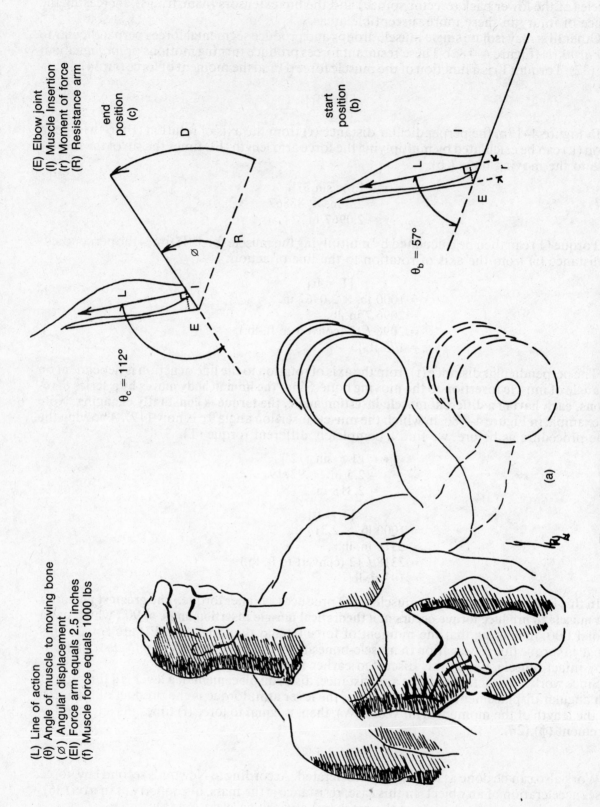

(L) Line of action
(θ) Angle of muscle to moving bone
(∅) Angular displacement
(EI) Force arm equals 2.5 inches
(f) Muscle force equals 1000 lbs

(E) Elbow joint
(I) Muscle Insertion
(r) Moment of force
(R) Resistance arm

Figure 4–18. Torque and Angular Displacement.

In addition, this force causes acceleration of an object and motion parallel to the force with the resistance as the mass, therefore satisfying the definition of work. Since work (W) is a function of force (f) and displacement (d), and force (f) is equal to mass (m) times acceleration (a), then (26):

$$[W = fd = mad]$$

This also holds true for angular acceleration. An angular analog of Newton's second law of motion states that angular acceleration produced by an unbalanced torque acting on a body is proportional to the net torque, in the same direction as the torque, and inversely proportional to the moment of inertia of the body (3). Torque (T) is the angular equivalent of force. Newton's first law of motion imputes to material bodies the tendency to resist motion. Mass is the linear measure of this tendency, whereas the *moment of inertia* is the angular counterpart of mass. Since work is a function of torque and angular displacement (ϕ) and torque (T) is equal to the product of the moment of inertia (I) and angular acceleration ($\propto$), then:

$$[W = T \phi = I \propto \phi]$$

This means that in speed activities (as in lifting free weights with maximum velocity) where leverage and torque are variable, muscle force remains constant throughout a large range of motion. As the muscle-bone lever approaches the most productive angles for producing force, acceleration increases as mass remains constant, thereby **maintaining a constant workload as well as muscle tension throughout most of the range in dynamic movement** (17, 35) (see Chapter 3 for application to anaerobic power).

Energy

Anything having the capacity to do work possesses energy. In humans, energy exists in many different forms, both chemical and mechanical (see Chapters 1 and 2). In mechanical terms, the ability to do work because of position or form is often called *potential* or stored energy. Potential energy (PE) increases when work is done in an effort to overcome gravity, as when a weight is held above the head. When deformed objects like spring or elastic devices (some of which have been suggested for use in resistive exercise) are used, resistance increases as the device is stretched. Consequently, **resistance is not constant,** and the force necessary to overcome the resistance must also increase as the distortion increases. Use of such exercise devices does not result in movement patterns that simulate sport activities and is not specific to the dynamics of muscular strength and power.

Elastic storage of energy does occur as a normal muscular function during the preparation phase of many ballistic movements. Such is the case with jumping and other propulsive activities in which the hip and knee extensors are stretched prior to contraction. This stretching action causes about a 3% lengthening of the series elastic components (34) located at the Z disc in skeletal muscle tissue (see Chapter 1). This storage of energy is released during the propulsive phases of the movement and, along with the *stretch reflex,* potentiates the quality of force production by the muscle. The factors governing this physio-mechanical phenomenon can be conditioned through *plyometric training,* thus improving the reactive ability of the muscle and subsequent power production. More discussion on plyometrics appears later in this chapter.

Another form of mechanical energy, called *kinetic energy* (KE), is related to the velocity of an object and is defined as the energy of motion. As movement produces work, KE becomes a function of mass (m) and velocity (v) such that:

$$[KE = 1/2 \ mv^2]$$

Thus kinetic energy becomes the energy of mechanical work. Since the *law of conservation of energy* states that energy cannot be created or destroyed, potential energy (PE) decreases as kinetic energy increases. Therefore, as an object is allowed to fall with the force of gravity pulling on it, the object's PE decreases while its KE increases. As the object accelerates, KE increases even more and more force is required to stop it. **Overcoming accelerations at the end of lifts and imparting forces to accelerate at the beginning of lifts have greater potential for injury.** Such movement dynamics are often unavoidable because they exist inherently in many sport-specific lifts. Nevertheless, poor body position at the beginning and/or conclusion of lifts can set up undesirable moments and result in injury of supporting tissues, particularly the lower back. In 1974, Frankel (15) and Noyes (31) studied energy absorption related to speed of loading on body tissue. Frankel found that with fast loading a bone can withstand greater loads before its failure (15), whereas Noyes determined that such speed produced the potential for more ligament failures (31). Study of heavy lifting has revealed that overcoming inertia at the beginning and possibly also at the end of a lift produces the greatest stress to the back (10, 20), with the highest stress found within the first 0.4 second of the lift (20).

Others have concluded that acceleration, both positive and negative, plays an important role in stress components on the musculoskeletal system (2). This finding lends further support to the notion that proper body mechanics must be performed during heavy or fast weightlifting, with much emphasis on stabilizing the lower back. Making this problem more complex is the increasing difficulty of keeping correct body position as velocity increases. Either through loss of concentration or decreased time for relocation (or both), poor mechanics are likely to occur during lifting attempts at heavy weights and/or high velocities. Yet high velocity lifts are essential for the training of strength-power athletes as they strive to simulate sport-specific neuromuscular dynamics and consequently stimulate fast twitch motor units (see Chapter 1). Even recreational lifters and individuals striving for desirable changes in body composition (particularly for body weight control) may select lifts because of their high metabolic requirements; many of these lifts also fall into the category of *fast velocity* exercises. Persons who use such lifts should follow these precautions:

- Keep the back straight and the head up (during squats, pulls, cleans, etc.), particularly at the beginning and end of lifts.
- Use weight rack or rubber plates to decelerate (break the fall of weights) when performing heavy suspension lifts (hang cleans, clean pulls, etc.).
- Avoid unnecessary or sudden deceleration of weights at the end of heavy suspension lifts if supportive devices are not available.
- Use a weight belt; a belt provides extra support for the lower back area through increased intra-abdominal pressure.
- Keep the weight close to the body and centered directly over the base of support.
- Avoid exaggerated forward lean.
- Keep the direction of lifts vertical so undue stress from horizontal forces is not placed on the smaller stabilizing muscles.
- Initiate the beginning of pull-type lifts (cleans, etc.) with the large muscles of the legs and hip rather than the back.
- Establish a strength base prior to much speed training.
- Mentally prepare before and concentrate during the execution of a lift, stressing proper body position.

Plyometrics

The combination of eccentric and concentric training is thought to enhance muscular strength and power to a greater degree than concentric training alone (22). Plyometrics relate to specific exercises that involve a rapid stretching of the muscle undergoing eccentric stress, followed by a concentric contraction of that muscle (6). A major purpose of such exercise is to heighten the excitability of the nervous system for improved reactive ability of the neuromuscular mechanism. To put it simply, plyometrics can be considered the link between strength and speed (6).

The theoretical basis for plyometric training lies in the rebound movement patterns so prevalent in sport activities. There is an *amortization phase,* which includes the electromechanical delay (EMD) between eccentric and concentric contraction, during which the muscle must rapidly switch from overcoming work to imparting the necessary amount of acceleration in the required direction (7). Explosive power from the knee and hip extensor muscles in jumping provides the type of ballistic movement characteristics exhibited in most anaerobic sports. Likewise, biomechanical analyses reveal a strong similarity between the mechanics of the bone-muscle levers while jumping and the sport-specific movement patterns for lower limb propulsion required in weightlifting (18) and many other strength-power activities (9). Consequently, it is not surprising that strong relationships have been reported in the literature between jumping ability and athletic performance (8, 9, 11, 12, 29, 30). Some major muscles involved in jumping, as in other strength-power activities, are the quadriceps, hamstrings, erector spinae, gluteals, deltoids, trapezius, and gastrocnemius (9).

Traditionally, much emphasis has been placed on the quads by strength programs with neglect of some other muscles, particularly the hamstrings. Recent data suggest that the hamstring muscle group may contribute a great deal to the overall movements requiring leg propulsion (28) and should be emphasized in anaerobic conditioning programs (9). Simple weight training alone may not fulfill jumping potential (Figure 4–19) because it may not maximize one's speed in switching from eccentric to concentric contractions within a counter-type movement (9, 37, 38). During rebound movements, mechanical energy is absorbed by the muscle during eccentric contraction and released during the subsequent propulsive phase (concentric contraction). The prestretch of the knee and hip extensors activates the myototic (stretch) reflex to potentiate the force of shortening and propel the jumper higher than could be obtained without the downward rebound movement.

A progression of weight training, jump drills, and plyometrics is recommended to further develop strength, quicken reactions, and increase agility. A strength base is considered an important prerequisite and therefore should be a precedent to bounding as well as plyometric training phases (9).

Jump Training

Bounding drills usually follow weight training as one moves from strength to power training. These movements typically involve a series of horizontal jumps, vertical jumps, or a combination of jumps done first from both feet and later with single leg variations. Figure 4–20 illustrates two such bounding drills. Amplitude and thus intensity should be placed on a progressive resistance model to allow adequate physiological and neurological adaptation to the stress overloads.

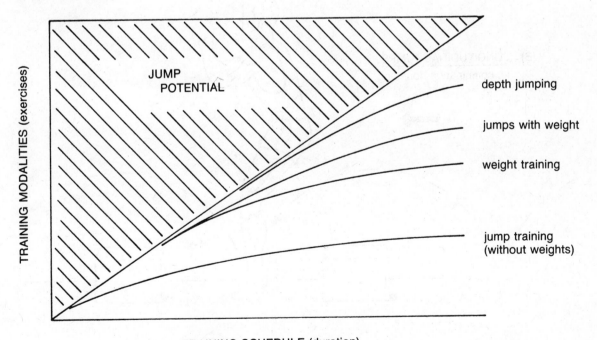

Figure 4–19. Exercises to Fulfill Jumping Potential.

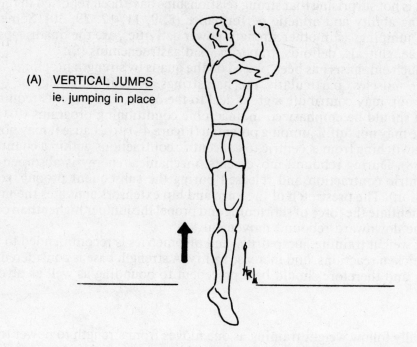

(A) <u>VERTICAL JUMPS</u>
ie. jumping in place

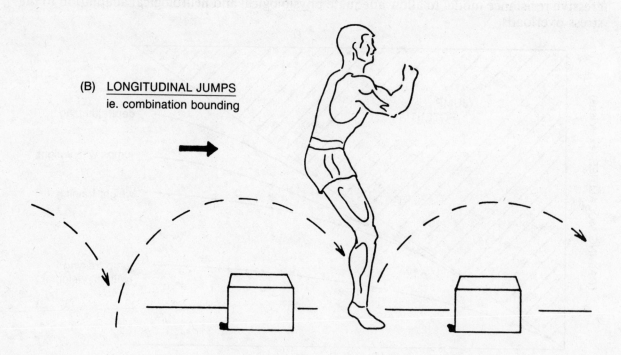

(B) <u>LONGITUDINAL JUMPS</u>
ie. combination bounding

Figure 4–20. Bounding Drills.

Box Drills

Weight and jump training is followed by *box drills* or rebound jumping from platforms (see Chapter 10 for photo illustration). These exercises are accomplished from an elevated surface from which the person leaves and is accelerated by gravity to the ground. Upon contact with the ground a maximal jump movement is executed as quickly as possible vertically, horizontally, or in combination. Figure 4–21 illustrates a typical box drill. As with all jump training, progression should be maintained while attempting double leg, single leg, weighted, or unweighted variations that serve to increase intensity. A variety of different box heights (typically 18 to 22 inches) have been used. Box height may be related to leg and hip strength (9) and to individual body weight to an even greater extent (13). As yet no exact method of determining box height has been developed.

Some other variations in plyometric exercise are particularly useful with the large, heavy athlete weighing over 230 pounds. Among them are *static* and *weighted release* jumps (see Chapter 10 for photo illustration). Even though they are quite strong, large athletes (shotputters, etc.), can experience joint trauma and undue stress upon the connective tissue during the deceleration phase of orthodox plyometric drills. An effective alternative may be to use weight drills that incorporate speed work, with less emphasis on deceleration and more emphasis on the acceleration of jumping mechanics. A countertype jump with dumbbells may provide the required prestretch minus the trauma. The weighted-release jump, in which dumbbells are released just before the moment of takeoff, may serve to accelerate the concentric contraction, with the possibility of further enhancing the neuromuscular apparatus.

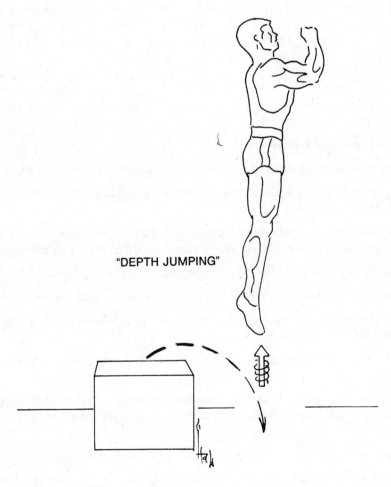

"DEPTH JUMPING"

Figure 4–21. Plyometric Box Drill.

Table 4–1. Optimum volume table for plyometrics.*

Phase	Total repetitions
Low intensity (LI)	400
Moderate intensity (MI)	350
High intensity (HI)	300
Very intense (VI)	200

*Note: The upper and lower body can be treated separately.

Table 4–2. Volume per individual plyometric exercise.

Phase	Volume
Low intensity (LI)	10 sets of 12 reps
Moderate intensity (MI)	7 sets of 10 reps
High intensity (HI)	5 sets of 8 reps
Very intense (VI)	3 sets of 6 reps

Still other modifications to the jumping mechanics can include statically held half squat (3-second hold) prior to the concentric phases of muscle dynamics. Elastic recoil may be used even more effectively in this movement of smaller amplitude (36), which minimizes the energy that is ordinarily wasted during cross-bridge detachment (sarcomere give) (4). Principles for progressive intensity can be maintained with increments of heavier dumbbells, either held or released upon takeoff. There appears to be little agreement among the few recognized authorities on the optimum volume for plyometric training (33). Some East German studies (16) have recommended 6 to 10 sets for most plyometric exercises, whereas Verkhoshanskiy (38) suggests 3 to 6 sets for the intense drills. Fewer repetitions of the intense exercises are likely to be done, particularly during the later phases of training. Usually, more repetitions are recommended during the onset of a plyometric conditioning program, when less intensity will be stressed. In general, the number of repetitions suggested ranges from 8 to 10 per plyometric exercise (33). Table 4–1 lists the suggested optimum volume per training session for plyometric conditioning according to intensity level. Table 4–2 lists the suggested volume of training per individual type of plyometric exercise. The values in Table 4–1 can be altered for a total conditioning approach or if additional modes of exercise are used.

The following list includes some plyometric exercises suggested by the authors and others (33), their classification, and their relative intensity (low intensity = LI, moderate intensity = MI, high intensity = HI, and very intense = VI. For further clarification, Chapter 10 contains photo sequences of some plyometric exercises.

A. Jump Training: Double Leg Using Low Boxes

(LI)   1. Double leg vertical jump upward with own body weight, as shown in Figure 4–20a.

(LI)   2. Double leg bound outward and upward. Movement is forward and upward to gain maximum height and horizontal distance.

(MI)   3. Double leg box bound on and off box. Similar to Figure 4–20b, but with the addition of landing on and taking off from boxes alternating with jumps from and onto the floor.

(MI)   4. Double leg incline bound up hill. As in jumping horizonally up hill.

(HI)   5. Double leg decline bound down hill. Opposite of A–4 but with a ricochet action.

(MI)   6. Double leg twisting box bound on and off boxes. As in A–3, but with ¼ or ⅛ turn, alternating right and left on landing.

(LI)   7. Double leg side hop sideways alternately. Similar to A–3 but landing either to the right or left of the box.

(LI)   8. Double leg angle hop with incline box. Bounding sideways with the aid of two boxes set approximately 3 to 6 ft. apart having top surfaces canted inward at the appropriate angles.

(MI)   9. Double leg twisting side hop sideways alternatively. A combination of A–6 and A–7.

(MI)   10. Side hop and sprint. Double leg jump sideways over box. Upon landing, immediately explode forward and run with as much speed as possible for about 10 to 30 yd.

B. Jump Training: Single Leg Using Low Boxes

(LI)   1.   Alternate leg bound. As in A–2, but alternating off one leg, then the other.

(MI)   2.   Alternate leg box drill. As in A–3, but alternating off one leg, then the other.

(MI)   3.   Alternate leg lateral bound. As in A–8, but alternating off one leg, then the other.

(MI)   4.   Single leg stride jump. Begin with one foot up on the box and the other foot on the ground to the side. Using the inside leg for power, jump upward. Upon landing with one foot on the box and one foot off as in starting position, immediately execute another repetition and continue until the end of the set. Switch sides facing opposite direction and execute exercise on the other leg.

(MI)   5.   Stride jump crossover. Same as in B–4 above, but landing on and taking off from alternate sides of the box with alternate legs.

C. Plyometric: Depth Jumps

(MI)   1.   Depth jump off box 14 in.-18 in. high. As in Figure 4–21, begin with balls of feet on edge of box, step off and land on floor with both feet; immediately execute an explosive jump upward.

(HI)   2.   Depth jump off box 22 in.-26 in. high. See C–1.

(VI)   3.   Depth jump off box 30 in.-34 in. high. See C–1.

(MI)   4.   Depth jump with double leg leap forward. As in C–1, but with jump upward and outward for both vertical and horizontal distance.

(HI)   5.   Depth jump with double leg leap forward. A higher order of progression from C–4 using the box height of C–2.

(VI)   6.   Depth jump with double leg leap forward. A higher order of progression from C–5 using the box height of C–3.

(MI)   7.   Depth jump with double leg leap to the box. As in C–1, but jumping outward and upward to land on a second box of the same or different height.

(HI)   8.   Depth jump with double leg leap to box. A higher order of progression performed as in C–7, but with a depth jump from a higher box, as in C–2.

(VI)   9.   Depth jump with double leg leap to box. A higher order of progression performed as in C–7, but with a depth jump from a higher box, as in C–3.

D. Drills With Dumbbells or Weight Vest
Note: Drills numbered D–1 through D–5 work well as alternatives to depth jumps for the heavy athlete (230 pounds and over).

(HI)   1.   Counter-type vertical jump. Performed as in Figure 4–20a, but with increasing amounts of additional resistance.

(HI)   2.   Static-type vertical jump. As in D–1 above, but beginning from a starting position of a half squat statically held for 3 seconds, then jumping straight upward without any preparatory counter movement.

(HI)   3.   Same as D–1, but with release of weight at bottom.

(HI)   4.   Same as D–2, but with release at takeoff.

(HI)   5.   Same as D–1, but with release at takeoff.

(VI)   6.   Jump to box. Jump from floor upward and forward to land on box. Progressively higher orders of intensity can be achieved by increasing box heights or using increasing amounts of additional resistance.

(VI)   7. Depth jump. As in C–1 through C–3.

(VI)   8. Depth jump with double leg leap forward. As in C–4 through C–6.

(VI)   9. Depth jump with double leg leap to box. As in C–7 through C–9.

E. Upper Body Drills: Anterior-Posterior Plane

(LI)   1. Vertical dumbbell swing. Execute a series of vertical jumps while swinging a dumbbell or swingbell with arms extended in front of body. Swing weight first upward on takeoff and then downward upon landing.

(MI)   2. Vertical medicine ball toss. From a half-squat position with legs slightly greater than shoulder width apart, use a scooping action and throw the weighted ball upward and catch it on the way down with each repetition.

(MI)   3. Medicine ball chest pass. Using a chest pass, toss the weighted ball back and forth between partners.

(HI)   4. Medicine ball sit-up throw. From a standard sit-up position, continue the motion as the sit-up is finished by using a chest pass and toss the weighted ball forward to a waiting partner who tosses it back to be caught at the onset of the next sit-up.

(MI)   5. Heavy bag forward thrust. Using a suspended heavy boxing bag, push the bag forward like a pendulum and decelerate the bag as it swings backward to execute another repetition.

(VI)   6. Medicine ball supine toss from drop. From a lying position as if performing a supine bench press, have a partner drop the ball from above to be caught about at the chest. Immediately use a chest pass to toss the weighted ball upward back to the level it was dropped from.

(VI)   7. Push-up drop from benches. Using two benches or chairs placed slightly wider than shoulder width apart, assume a push-up position with hands on the top of the benches. Drop from the benches to a push-up position on the floor between the benches and immediately execute an explosive push-up action to achieve a position on top of the benches ready to perform another repetition.

F. Torso Drills: Trunk Torque

(MI)   1. Horizontal dumbbell swing. From an upright shoulder width stance, arms extended forward from the chest, swing the dumbbell sideways with a twisting action of the upper body.

(HI)   2. Medicine ball twist pass. With extended arms and a twisting action of the upper body, toss the weighted ball sideways to a partner who will do likewise in the same fashion so that the ball must be caught in the reverse manner.

(HI)   3. Sideways heavy bag thrust. As in E–5, but performed with a trunk twisting action sideways.

(VI)   4. Supine one arm shotput toss. As in E–6, but with weighted ball caught at the side and thrust upward using a trunk twisting action, using only one arm at a time.

(MI)   5. Push-up from single bench. Perform an explosive push-up action from a position in which one arm is up on a low bench and the other is to the side down on the floor. Movement should be vigorous enough to allow the upper hand to clear the bench. Repetitions rapidly follow in succession after each downward movement and subsequent deceleration.

(VI)   6. Sit-up, one arm, shotput. As in E–4, but with the tossing and catching action executed by a trunk twisting movement and one arm.

(VI)   7. Roman chair sit-up, shotput, Similar to F–7, but from a roman chair sit-up, shotput a weighted ball to a waiting partner as a continuation of the sit-up movement. Partner then passes it back at the onset of the next sit-up.

Table 4–3. Plyometrics integrated with weight training (suggested 12-week periodization cycle).

Duration	3 weeks	2 weeks	3 weeks	2 weeks	1 week	1 week
Major exercises	5 × 10	3 × 5	3 × 10	3× 5 (1 × 10)*	3 × 3 (1 × 10)*	3 × 2 (2 × 5)†
Supplemental exercises	3 × 10 etc.	→				
Plyometric exercises		LI	LI–MI	MI–HI	MI–HI	HI–VI

Note: *Speed work to be done with approximately 70% initial 1RM intensity.
†Speed work to be done with approximately 75%–80% initial 1RM intensity.

The volume and intensity of plyometric conditioning should follow the same principles of periodization training described in Chapter 6. Table 4–3 is provided as a suggested guide for integrating plyometrics with a periodized weight-training approach.

Summary

The following summary is provided as a suggested guide to be used when designing drills and administering a plyometric conditioning program.

1. Alternate days of training (no two consecutive days).

2. Start on double leg and progress to single leg drills.

3. Use progressive resistance principles when increasing intensity. (Progress from less to more intense drills.)

4. Remember that speed may be more important than resistance.

5. Remember that specificity of movement is necessary for carryover to athletic activities.

6. Use good footwear and a padded surface for jumping.

7. Remember that intensity, volume, and frequency depend on the strength level and experience of the individual.

8. Use complete rest or low intensity exercises between jumping drills (stretching, relaxation, etc.).

9. Discontinue depth jumps 10 to 14 days prior to athletic competition.

10. Do not overuse depth jump training in season.

11. Use 3 to 10 sets of 5 to 12 reps per exercise, depending on the intensity of plyometric exercise and the nature of supplemental conditioning.

12. Allow 1 to 5 minutes of rest between plyometric exercises, depending on the volume and the intensity level of the drill.

13. Perform each plyometric exercise to maximum to stimulate the neuromuscular system.

14. Build a good strength base before extensive plyometric training.

15. Use bounding skills for horizontal distance to improve longitudinal jumping.

16. Jump from a static position from time to time to develop maximum cross-bridge interaction in the absence of sarcomere give.

17. In general, alternative drills to depth jumping should be provided for the heavy athlete (230 pounds and over).

18. Some simple, low intensity jumping drills (vertical jumps, vertical tuck jumps, and vertical pike jumps) can be integrated into warmups prior to a normal exercise routine.

References

1. Assmussen, E., O. Hansen, and O. Lammert. 1965. The relationship between isometric and dynamic muscle strength in man. Communications from the Danish National Association for Infantile Paralysis, No. 20.

2. Ayoub, M., R. Dryden, and J. McDaniel. 1974. Models for lifting activities. In Nelson, R., and C. Morehouse (Eds.). *Biomechanics IV.* Baltimore: University Park Press, pp. 30–36.

3. Barham, J. 1978. *Mechanical Kinesiology.* St. Louis: C. V. Mosby Co.

4. Bosco, C., and P. Komi. 1980. Influence of countermovement amplitude in potentiation of muscular performance. In *Biomechanics VII.* Baltimore: University Park Press, pp. 129–135.

5. Bosco, C., and P. Komi. 1980. Mechanical characteristics and fiber composition of human leg extensor muscles. *European Journal of Applied Physiology* 41:275–284.

6. Chu, D. 1983. Plyometrics: The link between strength and speed. *National Strength and Conditioning Association Journal* 5(2):20–21.

7. Chu, D. 1984. Plyometric exercise. *National Strength and Conditioning Association Journal* 5(6):56–59; 61–63.

8. Clarke, H. 1971. *Physical and Motor Tests in The Medford Boy's Growth Study.* Englewood Cliffs, N.J.: Prentice-Hall, Inc.

9. Coaches Roundtable, Improving jumping ability. 1984. *National Strength and Conditioning Association Journal* 6(2):10–20.

10. Davis, P., J. Troup, and J. Burnard. 1965. Movements of the thoracic and lumbar spine when lifting: A chronocyclophotographic study. *Journal of Anatomy* 99:13–26.

11. DiGiovanna, V. 1943. The relationship of selected structural and functional measures to success in college athletes. *Research Quarterly* 14:199.

12. Everett, P. 1952. The prediction of baseball ability. *Research Quarterly* 23:15.

13. Evitt, D., and H. O'Bryant. 1985. Determination of optimal box height for individualized plyometric training. Unpublished master's thesis, Appalachian State University, Boone, N.C.

14. Fox, E., and D. Mathews. 1981. *The Physiological Basis of Physical Education and Athletics* (3rd edition). Philadelphia: Saunders College Publishing.

15. Frankel, V. 1974. Biomechanics of bone. Paper presented at the American Academy of Orthopedic Surgeons, Buena Vista, Fla., April 2–5.

16. Gambetta, V. 1981. Plyometric training. In *Track and Field Coaching Manual.* V. Gambetta (Ed.) New York: Leisure Press.

17. Garhammer, J. 1979. Muscle fiber types and the specificity concept related to athletic weight training. Personal Communication.

18. Garhammer, J., and R. Gregor. 1979. Force plate evaluations of weightlifting and vertical jumping (Abstract). *Medicine and Science in Sports* 11(1):106.

19. Gordon, A., A. Huxley, and F. Julian. 1966. Variation in isometric tension with sarcomere length in vertebrate muscle fibers. *Journal of Physiology* (London) 184:170–192.

20. Grieve, D. 1974. Dynamic characteristics of man during crouch and stoop-lifting. In Nelson, R., and C. Morehouse (Eds.). *Biomechanics IV.* Baltimore: University Park Press, pp. 19–29.

21. Guyton, A. 1981. *Textbook of Medical Physiology* (6th edition). Philadelphia: W. B. Saunders Co.

22. Hakkinen, K., and P. Komi. 1982. Specificity of training-induced change in strength performance considering the integrating functions of the neuro-muscular system. *International Weightlifting Federation* 5:44–46.

23. Komi, P. 1973. Measurement of the force-velocity relationship in human muscle under concentric and eccentric contractions. In Cerguiglini (Ed.). *Biomechanics III.* pp. 224–229.

24. Komi, P. 1979. Neuromuscular performance: Factors influencing force and speed production. *Scandinavian Journal of Sports Science* 1:2–15.

25. Komi, P., and E. Buskirk. 1972. Effect of eccentric and concentric muscle conditioning on tension and electrical activity of human muscle. *Ergonomics* 15:417–434.

26. LeVeau, B. 1977. *Williams and Lissner: Biomechanics of Human Motion* (2nd edition). Philadelphia: W. B. Saunders Co.

27. Levin, A., and J. Wyman. 1927. The viscous elastic properties of muscle. *Proceedings of Royal Society of London.* 101:213–243.

28. Mattox, K., H. O'Bryant, and V. Christian. 1983. The relationship of training in aerobically and anaerobically conditioned females on vertical jump. Poster presentation at NCAHPERD Conference, Hyatt Convention Center, Winston-Salem, N.C., Nov. 18.

29. Moulds, B., D. Carter, J. Coleman, and M. Stone. 1979. Physical responses of a women's basketball team to a preseason conditioning program. *Science In Sports.* In Terauds, J. (Ed.), pp. 203–210.

30. Ness, P., and C. Sharos. 1956. The effect of weight training on leg strength and vertical jump. Master's thesis, Springfield College.

31. Noyes, F. 1974. Biomechanics of anterior cruciate ligament failure: An analysis of strain-rate sensitivity and mechanism of failure in primates. *Journal of Bone Joint Surgery* 56A:236–253.

32. O'Connell, A., and E. Gardner. 1972. *Understanding the Scientific Bases of Human Motion.* Baltimore: The Williams & Wilkins Co.

33. Radcliffe, J., and R. Farentinos. 1984. *Plyometrics: Explosive Power Training.* Boulder, Colorado: ExerTechnics Publishers.

34. Rasch, P., and R. Burke. 1974. *Kinesiology and Applied Anatomy: The Science of Human Movement* (5th edition). Philadelphia: Lea & Febiger.

35. Sawhill, J. 1981. Biomechanical characteristics of rotational velocity and movement complexity in isokinetic performance. Doctoral dissertation, University of Oregon.

36. Thys, H., G. Cavagna, and R. Margaria. 1975. The role played by elasticity in an exercise involving movements of small amplitude. *Pflugers Arch. Europ. J. Physiology* 354:281–286.

37. Tschiene, P. 1973. Power training principles for top-class throwers. *Track Techniques* 52:1642–1654.

38. Verkhoshanskiy, Y. 1966. Perspectives in the improvement of speed-strength preparation of jumpers. *Track and Field* 9:11–12.

Considerations for Gaining a Strength-Power Training Effect: Training Principles and Modes and Methods

Two important considerations in planning a resistive training program are to determine what set and repetition protocol (method) will be used and to determine what equipment (mode) will be used. This chapter presents information concerning basic training principles and how they relate to method and mode selection and will consider machine versus free-weight training.

Basic Principles

Training Principles

A brief discussion of the basic principles of training and the mechanisms of strength display and strength gain will be helpful in understanding various modes and methods of training. For detailed discussions of training principles, see references 16 and 65. The basic training principles are the principles of volume, intensity, variation, and specificity.

Volume

The duration and frequency of training are related to the total volume of work. Duration is the amount of time spent exercising. Frequency refers to the number of training sessions per day, week, month, etc. The higher the duration or frequency, the greater the total workload or volume. As pointed out in Chapters 6 and 7, weight-training volume can be estimated as the total number of repetitions during a given period.

Intensity

The intensity of exercise (or training) is equal to the power output (rate of work). Intensity is a key factor for progress in a variety of programs, but it is especially important for strength training. Figure 4–6, which shows a force-velocity curve, represents a capacity curve. The closer one trains to the curve, the greater the intensity and the greater the training effect (16)]. Although this relationship was originally shown in isolated muscle, it holds for intact single joint (33) and multi-joint, multi-segment movements (19, 33). Appropriate resistive training can shift this curve (concentric portion) to the right, effecting a gain in power ($P = f \times V$) at nearly all points on the curve (Figure 5–1). Continued heavy resistive training may cause further shifts of the lower portion of the curve to the right (Figure 5–2) (unpublished observations). It **may be** possible to positively effect the upper portion of the curve with specific, specialized types of high

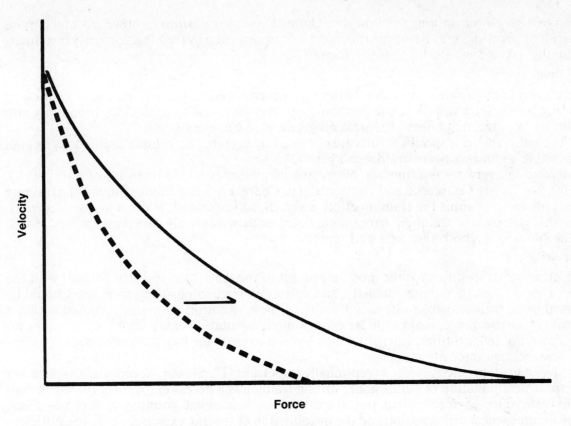

Figure 5–1. Force-velocity adaptations to training.

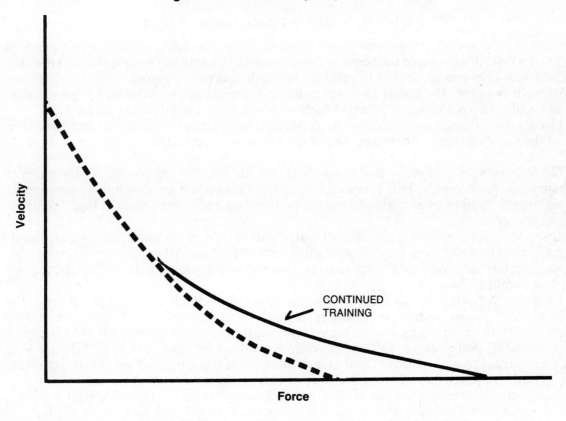

Figure 5–2. Force-velocity adaptations (continued training).

speed or high power training (unpublished data). The upper portion is, however, much more difficult to effect and may be more influenced by heredity than by training. Intensity is estimated by the average weight lifted (see Chapter 7).

Variation

The principle of variation probably is the most overlooked training principle. Variation in training is necessary to reduce the possibility of overwork and to reduce the monotony and potentiate the training effect of typical programs (see Chapters 6 and 7).

Typically, superior **specific** results are obtained by keeping the volume or intensity as high as possible so long as overwork doesn't result.

Reducing overwork is a function of varying the volume and the intensity of training (12, 37, 60, 64, 75) (see Chapters 6 and 7). As noted in Chapter 6, monotonous, unvarying training programs can also limit the training effect, even though overwork is not a major factor. To limit this type of "overtraining," care should be taken to periodically vary the exercises, as well as the training methods (i.e., sets and reps).

Specificity

The principle of specificity is the most important of the training principles. It deals with the proper application of volume, intensity, and variation. High intensity performance should be trained using primarily high intensity training. Unless variation in intensity is used within a relatively narrow range, inappropriate or unwanted adaptations may occur (see Chapter 6.) (*Occasionally,* inappropriate intensities may be used to break the monotony and strenuousness of constant high intensity training.)

Mechanical specificity is also exceptionally important (22, 51, 60). Appropriate application of mechanical imitation of performance during training is a necessity (51, 60). However, **constant** adherence to mechanical imitation may be somewhat counterproductive. Thus, appropriate mechanical variation and the introduction of specific exercises following sufficient physiological preparation will lead to an enhancement of the desired training effect (60, 64, 65).

Mechanism of Strength Production and Gain

A second important consideration pertinent to a detailed presentation of machines versus free weights is a brief discussion of the possible mechanisms of underlying force (strength) production and how they can be altered to produce strength and power gains.

Strength is simply the ability to produce force. Strength can be exhibited isometrically, concentrically, or eccentrically. Strength largely depends on the following factors:

The number of motor units involved (6, 16, 36, 53). A motor unit consists of a motor neuron and all the muscle fibers it innervates. The more motor units activated, the greater is the force produced.

The frequency (rate) of motor unit firing (3, 16, 28, 36, 39). The tension output increases as the rate of firing increases. This becomes increasingly important as recruitment approaches the maximum number of available motor units. It is especially important in high intensity, high force work.

Motor unit synchronization (28, 36, 39). Large numbers of motor units can contract simultaneously, briefly producing very forceful muscle contractions. Although controversial, this mechanism may aid some types of movements (such as near maximum deadlifts) that require high force contractions.

The pattern of motor unit and whole muscle contraction (7, 9, 16, 19, 51). The timing of the contraction of specific patterns of motor units (and whole muscles) is critical to performing athletic and training activities. For example, if an antagonistic muscle contracts at an inappropriate moment, performance will be reduced. Strength exhibition is a skill. Greater skill proficiency leads to more efficient and greater maximum force production. Thus, acquiring skill through training is an important aspect of increasing maximum strength.

Many activities require the use of elastic energy (see Chapter 4). Utilizing elastic energy, which is created by stretching the muscle, is an important consideration in producing force in many activities. Using elastic energy efficiently is a skill that can increase force production in plyometric exercise.

Again, the patterning of motor unit and whole muscle contraction (and the use of elastic energy and myototic reflex), which is commonly referred to as skill, is very important in strength display. This is especially important to the specificity of mechanics, which is discussed later in this chapter.

The degree of neuromuscular inhibition (6, 16, 30, 42, 46). Inhibitory influences from Golgi tendon organs, etc., as well as conscious aversion to maximal and near maximal exertion, can limit force output. The degree of inhibition is related to skill acquisition.

The muscle fiber type (4, 5, 13, 14, 15, 30, 48, 54). Fast twitch motor units produce a greater force output and contract with a greater velocity than slow twitch fibers (Table 5–1). The recruitment patterns are consistent with their biomechanical properties (Figure 5–3).

The degree of muscle hypertrophy (1, 45, 52). Strong correlations can be demonstrated between muscle cross sectional area and force output. Given equal training time, the amount of lean body mass (degree of hypertrophy) probably is the most important factor in determining absolute maximum strength (52). Support for this can be found by considering the amount of weight lifted by weightlifters in different weight classes.

Anthropometrics-Biomechanics (17, 33, 60). The point of muscle (tendon) insertion, limb length, and angle of muscle pull all have an influence on force output. The muscle lever system is important in determining maximum strength levels (see Chapter 4). The characteristic force-velocity relationship may also be influenced by different training methods (Figure 4–6).

Strength-Power Gains

Resistive training may cause profound changes in the above mechanisms, excluding such anthropometric variables as limb length and point of muscle insertion. When properly performed, strength training may induce central nervous system changes, causing an enhanced motor unit recruitment; increase firing rate, perhaps at lower force outputs; cause synchronization at lower force outputs; enhance motor unit firing patterns for specific movements; and cause deinhibition (6, 14, 28, 33, 39, 42). Although these five determinants relate to learning and are most obviously changed during the first few weeks of the training of beginners (Figure 5–4), they contribute to strength and power gains during an athlete's entire training career (15, 39, 42). A predominance of fast twitch fibers provides an advantage in gaining strength and power (13, 26). Typically, fast twitch fibers gain hypertrophy at a faster rate than slow twitch fibers during resistive training (39, 51) (see Chapter 1). A pre-existing large muscle mass also potentiates strength gains (1, 64, 65). Strength training also can cause considerable muscle (and connective tissue) hypertrophy and perhaps hyperplasia, thus adding contractile tissue (24, 42).

Volume of Training

Numerous studies have suggested a moderate relationship between total workload of training and changes in performance, and a strong relationship between total workload and measurable physiological variables (3, 40, 65, 71) (see Chapter 3). Typically, athletes increase their volume of training from year to year (3, 71).

Table 5–1. Biomechanical and physiological characteristics of various motor unit types.*

Isometric tension development	IIb > IIc > Ia
Isometric time to peak tension	Ia > IIc > IIb
Power production	IIb > IIc > Ia
Endurance	Ia > IIc > IIb
Glycolytic capacity	IIb > IIc > Ia
Oxidative capacity	Ia > IIc > IIb[†]
Ca^{2+} activated myosin ATPase	IIb > IIc > Ia

*Adapted from 5, 14, 15, 16, 30, 48, 52, 54.
[†]A few studies suggest that with extensive endurance training some type II motor units may have oxidative capacities equal to or higher than some type I motor units.

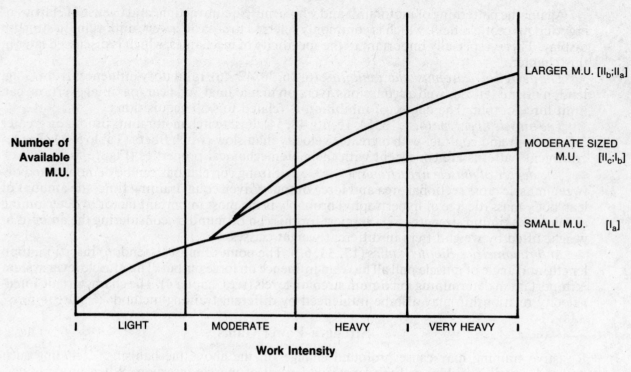

Figure 5–3. Typical motor unit recruitment (the size principle).

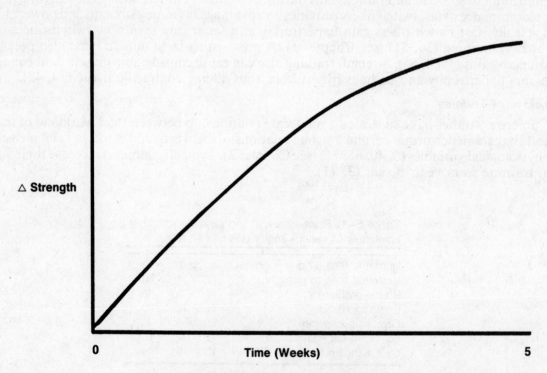

Figure 5–4. Strength gains: novice trainers.

Generally, total workload is strongly related to positive changes in body composition or to its maintenance (1, 64, 65) (see Chapters 3, 6, 7). Because muscle mass is an important factor in developing strength and power, it is reasonable to use training programs that cause muscular hypertrophy and efficiently reduce body fat. Considerable research has been devoted to methods of enhancing muscle hypertrophy. Clearly, multiple sets (5–10) of higher repetitions (7–12) are superior to smaller workloads in producing hypertrophy (1, 64, 65). From a practical standpoint, consider the training of high level bodybuilders, who typically use large volumes of work in their training.

At least one machine manufacturer recommends that only one set of an exercise be performed to exhaustion and that this represents a sufficient workload for gains in hypertrophy and strength (11, 43). This method of training greatly reduces the total workload made possible by multiple sets, which means the activated motor units receive less training. Part of the reasoning behind using sets to exhaustion is that, due to fatigue, the nth repetition would be maximal using an RM repetition scheme. This confuses relative and absolute maximum tensions; fatigue inhibits the use of some fibers, whereas all fibers are active with absolute maximum tension (3). Tension, not fatigue, is the major factor in developing maximum strength (3). One set to exhaustion likely reduces the training effect and produces small gains in lean body mass. Stowers et al. (67) observed inferior performance gains (1 RM squat, VJ and VJ power) from one set to exhaustion compared to multiple exhaustion sets and a training program "periodized" over 7 weeks.

High volume should not be used for too long a period. Multiple sets to exhaustion have been advocated as a superior training method, but this type of training can quickly lead to overtraining (65, 66).

Economy of Training

Another aspect of the principle of volume concerns economy of training. Garhammer (19, 21, 22) has pointed out the superiority of multi-segment free-weight exercises in enhancing power-oriented performance, as discussed later in this chapter. Another factor in favor of multi-segment training concerns economy of exercise, which means the same or a larger muscle mass can be trained with fewer exercises. For example, power snatches greatly stress the trapezius quadriceps, gluteus maximus, hamstrings, and gastrocnemius and apply considerable stress to the erector spinae (static) and to the deltoids and triceps (overhead support), as well as to various muscles that stabilize joints. This one multi-segment exercise can work as much muscle mass as 4 or 5 single or double segment exercises performed with various machines. Economy of training becomes very important when time is a primary consideration. The important point is that multi-segment exercises produce a greater workload per repetition **and** work a larger muscle mass per repetition (56, 60). (see Chapter 3).

Intensity of Training

The primary factor differentiating athletes in most sports is power output (20, 61). High maximum power output is a most desirable outcome of a resistive training program. Power (intensity) is force × velocity or the rate of performing work. High power exercise (or training) may take the form of very high force exercise or high speed exercise or some combination of the two. (20, 62). However, faster movements such as the snatch have created the highest human power outputs (19, 20). Although a few studies have suggested that fast motor units may be recruited first or solely during fast movements (33, 41), the majority of studies strongly suggest that motor units are recruited in order of size (smallest to largest), and that this recruitment is largely a function of the force of muscle contraction (14, 15, 16, 33, 39). Fast motor units generally are the larger motor units (33, 36, 39). As greater forces are needed, more fast motor units may be recruited (30, 39). Thus, the functional characteristics of the neuromuscular system are consistent with the biochemical and biomechanical properties of the various motor units (see Chapter 1).

Both high force and high speed exercise recruit fast twitch fibers (5, 14, 15, 33, 36, 48, 51, 59). Some authors (2, 11, 31, 43) have recommended purposefully slow movements. This type of training moves away from the force-velocity capacity curve, reduces the power output, and decreases the training effect (3, 16, 62). The reasons for the smaller training effect **could** include (1) reduced motor unit recruitment due to a lower muscle force, which means fewer fast motor units would be recruited and, therefore, fast motor units that are used during high level strength-power performance would not be trained effectively; (2) the lower force output reduces the need to increase the rate of motor unit firing; (3) the lower force output may reduce the possibility of synchronization; (4) Perrine and Edgerton (46) have shown that voluntary attempts at maximum concentric force production result in inhibitory responses. High force training can reduce this inhibition (6), likely better than purposeful, slow lower force movements (62).

Variation of Training

Variation of volume and intensity is an essential element in successful training programs. The importance of this type of variation is addressed in Chapter 6. Many machine companies recommend monotonous, unchanging training programs, but this type of training does not produce the most effective training programs. In fact, the usefulness of many machines may be enhanced by not following the recommended training programs.

Mechanical variation is also important. Constant use of a single type of contraction is not as effective as a mixture. For example, using only concentric contractions as opposed to a combination of concentric and eccentric contractions leads to inferior gains in strength (25, 26). Some machines, primarily isokinetic devices, do not provide eccentric loading.

Subtle differences such as changes in hand or foot placement or body position are also valuable in producing continued strength and power gains (21). A cursory inspection of most machines reveals limited room for this type of variation. Typically, most machines allow for only a single exercise with little room for any variation in body position, etc. In general, typical machine training provides monotonously few exercises (even with a company's entire line), limits mechanical variation, and increases the possibility of overtraining. On the other hand, the variety of exercises possible and the possible exercise variations are limitless using free weights (21). A word of caution: Too much variation (such as changing exercises every week) is also somewhat counterproductive. Sufficient adaptation time (4–8 weeks) must be allowed before making major variations in exercises.

Specificity of Training

Metabolic specificity is an important consideration for training. Changes in physiology, which are responsible for observed changes in performance, are covered in Chapters 1, 2, 3, and 6. This section deals with mechanical specificity and its relationship to the use of machines as compared to free weights. To understand mechanical specificity, a discussion of strength and related parameters is necessary.

It is becoming increasingly clear that strength is the **ability** to produce force (3). The known underlying physiological determinants of this ability or skill have been previously described in this chapter. It is important to understand that strength, using this definition, is not simple muscle tension but rather the resulting measureable force, which can range from 0–100% (maximum). Thus, maximum strength is the maximum ability to produce force (power is force × velocity; strength and power are not the same thing).

Strength can be displayed isometrically, by an increase in force with no change in muscle length, or dynamically, by an increase in force with a change in muscle length. The relationship of maximum force production to velocity of contraction is shown in Figure 4–6.

Isometric Strength

Isometrics are discussed in detail in Chapter 7. A short summary is given here. Isometric maximum strength is not necessarily strongly related to dynamic maximum strength. The relationship depends on body and limb positioning (3), the speed of dynamic contraction, and the degree of inhibition (17). In fact, due to inhibition, untrained humans display marked plateauing and even reductions in maximum strength as the isometric condition is approached (46). Isometric training generally produces gains in maximum strength that are joint-angle-specific (3, 17) and that may even produce decreases in speed of movement and power (17). Motivation is a problem with isometrics because there is no visual feedback; lack of visual feedback also makes it difficult to determine the intensity of contraction (17).

In general, the results of isometric research strongly support the specificity concept (17, 51). Dynamic performance is best improved by dynamic training and isometric performance is best improved by isometric training (17). Although isometrics may be useful in some rehabilitation programs, they are **generally** not useful in enhancing typical athletic types of performance (17) (see Chapter 7).

Dynamic Strength

Dynamic strength can be displayed isotonically or isokinetically, both of which can be performed concentrically, eccentrically, or with a combination of concentric and eccentric contractions. It must be emphasized, however, that concentric or eccentric muscle loading can occur with an infinite variety of speeds and that various speeds are the result of different applied forces (3). Furthermore, different training speeds produce different results in strength and power, and these results can affect other athletic performances such as jumping and throwing (3, 16).

Isotonic means "same tone or force." Isotonic contractions are possible only in isolated muscle. Isotonic contractions occur with a constant tension (3, 16). Because a human being has a muscle-level system, different muscle tensions and measurable forces are produced through a range of motion about a joint (see Chapter 4). Although the term isotonic is commonly used, it is a misnomer.

During most movements using free weights the majority of the forces exerted are verticle (17). Thus Newton's second law can be applied to human movement using free weights (17, 19, 21) (see Chapter 4):

$$F = W + MA$$

F = upward vertical force

W = weight lifted (effect of gravity)

M = mass lifted

A = resulting vertical acceleration

This equation allows a description of several important aspects of human movement. First of all, it describes (simplistically) the relationship between force and speed of movement for a given resistance. As the force of movement increases, the acceleration, and thus velocity, increases. Secondly, as apparent in Figures 4–8 through 4–10, there are weak and strong points in the range of motion about a joint. Because of this, as a joint or a series of joints moves into strong angles, a free weight will accomodate by accelerating. *This description typifies most athletic movements.* Small muscle mass exercises that close in on themselves (curls or flys, for example) may deviate from this pattern somewhat, as discussed later.

Variable resistance exercise represents a special case of dynamic exercise. Variable resistance is an attempt to match resistance to the joint angle-force curve. Theoretically, such a match would allow a maximum contraction throughout a range of motion, provided maximum force is used (Chapter 4). Several manufacturers have developed variable resistance machines (e.g., Nautilus and Universal). Figures 4–8 through 4–10 represent the force outputs of various limb extension and flexions. These figures represent the **average** of several hundred subjects; individuals may vary markedly from the mean. Individual variation could be caused by physical differences, such as the point of muscle attachment, muscle architecture, limb length, limb mass, or velocity of movement. By attempting to apply varying resistance as the force changes through various angles, only an average or some arbitrary force angle curve can be considered. Individuals may be restricted in the usable workload because increasing resistance would be applied at inappropriate angles. An important factor is that this will not occur using free weights because the athlete can easily move into a leverage position in which he can exert greater force, causing the free bar to accomodate by accelerating.

Another factor of interest is whether attempts at variable resistance are in fact accurate. One biomechanical analysis showed that for 5 Nautilus machines investigated, none of the resistance curves matched the **average** joint angle-force curves (27). This problem may further reduce the usefulness of the machine by again inappropriately applying resistances (i.e., high resistance-low muscle output).

Isokinetic literally means equal movement. Theoretically, isokinetic exercise permits continuous (through a range of motion) force against a resisting surface that recedes at a constant velocity (3). By constraining the motion of the structure providing the resistance so that it follows a path with an instant center coincident with a joint center of rotation, the muscles, again theoretically, can be caused to contract at a constant velocity (3). Because the resistance cannot be accelerated, any unbalanced force exerted against it is resisted by an equal and opposite reaction force (3). This force can be measured, and other variables like power and work can be derived (3, 29). Therefore, provided the subject actually performs maximally, a maximum force is possible throughout a range of motion.

However, current technology may not provide true isokinetic exercise (i.e., constant muscle shortening). It is very unlikely that the centers of rotation of a joint and machine can be held coincident; many muscles cross two joints, and many muscles follow twisted and curving paths during contraction (3, 29). Thus, isokinetic can only be considered exercise in which the movement occurs at a constant velocity (3, 29).

Another factor concerns whether constant velocity of movement can actually be realized using most current instrumentation. First of all, there is a time lag between initiation of movement and when the limb "catches up" with the speed of the machine and actually produces meaningful force (21, 34, 55). At the point of catching up, there will be a brief momentary collision force, with a second peaking force occurring as the most efficient joint angle is reached (35). Investigations of a cybex leg extension/flexion device and bench press machines revealed that the device was not totally isokenetic at any speed and that the percentage of the isokenetic range of motion decreased drastically as the velocity of movement was increased (35, 55). (35, 55). These factors create vastly different proprioceptive feedback when compared to freely moving exercises and may limit progress. Furthermore, no eccentric contraction is provided with most currently available commercial devices, nor do they provide speeds of movement that are in the range of fast athletic movements (34).

Mechanical Specificity

A major concern of the coach-athlete is the transfer of training to performance. There is little doubt from motor learning and other studies that similar training activities result in increased performance (10, 47, 51, 57, 58, 74).

Many so-called nonspecific exercises can in fact be quite specific. For example, the incline press (with bar or dumbells) is similar to a shotputter's arm movement. Using cinematographical and force plate techniques, Garhammer (18, 22) has shown great similarity between the double knee bend pull (see Chapter 10) and the vertical jump. Because of the respective mechanical similarities, these movements should be used in the enhancement of activities like shotputting and jumping.

The reasons for the carryover of many mechanically similar strength-power training exercises to other athletic activities are not well understood. Possibly the pattern of motor unit firing is stabilized or enhanced, perhaps additional or previously inactive motor units are activated (39, 53), or perhaps an increased firing rate occurs (39). In some movements the early appearance or enhancement of synchronization may aid performance (28). Proprioceptive feedback and kinesthetic awareness may be enhanced. An important point here is that with free weights an individual's own pattern of motor unit and whole muscle contraction, which is similar to that used in non-weight-training free moving performance, can be simulated rather closely, including balance and stabilizing factors. This is possible because the freely moving bar is not being guided or otherwise restrained as is the case with machines (21, 35, 60).

Another aspect of specificity concerns the appropriate time to use mechanically similar exercises. Accumulating evidence indicates that year-round emphasis on technique work, including strength-power exercise, may lead to stagnation and overtraining, especially during high volume training (9, 32, 49, 57, 58, 67, 69, 75). Matveyev (37) and others (12, 64, 65, 66, 70) suggest that a superior method of training includes an increasing emphasis on technique as the competition approaches, "instep" with increasing strength and power. Thus, technique can be stabilized or improved after an appropriate preparation. This does not mean that some mechanical specificity should not be used throughout the program, nor does it mean that sloppy techniques should be tolerated at any time. Instead, it suggests that training should move from a period with a low percentage of mechanically specific exercises to a period with a large percentage of mechanically specific exercises. This type of progression is exceptionally—and perhaps impossibly—difficult to produce using machines alone(21).

Elastic Energy and Myototic Reflex

With few exceptions, athletic movements and other work tasks require both eccentric and concentric movements. Typically the movement is begun by an eccentric contraction and quickly followed by a concentric movement. Plyometrics is a term used to describe this type of eccentric to concentric movement and contraction (7). Plyometrics represent the most common type of movement.

Elastic energy can be described simplistically as a pulling back of muscle and connective tissue (series elastic elements) against a stretch (3, 7, 19) (see Figures 4–5 and 4–6). A myototic reflex involves the muscle spindle and its ability to recruit additional motor units when forcefully stretched (16, 21). These two properties of the neuromuscular system are referred to collectively as elastic energy in this chapter.

The enhancement of elastic energy may be most appropriately accomplished by eccentric work. As can be seen from Figure 4–6, faster lengthening rates produce higher force outputs **to a point.** To produce superior elastic energy utilization and enhanced concentric contraction, the eccentric phase apparently should occur at relatively fast rates and the amortization phase must occur at rapid rates (7, 33). The amortization phase refers to the transition between the eccentric and concentric contractions (7). Factors that effect elastic energy and its utilization include fiber type (33), limb length and relative body segment lengths (33), and initial strength levels (33). Using depth jumping as an example, the optimum box drop height that produces the best vertical jump varies with the individual (33). This individual variation probably depends on the same factors that effect elastic energy utilization.

The basic premise of plyometric exercise is to make adaptations that shorten the amortization phase of plyometric work and increase elastic energy utilization and the force of concentric contraction. The longer the amortization phase, the greater the dissipation of elastic energy. This relationship can be easily seen by comparing the jumping height of a statically held jump (bottom position 2–3 seconds) to a typical countermovement vertical jump (33).

Typical plymoteric exercises include various jumping and bounding exercises, squatting movements, push presses, push jerks, split jerks, and the double knee bend pull (lower body); various types of full and partial presses; and the medicine ball catch and throw (upper body) (see Chapter 4). Although many machines offer eccentric resistance, Garhammer (21) points out that the requirements for the loading of eccentric, or countermovement, contractions that produce efficient and productive elastic energy utilization are not impossible with many machines because of the absence of a loaded countermovement (e.g., weight stack support upon impact or perceived impact). Because the majority of athletic and other movements are plyometric in nature, machines may not offer the best training mode for increasing elastic energy utilization and therefore plyometric performance (see also Chapter 4).

Metabolic Turnover and Energy Cost

Large muscle mass exercises like squats, pulls, and jumps require more energy than small muscle mass exercises because the loading is greater and the weight is moved a greater distance, thus producing more work (W = f × d). Therefore, per repetition, a greater energy cost occurs (56). This result is most important in changing physiology (see the section on volume of training and Chapter 3). Although some machines work relatively large muscle masses (e.g., leg press, hip extensions), most machines are geared toward smaller muscle mass exercises (e.g., leg extension, curls, etc.). Because of the ease with which large muscle mass exercises can be performed using free weights (see Chapter 7), raising the metabolic turnover rate and total energy cost are superior using free weights.

Exercise Choice and Importance

In general, large muscle mass exercises such as squats, pulling movements, weighted jumping, push presses, and jerks must be considered superior in terms of carryover for several reasons (18, 19, 20, 21, 22, 45, 56). These core exercises should in general be used both for athletic and daily performance movements because: (1) They use the same muscles that are used in throwing, pushing, lifting, carrying, and stabilizing. (2) They can produce proprioceptive-kinesthetic feedback similar to many performance activities; that is, they provide greater mechanical specificity. For example, both variable resistance and isokinetic devices can retard normal acceleration. (3) From an energy cost standpoint, large muscle mass exercises produce a higher rate of caloric cost as well as a higher total energy cost (at equal total repetitions) compared to small muscle mass exercise.

Because of the above considerations, the majority of exercises in a resistive training program should be made up of large muscle mass exercises. These large muscle mass, multi-segment exercises are more easily accomplished using free weights.

Small muscle mass exercises, which close in on themselves and are important for isolating specific muscles, can be performed beneficially through specific machine exercise. When typically performed, small muscle mass exercises using free weights (curls, flys, etc.) may have the imposed resistance (effect of gravity) diminished toward the ends of the range of motion. Some machines, especially pullies, avoid this difficulty and keep the resistance high through a greater range of motion. This may be important in hypertrophy production. Appropriate variation of free weights can overcome this problem, but more exercises may be required.

Research: Comparisons of Modes and Methods

The theoretical data and arguments presented, so far suggest that free weights produce superior results compared to machines, especially in terms of strength and power gains and carryover to other activities. This is largely due to the great versatility, mechanical specificity, and ease of performing large muscle mass, multi-segment exercises.

In comparing the training adaptations afforded by various modes of exercise, it becomes quickly apparent that equalizing workloads is exceptionally difficult if not impossible to achieve, even when set and repetition combinations are the same. This is because the machines use a variety of ways to produce resistance, including combinations of springs, weights, levers, and pullies of various shapes. In practice, it is doubtful that training protocols with equal workloads are ever chosen. Indeed, training protocols are chosen because they are believed to produce desired results.

Short-term studies comparing modes of training support the theoretical and empirical data concerning strength and power that have been presented. These studies include both those in which exercise selection or repetition schemes were made as similar as possible in comparing modes and those more important practical studies in which the modes were compared using commonly used methods (set and repetition schemes). The studies considered below were divided into those that considered overall training programs and those that considered small muscle mass or isolated muscle groups.

Machines Versus Machines (Overall Training Programs)

The literature generally suggests that various machines produce essentially equal gains in muscular strength and power (8, 23, 47, and Reference Note 1). Differences in training adaptations with machines may be limited due to the large number of small muscle mass exercises used or to poorly planned training protocols (Reference Note 1).

Machines Versus Machines (Small Muscle Mass—Isolated Groups)

These studies have made short-term comparisons, primarily using isokinetic devices and comparing them to some other dynamic or isometric form of training.

In his review, "Strengthening Muscle," Atha (3) points out that isokinetics were quickly adapted worldwide and were thought to be "the superior method of strength training." This enthusiasm was reminiscent of that accompanying isometrics 25 years ago.

Most of this enthusiasm was based on being able to adjust speed (approximately 0–300°/sec) and to the ability of isokinetics to recruit more motor units. The ability to recruit more motor units is based on studies comparing the integrated electrical activity of the active muscle (IEMG). Using the leg extensors, Thistle et al. (69) found the IEMG values to be 3.17 mv/sec for isokinetics, 3.09 mv/sec for isotonics, and 2.98 mv/sec for isometrics, the isometric value being significantly different from the isokinetic value. These results agree with later studies (3). What this result suggests is that in **isolated, confined movements** isokinetics may result in higher forces—at least peak forces—being produced. The ability of isokinetic devices to produce force was investigated by Lander et al. (35). In that study, isokinetic bench pressing (cybex) compared to free weights did produce higher but nonsignificant forces in the middle of the range of motion, whereas the free weights produced higher forces at the beginning and end of the range of motion. The authors (35) speculated that the difference in the middle range of motion occurred because energy must be used to balance the free weight, a situation that is close to what is encountered in typical daily and athletic movements. Interestingly, Meadors et al. (38), in comparing cybex isokinetic equipment to universal plus free weight training, found that the isokinetic devices produced inferior results in young women after 8 weeks.

Machines Versus Free Weights

The studies and observations presented in this section are of a practical nature. They compare free-weight training programs to machines using recommended training programs.

Free weights generally produce superior results in strength compared to machines (63, 72, 73, Reference Note 2) as well as superior results in a power movement (e.g., vertical jump) (63, 68, 72).

Empirical Data

One must consider the training and opinions of athletes, teachers, coaches, trainers, and researchers who have spent major portions of their lives searching for superior methods of improving strength, power, and underlying physiology. Experienced bodybuilders and gym owners (21); strength-power athletes including throwers, powerlifters, and weightlifters (21, 60); strength coaches; rehabilitation specialists (44); and researchers (21, 60) consistently advocate the primary use of free weights in training programs. As Garhammer (21) points out, competitive weightlifters as a group are the strongest and most powerful athletes. If machines produced superior gains in maximum strength and power compared to free weights, then weightlifters would be using them as a major portion of their training. This is clearly not the case.

Practical Considerations

Although theoretical (21, 27, 44, 60), empirical (21, 44, 60), and research (8, 68, 72, 73) evidence strongly indicates that free weights can produce superior results, especially in terms of strength and power, practicalities must be considered. To a large extent, these factors can be considered matters of cost/benefit and personal choice.

1. The use of spotters is necessary in a few free-weight and machine exercises (i.e., for some squatting and pressing movements and negative work). In the opinion of the authors, spotters are necessary for, in order of importance: insuring proper technique, helping to provide motivation, catching the weight if a repetition is missed, and providing socialization, which may not be as important in the athletic as in the nonathletic situation and could possibly be associated with stress reduction. From this standpoint, spotters may be useful regardless of training mode.

2. Although the technique required for some free-weight exercises (especially large muscle mass, multi-segment exercises) may require more time to learn, the benefits (mechanical specificity, energy requirements, etc.) may outweigh any time spent learning a new skill.

3. Time may be a factor in some training situations, but it is a common misconception that machines always save time in training. If during circuit weight training, the rest pe-

riods between sets are extremely short (< 30 sec), the ease of moving a pin (weight stack) may be an advantage. However, in more typical situations, and especially in priority training, rest periods are more a function of loading (repetitions × weight). Thus changing weights is not a problem.

4. Although moving a pin is easier than changing weights on a bar, typical machines offer incremental jumps on the order of 7.5–12.5 kg. With free weights incremental jumps typically can be made from approximately 0.5 kg to 45 kg. Thus free weights may allow easier progression and will allow more accurate loading, especially if percentages of maximum are employed in training.

5. Depending on conditions such as pain threshold and extent of damage, machines may be more useful in certain rehabilitation situations.

6. Isolating specific small muscle groups can be more easily accomplished using some machines, especially pullies. Being able to do so may be important in some bodybuilding and athletic training procedures, or in injury prevention programs. These procedures may include exercises such as lat work and leg curls. Appropriate, although at times extensive, free-weight exercise variation can, however, produce equal or superior results.

7. Injury potential is commonly believed to be greater using free weights. But there have as yet been no studies that compare the injury rates of various modes of resistive training. Injuries occur using both free weights and machines. The injury potential of resistive training is small compared to most other athletic endeavors, and even rehabilitation situations, including cardiac rehabilitation (50).

8. Storage can be an important consideration. Space is not usually a problem in YMCAs, health clubs, and typical gymnasiums, but it can be in some situations. Storage space in homes is often limited, and providing adequate storage space aboard ships or submarines (for military use) is no doubt difficult. Barbells are not easy to store or transport compared to some machines, including springs and elastic band devices.

9. **Generally,** machines are expensive compared to free weights. Considering the cost of many multi-station devices or buying several single exercise machines, more free-weight equipment can be purchased for the same price. Free-weight equipment also allows several people to be trained simultaneously for the same cost.

Factors concerning the use of various modes are summarized in Table 5–2.

Table 5–2. Factors relating to choice of training mode

Factor*	Free weights (FW)	Nonvariable resistance machines (NVRM)	Variable resistance machines (VRM)	Elastic bands (spring) (EB)	Isokinectic devices (IK)	Isometric devices (IM)
Potential for strength gain	1	3	3	3–4	2–3	2–3
Potential for power gain	1	3	3	3	2–3	5
Ease of performance	2	1–2†	1–2†	1–2†	1–2†	1
Progress assessment	1	3–4	3–4	5	4	5
Mechanical specificity	1	3	3	2–3	2–3	5
Ease of producing high metabolic rate	1	3	3	2–3	2–3	5
Injury potential	2–3	2–3	2–3	3	3	2–4
Muscle soreness	2–4	2–3	2–3	2–3	2–3	1
Isolating small muscle masses	3–4	1–3	1–3	3–5	1–4	1–3
Training tendons and ligaments	1	3	3	3–4	3	4

*These factors, to an extent, depend on the training method (sets and reps.)
†May be difficult for children attempting to use adult size machines.
1 = Superior   4 = I
2 = I   5 = Poor
3 = Fair

Summary

Adhering to the basic principles of training produces enhanced results regardless of training mode. In terms of many typical athletic movements, small muscle mass, isolated movements do not transfer as well as large muscle mass, multi-segment exercises.

Free weights produce superior results compared to machines because of mechanical specificity, greater versatility (exercise variation), and the ease of performing multi-segment exercises, which is important for mechanical specificity and energy cost considerations. Although free weights produce superior results, secondary factors associated with personal choice and cost/benefit must be considered in choosing a training mode.

In situations in which special requirements such as injury prevention are important, machines—because of their ability to isolate small muscle masses— should be integrated into training programs. An ideal program would use primarily free weights, with multi-segment exercises predominating, and machines for special purposes.

References

1. Alexeev, V., and R. A. Roman. 1976. Theory and practice of physical culture. *Yessis Reviews* 13, 14–17.

2. Allman, F. L. 1976. Prevention of sports injuries. *Athletic Journal* 56:74.

3. Atha, J. 1981. Strengthening muscle. *Exercise and Sports Sciences Reviews* (A. I. Miller, Ed.) Franklin Institute Press 9:1–73.

4. Bosco, C., P. V. Komi, J. Tihanyi, et al. 1983. Mechanical power test and fiber composition of human leg extensor muscles. *European Journal of Applied Physiology* 51:129–135.

5. Burke, R. E., and V. R. Edgerton. 1975. Motor unit properties and selective involvement in movement. In *Exercise and Sport Sciences Reviews* (J. Wilmore and J. Keough, Eds.). New York: Academic Press.

6. Caiozzo, V. J., J. J. Perrine, and V. R. Edgerton. 1981. Training-induced alterations of the in vivo force velocity relationships of human muscle. *Journal of Applied Physiology* 51(3):750–754.

7. Chu, D. 1983. Plyometrics: The link between strength and speed. *National Strength and Conditioning Association Journal* 5(2):20–21.

8. Coleman, A. E. 1977. Nautilus vs. Universal gym strength training in adult males. *American Corrective Therapy Journal* 31:103–107.

9. Cotten, D. J., J. R. Thomas, W. R. Spieth, and J. Biasotto. 1972. Temporary fatigue effects in a gross motor skill. *Journal of Motor Behavior* 4:217–222.

10. Cratty, B. J. 1979. *Teaching Motor Skills.* Englewood Cliffs, Ca.: Prentice-Hall, Inc.

11. Darden, E. 1975. Frequently asked questions about muscle, fat and exercise. *Athletic Journal* 56:85–89.

12. Dick, F. 1975. Periodization: An approach to the training year. *Track Technique* 62:1968–1969.

13. Dons, B., K. Bollerup, F. Bonde-Peterson, and S. Hancke. 1979. The effect of weightlifting exercise related to muscle fiber composition and muscle cross-sectional area in humans. *European Journal of Applied Physiology* 40:95–106.

14. Edgerton, V. R. 1976. Neuromuscular adaptation to power and endurance work. *Canadian Journal of Applied Sports Sciences* 1:49–58.

15. Edgerton, V. R. 1978. Mammalian muscle fiber types and their adaptability. *American Zoology* 18:113–125.

16. Edington, N., and V. R. Edgerton. 1976. *The Biology of Physical Activity.* Boston: Houghton Mifflin Co.

17. Fleck, S. J., and R. C. Schutt. 1983. Types of strength training. ORTHOPEDIC CLINICS 14(2):449–458.

18. Garhammer, J. 1976. Force plate analysis of the snatch lift. *International Olympic Lifter* 3:22–27.

19. Garhammer, J. 1980. Evaluation of human power capacity through Olympic weightlifting analysis. Doctoral dissertation, University of California at Los Angeles.

20. Garhammer, J. 1980. Power production by Olympic weightlighters. *Medicine and Science in Sports* 12:54–60.

21. Garhammer, J. 1981. Equipment for the development of athletic strength and power. *National Strength and Conditioning Association Journal* 3(6):24–26.

22. Garhammer, J., and R. Gregor. 1979. Force plate evaluations of weightlifting and vertical jumping (Abstract). *Medicine and Science in Sports* 11:106.

23. Gettman, L. R., L. Culter, and T. Stratham. 1979. Isotonic vs. isokinetic circuit strength training—physiological changes after 20 weeks (Abstract). *Medicine and Science in Sports* 11(1):81.

24. Gonyea, W., D. Sale, and J. A. Dixon. 1983. Increase in muscle fiber number in response to weight-lifting exercise (Abstract). *Medicine and Science in Sports and Exercise* 15(2):135.

25. Häkkinen, K., P. V. Komi. 1981. Effect of different combined concentric and eccentric muscle work regimens on maximal strength development. *Journal of Human Movement Studies* 7:33–44.

26. Häkkinen, K., and P. V. Komi. 1982. Specificity of training-induced changes in strength performance considering the integrative functions of the neuromuscular system. *World Weightlifting* 3:44–46.

27. Harmen, E. 1983. Resistive torque analysis of 5 Nautilus exercise machines. *Medicine and Science in Sports and Exercise* 15(2):113.

28. Hayes, K. C. 1978. A theory of the mechanism of muscular strength development based upon EMG evidence of motor unit synchronization. In *Biomechanics of Sports and Kinanthropometry* (F. Landry and W. Orban, Eds.). Symposia Specialists, Inc. Miami, Florida, pp. 69–77.

29. Hinson, M. N., W. C. Smith, and S. Funk. 1979. Isokinetics: A clarification. *Research Quarterly* 50:30–35.

30. Hopper, B. 1980. Getting a grip on strength. *Swimming Technique,* pp. 10–12, August.

31. Jesse, J. P. 1977. Olympic lifting movements endanger adolescents. *The Physician and Sports Medicine,* pp. 61–67, September.

32. Komarova, A. 1976. Strength and technique (track and field). *Yessis Reviews* 11:10–13.

33. Komi, P. V. 1979. Neuromuscular performance: Factors influencing force and speed production. *Scandinavian Journal of Sports Sciences* 1:2–15.

34. Lander, J. 1985. Personal communication.

35. Lander, J. E., B. T. Bates, J. A. Sawhill, and J. Hamill. 1985. A comparison between free-weight and isokinetic bench pressing. *Medicine and Science in Sports and Exercise* 17:344–353.

36. Maton, B. 1976. Motor unit differentiation and integrated surface EMG in voluntary isometric contraction. *European Journal of Applied Physiology* 35:149–157.

37. Matveyev, L. P. 1972. Perodisienang das sportlichen training (translated into German by P. Tschiene with a chapter by A. Kruger). Berlin: Beles and Wernitz.

38. Meadors. W. J., T. R. Crews, and K. Adeyonju. 1983. A comparison of three conditioning protocols and muscular strength and endurance of sedentary college women. Athletic training Fall:240–242.

39. McDonach, M. J. N., and C. T. M. Davies. 1984. Adapative response of mammalian skeletal muscle to exercise with high loads. *European Journal of Applied Physiology* 52:139–155.

40. McQueen, I. J. 1954. Recent advances in the technique of progressive resistance exercise. *British Medical Journal* 11:1193–1198.

41. Minagana, T., H. Matoba, S. Morita, et al. 1978. Physiological properties of motor units (E. Asmussen and K. Jorgensen, Eds.). Biomechanics VIA Baltimore: University Park Press, pp. 201–206.

42. Moratoni, T., and H. A. DeVries. 1979. Neural factors versus hypertrophy in the time course of muscle strength gain. *American Journal of Physical Medicine* 58(3):115–130.

43. *Nautilus Instruction Manual.* 1980. Nautilus Sports/Medical Industries, March.

44. O'Donahue, D. H. 1976. *Treatment of Injuries to Athletes* (3rd edition). Philadelphia: W. B. Saunders.

45. O'Shea, J. P. 1976. *Scientific Principles and Methods of Strength Fitness* (2nd edition). Reading, Mass.: Addison-Wesley Publishing Co.

46. Perrine, J. J., and V. R. Edgerton. 1978. Muscle force-velocity and power-velocity relationships under isokinetic loading. *Medicine and Science in Sports* 10:159–166.

47. Pipes, T. V. 1977. The acquisition of muscular strength through constant and variable resistance strength training. *Athletic Training* 12:146–151.

48. Prince, F. P., R. S. Hikida, and F. C. Haggermen. 1976. Human muscle fiber types in powerlifters, distance runners, and untrained subjects. *Pflugers Archives* 363:19–26.

49. Sage, G. H. 1977. *Introduction to Motor Behavior: A Neuropsychological Approach* (2nd edition). Reading, Mass.: Addison-Wesley Publishing Co.

50. Saldiver, M., W. M. Frye, C. M. Pratt, and J. A. Herd. 1983. Safety of a low weight, low repetition strength training program in patients with heart disease (Abstract). *Medicine and Science in Sports and Exercise* 15(2):119.

51. Sale, D., and D. MacDougall. 1981. Specificity in strength training: A review for the coach and athlete. *Sports* (Science periodical on research and technology in sport) March: 1–6.

52. Sale, D. G., J. D. MacDougall, S. E. Alway, and J. R. Sutton. 1983. Muscle cross-sectional area, fibre type distribution and voluntary strength in humans (Abstract). *Canadian Journal of Applied Sport Sciences* 221.

53. Sale, D. G., D. MacDougall, A. R. M. Upton, et al. 1983. Effects of strength training upon motoneuron excitability in man. *Medicine and Science in Sports and Exercise* 15:57–62.

54. Salmons, S., and J. Henriksson. 1981. The adaptive responses of skeletal muscle to increased use. *Muscle and Nerve* 4:94–105.

55. Sawhill, J. A. 1981. Biomechanical characteristics of rotational velocity and movement complexity in isokinetic performance. Doctoral dissertation, University of Oregon.

56. Scala, D. 1984. Oxygen uptake, oxygen debt and energy cost of high volume non-circuit Olympic style weight-training. Master's thesis, Auburn University.

57. Singer, R. 1980. *Motor Learning and Human Performance* (3rd edition). New York: McMillan.

58. Singer, R. 1981. Personal Communication, September 15.

59. Spectar, S. A., P. F. Gardiner, R. F. Zernicke, et al. 1980. Muscle architecture and force-velocity characteristics of cat soleus and medical gastrocnemius: Implications for motor control. *Journal of Neurophysiology* 44:951–960.

60. Stone, M. H. 1982. Considerations in gaining a strength-power training effect. *National Strength and Conditioning Association Journal* 4(1):22–24.

61. Stone, M. H., R. Byrd, J. Tew, and M. Wood. 1980. Relationship between anaerobic power and olympic weightlifting performance. *Journal of Sports Medicine and Physical Fitness* 20:99–102.

62. Stone, M. H., and J. Garhammer. 1981. Some thoughts on strength and power: The Nautilus controversy. *The National Strength Conditioning Association Journal* 3(5):24–40.

63. Stone, M. H., R. L. Johnson, and D. R. Carter. 1979. A short term comparison of two different methods of resistance training on leg strength and power. *Athletic Training* 14:158–160.

64. Stone, M. H., H. O'Bryant, and J. G. Garhammer. 1981. A hypothical model for strength training. *Journal of Sports Medicine and Physical Fitness* 21:342–351.

65. Stone, M. H., H. O'Bryant, J. Garhammer, et al. 1982. A theoretical model of strength training. *National Strength and Conditioning Association Journal* 4(4):36–39.

66. Stowers, T., J. McMillan, D. Scala, et al. 1983. The short-term effects of three different strength-power training methods. *National Strength and Conditioning Association Journal* 5(3):24–27.

67. Strength-specificity and sequence. A summary of studies in the U.S.S.R. *Modern Athlete and Coach* 9:8–11, 1974.

68. Sylvester, L. F., C. Stiggins, C. McGown, and G. R. Bryan. 1981. The effect of variable resistance and free-weight training programs on strength and vertical jump. *National Strength and Conditioning Association Journal* 3(6):30–33.

69. Thistle, H. G., H. J. Hislop, M. Moffroid, and E. W. Lowman. 1967. Isokinetic contractions: A new concept of resistive exercise. *Archives of Physical and Medical Rehabilitation* 48:279–282.

70. Tschiene, P. 1979. The distinction of training structure in different stages of the preparation of athletes. Paper presented at the International Congress of Sports Sciences. Edmonton, Alberta, Canada, July 25–29.

71. Vorobeyev, A. 1978. *Weightlifting.* Budapest: International Weightlifting Federation (Translated from Russian by W. Jeffrey Brice).

72. Wathen, D. 1980. A comparison of the effects of selected isotonic and isokinetic exercises, modalities, and programs on the vertical jump in college football players. *National Strength Coaches Association Journal* 2:47–48.

73. Wathen, D., and M. Shutes. 1982. A comparison of the effects of selected isotonic and isokinetic exercises, modalities and programs on the acquisition of strength and power in collegiate football players. *National Strength and Conditioning Association Journal* 4(1):40–42.

74. Williams, L. R. T., J. G. Daniell-Smith, and L. K. Gunson. 1976. Specificity of training for motor skills under physical fatigue. *Medicine and Science in Sports* 8:162–167.

75. Yessis, M. 1981. Variety: The key to strength development. *National Strength and Conditioning Association Journal* 3(3):32–34.

Reference Notes

1. Garfield, D. S., R. Cobb, R. Coulson, and P. Ward. Comparative strength research, Syracuse University, 1978.

2. Everson, J. M. Variable resistance vs. isotonic weight trainii in monozygotic male twins. Case study compiled for Dr. F. Nagle, Independent Study.

Training Theory and Its Adaptation to Resistance Training

Overtraining is an unusually common phenomenon among weight trainers (15, 45). Its causes may be physiological, from simple overwork (13, 24, 41, 45), or an adaptation of the central nervous system to monotonous unvarying training routines (15, 41). The symptoms of overtraining are not always the same but can include loss or plateauing of performance, chronic fatigue, loss of appetite, loss of bodyweight and lean body mass (LBM), increased injury potential, and increased illness potential (24, 42, 45). This chapter describes a method of resistance training that reduces the possibility of overtraining and that brings strength and power to peak levels.

Basic Principles and Concepts

In the early 1930s, Selye developed the general adaptation syndrome (GAS), which describes a person's changing ability to adapt to stress through his lifetime. Garhammer (14) has presented basic concepts of GAS as they relate to exercise and training. Briefly, the GAS theory suggests that an athlete or noncompetitive trainee is subject to 3 distinct phases of adaptation during a training period (Figure 6–1). The first phase, the *alarm stage,* deals with the initial response to a stimulus. This could represent a temporary drop in performance due to stiffness or soreness during the first few days of a new training program or cycle. The second stage, *resistance,* relates to the period of training during which the athlete adapts by making various biochemical, structural, mechanical, and likely psychological adjustments that lead to increased performance. If the total stress imposed by training (or other areas of the athlete's life) is too great, the third stage of GAS, *exhaustion or overwork,* is reached. During this third stage, desired adaptations are no longer possible. Due to central nervous system overadaptation (15, 45), monotonous routines will limit adaptation and progress, even though overwork may not be the cause. Other stresses besides training can contribute to overtraining; the coach-athlete must be aware of these factors in planning training regimens (Figure 6–2).

The basic principles of training are frequency, duration, intensity, variation, and, most importantly, specificity (12). These principles must be considered in all training programs; applying them properly reduces the potential for overtraining. The concept of periodization, originally proposed by Matveyev in 1961 (28, 41), embodies and manipulates these basic training principles in a manner that reduces the potential for overtraining and brings performance to optimum or peak levels (28, 41).

Generally, overtraining can be reduced through variation in volume (frequency and duration) and intensity, and through variation in the amount of technique and other specialized work performed. Figure 6–3a presents a model of training suitable for novice and beginning

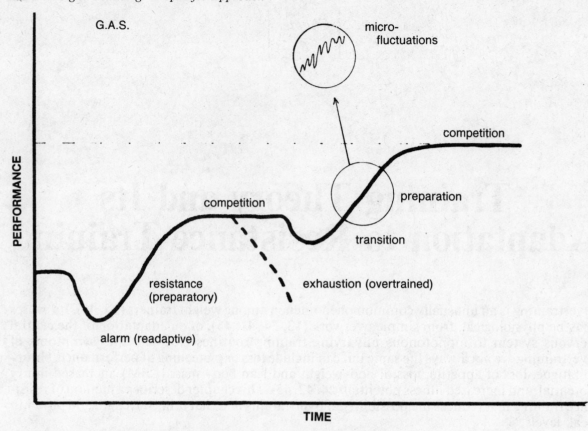

Figure 6-1. The general adaptation syndrome.

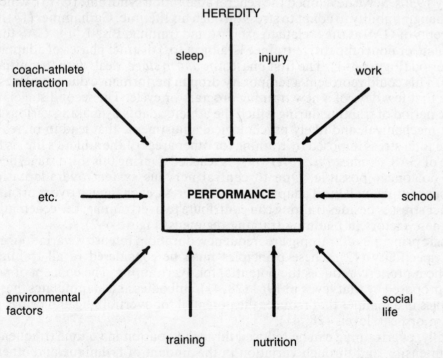

Figure 6-2. Factors (stressors) contributing to the possibility of overtraining or increased performance.

athletes. Volume, which can be estimated by the total repetitions, begins high and decreases through the training year. Intensity, average bar weight, begins low and increases over the training period. With beginners, relatively subtle changes in volume and intensity are appropriate (28, 38, 41).

Because of years of training, advanced athletes have made physiological adaptations that allow them to train at higher initial volumes and intensities (Figure 6–3b). Further studies, primarily by European sport scientists (28, 41), strongly suggest that the establishment of volume and intensity variations on the mesocycle (months) and microcycle (weekly) level further reduce the possibility of overtraining and enhance performance peaks. This entails relatively high loading (volume × intensity) for 2–3 weeks followed by a light week throughout the macrocycle (period) (Figure 6–3b). Matveyev's basic premise is still intact: volume is high at the beginning of the period and decreases toward the climax; intensity begins relatively low and increases.

Table 6–1 presents a model of strength-power training that conforms to the basic tenants of periodization. This model was developed using both empirical observation and objective research. To date, seventeen research projects investigating the effectiveness of this model compared to other training programs have been completed. Most of these studies have been carried out on the mesocycle level and have lasted 6–15 weeks. The subjects have included untrained men and women, a high school football team, a women's softball team, advanced weight trainers, weightlifters, and various other athletes. Empirical data as to the effectiveness of this model have been collected from various professional and collegiate coaches as well as from national and international class athletes. Two papers have been published describing the basic concepts and presenting some of the early data and observations about the superiority of this model of strength-power training over more traditional methods (37, 38).

Table 6–1. Theoretical model of strength training (associated with Matveyev's periodization model).

Phase	Preparation		Transition	Competition	Transition 2
	Hypertrophy	Basic strength	Strength and power	Peaking or maintenance*	Active rest
Sets[†]	3–10	3–5	3–5	1–3	S e e
Repetitions	8–12	4–6	2–3	1–3	e
Days/week	3–4	3–5	3–5	1–5	
Times/day	1–3	1–3	1–2	1	T e x t
Intensity cycle (weeks)[‡]	2–3/1	2–4/1	2–3/1	–	
Intensity	low	high	high	very high to low	
Volume	high	moderate to high	low	very low	

*Peaking for sports with a definite climax or maintenance for sports with a long season such as football.
†Does not include warmup sets.
‡Ratio of number of heavy training weeks to light training weeks.

Matveyev's Model of Periodization

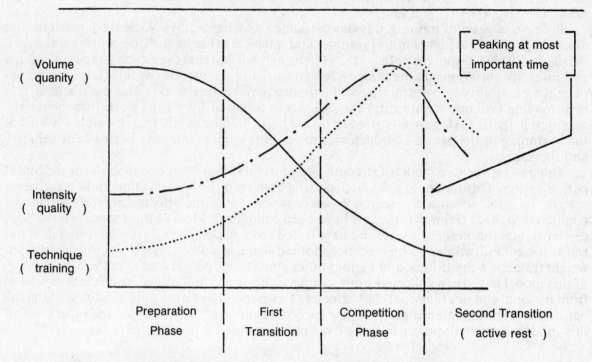

Figure 6–3a. Matveyev's model of periodization (modified).

Modification for Advanced Athletes

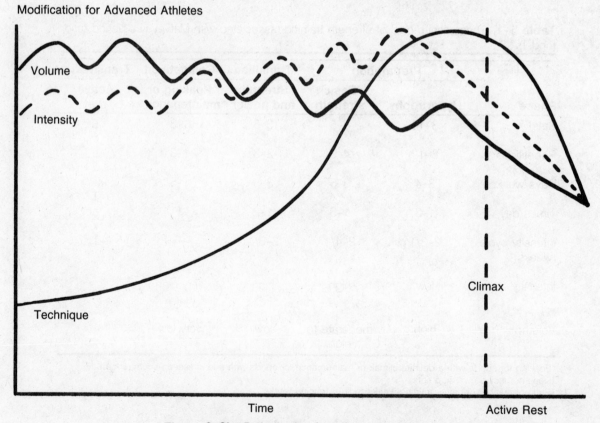

Figure 6–3b. Periodization for advanced athletes.

Results of Research

Various measurements have been used in the seventeen studies. The following major variables were measured in many or all of these studies:

- Leg and hip strength (1RM squat)
- Leg and hip power
- – Vertical jump and Lewis formula ($P = \sqrt{4.9} \times BW_{kg} \times \sqrt{VJ_m}$)
- – Power clean
- Upper body strength (1RM bench press)
- Body weight
- Body composition [percentage of fat and lean body mass (LBM)] measured by hydrostatic or skinfolds methods.

Typically, the following changes would be expected to occur through the various stages. An example of these changes over 15 weeks is shown in Figures 6–5 through 6–9.

Hypertrophy Stage

This stage is an early preparation phase designed to allow the athlete to make certain specific physiological adaptations that prepare him to perform high intensity and high-intensity-technique-oriented training. During this phase, two important adaptations **beyond those of typical programs,** can be expected to occur. The first is a positive change in body composition. High volume training (8–12 reps/set) has been shown to produce greater gains in LBM (hypertrophy) and greater decreases in percentages of fat than low volume training (1, 30, 37, 38) (Figure 6–4). Increases in muscle mass (hypertrophy) increase an athlete's potential to gain strength and power (30, 32, 43).

A second important adaptation occurring with high volume training is an increase in short-term endurance (expansion of anaerobic capacity), especially in terms of performing high intensity work (3, 25, 30, 32, 35, 38). The development of expanded anaerobic capacity is a major factor in reducing fatigue during the later stages of training, when high intensity (high power), technique-oriented work is performed. Therefore, this hypertrophy stage is most important in laying the proper foundation and preparing the athlete for higher intensity work by positively altering body composition and anaerobic capacity (32, 37, 38, 39). These adaptations are best produced by using sets of 10 repetitions (Figure 6–4).

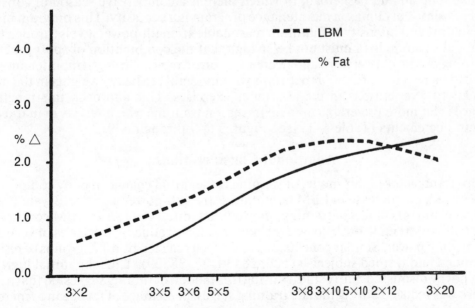

Figure 6–4. Short-term comparison of different combinations of sets and repetitions and their ability to produce muscle hypertrophy. These fourteen studies lasted from 4 to 6 weeks. All studies used male subjects. The results are in general agreement with other researchers and their observations (1, 17).

Leg and hip strength and power will increase during this phase to about the same level as that realized using 3×6 RM during short-term (2–4 weeks) programs with untrained subjects. The bench press may show only slight increases or no change. However, advanced athletes may actually show slight decreases in their 1RM strength (especially lower back, leg, and hip strength) and maximum power output. This may be due in part to fatigue. It must be remembered that this is a preparation primarily designed to increase LBM and anaerobic capacity.

Basic Strength Stage

Basic strength refers to the 1RM strength gain in movements that are basic to the sport in question. In most sports, this refers to squatting, pulling, and pressing movements. After the hypertrophy stage, strength can be trained using 3 sets of 5 repetitions. This represents a **late stage of preparation.** The gain in basic strength provides the appropriate foundation for power specialization and further high intensity work. Strength, especially of the leg and hip, increases sharply during this phase.

Strength-Power Stage

Adhering to the concepts of Matveyev and to the principle of specificity, strength and power can be brought to higher levels using 3–5 sets of 2–3 repetitions. A sharp rise in vertical jump and vertical jump power can be expected during this phase. This rise in power is a result of increased leg and hip strength and a reduction of fatigue in response to decreasing workloads (volume).

Peaking Stage

Again, conforming to specificity of training and to the concept of periodization, power and strength can be brought to a peak by further volume reductions and accompanying increases in intensity. In many sports (e.g., olympic weightlifting) increased emphasis should be placed on speed of movement, increases in elastic energy, and technique work through the final stages, with the greatest emphasis during the peaking phase. Athletes using this method of training typically use 2 or 3 sets of 1–3 repetitions (after warmup) during a peaking phase with excellent results.

Maintenance

In sports like football and basketball, in which there is a competitive season of considerable length with no clear-cut climax, a maintenance program is a necessity. This program must be of sufficient volume and intensity to maintain reasonable strength-power levels through the playing season, but the total load must not be so high that the combination of sport practice plus weight training produces overwork and decreased performance. Strength maintenance may be accomplished using 3 sets of 2 or 3 repetitions with moderate to heavy weights in the major exercises and 3 to 5 repetitions in the assistance exercises. This approach to strength-power maintenance is far more preferable than no in-season training, which results in marked power and strength decrements (Table 6–1) (see Figures 6–5 through 6–9).

Additional Considerations

A most important factor in this model of training is the initial change in body composition. As previously stated, the increase in LBM potentiates strength-power gains. O'Bryant (32), using untrained men and this model of training, showed that initial changes in LBM contributed not only to leg and hip strength, but also was the major factor producing increases in vertical jump and vertical jump power. Similar conclusions have been reached by other groups of researchers using untrained and trained subjects (1, 23, 28, 30, 37, 38, 39). Thus the initial high volume work must not be dismissed. Early studies using this model of training suggested that as the volume of work was reduced during the late training stages, percentage of fat began to increase and LBM had a slight tendency to decrease. Later studies **suggested** that this negative effect on body composition can be reduced by introducing a warmdown set of 1×10 repetitions. Even with warmdown sets included, there is a sharp decrease in volume across the training cycle.

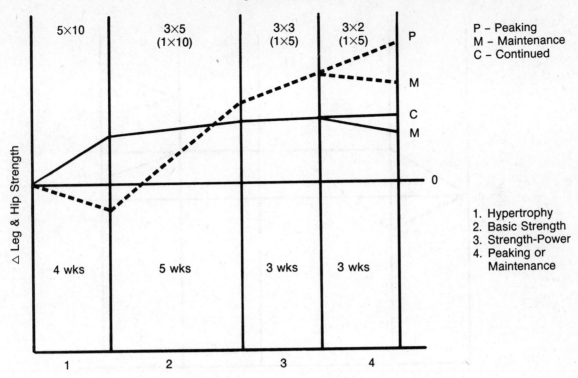

Figure 6–5. Example, changes in leg and hip strength (1RM squat) compared to traditional methods of training.

Model – – – – – –
Traditional _____ (3×6, pyramids, etc.)

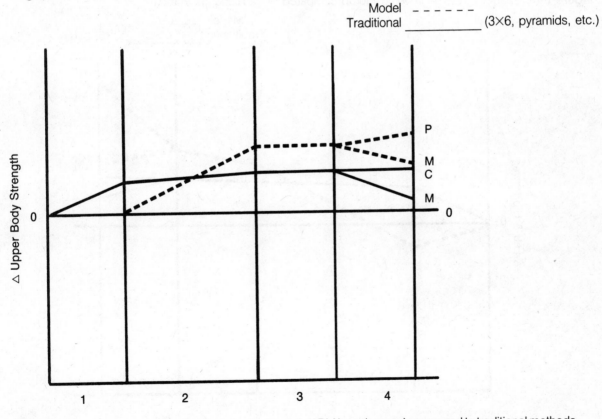

Figure 6–6. Example, changes in upper body strength (1RM bench press) compared to traditional methods.

Model – – – – – –
Traditional _____ (3×6, pyramids, etc.)

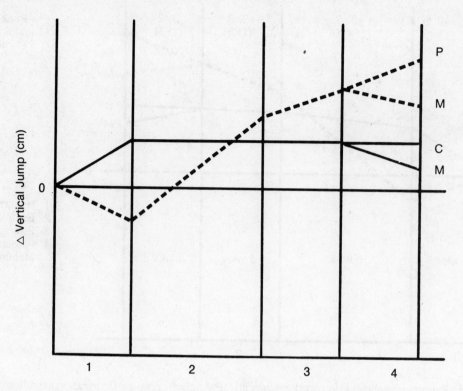

Figure 6–7. Example, change in vertical jump compared to traditional methods.

Model _ _ _ _ _ _
Traditional _____ (3×6, pyramids, etc.)

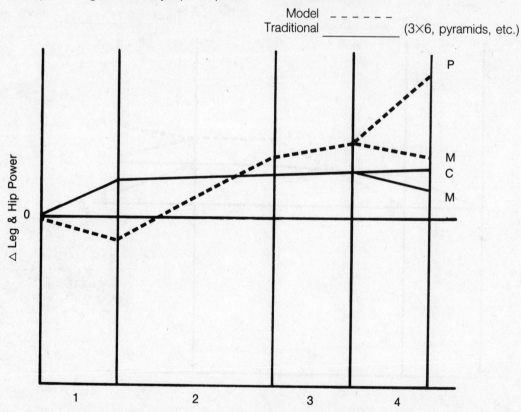

Figure 6–8. Example, change in leg and hip power (Lewis formula) compared to traditional methods.

Model _ _ _ _ _ _
Traditional _____ (3×6, pyramids, etc.)

1. Hypertrophy
2. Basic Strength
3. Strength-Power
4. Peaking or Maintenance

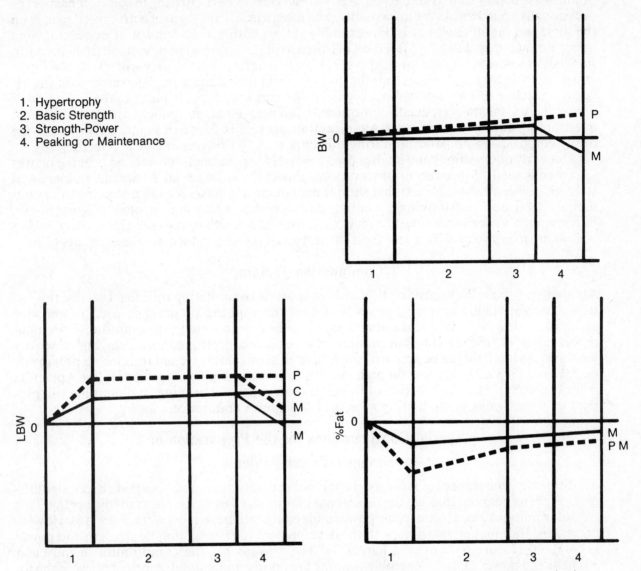

Figure 6–9. Example, changes in body weight and body composition compared to traditional methods.

Model ‒ ‒ ‒ ‒ ‒ ‒
Traditional ‒‒‒‒‒‒ (3×6, pyramids, etc.)

Notice the sharp break in volume and the sharp increase in intensity from phase to phase (Table 6–1 and Figures 6–3a and 6–3b). We have observed that this produces better progress, especially in advanced athletes, an observation with which other researchers (28, 41) agree. This phenomenon may be due to reducing monotony or perhaps to "shocking" the central nervous system.

Advanced athletes may require greater planned variation in volume and intensity in order to continue progressing. Figure 6–3b illustrates a method by which this can be accomplished. Basically, this is concerned with introducing microcycles into the overall cycle (several microcycles could make up a mesocycle) and training 2–3 weeks with increasing loads followed by an unload week. Additional variation, such as changing the type of exercise or speed of training, may also be helpful.

Active rest is another important factor that contributes to long-term progress. If an athlete simply moves right into hard training after peaking or after a season of playing some sport, progress will be diminished. Complete rest, while sometimes necessary, also does not seem to produce as good a result as active rest. Active rest refers to participating in some other sport or occasionally your own at very low volumes and intensities. The length of active rest depends on the sport and the athlete's needs. For example, the weightlifters at Auburn, after peaking for a meet, are encouraged to take a few days off, then to play racketball or basketball for a few additional days before beginning the next cycle. After two or three cycles, they will take 3 or 4 weeks and do nothing, as far as weight training, but very light technique work. The reasons for the necessity of active rest are not completely clear, but certainly it contributes to the reduction of physical and mental (especially emotional) fatigue. Thus, it reduces the possibility of overtraining during the next cycle. A typical training year is shown in Figure 6–10. Notice the heavy emphasis on preparation during the early part of this training year (macrocycle).

Our early observations and studies used relatively long strength-power and peaking phases (3–5 weeks total). More recent observations, especially with advanced weight trainers and strength-power athletes, suggest that shorter high intensity phases lead to decreased injury potential, decreased overtraining potential, and a higher performance peak (Figure 6–10). Furthermore, under some circumstances (i.e., time and holiday considerations) two or more very short mesocycles with a few days off in between can produce excellent results (32).

Combination Training

Another very important consideration in most sports is combination training. Usually, this entails a weight training-running protocol. Often the running program is used to enhance endurance. However, aerobic training (long distance running, etc.) can compromise strength-power gains (11, 17, 33). Gains in endurance, especially concerning short-term, high intensity work such as football, can be accomplished through high volume weight training, as previously pointed out (3, 32, 35, 39), and through interval running and jumping programs (see Appendix A for examples). The combination of weight training, interval running, and jumping will produce excellent gains in strength, power, and short-term endurance.

Special Considerations for the Preparation of
Strength-Power Athletes

Traditionally, endurance for most sports, including highly anaerobic sports such as weightlifting, has been enhanced through the regular use of prolonged exercise, particularly jogging. This type of training can enhance aerobic power and reduce fatigue in most work tasks (16). However, aerobic training can interfere with the development of skeletal muscle strength and power (11, 17, 33) (Figure 6–11) (see Chapter 1). The reasons for the compromise in muscular strength and power caused by aerobic training are poorly understood. A brief review of the literature allows several interesting speculations on how aerobic training may compromise performance among strength-power athletes. Aerobic training may cause a reduction of myosin ATPase in type IIb and other skeletal muscle fibers (i.e., it may cause a change in fiber type) (2, 4, 5, 19, 22, 36) and a reduction in the concentration of anaerobic enzymes (42). Aerobic training may also produce an increase in skeletal muscle catabolism, possibly resulting in a smaller muscle mass (10, 26). Increased catabolism (or reduced anabolism) may be influenced by the way aerobic exercise and training affect various hormones (10, 34) and proteolytic enzymes (7). Empirical support for this catabolic effect may be found in the comparison of the physical characteristics of long distance runners and sprinters or weightlifters (see Chapter 1). Furthermore, it is possible that the mechanics of typical aerobic training such as distance running negatively affect the weightlifting-specific pattern of motor unit recruitment and whole muscle contraction (33, 44). Finally, among serious strength-power athletes, especially weightlifters, already handling near maximum training workloads, the addition of extra work (jogging, swimming, etc.) may lead to overtraining (38). Regardless of the mechanism of compromise, at the top levels of strength-power athletics, mixed training methods produce mixed results.

Considering the evidence that aerobic training can interfere with the development and maintenance of high levels of muscular strength and power, more specific methods of enhanc-

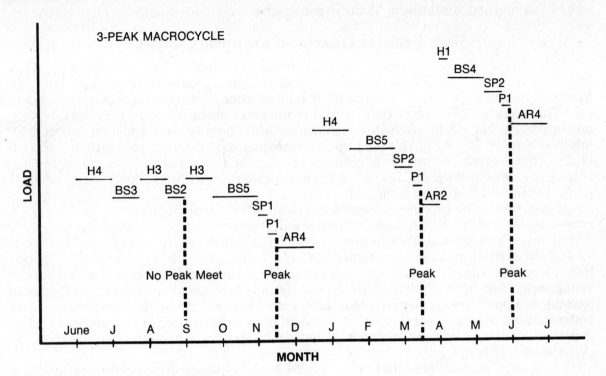

Figure 6-10. Three-peak macrocycle.
H = Hypertrophy   SP = Strength power
BS = Basic strength   P = Peaking
*The number beside the letter indicates the number of weeks spent in that subphase.
†Load = repetitions × weight used.

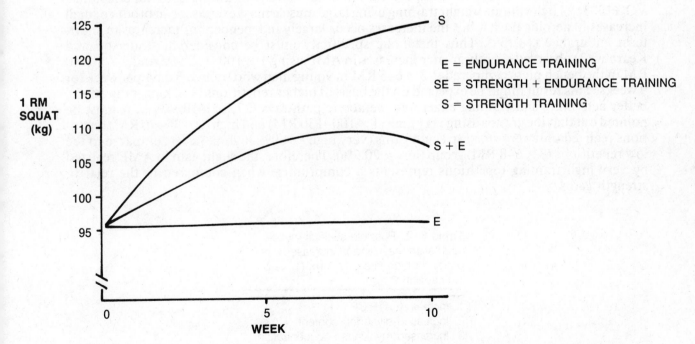

Figure 6-11. Example of a compromise in strength produced by combined strength and endurance training. The effect (compromise) is most apparent at high levels of strength, where actual decreases may occur. Modified from Hickson, R. C., 1980 (17).

ing endurance must be considered. An important consideration in improving endurance for weight training and weightlifting is the expansion of *anaerobic capacity.*

Basic Concepts Concerning Anaerobic Capacity

Absolute muscular endurance (AME) refers to the ability to maintain an absolute submaximal force output during work relying primarily on anaerobic metabolism until exhaustion (9, 25). Muscular endurance largely depends on the maximum strength level of the muscles being used (25). The advantage of higher strength levels becomes more apparent as the required force output increases; that is, the strength advantage in AME tests is most apparent during high intensity work (9, 25). Weight training enhances AME through increases in maximum strength (9, 25). Thus, one possible method of reducing the onset of fatigue associated with high intensity work (e.g., weight-training) is by increasing maximum strength. Strength may be a key factor in the enhancement of short-term endurance.

As each motor unit becomes stronger with training, fewer motor units are needed at a given submaximal workload, leaving a greater motor unit reserve available for continued work (25). The increase in motor unit strength may be associated with an increase in the cross-sectional area of the skeletal muscle being trained (18, 25). Increases in LBM accompanying weight training may be related to increased strength and to enhanced AME. In previously untrained young men, O'Bryant (32) showed strong correlations between gains in LBM and gains in strength and power. Note, however, that the correlation between muscle cross-sectional area and maximum strength is **not** r = 1.0 (23). Strength gains and therefore AME gains may be due, in part, to changes in the central nervous system (such as greater motor unit recruitment or synchronization) (23).

The skeletal muscle concentrations of ATP-CP and glycogen are crucial to maintaining high intensity workloads and workrates (25). Increases in ATP-CP, glycogen, and the myokinase reaction (2 ADP $\rightarrow$ ATP + AMP) have been observed after strength training (27, 40). Therefore, biochemical adaptations within the skeletal muscle that accompany weight training may also contribute to increased endurance during high intensity work (Table 6–2).

Weight-training-induced increases in aerobic power could also contribute to success in short-term endurance (16). However, typical low volume weight training does not effect max $\dot{V}O_2$ (13, 31). High volume weight training using large muscle mass exercises can produce small increases in aerobic power, but the increases occur largely independent of increases in short-term endurance (18, 39). Thus metabolic specificity must be considered. Anderson and Kearney (3) observed slightly greater increases in AME using 1 $\times$ 100–150 RM and 2 $\times$ 30–40 RM in the bench press compared to 3 $\times$ 6–8 RM in young men who trained 3 days per week for 9 weeks. This result might be expected on the basis of higher repetitions (i.e., longer duration), better activating and training anaerobic metabolic pathways (27, 35). However, it must be pointed out that the groups using very high (1 $\times$ 100–150 RM) and high (2 $\times$ 30–40 RM) repetitions realized only very small strength gains (very high = 4.9%, high = 8.2%) compared to the low repetitions (3 $\times$ 6–8 RM) group (low = 20.2%). Therefore, the slight gain in AME realized by very high training repetitions represents a compromise when compared to the relative strength gains.

Table 6–2. Possible skeletal muscle adaptations resulting in increased capacity for high intensity work (anaerobic capacity)

1. Increased ATP-CP
2. Increased glycogen content
3. Increased myokinase concentration
4. Increased strength
5. Increased volitional drive

In light of the considerations discussed previously, the preparation phase of weightlifters and other strength-power athletes must entail the following objectives:

1. Raising endurance capabilities without using extensive aerobic training, which compromises strength and power.

2. Effectively enhancing anaerobic capacity along with reasonable strength-power gains, or reducing the compromise of strength and power associated with typical endurance/high volume training.

3. Realizing positive changes in body composition (LBM and % fat), which potentiates gains in strength, power, and probably short-term endurance (anaerobic capacity).

4. Preparing for additional high intensity, high quality training.

The ability to delay fatigue or continue working during fatigued states is very important in many types of athletic activities, including weight training and weightlifting. Aerobic training has been advocated as a method of increasing short-term endurance, even for highly anaerobic events such as weightlifting (21). However, as previously pointed out, aerobic training is likely to reduce the ability of strength-power athletes to perform (17, 33). Weight training, and perhaps other forms of anaerobic training such as interval sprints, may increase short-term endurance without a simultaneous compromise in performance.

Weight training using high volumes (multiple sets of 8–12 repetitions) and large muscle mass exercises has been shown to meet the above four objectives of the preparation phase for strength-power athletes (1, 29, 32, 37, 38, 39). The principles outlined in this chapter satisfy the preparation criteria and allow development of the characteristics necessary for successful athletic competition (see Appendix A).

Summary

Although no clear-cut distinction can be made between muscle training and nerve training, our approach has been to emphasize the muscle during the early preparation (high volume) and then to emphasize the central nervous system (high intensity and increased technique work and other specialized work) during the later stages of training. Our own research and observations, specific observations of other researchers (1, 29), and the subjective evaluations of athletes and coaches who have tried this method lead us to believe that this approach is a superior method of strength-power training.

This model of training has been compared to various methods of strength-power training, including 3 sets of 6 RM, pyramiding, low repetitions, and various sets to exhaustion (6, 8, 20, 32). Based on these comparisons, the following conclusions were reached:

1. The model produced superior gains in leg and hip strength (1RM squat).

2. The model produced superior gains in leg and hip power (VJ and Lewis formula) and the power clean.

3. The model generally produced superior gains in upper body strength (1RM bench press). (A few studies showed equal gains when compared to 3 × 6 RM and pyramiding over a short term (6–12 weeks).

4. Positive changes in body composition (% fat and LBM) were greater in those subjects using the training model in most of the studies. This was especially evident after high volume training (sets of 10).

5. Based on cycle ergometry of increasing intensity to exhaustion, the model produced greater gains in short-term endurance. This was especially apparent after high volume training (sets of 10).

While this method of training is not the final answer, it is based on sound concepts and principles and will provide the coach-athlete with a superior training program.

References

1. Alexeev, V., and R. A. Roman. 1976. Theory and practice of physical culture *Yessis—Reviews* 13:14–17.

2. Andersen, P., and J. Henriksson. 1981. Training induced changes in subgroups of human type II skeletal muscle fibers *Acta Physiologica Scandinavica* 113:9–16.

3. Andersen, T., and J. T. Kearney. 1982. Effects of three resistance training programs on muscular strength and absolute and relative endurance. *Research Quarterly for Exercise and Sport* 53:1–7.

4. Baldwin, K. M., O. M. Martinex, and W. G. Cheadle. 1976. Enzymatic changes in hypertrophical fast-twitch skeletal muscle. *Pflugers Archiv* 364:229–234.

5. Belcastro, A. N., H. Wenger, T. Nibel, et al. 1980. Functional overload of rat fast-twitch skeletal muscle during development. *Journal of Applied Physiology* 49:583–588.

6. Clarke, D. H. 1973. Adaptations in strength and muscular endurance resulting from exercise. *Exercise and Sport Sciences Reviews* 1: 73–102.

7. Dahlmann, B., A. Widjaja, and H. Reinauer. 1981. Antagonistic effects of endurance training and testosterone on alkaline proteolytic activity in rat skeletal muscles. *European Journal of Applied Physiology* 46:229–235.

8. Darden, E. 1975. Frequently asked questions about muscle, fat and exercise. *Athletic Journal* 56:85–89.

9. deVries, H. A. 1980. *Physiology of Exercise* (3rd edition). Dubuque, Iowa: Wm. C. Brown.

10. Dohm, G. L., and T. M. Louis. 1978. Changes in androstenediome, testosterone, and protein metabolism as a result of exercise. *Proceedings of the Society for Experimental Biology and Medicine* 158:622–625.

11. Dudley, G. A., and R. Djamil. 1985. Incompatibility of endurance and strength training modes of exercise (Abstract). *Medicine and Science in Sport and Exercise* 17:184.

12. Edington, N., and V. R. Edgerton. 1976. *The Biology of Physical Activity.* Boston: Houghton Mifflin Co.

13. Fahey, T. D., and C. H. Brown. 1973. The effects of an anabolic steroid on the strength, body composition, and endurance of college males when accompanied by a weight training program. *Medicine and Science in Sports* 5:272–276.

14. Garhammer, J. 1979. Periodization of strength training for athletes. *Track Technique* 73:2398–2399.

15. Hakkinen, K., and P. V. Komi. 1981. Specificity of training-induced changes in strength performance considering the integrative functions of the neuromuscular system. *World Weightlifting* 3:44–46.

16. Harrison, M. H., G. A. Brown, and L. A. Cochrone. 1980. Maximal oxygen uptake: Its measurement, application, and limitations. *Aviation Space and Environmental Medicine* 5:1123–1127.

17. Hickson, R. C. 1980. Interference of strength development by simultaneously training for strength and endurance. *European Journal of Applied Physiology* 215:255–263.

18. Hickson, R. C., M. A. Rosenkoetter, and M. M. Brown. 1980. Strength training effects on aerobic power and short-term endurance. *Medicine and Science in Sports and Exercise* 12:336–339.

19. Janssan, E., B. Sjudin, and P. Tesch. 1978. Changes in muscle fibre type distribution in man after physical training. *Acta Physiologica Scandinavica* 104:235–237.

20. Jones, A. 1976. Time. . .as a factor in exercise. Deland, Florida. *Nautilus Sports/Medical Industries Publication.*

21. Keul, J. 1975. The relationship between circulation and metabolism during exercise. *Medicine and Science in Sports* 5:209–219.

22. Klausen, K., L. B. Andersen, and I. Pelle. 1981. Adaptive changes in work capacity, skeletal muscle capillarization and enzyme levels during training and detraining. *Acta Physiologica Scandinavica* 113:9–16.

23. Komi, P. V. 1979. Neuromuscular performance: Factors influencing force and speed production. *Scandinavian Journal of Sports Sciences* 1:2–15.

24. Kristensen, J. E. 1977. Overtrained: The problematic effects of overtraining. *International Olympic Lifter* 4:8–26.

25. Lamb, D. R. 1978. *Physiology of Exercise.* New York: MacMillan Co.

26. Lemon, P. W. R., and F. J. Nagle. 1981. Effects of exercise on protein and amino acid metabolism. *Medicine and Science in Sports and Exercise* 13:141–149.

27. MacDougall, J. D., G. R. Ward, D. G. Sale et al. 1977. Biochemical adaptations of human skeletal muscle to heavy resistance training and immobilization. *Journal of Applied Physiology* 43:700–703.

28. Matveyev, L. P. 1972. Periodisienang das sportlichen training (translated into German by P. Tschiene with a chapter by A. Kruger). Berlin: Beles and Wernitz.

29. Medvedev, A. S., V. F. Rodionov, V. N. Rogozykn, and A. E. Gulyants. 1981. Training content of weightlifters in preparation period (translated by Michael Yessis). *Teoriya i Praktika Fizicheskoi Kultury* 12:5–7.

30. Morehouse, L. E., and A. T. Miller. 1976. *Physiology of Exercise* (7th edition). St. Louis: C. V. Mosby Co.

31. Nagle, F., and I. Irwin. 1960. Effects of two systems of weight training and circulorespiratory endurance and related physiological factors. *Research Quarterly* 31:607–615.

32. O'Bryant, H. 1982. Periodization: A hypothetical training model for strength and power. Doctoral dissertation, School of Health, Physical Education, Recreation, and Dance, Louisiana State University.

33. Ono, M., M. Miyashita, and T. Asami. 1976. Inhibitory effect of long distance running training on the vertical jump and other performances among aged males. *Biomechanics V-B.* Baltimore: University Park Press, pp. 94–100.

34. Pesquies, P. C., R. Morville, C. Y. Guezennec, and B. D. Servarier. 1981. Effects of prolonged physical exercise on blood concentrations of adrenal and testicular androgens. In *Biochemistry of Exercise IV-B* (J. Pourtmans and G. Niset, Eds.). Baltimore: University Park Press.

35. Sale, D., and D. MacDougall. 1981. Specificity in strength training: A review for the coach and athlete. *Sports* (Science periodical on research and technology in sport), March, pp. 1–6.

36. Salmons, S., and J. Henriksson. 1981. The adaptive response of skeletal muscle to increased use. *Muscle and Nerve* 4:94–105.

37. Stone, M. H., H. O'Bryant, and J. Garhammer. 1981. A hypothetical model for strength training. *Journal of Sports Medicine and Physical Fitness* 21:342–351.

38. Stone, M. H., H. O'Bryant, J. Garhammer, et al. 1982. A theoretical model of strength training. *National Strength and Conditioning Association Journal* 4(4):36–39.

39. Stone, M. H., G. D. Wilson, D. Blessing, and R. Rozenek. 1983. Cardiovascular responses to short-term olympic style weight training in young men. *Canadian Journal of Applied Sports Sciences* 8:134–139.

40. Thorstensson, A. 1976. Muscle strength, fibre types, and enzymes in man. *Acta Physiologica Scandinavica Supplementum)* 443.

41. Tschiene, P. 1979. The distinction of training structure in different stages of athlete's preparation. Paper presented at the International Congress of Sport Sciences, Edmonton, Alberta, Canada, July 25–29.

42. Vihko, V., A. Salminen, and J. Rontumaki. 1978. Oxidative and lysomal capacity in skeletal muscle of mice after endurance training of different intensities. *Acta Physiologica Scandinavica* 104:74–81.

43. Ward, T., J. L. Groppel, and M. Stone. 1979. Anthropometry and performance in master and first class olympic weight lifters. *Journal of Sports Medicine and Physical Fitness* 19:205–212.

44. Williams, L. R. T., E. A. S. McEwen, C. D. Watkins, et al. 1979. Motor learning and performance under physical fatigue and the specificity principle. *Canadian Journal of Applied Sport Sciences* 4:302–308.

45. Wolf, W. 1961. Contribution to the question of overtraining. *Health and Fitness in the Modern World*. Chicago: Athletic Institute Press, pp. 291–301.

Practical Considerations for Weight Training

The weight trainer is often confronted with basic questions that can range from how to calculate workloads to what are the most efficient breathing patterns. The purpose of this chapter is to present information that will help the weight trainer create reasonable solutions to those problems and produce more efficient training programs. It must be pointed out that many of these problems have not been well researched, and empirical evidence must serve as the primary guide.

Estimation of Workload

Work is equal to force (strength) × vertical displacement. Total work is proportional to the total energy cost of training (98, 135, 161, 162) (See Chapter 4). To calculate total work for weight training the distance for each movement must be multiplied by the weight and the number of repetitions. Furthermore, negative (eccentric) work must be considered. While this method is reasonable for some research studies, a few trial calculations will quickly show the impractical nature of this method. With adults the distance the weight moves for each exercise is basically constant, thus the work or *load* may be estimated by multiplying the weight × repetitions (135) (Table 7–1).

The volume of training is actually equal to the load (or tonnage), but it may be estimated by the total number of repetitions (28, 102). The relationship of repetitions to load is demonstrated in Table 7–1. Thus, volume can be estimated simply by keeping track of the total repetitions.

Power is work per unit of time or force × velocity of movement (Table 7–2). The intensity of exercise is equal to the power output and is proportional to the rate at which energy is used (9, 135).

The intensity of exercise is proportional to the average weight of the bar. As shown in Table 7–2, the heavier the bar, the less time it takes to complete the exercise. Thus, the heavier the weight lifted, the higher the power output (provided reasonable weights are used). When the same weight is lifted the same number of repetitions, speed of movement is the factor determining power output.

The olympic weightlifters at Auburn University have been keeping training logs. Figure 7–1 represents the mean load, volume, and intensity of training for 5 of these weightlifters

Table 7–1. Calculation of training load.*

Work = f × d	Example:
Assume for adults d is constant	10 reps × 200 kg = 2000 kg
Workload = weight × reps	
Work ≅ repetitions	5 reps × 250 kg = 1250 kg

*Notice in the example that the repetitions are proportional to the load. Thus, the volume (total load) can be estimated simply by keeping track of the total repetitions.

Table 7–2. Estimation of training (exercise) intensity.*

Power = f × v = intensity of exercise
Intensity ≅ average weight lifted
Example:

$$\frac{10 \text{ reps} \times 200 \text{ kg}}{40 \text{ sec}} = 50 \text{ keg/sec}$$

$$\frac{5 \text{ reps} \times 250 \text{ kg}}{15 \text{ sec}} = 83.3 \text{ kg/sec}$$

*The weight lifted is proportional to the power output.

(major exercises) for the 12 weeks immediately prior to the 1981 Collegiate National Championships (won by Auburn). Notice that volume (repetitions) generally increases or decreases with the load, but intensity (average weight lifted) does not. By charting the variations of volume, intensity, and load, comparisons can be made from cycle to cycle and from year to year to help determine the effectiveness of particular programs in producing desired results. Furthermore, the total energy cost of training is proportional to the load and therefore the volume, and the rate of energy expenditure is proportional to the intensity of training. Thus, rough qualitative estimates of energy expenditure can be calculated from volume and intensity. This estimate of energy expenditure can be useful in reducing overwork (chronic fatigue). For example, if a particular phase of training produces chronic fatigue, a reduction in volume and/or intensity in the next cycle may be helpful.

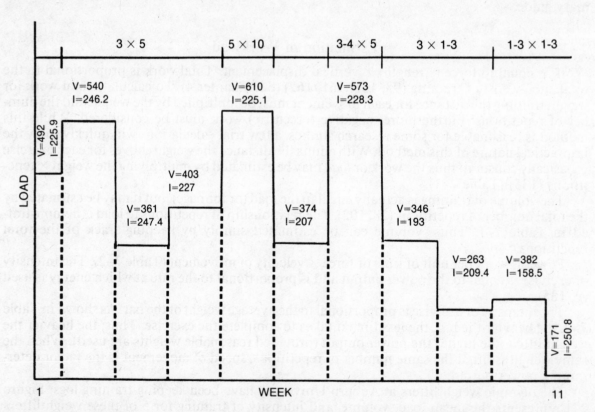

Figure 7–1. Example of load, volume, and intensity estimates. The basic training program is presented at the top of the figure.
V = volume (repetitions) = workload
I = intensity (average weight lifted) = power output

Methods of Varying Intensity, Volume, and Load

As pointed out in Chapter 6, appropriate variation in volume and intensity is crucial to realizing superior strength-power gains. The variation in volume and intensity (and therefore load) should occur over the macrocycle, the mesocycle, and the microcycle.

One method of variation is to base the various exercises on the 1RM for each movement. Considering empirical observation (119, 154) and data reported by various researchers (17, 37, 124) the following percentages seem appropriate for various sets and repetitions, and could be worked into appropriate variations from day to day:

Sets	Repetitions	Percentage range
1	1RM	100
1–3	2	90–95+
1–3	3	87.5–95
3–5	5	75–87.5
3–5	10	60–80

A drawback to this method is that the maximum value (1RM) can change considerably from the beginning of a cycle to the end. If the percentages are calculated based on an initial 1RM, then later in the cycle the weights handled may be too light. An overestimate of the final 1RM at the end of the cycle produces the opposite results and leads quickly to overtraining. (It has been the author's observation that weight trainers using this method often overestimate their 1RM.) A method used by the weightlifters at Auburn University and other weightlifters and strength-power athletes (58, 119, 154, 158) is to base the percentages of weight lifted on a projected maximum for sets and repetitions during each phase of training. Using this method requires the creation of an intensity table (see Appendix A) that can be used from training phase to training phase. An example of an intensity table is presented in Table 7–3. The intensity table can be used in conjunction with a variation table (Table 7–4). In keeping with the principles outlined in Chapter 6, heavy days should not follow heavy days, thus facilitating recuperation. In training that combines running and weight training, for example, care must be taken not to plan heavy running on a light to moderate weight training day. Doing so would turn a light training day into a heavy day and increase the potential for overtraining.

Table 7–3. Example of an intensity table.*

Intensity	Percentage range for sets and repetitions
Very heavy (VH)	95–100
Heavy (H)	90–95
Moderately heavy (MH)	85–90
Moderate (M)	80–85
Moderately light (ML)	75–80
Light (L)	70–75
Very light (VL)	65–70

*This table can be used in conjunction with the variation table (Table 7–4) in helping to establish appropriate variation in intensity and loading.

Table 7–4. Example of a variation table.*

Week	Monday	Tuesday	Wednesday	Thursday	Friday	Saturday	Sunday
1	MH	L	Rest	ML	Rest	L	Rest
2	H	ML	Rest	M	Rest	ML	Rest
3	VH	M	Rest	H	Rest	M	Rest
4	L	L	Rest	ML	Rest	L	Rest

*This table is used in conjunction with the intensity table. Notice that, to insure adequate recovery, heavy and very heavy days are not followed by higher than moderate intensity days.

An example of this method of variation in intensity is shown in Figure 7–2. In this example, an olympic weightlifter was emphasizing the squat in trying to increase leg and hip extension strength during an early basic strength phase before the 1982 American Championships. The weightlifter performed squats on Mondays and Thursdays along with quarter squats and upper body movements; Tuesdays and Saturdays were devoted to pulling movements. He used the intensity cycle shown in Table 7–3 and the variation cycle shown in Table 7–4. Notice that the heaviest day of each week is placed first (Monday); this is done because accumulative fatigue through the week might reduce the possible training load if the heavy day were placed toward the end of the week. This is consistent with the observations of other coaches and athletes (10, 119, 154, 158, 162).

An advantage of using intensity variations based on sets and repetitions rather than 1RM is that the projection of 100% is made only a few weeks ahead, which increases the accuracy of prediction (as opposed to trying to project an estimated 1RM many weeks later). Additionally, projected weights become easier to make after a few cycles have been completed. Projections based on regression equations can facilitate planned variation based on either method. Developing the equations would require considerable effort, as would revalidating the equations periodically. These equations would be of assistance in planning training programs for large groups.

For the novice weight trainer the following percentages, which are based on empirical evidence, appear to be reasonable starting percentages for a *first* mesocycle (based on 1RM):

Sets	Repetitions	Percentage based on initial 1RM
3-5	10	60-67.5
3	5	70-75
3	3	85-90

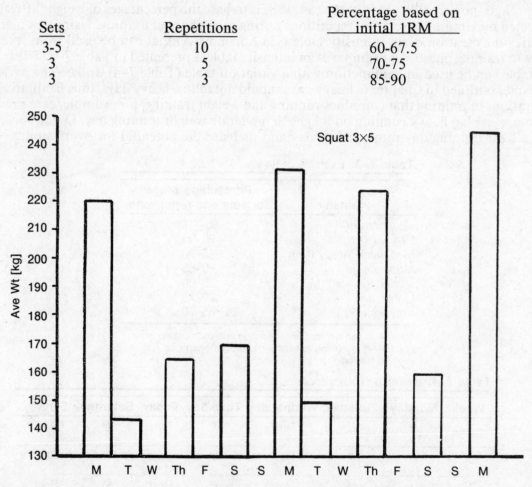

Figure 7–2. Microcycle variation with emphasis on the squat. Monday was the heaviest day of the week. The fourth week was a light training week, producing a 3:1 intensity cycle.

Adherence to these practical methods will enhance the weight-training program and help to produce superior results (see Chapter 6.) Note: highly technical lifts like the snatch or the clean and jerk should not be performed for more than 2–3 repetitions (see Chapter 2).

Frequency of Training

Exercise scientists and physical educators generally have recommended training 3 days per week (17, 30, 126). This recommendation has been based largely on experiments dealing with various sets, repetitions, exercises, and days per week of training and generally using **untrained** subjects (17, 30). It has been believed that training 3 days per week provides optimum recovery and allows efficient increases in strength and accompanying physiology. But many athletes, including weightlifters, train 5 and 6 days per week and often use multiple training sessions each day. Furthermore, they may train the same muscle mass several days in succession with superior results. Gillam (63) observed that increased frequency (2–5 days) of training produced superior results in the bench press, lending additional credence to empirical evidence.

Training theory and principles (Chapter 6) suggest that the frequency of training should be as high as possible *without* overtraining. Weight training is no exception. As pointed out in Chapter 6, overtraining (overwork) can be reduced through variation in volume and intensity. Thus, the frequency of training can be high if proper variation is introduced.

Various factors can affect the frequency of training. The volume of training is related to the total energy cost. If a high volume of training per day is used, then additional recovery time or lighter subsequent workouts are necessary to reduce the possibility of overtraining. This principle is also very important if combination training is being used.

Another factor that affects frequency of training is the muscle mass being trained. Volkov, Milner, and Nosov (161) observed that the forearm extensors returned to initial strengths and isometric endurance levels faster than did leg and hip extensors after heavy loading. Unpublished data (Stone, 1978) suggest that the order of recovery from heavy loading (5×10 at 70% of 1RM) is first, upper body; second, leg extensors; and third, lower back. This finding agrees with the observations of other coaches, athletes, and researchers (119, 158, 162). This order of recovery means that training days that markedly stress the lower back should be followed by rest or light training days. Furthermore, upper body training **may** be performed more often without overtraining.

A third factor concerns the training status of the athlete. As in other sports and activities (9, 43, 58, 119, 127, 130, 148), beginners may not have made sufficient adaptations to the stress of weight training to allow them to recover as fast as advanced weight trainers. Beginners may need more days of rest to avoid overtraining. This finding is consistent with the observation that weight lifters, as well as other athletes, tend to increase their training volume (duration and frequency) from year to year, not only by adding sets, but also by adding training days and multiple workouts per days (119, 148, 158, 162).

Individual biological variation is an important factor. Although everyone can improve their recovery powers through reasonable training, some trainees simply need more rest than others, and this recovery time must be built into their programs.

To a large extent, frequency of training depends on the goals of the individual. Three days of training per week may fit the physical and psychological needs of some weight trainers, but both empirical evidence and careful scientific observation strongly suggest that frequencies greater than typical 3-day-per-week training can produce superior results in strength, power, and other accompanying physiology (28, 63, 119, 148, 162), especially in advanced weight trainers, including weightlifters, powerlifters, and bodybuilders. In weightlifting and in other advanced training, frequency of training is related to and will change with the volume of training and will decrease with the peaking of strength and power (28, 148, 162).

Workout Length

The length of a training session depends on the total volume of training, the repetitions per set, the type of exercise, and the rest time taken between sets. Table 7–5 presents the approximate

Table 7–5. Approximate time of training and rest periods for various exercises and repetitions per set using a priority system (133, 135, and unpublished data).

Exercise	Repetitions per set	Exercise time (sec) at 100% for sets and reps	Rest time between sets (min) Untrained	Weightlifters
Squats	10	45–60	4.0	3.5
	5	20–30	3.5	3.0
	3	10–15	3.0	3.1
Clean pulls	10	45–50	4.3	3.5
	5	25–30	3.2	3.0
	3	12–16	3.0	3.2
Bench press	10	35–40	3.3	3.4
	5	15–20	3.0	3.1
	3	8–16	2.9	3.1

time to complete various exercises and the approximate time for rest periods between exercises for untrained males and weightlifters (135, 149, 162, and unpublished data). Notice that the weightlifters and untrained subjects used the same amount of time to complete the exercises. For both groups, rest time decreased slightly from sets of 10 to sets of 3. The weightlifters used less recovery time with the higher volume work, perhaps reflecting superior recuperative powers developed through training. However, rest time for the lower volume work (sets of 3) was nearly equal, the weightlifters using slightly more time. As noted in Chapter 6, as the volume is reduced, more emphasis is placed on the **quality** of exercise. Therefore, relatively more time can be taken between sets to insure reasonable levels of high quality, high intensity work (162, 164). When weightlifters are peaking for a meet and performing single attempts in the two olympic-style lifts, they may rest 4–8 minutes between sets to insure recovery and quality of performance (154, 162).

Recovery of muscle strength after high intensity, anaerobic work is at best poorly understood (see Chapter 1 and the sections on metabolic cost and nutrition in Chapter 2). Bioenergetics is an important factor. Work using few repetitions probably is supported primarily using phosphogens (ATP-CP system). Phosphogen stores are completely replenished in 2½ to 3 minutes. Thus, the time taken by the subjects in Table 7–5 probably was sufficient for phosphogen repletion for the lower repetitions. However, higher repetition training, can produce high blood lactates, indicating considerable involvement of anaerobic gylcolysis (133, 134). The longer rest periods taken after high volume work probably indicate a need to replenish phosphogens and to recover from low muscle pH.

Goal-oriented factors also can affect length of training, rest periods, etc. For example, bodybuilders often use short recovery periods, believing that short rest periods allow them to achieve a better "muscle pump" and greater hypertrophy (164). Priority training entails using a specific order of exercises, whereas circuit weight training often alternates upper and lower body exercises and typically uses very short rest periods between sets (15–45 seconds) to enhance the use of aerobic mechanisms. Circuit training may enhance aerobic capacity and shorten training time (see Chapter 1, but it also forces the use of lighter weights (40%–45% of 1RM) and produces a compromise in strength and power gains (61, 62).

Using shorter rest periods may enhance adaptations, resulting in increased endurance (133, 134). According to many bodybuilders, it results in greater gains in hypertrophy. However, adequate time must be given for sufficient recovery to accomplish continued work, especially when performing high quality, technique-oriented work.

Exercise Order

The alternation of prime movers, usually upper body exercise being performed alternately with lower body exercises, has been suggested as a means of facilitating recovery (164). While this means may be appropriate for circuit training, it is not appropriate for work emphasizing strength and/or power development (127, 148).

The priority system emphasizes training with a definite order of exercises. Large muscle mass exercises such as squatting and pulling movements should come first in the exercise session. This is important for the following reasons:

1. Large muscle mass exercises use the heaviest weights and are fundamental to basic strength development (127, 148, 162). They should be trained while the athlete is fresh.

2. Large muscle mass exercises have relatively high energy cost (135) and produce both general and local muscular fatigue. Furthermore, empirical data suggest that these exercises require considerable mental effort and concentration to perform. Placing them later in the training or alternating them with small muscle mass exercises is likely to diminish the high levels of concentration necessary for performing these important exercises. The required mental effort often includes mental imagery.

3. Because of the high energy cost of large muscle mass exercises, the placement of lower energy cost small muscle mass exercises at the end of a workout can provide a metabolic warmdown (135, 162).

4. Working small muscle mass exercises first or alternately fatigues the synergistic and supporting musculature necessary for producing proper technique (form) in the large muscle mass exercises. Fatigue increases the chance of getting out of position, using poor technique, and thus increases injury potential. Furthermore, fatigue increases the chance of practicing poor technique, thus discouraging the acquisition of high skill levels.

Vorobeyev (162) suggests that all workouts should be preceded by a speed-strength exercise such as the power snatch and points out that placing this type of exercise first has a positive influence on subsequent movements. While this is certainly reasonable for weightlifters and other athletes, it is also reasonable for nonathletes in that it would act as a general warmup as well as provide a high energy cost exercise important in weight control (see Chapter 2).

In the case of weightlifters (and other strength power athletes), where the meet may last several hours, it is occasionally necessary to place competition movements toward the end of a workout in order to train them against a background of fatigue (162). The athlete will then have to draw on his stamina and recuperative powers, which is in keeping with what can actually occur under meet conditions. Success often depends on mental and physical reserves.

Realizing reasonable strength-power gains depends on reasonable exercise selection and exercise order. Wise selection is especially important for the athlete who is interested in superior strength-power gains.

Exercise Selection

Exercise selection is largely a matter of equipment availability and the trainer's goals. Empirical evidence, logical application of training principles, extension of basic research, and objective comparisons of training modes strongly suggest that superior results can be derived from free weights in terms of strength and power gains (see Chapter 5). If only machines are available the trainer should make efforts to simulate as closely as possible the basic large muscle mass exercises suggested in this section.

O'Shea (127) considers power cleans, squats, and pressing movements to be the core exercises and the foundation of every program. Certainly large muscle mass, multiple joint exercises should be the core of all weight-training programs because of their contribution to overall strength, power, and changes in body composition.

Typical 3-day-per-week small muscle mass training does not stimulate metabolic turnover as much as do these multiple joint exercises (see Chapter 2). Because of this, the stimulus for reduction of fat and general changes in body composition is not as high as with multiple joint exercises. Performing such exercises is no problem for weightlifters, powerlifters, and many other athletes because they are directly related to their performance. But many weight trainers may be unfamiliar with them. These exercises include the following:

Exercise*	Major muscles
Push press and push jerks	Knee extensors
	Arm and shoulder abductors and extensors
Back squats and front squats	Knee and hip extensors
	(trunk extensors—static)
Pulls (snatch and clean grip)	Plantar flexors
	Knee and hip extensors
	Shoulder elevators (trunk
	extensor—static)

*See Chapter 10 for detailed descriptions.

Because these exercises use large muscle masses, they can be time efficient and thus a good choice for those with limited workout time. One of these exercises can produce as much work as several single joint, muscle isolation exercises.

In accordance with the principles outlined in the section on exercise order, these multiple joint exercises should be placed at the beginning of the training session. Small muscle mass or single joint muscle group isolation exercises can be placed later in the workout.

Isolated muscle group exercises, such as leg curls (hamstrings), are useful for a number of reasons. Bodybuilders may use training programs largely made up of small muscle mass exercises in order to produce hypertrophy, to a greater or lesser degree, resulting in overall muscularity and symmetry. Small muscle mass exercises and isolated muscle exercises may be used to correct specific muscle weaknesses. In this context, these exercises are excellent for both injury prevention and rehabilitation (see Chapter 3).

One important area in which isolated muscle exercises can play a significant role is in muscle strength balance. When a specific muscle group becomes considerably stronger than its antagonistic group, the weaker group may have an increased injury potential (164). This does not mean that the opposing muscle groups should be equal in strength; larger muscle groups (e.g., quadriceps) should be stronger, in absolute terms, than smaller opposing groups (e.g., hamstrings). Constant use of exercises that produce the same basic movement pattern, such as strengthening the quadriceps and neglecting the hamstrings, could produce muscle imbalances; adding a few appropriate antagonistic muscle group exercises may avert imbalance and reduce the potential for injury. In some sports, especially those using body weight classes, stressing both sides of every joint may be counterproductive. For example, in olympic weightlifting, the biceps are not important to performance. Exercise stressing the biceps, producing excessive hypertrophy (and body weight), may retard performance by adding muscle to a structure that is not directly used in performance or in typical training. Furthermore, a larger bicep may restrict racking the bar in the clean, again reducing performance.

Exercise Speed

This section summarizes briefly the information presented in Chapters 4 and 5.

In a concentric movement, resistance and speed of movement are inversely related in a hyperbolic manner. Simply stated, 20 kg can be lifted faster than 200 kg. The training principle of intensity indicates that high intensity work has a greater training stimulus than does lower intensity work. Specificity of training suggests that intensity, along with other training principles, must be applied appropriately to gain the desired results. For example, although high intensity aerobic training will affect max $\dot{V}O_2$ positively, it will not increase strength; training the arms will do little for the legs.

With the above principles in mind, consider the following:

1. Appropriate resistive training can increase speed of movement, strength, power, and short-term endurance (5, 16, 30, 31, 68, 108, 112, 124, 130, 134, 137, 143, 144).

2. Slow *high force* movements can produce superior gains in strength, power, and speed of movement when compared to purposefully slow, lower force movements (57, 146, 147).

3. Provided that reasonable exercises and weight selections are used, high speed weight training is likely to be superior to slow speed movements in producing increases in performance speed and increases in power output. This conclusion is based on careful observation of the training of various athletes (148, 154, 158), logical extension of related research (34, 105, 147, 151, 156), and scientific observation (36, 49, 57, 72).

4. The most efficient way to produce increases in strength, power, and speed of movement is to use a logical progression and combination of training speeds (124, 148). Simplistically, this method entails developing a strength base (high force work) before moving to high speed, high power work (see Chapter 6).

5. Based on objective and theoretical considerations, purposefully slow movements may not be as effective in producing gains in muscle size as moderate speed or fast movements (36, 148). Hypertrophy probably is more closely related to the intensity, volume, and total load used during training (37, 109, 148).

Until evidence is presented obviating the 5 points presented above, it is reasonable to use training speeds that are limited by the exercise resistance and movement pattern. The speed of movement used in training is to a large extent related to desired goals. This is in agreement with the training principles of intensity and specificity.

Effective Resistance (Overload)

The amount of weight lifted that can produce strength gains during training is believed to be a percentage of one's maximum (30, 73). It is unclear, however, exactly what constitutes the effective resistance.

Isometric training has been shown to produce strength gains when using as little as 35% of maximum force, although greater percentages produced better results (77). Berger (18) reported experimental evidence suggesting that the effective resistance was above 66% of the 1RM for the squat after 6 weeks of training. But several studies (61, 62) that used circuit weight training and percentages as low as 45% of the 1RM produced significant strength gains. Berger used sets of 1–6 repetitions. The circuit training studies used high repetitions and short recovery periods. Effective resistance probably depends on the number of repetitions per set, the frequency of training, and the total load of training (the underlying mechanism being unclear).

Three important observations must be emphasized: First, it is clear that intensity of training is the major factor in producing strength and other performance gains. In Berger's study (18), training 3 days per week with 66% of the 1RM was significantly inferior to training 2 days per week at 66% of 1RM plus 1 day per week at 1RM. This and other studies (71, 73) suggest that performance gains are related to training intensity. Second, this training combination (66% of 1RM for 2 days plus 1RM for 1 day) produced greater, though statistically equal, gains compared to 2 days at 80% or 90% of 1RM plus 1 day at 1RM. This result suggests that the combination of low and high intensity training is at least equal to combinations of moderate and high intensity combination training. Furthermore, Berger (18) speculated that if the training period had been carried out longer than 6 weeks the low plus high intensity training might have produced a significant difference compared to 3-day-per-week very high intensity training. Third, normal consequence of training is cumulative fatigue through the training week (148, 161, 162), especially during high volume training. Fatigue **may** reduce effective resistance. Periodic lowered intensities **may** produce sufficient overload during fatigue states, as well as allow some recovery.

Berger's study and other observations (148, 161) strongly suggest that appropriate periodic reductions of intensity (variation of intensity) **will not** impede performance gains but are likely to enhance performance by reducing the overtraining potential.

The above arguments are consistent with the principles of intensity and variation. They also are consistent with observations concerning the achievement of a strength training overload made by Hellebrandt and Howtz (73) in 1956 and with subsequent investigations and observations concerning overload.

In summary, then:

1. Strength gains are proportional to the intensity of training.

2. Cumulative fatigue through the training week may lower the intensity, constituting an overload.

3. Strength gains derived from combining light and heavy days are likely to be superior to constant high intensity training.

4. The effective resistance needed to produce performance or positive physiological changes probably depends on the number of repetitions per set, total workload, etc.

Methods of Strength Training

This section deals with various priority methods of resistive training. All of these methods are directly or indirectly related; all of these programs use various numbers of sets and repetitions per set. These various methods have been created by weight trainers with specific goals in mind (109, 130).

Light→Heavy Sets

Each set is made heavier until either a predetermined weight is reached or no more than 1 repetition can be performed. The latter method is called pyramiding and has been widely used since at least the 1930s.

Heavy→Light Sets

This is a reversal of the above technique, in that, after a brief warmup, the heaviest set is first. This method was investigated by Zinovieff (167) in an effort to reduce the fatigue associated with the DeLorme technique (37), which was a light→heavy set method. The Oxford technique (167), as this method is termed, is an attempt to allow the muscle to continue working at reasonable levels even though fatigue is reducing its strength level. McMorris and Elkins (114) found the Oxford technique to be superior to the DeLorme method in producing strength gains. However, they pointed out the need for further research.

Light→Heavy→Light Sets

This is a combination of the DeLorme and Oxford methods. Typically, the weight trainer will work up to a single heavy repetition in pyramid form and then remove weight from each set and perform a reverse pyramid.

Multiple Sets

Until the early 1940s, most weight trainers used one of the above methods (130). The multiple sets method uses a warmup of increasing weight per set (2–3) until the workout weight is reached at which multiple sets with this same weight are performed. Several studies have suggested that 3 sets of 5 or 6 repetitions (after warmup) produce superior strength gains when compared to other sets and repetitions (17, 30, 127). Advanced weight trainers may perform many more than 3 sets, consistent with their goals (127, 148, 162).

Super Sets

This method uses multiple sets in which each set is alternated with an exercise for the antagonist (e.g., quadriceps versus hamstrings).

Sets to Exhaustion

One set (35) or multiple sets (141) to exhaustion have been advocated as producing superior results in terms of strength and hypertrophy. Many weight trainers, especially bodybuilders, use sets to exhaustion with good results. It is believed that this method would better train a greater number of motor units (141). Often, this method is used in conjunction with **forced repetitions** (additional repetitions performed with the assistance of a training partner).

Periodization Training

This training concept uses the basic principles of periodization discussed in Chapter 6. It entails a logical progression of different combinations of sets and repetitions, each with specific major goals, that results in superior strength and power gains when compared with the methods described above (125, 148, 150). (Depending on the phase of training, periodized training may use one or more of the methods presented above.) A major advantage to this concept is its adherence to the principle of variation, not found in solely using any of the other methods.

Repetitions per Set

The number of repetitions per set is largely a matter of the goals of the weight trainer. From a performance standpoint, many repetitions per set are more conducive to producing endurance, and lower repetitions are more conducive to producing strength and power (109, 127, 148, 162). This is in agreement with specificity of training (49, 148). In terms of building muscle (hypertrophy), using a moderately high number of repetitions appears to be most efficient (109, 125, 148).

As pointed out in previous sections and in Chapter 6, superior results in strength and power and increases in anaerobic capacity can be attained with reasonable variations in volume (repetitions) intensity and exercise.

Isometric Training

Isometric means same length. An isometric contraction occurs when the muscle gains tension but does not change its length. Technically the muscle-lever system performs no work.

Isometric training produces strength gains specific to the joint angle trained (54, 107). Therefore, to effect strength gains throughout the range of motion, many joint angles must be trained. Some studies have found that isometric training increases speed of contraction (29, 31, 105, 112, 143, 144). Other studies have found that isometric training has no effect (105, 112, 156) or can retard speed of movement and power production (113, 151).

Isometric and dynamic measures of strength are not necessarily strongly or even moderately related (16, 60, 113, 128), especially for fast movements (105). Therefore, it is no surprise that isometric training does not produce proportional gains in dynamic strength (16, 113), or vice versa. Training for sports or other activities that require dynamic strength is best performed dynamically.

Training that combines isometrics with dynamic training may produce the advantages of both forms (127). One type of combined training, termed functional isometrics, has been reviewed by O'Shea (127).

In summary, most physical activities are primarily dynamic in nature, and increases in dynamic strength, speed, and power would likely be beneficial to their performance. In agreement with the concept of specificity (134), dynamic strength training is more likely than isometric training to enhance these qualities (16, 113, 127). Isometric training may, however, be useful in the absence of dynamic training devices.

Eccentric Training

Maximal eccentric contractions produce higher tension levels than do isometric or concentric contractions (80). However, solely eccentric training has not been shown to be superior to solely concentric training (80). In general, a combination of the two is likely to be superior (67, 69).

Warmup

Although there has been some controversy over the need for warmup, compelling evidence supports the use of both general and specific warmup.

Effects on Hemodynamics and $\dot{V}O_2$

Several observations have suggested that physiologically increased muscle or rectal temperature facilitates transfer of gases at the level of working tissues (6, 9, 110), increased muscle blood flow (66), lowers lactate levels (38, 110), and in general raises muscle metabolism (8, 9, 110). Max $\dot{V}O_2$ can be increased with warmup (6, 110).

Effects on Muscle and Nerve Tissue

Nerve conduction rate is faster at higher temperatures (9). Several studies and observations suggest that muscle contractile force and speed are enhanced by increased muscle temperature (19, 78, 157).

Effects on Injury Potential

It is generally accepted among coaches, athletes, and most sports scientists that lack of proper warmup increases injury potential (14, 43, 115, 130). The elasticity of muscle can be increased and the viscosity of muscle can be decreased with increased muscle temperature (43, 115), which is likely to reduce the chance of strains and tears. Barnard and coworkers (13, 14, 15) have demonstrated adverse cardiovascular responses, including tachycardia, pre-ventricular contractions, and greatly elevated blood pressures during intense exercise. Warmup eliminated or reduced these abnormalities in nearly all the subjects used in the study.

Effects on Performance

Based on the above discussions and on a variety of empirical (14, 117, 119, 158) as well as scientific observations and studies (22, 129, 131, 132, 157), the following conclusions would appear to be reasonable concerning the effect of warmup on performance. In general, it appears that (1) Performance is positively affected by warmup; (2) Although both active and passive warmup may enhance subsequent performance, vigorous active warmup is preferred; (3) General warmup may be superior to local warmup, but the combination of general plus local warmup may be superior to either alone. (It should be pointed out that specific warmup, besides increasing local muscle temperature, may provide practice, thus facilitating performance). (4) Warmup may prevent injuries, especially to the cardiovascular system.

Warmup for Weight Training

Considering the above discussion, the following guidelines are suggested for proper warmup preceding weight training:

- For general warmup:
  - Stretching of muscles crossing all joints.
  - **Light** large muscle mass (multiple joint) exercises such as power snatches or push presses.
- For specific warmup:
  - Light→moderate warmup sets for each major weight-training exercise.

Breathing During Weight-Training Exercise

Proper breathing during weight-training exercises is very important. Completely holding the breath (closed glottis) during heavy exertion can produce the valsalva effect, or semi-valsalva, with the following associated effects (43, 95):

- Intrathoracic pressure may rise to 200+ mm Hg.
- Blood pressure (both systolic and diastolic) will show a sharp rise that parallels intrathoracic and muscular pressures.
- Intrathoracic and muscular pressure will occlude venous return to the right heart. Cardiac output **may** drop or rise slightly, depending on the degree of occlusion and its time course (84, 104). During a true valsalva effect, fainting could occur due to a fall in cardiac output.
- Release of the straining activity **may** cause a momentary precipitous fall in blood pressure. This can occur in the cerebral vasculature and cause fainting. Reflex mechanisms quickly return pressure, flow, and cardiac output to normal values, however. If blackout occurs, it generally happens during the first few seconds after the exercise—usually a heavy attempt)is completed and the subject is no longer straining.

Trainers with hypertension or other cardiovascular abnormalities should use caution considering the possible effects associated with straining. (Fainting while holding a bar or postexercise may also result in injury.) Damage to the normal cardiovascular system is at best rare (130) if not nonexistent.

Some breathholding is desirable. Increases in intra-abdominal pressure can contribute to vertebral stabilization during multi-joint exercises, and can contribute to stabilized thoracic and shoulder girdle structures during pressing and other movements (65, 94). This type of stabilization may contribute to decreased musculo-skeletal injury potential and increased lifting potential (65, 94).

Generally the breathing pattern is to inspire at the beginning of the eccentric contraction and exhale during the last two-thirds of the concentric contraction. For example, breathing correctly while performing the bench press or squat would be described as follows:

1. Remove bar from rack and stabilize.

2. Inspire deeply, thus stabilizing appropriate structures.

3. Lower the weight (eccentric work).

4. Raise the weight (concentric work) and expire during the last one-half to two-thirds of the upward movement.

5. Repeat the cycle.

In summary, a true valsalva maneuver is to be avoided in exercise. Proper breathing can be beneficial in avoiding injuries and can allow greater weight to be handled because it encourages improved mechanics (technique).

Factors That Affect Strength, Power, and Muscular Endurance

Age

Astrand and Rodahl (9), using cross-sectional data, show that in untrained individuals, peak strength levels are reached at about 20 yrs (males) and 18 yrs. (females). Strength levels decline until at age 70, the peak levels are about the same as at age 15. Considerable empirical data (162 and unpublished data) suggest that appropriate weight training can decrease the expected age-related strength decline, although other types of training (47) may not alter the decline. It is known that there is an aging-related loss of muscle tissue (2, 9, 96, 97) and that fast motor units may be lost at a greater rate than slow motor units (96, 97). Perhaps weight training delays the loss of muscle tissue, thus helping to maintain strength/power/muscular endurance levels. It is also of interest to note that muscular endurance does not decline as fast as does maximum strength (47, 96, 97) and that both weight training (162 and unpublished data) and endurance training (47) may reduce the rate of decline in muscular endurance. The slower decline in muscular endurance compared to maximum strength could be a result of the retention of slow motor units during aging (96, 97).

Increases in strength-power-muscular endurance in preadolescent children as a result of resistive training has been a controversial issue. Critics of strength training for children in this group suggest that increased maximum strength beyond what occurs with normal growth is not likely to develop because muscle growth cannot be stimulated due to low hormone levels (estrogen or testosterone) (4, 103, 120). Although the stimulation of additional muscle growth through strength training may be minimal, adaptations in the central nervous system are still likely to occur (i.e., there is likely to be increased motor unit recruitment, etc.).

Empirical data and even casual observation of preadolescent gymnastics, weight training, and other high resistive activities suggest that children engaged in these programs are stronger than their untrained counterparts. Recent research suggest that preadolescents can substantially increase their maximum strength through resistive training (46, 48, 139, 140).

For 11- to 20-year-olds, weightlifting training may produce gains in strength, power, and speed-related movements better than other forms of training such as track and field (46, 48).

Furthermore, weightlifting training may enhance other health-related factors, including cardiovascular parameters in children (46, 139).

Sex

Given similar ages, total body mass, and training state, females have less muscle mass than males (20, 45, 123). Although the maximum isometric strength per unit of muscle is similar among males and females over a wide age range (123, 136), differences in absolute and relative dynamic and isometric strength result from differences in muscle mass. However, females appear to have a different distribution of their muscle mass, more of it being in the lower body (20, 123, 136). Furthermore, the diameter of muscle fibers is about 30% larger in males (45). These differences are in part due to differences in testosterone levels.

Additionally, there are skeletal differences between men and women that could contribute to strength differences. For example, women have a wider, shallower pelvis, which increases the Q angle (increasing the potential for genu valgum or "knock knees"). A larger Q angle may decrease the efficiency of the quadriceps.

Men have a higher absolute ($\geq$ 20%) and relative (body mass) ($\geq$ 12%) maximum total body strength than women (100, 123). When maximum strength is expressed per kg of LBM, men have a higher maximum upper body strength with similar lower body values (20, 45).

Delayed Muscle Soreness

Delayed muscle soreness (DMS) as a result of exercise can be an annoyance or can become a major problem. Loss of training time or temporary reduction in exercise intensity as a result of DMS may ultimately affect performance. Thus, an understanding of the mechanism of DMS and how to reduce DMS are reasonable objectives.

The problems associated with DMS were recognized as early as 3000 B.C. (106), and various mechanisms for its appearance were proposed around 1900 (64, 79). There are four basic theories as to the mechanism of DMS: (1) tonic spasms in localized motor units (39–43); (2) damage to muscle tissue (1, 7, 79); (3) damage to connective tissue (1, 7, 79); and (4) some combination of the above factors.

The muscle spasm theory is supported by the work of deVries (39–43), who noted that static stretching, which may relieve cramps, furnishes some degree of DMS prevention as well as momentary relief and that where DMS exists there is markedly higher electromygraphic (EMG) activity. DeVries used unipolar electrode EMG. When using bipolar electrodes, a more accurate procedure, higher EMG activity is not always produced (1). Furthermore, Abraham (1) suggests that the changes in EMG activity and soreness resulting from stretching are transient and can easily be accomplished by slowly flexing and extending the limbs. Thus the tonic spasm theory is not well supported by experimental evidence (1, 11).

As early as 1902, Hough (79) postulated that DMS was due to tearing of muscle/connective tissue. The recent electron microscopic work of Friden et al. (52, 53) lends some support to this hypothesis (79) by showing evidence of Z-band distortion and disruption after eccentric work. Indirect evidence of tissue damage or at least a change in cell membrane permeability has been provided recently by studies associating DMS with an increase of intracellular substances in the plasma or urine (1, 7, 82, 138). These substances include creatinine, creatinphosphate (CP), hydroxyproline, myoglobin, creatinphosphokinase (CPK), lactate dehydrogenase (LDH), and myokinase (MK).

Bansil and others (11, 12) have recently produced evidence that prostaglandins are involved in DMS. Prostaglandins are "hormones" formed from C-20 unsaturated fatty acids, usually arachidonic acid. It is well established that prostaglandins, especially the E (PGE) series, are pro-inflammatory, meaning that they act as potentiating agents for inflammatory substances such as histamine and bradykinin (44, 81). Furthermore, the synthesis of prostaglandins can be blocked by aspirin. Studies by Bansil et al. suggest that DMS is an inflammatory reaction brought about by the synthesis of sufficient amounts of PGE about 12–36 hours postexercise, which helps to explain the delay in DMS. Furthermore, it was shown that aspirin decreased soreness and serum PGE levels. (Empirical evidence lends support to this work because for years weightlifters have used aspirin to suppress muscle soreness.) In another study (145), a rise in neutrophils (an inflammatory response) was noted several hours after one-legged bench stepping; this finding also supports the concept of DMS as a result of an inflammatory process. In summary, considerable data suggest that DMS is an inflammatory response, **possibly** resulting from tissue damage.

Considering the above data and empirical evidence, the following statements can be made about DMS:

1. DMS is most easily produced by eccentric exercise.

2. There is a delay of about 12–48 hours postexercise before significant soreness appears. (Empirical evidence suggests that the delay is shorter (12–24 hours) in young athletes and longer (24–48 hours) in older athletes.)

3. DMS is an inflammatory reaction possibly induced by muscle or connective tissue damage. It is possible that the damage could induce some motor unit spasms.

4. The severity of DMS can be reduced by using aspirin or other antiprostaglandins and by using ice postexercise.

Injuries

[*We extend special thanks to Jeff Lander, Ph.D., National Strength Research Center, Auburn University, for his help in preparing this section.]

Although on rare occasions weight-training injuries can be severe (166), they are not numerous relative to other sports (74, 93) and typically result from overtraining or overuse (90, 111).

A brief discussion of theoretical considerations concerning ligament and tendon properties and the possible effects of training is useful in understanding injury potential. Also included are practical examples of possible training adaptations that may beneficially alter injury potential.

The effects of strength training on tendons and ligaments are difficult to ascertain. Little, if any, research has been directed at this problem (32, 33).

There have been some animal studies using endurance-type training. The results of these studies have been reviewed by Viidik (159), Tipton et al. (152), and Butler et al. (24). Endurance training does, in general, seem to enhance tendon and ligament strength. Sprint training (153) was found to produce marked increases in ligament weights and weight: length ratios, although it did not significantly affect junction (bone-ligament) strength. It does appear, based on limited animal studies, that training can positively influence ligament and tendon structure.

However, the animal studies have received two major criticisms (24, 165). First, the exercise studies compared trained animals to caged animals. Inactivity or disuse can cause considerable weakening and atrophy in visco-elastic tissue (24, 99, 121, 122, 165). The conditions imposed by confinement in a cage do not represent the conditions found in the wild (24, 165). The exercise may return the properties of the tendons and ligaments to what would be found in unconfined animals. Therefore, these animal studies may simply be reverse immobility research (99, 165).

Second, the strain rates used in many of these studies were below physiological rates. Therefore, it is difficult to generalize back to the normal intact animal (24). These slower strain rates also fail to answer the question of whether exercise strengthens tendons and ligaments under more normal conditions. Noyes et al. (121) have shown that visco-elastic tissue failure mechanisms are a function of the strain rate. At slow strain rates, failure is at the bone (junction); at faster strain rates it is in the tendon or ligament. Therefore, if the bone fails, the tendon or ligament is not being tested (24, 165). Until these criticisms have been obviated, there is little objective evidence from which to determine the extent any type of exercise, including strength training, causes positive adaptations in visco-elastic tissue.

Empirically the evidence is quite compelling. Consider weightlifting, for example. Although the forces generated during training and competition are quite high (10, 50, 55, 56, 57, 166), the visco-elastic tissue injury rate is not unusual and may, in fact, be lower than for sports like basketball and football (10, 51, 74, 75, 76, 93, 95).

Two important factors operate to minimize weightlifting injuries. The first factor is a basic property of visco-elastic tissue. The faster the strain rate, the greater is the maximum load (force) at failure and the larger is the energy of failure (24, 165). This basic property of these tissues offers some protection against potential injury with high force-high velocity movements like those found in weightlifting, football, basketball, shotput, etc.

Perhaps a more important factor is the possible physiological adaptation(s) to training. If a 16-year-old boy with no previous training attempted a 300 kg (660-lb.) squat, he could expect ruptured tendons and ligaments, plus assorted other injuries. But, with proper training procedures (safety precautions, technique, appropriate volumes and intensities) he might eventually make this lift. The same can be said of performing a 200 kg (44-lb.) clean and jerk or attempting to block a professional football linebacker. The important point is that physiological adaptations eventually allow high level activities to be accomplished. One of these adaptations is a strengthening of tendons and ligaments. The recent descriptive research of Hejna et al. (72) supports this argument.

Tendon rupture does occur, though rarely, in high force-high velocity sports like olympic weightlifting (166). It also occurs in many other sports and physical activities (10, 27, 59, 75, 92, 142), including low muscle force-low velocity sports like distance running (10, 75, 92). Visco-elastic tissue injuries may not be directly related to the force produced by a particular movement, such as high velocity weight training, as has been recently suggested (3), but rather to the inappropriate use of training volumes and intensities. High intensity training is known to cause connective tissue microtrauma (minute tears in the tissues). Microtrauma also may occur in the muscle (24, 165). The rate of healing may be slower in connective tissue than in muscle due to a relatively poor blood supply (24, 165). Frequent high intensity training may not allow sufficient healing in the ligament or tendon; high volume work can produce similar effects (overtraining). This may lead to the degenerative process generally termed tendinitis, and could eventually result in a ruptured tendon (or ligament) (101, 165). It is possible, and perhaps likely, that poorly planned training programs are more directly responsible for visco-elastic tissue injury, rather than the velocity of exercise.

Drug use also can contribute to injury. Anabolic steroids and testosterone are taken by large and increasing numbers of athletes, both men and women. It is likely in strength-power sports that the majority of athletes, even at low levels of competition, take different androgens in various amounts. Although the mechanism of action is unclear, androgens seem to facilitate recovery from large training loads (high volume or high intensity), allowing the athlete to train harder (higher loads) more often. This type of training may increase performance at rapid rates and perhaps, due to the drug, increase it to higher levels than otherwise could occur. However, the increased frequency of heavy loading may potentiate injuries (see Chapter 9).

It also has been speculated (165) that androgens can directly or indirectly result in a disproportionate strengthening of muscle compared to tendons. (Muscle has a superior blood supply compared to connective tissue, so it may grow faster.) The greatly increased strength of the muscle compared to the tendon may contribute to tendon rupture, especially in the presence of microtrauma in the connective tissue.

Cortico-steroids are commonly used anti-inflammatory agents. Often they are injected at the site of injury. Recent studies suggest that these drugs may in fact increase degeneration and add to the problem (27, 59). Therefore, they should be used with considerable caution.

Injury Prevention

Prevention of injury is largely related to proper preparation and the attainment of appropriate adaptations. These adaptations include changes in the central nervous system, structure, and biochemistry of the trainee. Preparation should include: increased awareness of safety factors; flexibility training; stabilization of technique; proper manipulation of volume, intensity, and technique work; reasonable exercise selection; and reasonable manipulation of exercise speeds (134, 148, 150).

There is little doubt that specificity of training is a valid concept. This concept includes specificity of velocity. Considerable evidence suggests that properly integrated high force-high velocity training is necessary to produce superior gains in strength and power (148, 150), and is therefore a necessity in the training of strength-power athletes. This assumption makes sense from an injury standpoint. If the performance of an athlete demands high force and/or high velocity exercise, then it is logical to assume that to avoid injuries during competition some of the training should be high force and high velocity. Specificity of training dictates specific adaptations to specific stresses; constant adherence to slow training is unlikely to lead to appropriate adaptations and may increase injury potential.

Flexibility training is essential for proper performance and injury prevention. The positions attained in sport performances are related to flexibility, both static and dynamic, and flexibility relates to technique. If poor technique is established because of poor flexibility, performance suffers. Furthermore, poor technique may increase injury potential, so, from a performance standpoint, flexibility is also related to injuries.

From purely an injury prevention standpoint, increased mobility about a joint may have its most obvious positive effects in contact sports. A severe blow to an inflexible joint can result in a tear (remember that flexibility is not joint laxity). Flexibility also is important in relation to cross-linking of collagen. The collagen fibers in connective tissue cross-link with age, and cross-linking probably increases injury potential. Flexibility work may decrease cross-linking and therefore injury potential (165).

Rehabilitation Following Injury

Various methods of rehabilitation should be used, just as with normal training procedures. A return to reasonable free-weight exercises should be made as soon as possible (95). These types of exercises produce superior strength-power gains during normal training, and there is no reason to believe this would not be true during rehabilitation training, provided it is beneath the pain threshold and is integrated with traditional modes of rehabilitation. The use of ice and some drugs, including aspirin and dimethylsulfoxide (DMSO) also may be beneficial (10, 74, 95).

Specific Injuries

Specific injuries related to weight training and especially competitive lifting, are discussed below.

Hand Injury

Torn calluses, blisters, etc., are likely to be the most common weight-training/weightlifting/powerlifting injuries (75, 93). Proper hand care, including trimming calluses and using hand cream, can help to prevent hand problems.

Long Bone Epiphyses

Case studies of epiphyseal damage due to weight training have recently appeared in the medical literature (21, 23). All of these injuries have been attributed to improperly performed lifts (10, 74, 75, 120). Epiphyseal damage (crushed epiphysis) may cause improper bone growth (10).

Dislocated Elbows

The authors are aware of the occurrence of dislocated elbow in six weightlifters. All of these injuries occurred during weightlifting meets during the snatch lift. Four occurred when lifters were trying to establish national or world records. All six occurred during lifts that were out of position while the lifter was trying to save the lift. All six weightlifters returned to competition within 6 months without further problems. Two of the six subsequently set national or world records.

Petellar Tendon Rupture

For a discussion of the biomechanics of petellar tendon rupture see Zernicke et al. (166). The authors are aware of the occurrence of complete or partial tears of the petellar tendon in six weightlifters and six powerlifters. Among the weightlifters, three injuries occurred during the eccentric portion of the jerk and three occurred at the bottom of the clean. Among the powerlifters, all injuries occurred during the eccentric phase of the squat; furthermore, several of the powerlifters tore the tendon/muscle at the point (beginning) of the knee wraps. (We also are aware of a partial rupture in an athlete who was using a cybex leg extension machine, but we have found no report of such an injury in the medical literature.) All but one of the competitive lifters returned to competition within 1 year, and two surpassed previous results. Interestingly, three of the competitive lifters had repeated injections of cortico-steroids, one within 2 days of the tear.

Lower Back Injury

Injuries to the small ligaments and muscles supporting the spine can result from overtraining or improper movements. Spondolysis and spondolysthesis may be produced by repeated hyperextension, although heredity may be especially significant to these injuries. (91). Ruptured discs also can result from heavy or improper lifting. Furthermore, pain that mimicks more serious lower back problems can be produced by "tendinitis" of the supporting connective tissue (10).

Although low back pain has been reported among a significant percentage of competitive lifters (91), it is rarely severe enough to cause missed or reduced training (10, 93). We know of at least one case in which a weightlifter had surgery for a disc rupture (with fusion) and went on to become world and Olympic champion. Back problems were much more prevalent among weightlifters prior to 1972 (91), when the press, which causes considerable hyperextension, was removed from competition. Back problems have decreased since that time (10, 93). Back pain, especially with accompanying symptoms of sciatica, should be reported to a physician promptly.

Knee Injury

Contrary to the commonly held view, weight training rarely produces knee injuries (10, 25, 26, 33, 74, 95). Petellar "tendinitis" accounts for the majority of the pain and injury experienced by competitive lifters (10, 74, 95).

Squatting, and especially squatting in which the top of the thigh goes below parallel, has been erroneously associated with damage to the meniscus and ligaments. Although bouncing and other improper techniques can cause knee damage, there is little evidence that squatting is harmful to a healthy knee.

Although it is a common view that squats can damage the knee (25, 89), only one researcher has offered any experimental evidence supporting this contention. Klein (85–89), primarily using data from paratroopers and weightlifters, found evidence that squatting movements produced instability in the medial-lateral collateral ligaments. Unfortunately, methodological problems preclude drawing any definitive conclusions from Klein's studies (25, 70, 155, 160). Subsequent studies by several researchers (83, 116, 118, 163) have revealed no detrimental effects of squatting movements on the collateral ligaments. Furthermore, Chandler (25, 26) was unable to find any change in knee stability due to changes in the anterior-posterior cruciate ligaments in two short-term longitudinal studies. Furthermore, there is no evidence of reduced knee stability among weightlifters and powerlifters who have done squatting for many years (10, 25, 26, 74, 76).

It also has been suggested that squatting can lead to degenerative changes in the knee joint (25, 51). No evidence suggesting an increased incidence in arthritis has been observed among experienced and older (master) weightlifters and powerlifters (25, 51, 76). Furthermore, it has been noted that athletes injured in other sports have become proficient weightlifters and powerlifters (25, 74, 76).

Thus, there is little evidence suggesting that properly executed squats harm healthy knees. It is possible that, because squatting is difficult both mechanically and metabolically, some coaches and athletes find an excuse to avoid its use.

Injuries: Strange occurrences in the weight room or you had to be there to believe it.

The following cases were observed by the authors and actually occurred. While this section has been written with cynicism, there are important points to consider.

Case #1

The scene: A typical cluttered weight room with a slick linoleum floor.

The victim: Harried young college student (male, about 20 yrs) who had been studying for finals. He had not slept at all the previous night and was rumored to have taken amphetamines.

The accident: Victim arrived at the weight room at about 6:00 P.M. and immediately began overhead pressing movements to exhaustion. Amazingly, the victim began to lose consciousness with the bar overhead, ran forward (and several other directions), and slipped on a plate left on the floor. Bar and hand hit the rack on a bench, severing his right index finger just distal to the second joint. The victim and part of his finger retrieved from the corner were rushed to the hospital, where the finger was reattached. Both are doing well.

Moral: If you can't figure this one out, don't go in the weight room.

Case #2

The scene: Typical unsupervised high school weight room.

The victim: High school football player (lineman) wearing a St. Christopher medal (no shirt on).

The accident: The victim proceeded to perform bench presses while bridging and violently bouncing the bar off his chest. Somehow the medal moved under the bar. It was driven into his pectoral muscle, sideways, about ½ inch. It was duly removed by a teammate (after the victim had yelled get it out several dozen times).

Moral: Don't wear St. Christopher medals or other jewelry while lifting and perform bench presses correctly.

Case #3

The scene: A typical college weight room.

The victim: A male college student intent on finding ways to lift more than he should be lifting.

The accident: The victim was performing bench presses to exhaustion. His technique was to drop the bar on his chest and throw it overhead by violently bridging. About the third repetition with about 300 pounds, both feet slipped. Before his spotters could catch the weight, he managed to stop the bar from hitting the floor by catching it with his mouth.

Moral: There are easier ways to develop a nice wide smile.

Case #4

The scene: A typical college weight room in the early 1970s.

The victim: A trusting college-aged male (a freshman, we think).

The accident: After watching several powerlifters use an early model hip and back machine loaded with several hundred pounds, the young victim asked, "Can I try that?" Older, wiser lifters decided to teach young victim a lesson by helping him into the machine and releasing the lever arm. Young victim was promptly folded into a pretzel, injuring his back and several other parts.

Moral: If you don't know how to use the equipment, don't use it.

Case #5

The scene: Athletic weight room at a major university.

The victim: A pentathlete on the women's track team.

The accident:	The weight-stack on the Nautilus leg extension machine hangs up (weights are suspended on the guide bars). The victim, rather than tapping the top of the weights, put her hand under the weight stack and pushed up. The weights mashed her hand nearly flat.
Moral:	If you don't know how to repair equipment, find someone who does.

Case #6

The scene:	Almost everyone has seen or heard of this one.
The victim:	Young college quasi-bodybuilder (Phenotypic mutant—no legs). "This thing'll never break."
The accident:	Neglecting to notice the frayed cable or the sign stating "DO NOT USE," the victim proceeded to perform lat work using a lat machine. The cable broke, knocking the young bodybuilder senseless.
Moral:	Make sure the equipment is in working order, and learn how to read.

All of these six accidents could have been avoided by simply taking proper precautions and using common sense. Stupidity is never a substitute for anything.

Free Weights Versus Machines

Using machines is often assumed to be safer than using free weights, but there is no evidence for this assumption. Injuries occur using both (10, 74). Injuries usually occur during improperly performed exercises or when equipment is misused.

In the authors' experience, severe injuries rarely occur during maximum attempts, regardless of equipment mode. They are more likely to occur when a lifter is fatigued or moves out of proper position. They often occur during sets to exhaustion when a lifter is moving out of position trying to produce one last repetition.

Periodic inspection of equipment is a must. Olympic bars should rotate properly, pullies should turn, weight stacks should not hang up, and cables should not be frayed. The authors are aware of several injuries, including a mashed hand (weight stack hung up) and assorted bumps on the head (lat machine cable broke), that were a result of poor maintenance. A few minutes of inspection each week may reduce injuries substantially.

Injuries Summary

There are several thousand weightlifters and powerlifters in the United States and more than a million worldwide. There are several million weight trainers in the United States alone. Considering the number of people who engage in weight training, serious injury is uncommon. A review of the medical literature and empirical data suggests that the following are reasonable conclusions:

1. Most weight-training injuries are of the overuse type (tendinitis, bursitis, etc.).

2. Most serious injuries occur during heavy eccentric movements, fatigued states, or moving out of position, and not during maximum (1 RM) attempts.

3. Proper spotting can reduce injuries.

4. Proper equipment maintenance can reduce injuries (see Chapter 11).

Finally, we must question why many weight-training (and other sports) exercises, especially squatting, are widely held to be dangerous, without solid evidence. It is possible that anytime someone offers evidence, even speculative, that something is harmful, this evidence is more widely disseminated than beneficial evidence and therefore has a great potential to be believed. Weight training is no more harmful than many other physical activities and is less so than most.

Summary

1. Weight-training volume may be estimated by keeping track of repetitions. Intensity is estimated by the average weight (mass) lifted.

2. Volume and intensity can be varied over the macrocycle, mesocycle, and microcycle. Variation can be based on the 1RM or on projected goals for sets and repetitions (see Appendix A).

3. Frequency of training (related to total volume) should be as high as possible (without overtraining) for maximum strength-power gains.

4. Workout length is a function of the number of sets, repetitions, and rest time. The time taken to complete a set and the rest time between sets is a function of the trainee (athletes versus nonathletes), specific goals and recovery powers.

5. Exercise order in a priority system should begin with large muscle mass exercises and proceed to small muscle mass exercises.

6. Generally, a weight-training program should center around large muscle mass/multi-segment exercises. These exercises provide a greater energy cost and a greater carryover to both athletic and daily tasks.

7. High force and/or high speed movements appear to be more effective in producing strength-power gains than purposefully slow movements.

8. Proper warmup is necessary to reduce injury and to enhance subsequent performance. Warmup should be of both a general and specific nature.

9. Proper breathing is necessary to prevent injuries and to enhance performance.

10. Children can safely gain strength from properly planned and supervised resistive training programs.

11. Serious injuries are not common as a result of weight-training. Injuries can be reduced by adhering to simple safety precautions (see Chapter 11).

References

1. Abraham, W. M. 1977. Factors in delayed muscle soreness. *Medicine and Science in Sports* 9:11–20.

2. Allen, T. H., E. C. Andersson, and W. H. Langham. 1960. Total body potassium and gross body composition in relation to age. *Journal of Gerontology* 15:348–357.

3. Allman, F. L. 1982. Commentary on: Weight training-related injuries in the high school athlete. *The American Journal of Sports Medicine* 10:1–5.

4. American Academy of Pediatrics Committee on Sports Medicine. 1983. Weight training and weight lifting: Information for the pediatrician. *The Physician and Sports Medicine* 11:157–161.

5. Anderson, T., and J. T. Kearney. 1982. Effects of three resistance training programs on muscular strength and absolute and relative endurance. *Research Quarterly for Exercise and Sport* 53:1–7.

6. Andzel, W. D., and B. Gutin. 1976. Prior exercise and endurance performance: A test of the mobilization hypothesis. *Research Quarterly* 47:269–276.

7. Asmussen, E. 1956. Observations on experimental muscle soreness. *Acta Rheumatologica Scandinavica* 1:109–116.

8. Asmussen, E., and O. Boje. 1945. Body temperature and capacity for work. *Acta Physiologica Scandinavica* 10:1–22.

9. Astrand, P. O., and K. Rodahl. 1970. *Textbook of Work Physiology* (2nd ed.). New York: McGraw-Hill.

10. Banks, A. 1981. Injuries in strength-power activities. Presentation at the NSRC Strength-Power Symposium II, Auburn, Alabama, April 2–3.

11. Bansil, C. K., G. D. Wilson, and M. H. Stone. 1985. Role of protaglandins E and F2 alpha in exercise induced delayed muscle soreness (Abstract). *Medicine and Science in Sports and Exercise* 17:276, (Also doctoral dissertation, Auburn University, 1984).

12. Bansil, C. K., G. D. Wilson, M. H. Stone, and D. Blessing. 1982. Biochemical changes accompanying exercise induced muscle soreness. *Proceedings: World Federation for Physical Therapy IXth International Congress.* Stockholm, May 1982, pp. 35–39.

13. Bernard, R. J. 1975. Warm-up is important for the heart. *Sports Medicine Bulletin* (ACSM) January.

14. Bernard, R. J., G. W. Gardner, N. V. Diaco, et al. 1973. Cardiovascular responses to sudden strenuous exercise heartrate, blood pressure and ECG. *Journal Applied Physiology* 34:833–837.

15. Bernard, R. J., R. V. MacAlpin, A. A. Kettus, and G. D. Buckberg. 1973. Isometric responses to sudden strenuous exercise in healthy men. *Circulation* 48:936–942.

16. Berger, R. A. 1962. Comparisons of static and dynamic strength increases. *Research Quarterly* 33:329–333.

17. Berger, R. A. 1963. Comparative effects of three weight-training programs. *Research Quarterly* 34:396–398.

18. Berger, R. A. 1965. Comparison of the effect of various weight training protocols on strength 36:141–146.

19. Binkhorst, R. A., L. Hoofd, and C. A. Vissers. 1977. Temperature and the force-velocity relationship of human muscle. *Journal of Applied Physiology* 42:471–475.

20. Bishop, P. 1983. Biological determinants of the sex difference in muscular strength. Doctoral dissertation, University of Georgia.

21. Brady, T. A. 1982. Weight training-related injuries. *American Journal of Sports Medicine* 10:1–5.

22. Brown, P. T. 1972. Effects of three intensity levels of warm-up on the reaction and speed of movement in the baseball swing. *Completed Research in HPER* 14:107.

23. Brown, E. W., and R. G. Kimball. 1983. Medical history associated with adolescent powerlifting. *Pediatrics* 75:636–44.

24. Butler, D. L., E. S. Grood, F. R. Noyes, and R. F. Zernicke. 1978. Biomechanics of ligaments and tendons. *Exercise and Sport Sciences Reviews* 6:125–181.

25. Chandler, J. 1986. Knee stability related to the squat. Doctoral dissertation, Auburn University.

26. Chandler J., D. Wilson, M. Stone, and J. McMillan. 1985. The effect of the full squat exercise on knee stability (Abstract). Conference Abstracts of the 1985 SEACSM meeting, Boone, N.C., January.

27. Chechick, A., Y. Amit, A. Israeli, and H. Horoszowski. 1982. Recurrent rupture of the achilles tendon induced by corticosteroid injection. *British Journal of Sports Medicine* 16:89–90.

28. Cherniak, A. V., and L. N. Melnikova. 1974. The training of a skilled athlete. *1974 Soviet Weightlifting Yearbook.* Moscow: Fizkultura i Sport Publishing House. (Translated from Russian by B. W. Scheithauer, M.D.).

29. Chui, E. F. 1964. Effects of isometric and dynamic weight training exercises upon strength and speed of movement. *Research Quarterly* 35:246–257.

30. Clarke, D. H. 1943. Adaptations in strength and muscular endurance resulting from exercise. *Exercise and Sport Sciences Review* 1:73–102.

31. Clarke, D. H., and F. M. Henry. 1961. Neuromotor specificity and increase speed from strength and development. *Research Quarterly* 32:315–325.

32. Coaches Roundtable. 1984. Prevention of athletic injuries through strength training and conditioning. *National Strength and Conditioning Association Journal* 4:14–19.

33. Coaches Roundtable. 1984. The squat and its application to athletic performance. *National Strength and Conditioning Association Journal* 6(3):10–22.

34. Coyle, E. T., D. C. Feiring, T. C. Rutkis, et al. 1981. Specificity of power improvements through slow and fast isokinetic training. *Journal of Applied Physiology* 51:1437–1442.

35. Darden, E. 1975. Frequently asked questions about muscle, fat and exercise. *Athletic Journal* 56:85–89.

36. Delikov, S. I., and N. N. Saksonov. 1976. The growth of the strength of the leg muscles in relation to the tempo of performance of the squats. *1976 Soviet Weightlifting Yearbook.* (Translated from Russian by W. J. Bryce).

37. DeLorme, T. L., and A. L. Watkins. 1978. Techniques of progressive resistance exercise. *Archives of Physical Medicine* 29:263.

38. deVries, H. A. 1959. Effects of various warm-up procedures on 100-yard times of competitive swimmers. *Research Quarterly* 30:11–20.

39. deVries, H. A. 1965. Muscle tonus in postural muscles. *American Journal of Physical Medicine* 44:275–291.

40. deVries, H. A. 1966. Quantitative electromyographic investigation of the spasm theory of muscle pain. *American Journal of Physical Medicine* 45:459–470.

41. deVries, H. A. 1968. EMG fatigue curves in postural muscles. A possible etiology for idiopathic low back pain. *American Journal of Physical Medicine* 47:175–181.

42. deVries, H. A. 1968. Immediate and long term effects of exercise upon resting action potential level. *Journal of Sports Medicine and Physical Fitness* 8:1–11.

43. deVries, H. A. 1980. *Physiology of Exercise* (third edition). Dubuque: Wm. C. Brown, 488–500.

44. DiRosa, M., J. P. Giroud, and D. A. Willoughby. 1971. Studies of the mediators of the acute inflammatory response induced in rats in different sites by carageenan and turpentine. *Journal of Pathology* 104:15–29.

45. Drinkwater, B. L. 1984. Women and exercise: Physiological aspects. *Exercise and Sport Science Reviews* 12:30–51.

46. Drozdov, V. F., and N. Y. Petrov. 1983. Physical development and health of weightlifting students. *1983 Soviet Weightlifting Yearbook.* (Translated from Russian by Andrew Charniga). Moscow: Fizkultura: Sport Publishers, Moscow, pp. 51–54.

47. Dummer, G. M., D. H. Clarke, P. Vaccaro, et al. 1985. Age-related differences in muscular strength and muscular endurance among female masters swimmers. *Research Quarterly* 56:97–110.

48. Dvorkin, L. S., and A. S. Medvedev. 1983. Age changes in muscular strength and speed-strength qualities. *1983 Weightlifting Yearbook.* (Translated from Russian by Andrew Charniga). Fizkultura: Sport Publishers, Moscow, pp. 43–51.

49. Edington, N., and V. R. Edgerton. 1976. *The Biology of Physical Activity.* Boston: Houghton Mifflin Co.

50. Enoka, R. M. 1979. The pull in Olympic weightlifting. *Medicine and Science in Sports* 11:131–137.

51. Fitzgerald, B., and G. P. McLatchie. 1980. Degenerative joint disease in weightlifters, fact or fiction? *British Journal of Sports Medicine* 14:97–101.

52. Friden, J., M. Sjostrom, and B. Ekblom. 1981. A morphological study of delayed muscle soreness. *Experientia* 37:506–507.

53. Friden, J., M. Sjostrom, and B. Ekblom. 1983. Myofibriller damage following intense eccentric exercise in man. *International Journal of Sports Medicine* 4:170–176.

54. Gardner, G. 1963. Specificity of strength changes of the exercised and non-exercised limb following isometric. *Research Quarterly* 34:98–101.

55. Garhammer, J. 1976. Force plate analysis of the snatch lift. 1976. *International Olympic Lifter* 3:22–27.

56. Garhammer, J. 1979. Performance evaluation of olympic weightlifters. *Medicine and Science in Sports* 11:284–287.

57. Garhammer, J. 1980. Power production by Olympic weightlifters. *Medicine and Science in Sports and Exercise* 12:54–60.

58. Garhammer, J. J. 1982. Strength Training. New York, Time/Life Inc.

59. Genety, J., and E. Brunet-Gadj. 1976. La tendinite achilleenne du sportif EMC first edition. *Apparei Locomotere* 151, C10, 101–102.

60. Greg, A., A. Mital, and S. S. Asfour. 1980. A comparison of isometric strength and dynamic lifting capability. *Ergonomics* 23:13–27.

61. Gettman, L. R., and J. J. Ayres. 1982. Aerobic changes through 10 weeks of slow and fast speed isokinetic training (Abstract). *Medicine and Science in Sports* 10:47.

62. Gettman, L. R. and M. Pollock. 1981. Circuit weight-training: A critical review of its physiological benefits. *Physician and Sports Medicine* 9:45–60.

63. Gillam, G. M. (In Press). Effects of frequency of weight training on muscle strength enhancement. *Journal of Sports Medicine and Physical Fitness.*

64. Gowers, W. R. 1904. Lumbago: Its lessons and analogues. *British Medical Journal* 1:117–121.

65. Gowitzke, B. A., and M. Milner. 1980. *Understanding the Scientific Basis of Human Movement* (2d edition). Baltimore: Williams, and Wilkins, p. 109.

66. Greenberg, R. S. 1972. The effects of hot packs and exercises on local blood flow. *Physical Therapy* 52:273–278.

67. Hakkinen, K., and P. V. Komi. 1981. Effects of different combined concentric and eccentric muscle work regimens and maximal strength development. *Journal of Human Movement Studies* 7:33–34.

68. Hakkinen, K., and P. Komi. 1982. Alterations of mechanical characteristics of human skeletal muscle during strength training. *European Journal of Applied Physiology* 50:161–172.

69. Hakkinen, K., and P. V. Komi. 1982. Specificity of training-induced changes in strength performance considering the integrative functions of the neuro-muscular system. *World Weightlifting* 3:44–46.

70. Hallen, L. G. and O. Lindahl. 1965. Rotation of the knee joint in experimental injury to the ligaments. *Acta Orthopedica Scandinavica* 36:400–407.

71. Hay, J. G., J. G. Andrews, and C. L. Vaughan. 1983. Effects of lifting rate on elbow torques exerted during arm curl exercises. *Medicine and Science in Sports Exercise* 15:63–71.

72. Hejna, W. F., A. Rosenberg, D. J. Butunusis, and A. Krieger. 1982. The prevention of sports injuries in high school students through strength training. *National Strength and Conditioning Association Journal* 4:28–31.

73. Hellebrandt, F. A., and S. J. Howtz. 1956. Mechanism of muscle training in man. *Physical Therapy Reviews* 36:371–383.

74. Herrick, R. 1981. Injuries in Strength-Power Activities. Presentation at the NSRC Strength-Power Symposium II, Auburn, Alabama, April 2–3.

75. Herrick, R. 1982. Personal Communication, August.

76. Herrick, R., M. Stone, and S. Herrick. 1984. Injuries in strength-power activities with special reference to the knee. Presentation at the 1984 Olympic Scientific Congress (Sports Medicine section), Eugene, Oregon, July.

77. Hettinger, T., and E. A. Mueller. 1953. Muskelleistung and muskel training. *Arbeitsphysiologic* 15:111–126.

78. Hill, A. V. 1956. The design of muscles. *British Medical Bulletin* 12:165.

79. Hough, T. 1902. Ergogenic studies on muscle soreness. *American Journal of Physiology* 7:76–92.

80. Johnson, B. L., and J. W. Ademczyk. 1975. A program of eccentric and concentric strength training. *American Corrective Therapy Journal* 29:13–16.

81. Karim, S. M. M. (Ed.). 1976. *Advances in Prostaglandin Research.* Baltimore: University Park Press.

82. Karlssen, J. 1979. Localized muscular fatigue: Role of muscle metabolism and substrate depletion. *Exercise and Sports Science Reviews* 7:1–42.

83. Karpovich, P. V., M. Singh, and C. M. Tipton. 1970. The effect of deep knee squats upon knee stability. *Teor Praxe tel Vvch* 18:112–122. (See reference #26).

84. Keul, J. 1973. The relationship between circulation and metabolism during exercise. *Medicine and Science in Sports* 5:209–219.

85. Klein, K. 1960. A preliminary study of the dynamics of force as applied to knee injury in athletics and as related to the supporting strength of the involved musculature. *Journal of the Association for Physical and Mental Rehabilitation* 14(2):33–37.

86. Klein, K. K. 1961. The deep squat exercise as utilized in weight training for athletes and its effect on the ligaments of the knee. *Journal of the Association for Physical and Mental Rehabilitation* 15:6–11.

87. Klein, K. K. 1962a. The knee and the ligaments. *The Journal of Bone and Joint Surgery* 44–A:1191–1193.

88. Klein, K. K. 1962b. An instrument for testing the medial and lateral collateral ligament stability of the knee. *American Journal of Surgery* 104:768–772.

89. Klein, K. K. 1962c. Squat right. *Scholastic Coach* 32(2):36–38, 70–71.

90. Kosar, B., and R. M. Lord. 1983. Overuse injury in the young athlete. *The Physician and Sports Medicine* 11:116–122.

91. Kontani, P. T., N. Ichikawa, W. Wakabayashi, et al. 1971. Studies of spondylolysis found among weightlifters. *British Journal of Sports Medicine* 6:4–7.

92. Krejci, K., and P. Mock. 1979. *Muscle and Tendon Injuries in Athletes.* Chicago: Yearbook Medical Publishers. (Translated by D. LeVay).

93. Kulund, D. N., J. B. Dewey, C. E. Brubaker, and J. R. Roberts. 1978. Olympic weightlifting injuries *The Physician and Sports Medicine* pp. 111–119, November.

94. Lander, J., B. Bates, and P. De Vita. 1985. The kinetics of the squat exercise using a modified center of mass bar (Abstract). *Medicine and Science in Sports and Exercise* 17:222, 1985. (See also J. Lander, Doctoral dissertation, University of Oregon, 1984).

95. Lander, J., and R. Herrick. 1985. Weight-training injuries and prevention. Symposium presented at the 1985 SEACSM meeting, Athens, Georgia, January.

96. Larsson, L., and J. Karlsson. 1978. Isometric and dynamic endurance as a function of age and skeletal muscle characteristics. *Acta Physiologica Scandinavica* 104:129–136.

97. Larsson, L., G. Grimoy, and J. Karlsson. 1979. Muscle strength and speed of movement in relation to age and muscle morphology. *Journal of Applied Physiology* 46:451–456.

98. Laritcheva, K. A., N. I. Yalovaya, V. I. Shubin, and P. V. Smirnov. 1978. Study of energy expenditure and protein needs of top weightlifters. *Nutrition, Physical Fitness and Health* 7:155–163.

99. Laros, G. S., C. M. Tipton, and R. R. Cooper. 1971. Influence of physical activity on ligament insertions in the knees of dogs. *Journal of Bone and Joint Surgery* 53A:275–286.

100. Laubach, L. 1976. Comparative muscular strength of men and women: A review of the literature. *Aviation, Space and Environmental Medicine* 47:534–542.

101. Leach, R. E., S. James, and S. Wasilewski. 1981. Achilles tendinitis. *The American Journal of Sports Medicine* 9:93–98.

102. Lear, J. 1980. *Weightlifting*. East Ardsley: EP Publishing Limited.

103. Legwold, G. 1982. Does lifting weights harm a prepubescent adolescent athlete? *The Physician and Sports Medicine* 10:141–144.

104. Lind, A., and G. McNicol. 1967. Muscular factors which determine the cardiovascular responses to sustained and rhythmic exercise. *Canadian Medical Association Journal* 96:706–714.

105. Lindh, M. 1979. Increase of muscle strength from isometric quadriceps exercises at different knee angles. *Scandinavian Journal of Rehabilitation Medicine* 11:33–36.

106. Litch, S. 1982. *Therapeutic Heat and Cold* (J. F. Lehmann, Ed.). Baltimore: Williams and Wilkins, pp. 1–30. (See also reference 12).

107. Logan, G. A. 1960. Differential applications of resistance and resulting strength measured at varying degrees of knee extension. Doctoral dissertation, University of South Carolina.

108. Logan, G. R., W. C. McKinney, W. Rowe, and J. Lumpe. 1966. Effect of resistance through a throwing range-of-motion on the velocity of a baseball. *Perceptual and Motor Skills* 23:55–58.

109. MacQueen, I. J. 1954. Recent advances in the technique of progressive resistance exercise. *British Medical Journal* 11:1193–1198.

110. Martin, B. J., S. Robinson, D. L. Wiegman, and L. H. Aulick. 1975. Effect of warm-up on metabolic responses to strenuous exercise. *Medicine and Science in Sports* 7:146–149.

111. Mason, T. A. 1977. Is weightlifting deleterious to the spines of young people? *British Journal of Sports Medicine* 5:61.

112. McIntosh, D. 1974. The structure and nature of strength. *Journal of Sports Medicine and Physical Fitness* 14:168–176.

113. McKethan, J. F., and J. L. Mayhew. 1974. Effects of isometric, isotonics and combined isometric-isotonics on quadriceps strength and vertical jump. *Journal of Sports Medicine and Physical Fitness* 14:224–229.

114. McMorris, R. O., and E. C. Elkins. 1954. A study of production and evaluation of muscular hypertrophy. *Archives of Physical Medicine* 35:420–426.

115. Mellornica, H., and G. Hansen. 1971. Conditioning. In *Encyclopedia of Sports Science and Medicine*. (L. A. Larson, Ed.). New York: MacMillan.

116. Meyers, E. J. 1971. Effect of selected exercise variables on ligament stability and flexibility of the knee. *The Research Quarterly* 42:411–422.

117. Miller, R. I. 1981. The science and practice of warming-up. *Athletic Journal* 31:28–30.

118. Morehouse, C. A. 1970. Evaluation of knee abduction and adduction; the effect of selected exercise programs on knee stability and its relationship to knee injuries in college football. Final Project Report RD-2815-M, U.S. Department of Health, Education, and Welfare, Pennsylvania State University.

119. Murphy, B. 1983. Personal communication. (Strength Coach, McNeese State University, Louisiana).

120. National Strength and Conditioning Association. 1985. Position paper on prepubescent strength training. *National Strength and Conditioning Association Journal* 7(4):27–29.

121. Noyes, F. R. 1977. Functional properties of knee ligaments and alterations induced by immobilization. A correlative biomechanical and histological study in primates. *Clinical Orthopaedics and Related Subjects* 123:210–242.

122. Noyes, F. R., N. S. Nussbaum, P. J. Torvik, and S. Cooper. 1975. Biomechanical and ultrastructural changes in ligaments and tendons after local corticosteroid injections. Proceedings of the Orthopaedic Research Society, 1975 Annual Meeting. *Journal of Bone and Joint Surgery* 57A:876.

123. NSCA Roundtable. 1985. Strength training and conditioning for the female athlete. *National Strength and Conditioning Association Journal* 7(8):10–29.

124. O'Bryant, H. 1982. Periodization: A hypothetical training model for strength and power. Doctoral Dissertation, Louisiana State University.

125. O'Bryant, H.S. (In press). Strength Training for the Young. *North Carolina AHPERD Journal,* Spring 1986.

126. O'Shea, J. P. 1966. The development of strength and muscle hypertrophy through selected weight programs. *Research Quarterly* 37:95–107.

127. O'Shea, J. P. 1976. *Scientific Principles and Methods of Strength Fitness.* (Second edition). Reading, Massachusetts: Addison-Wesley.

128. Osternig, L. R., B. T. Bates, and S. L. James. 1977. Isokinetic and isometric torque force relationships. *Archives of Physical Medicine and Rehabilitation* 58:254–256.

129. Pacfreo, B. A. 1959. Effectiveness of warm-up exercise in junior high school girls. *Research Quarterly* 30:202–213.

130. Rasch, P. J. 1982. *Weight Training.* (4th Edition). Dubuque, Iowa: Wm. C. Brown.

131. Richards, D. K. 1968. A two-factor theory of the warm-up effect in jumping performance. *Research Quarterly* 39:668–673.

132. Rochelle, R. H., V. Skubic, and E. D. Michael. 1960. Performance as affected by incentive and preliminary warm-up. *Research Quarterly* 31:499–504.

133. Rozenek, R. 1985. The effect of an acute bout of resistance exercise and self-administered anabolic steroids on Plasma levels of LH, Androgen, ACTH, cortisol, lactate and Psychological factors in athletes Doctoral Dissertation, Auburn University.

134. Sale, D., and D. MacDougall. 1981. Specificity in strength training: A review for the coach and athlete. *Sports* March:1–6.

135. Scala, D., J. McMillan, D. Blessing, et al. (In press). Metabolic cost of a preparatory phase of training in weightlifting: A practical observation. *Journal of Applied Sport Sciences Research.* (See also D. Scala, master's thesis, Auburn University, 1983.)

136. Schantz, P., E. Randall-Fox, W. Hutchinson, et al. 1983. Muscle fiber type distribution, muscle cross-sectional area and maximal voluntary strength in humans. *Acta Physiologica Scandinavica* 117:219–226.

137. Schmidbleicher, D., and G. Haralombie. 1981. Changes in contractile properties of muscle after strength training in man. *European Journal of Applied Physiology* 46:221–228.

138. Schwane, J. A., S. R. Johnson, C. B. Vandenakker, and R. B. Armstrong. 1983. Delayed onset of muscular soreness and plasma CPK and LDH activities after downhill running. *Medicine and Science in Sports and Exercise* 15:51–56.

139. Servidio, F. J., R. L. Bartels, R. L. Hamlin, et al. (Abstract). *Medicine Science Sports and Exercise* 17:288.

140. Sewall, L., and L. Micheli. (In press). Strength training for children. *Journal of Pediatric Orthopedics* 6:(2).

141. Silvester, L. J., C. Stiggins, C. McGowen, and G. R. Bryae. 1982. The effect of variable resistance and free-weight training programs on strength and vertical jump. *National Strength and Conditioning Association Journal* 3(6):30–33.

142. Skeoch, D. U. 1981. Spontaneous partial subcutaneous ruptures of the tendo achillis. *The American Journal of Sports Medicine* 9:20–22.

143. Smith, L. E., and L. D. Whitley, 1965. Influence of strengthening exercise on speed of limb movement. *Archives of Physical Medicine and Rehabilitation* 46:772–777.

144. Smith, L. E., and L. D. Whitley. 1966. Influence of three different training programs on strength and speed of limb movement. *Research Quarterly* 37:132–142.

145. Smith, L. L., W. G. Herbert, and F. C. Gwazdauskas. 1985. Markers of inflammation in delayed muscle soreness (DMS) (Abstract). Proceedings of the SEACSM meeting, Athens, Georgia, January, p. 12.

146. Stone, M. H., and J. Garhammer. 1981. Some thoughts on strength and power (the Nautilus controversy). *National Strength and Conditioning Association Journal* 3(5):36–50.

147. Stone, M. H., R. L. Johnson, and D. R. Carter. 1979. A short term comparison of two different methods of resistance training on leg strength and power. *Athletic Training* 14:158–160.

148. Stone, M. H., H. O'Bryant, J. Garhammer, et al. 1982. A theoretical model of strength training. *National Strength and Conditioning Association Journal* 3(5):36–39.

149. Stone, M. H., G. D. Wilson, D. Blessing, and R. Rozenek. 1983. Cardiovascular responses to short-term olympic style weight-training in young men. *Canadian Journal of Applied Sports Science* 8:134–139.

150. Stowers, T., J. McMillan, D. Scala, et al. 1983. The short-term effects of three different strength-power training methods. *National Strength and Conditioning Association Journal* 5(3):24–27.

151. Swegan, D. B. 1957. The comparison of static contraction with standard weight-training in effect on certain movement speeds and endurance. Doctoral dissertation, Pennsylvania State University.

152. Tipton, C. M., R. D. Matthes, J. A. Maynard, and R. A. Corey. 1975. The influence of physical activity on ligaments and tendons. *Medicine and Science in Sports* 7:165–175.

153. Tipton, C. M., R. D. Matthes, and D. S. Sandage. 1974. In situ measurements of junction strength and ligament elongation in rats. *Journal of Applied Physiology* 37:758–761.

154. Thomas, P. 1983. Personal communication, District Weightlifting Coach, Portland, Oregon.

155. Todd, T. 1984. Karl Klein and the squat. *National Strength and Conditioning Association Journal* June-July, 26–31, 67.

156. Tucker, R. M. 1957. Effects of isometric strength development on speed and power of resisted and non-resisted horizontal arm flexion. Masters thesis, Pennsylvania State University. (Also reference 126.)

157. Van Huss, W. D., N. R. Albrecht, and R. Hagerrman. 1962. Effect of overload warm-up on the velocity and accuracy of throwing. *Research Quarterly* 33:472–475.

158. Vermeil, A. (San Francisco 49'ers). 1980. Personal communication. (Also Al Miller, Denver Broncos, 1986.)

159. Viidik, A. 1973. Functional properties of collagenous tissues. *International Review of Connective Tissue Research* 6:127–215.

160. Vitale, M. E. 1976. A comparison of knee stability related to skeletal maturation of the knee among male and female skiers, swimmers, and non-athletes. Unpublished masters thesis, University of Colorado.

161. Volkov, V. M., G. E. Milner, and G. V. Nosov. 1975. The after effects of training loads. *1975 Soviet Weightlifting Yearbook.* Moscow: Fiskultura i Sport Publishing House. (Translated from Russian by B. W. Scheithauer, M.D.)

162. Vorobyev, A. V. 1978. *Weightlifting.* Budapest: International Weightlifting Federation. (Translated from Russian by W. J. Brice.)

163. Ward, L. 1970. The effects of the squat jump exercise on the lateral stability of the knee. Unpublished masters thesis, Pennsylvania State University, University Park.

164. Wescott, W. L. 1982. *Strength Fitness.* Boston: Allyn and Bacon.

165. Zernicke, R. F. (Department of Physiology, UCLA). 1982. Personal communication. (Also notes from advanced biomechanical classes at UCLA.)

166. Zernicke, R. F., J. J. Garhammer, and F. W. Jobe, 1977. Human patellor-tendon rupture. *Journal of Bone and Joint Surgery* 59A:179–185.

167. Zinovieff, A. N. 1959. Heavy-resistance exercise, the "Oxford Technique." *British Journal of Physical Medicine* 14:129.

| Chapter
| 8

Practical Testing
and Progress Evaluation

Determining Anaerobic Power

Muscular power is commonly used to indicate the ability to release maximum muscular force in the shortest possible time (10). With speed being the chief component, there is a composite interplay of both muscular strength and utilization rate of anaerobic energy sources (ATP-CP and anaerobic glycolysis) (18). The extent to which a person can develop power is a prime determinant of success for many athletes (jumpers, sprinters, shotputters, throwers, for example) (8, 14, 16, 18). The most common power test used is the vertical jump, although climbing stairs and various sprint distances also have been used. Consequently, the legs have generally been used as the primary indicator of one's power and potential (9, 12). Still other tests can be administered for determining anaerobic capacity.

Vertical Jump

The displacement of a person's center of mass will yield some measure of the person's jumping ability. There are a number of sophisticated and sport-specific ways this can be done, limited only by one's time constraints and creativity. Many of these procedures include confounding mechanical variables that are hard to control from one person to another. Nevertheless, an argument is sometimes made for the use of *spiking* type jumps from an approach (short run or jab step); such a measurement may be useful for certain sport-specific applications (11). But a standard approach that eliminates some of these confounding variables may be preferable in the classroom if not for general athletic use.

One widely accepted and easily administered method for vertical jump measurement is the *Sargent jump* (18). First a *base height* must be determined by having the person stand upright against a wall (or vertical jumping board), feet flat on the floor. The distance to the finger tip with both arms extended upward is then measured. Next, the subject is instructed to jump straight up, using a natural countertype movement, as high as possible for one practice followed by three trial jumps. **No jab step or preparatory run is permitted,** but the subject is encouraged to use both arms for unrestricted movement of the upper body. By measuring the maximum height reached by the subject's finger tips as she or he touches the wall, and taking the difference between base height and the best height of three trials, the subject's maximum vertical jump can be obtained.

Caution should be exercised when using the vertical jump to determine relative gain in improvement or validation of training programs. **The vertical jump is not a valid indication of leg and hip power unless mass and time are taken into consideration.** The use of the Lewis formula (18) will do this where:

$$\text{power index (kg–m/sec)} = \sqrt{\text{vertical jump (m)}} \times \text{body weight (kg)} \times \sqrt{4.9}$$

(See Appendix F for microcomputer program.)

Reading from the nomogram in Figure 8–1 will yield a quick estimate of a *power index* in kilogram-meters per second. By connecting the person's body weight (pounds) and their vertical jump (inches or centimeters) with a straight edge, power (kg-m/sec) can be read at the intercept. Example: for a 165-pound person (left scale) jumping 20 inches (right scale), the power index (read from the middle scale) is 118 kg-m/sec.

Margaria-Kalamen Test

The Margaria stair climbing test, which was later modified by Kalamen, is another test of anaerobic power (23, 25). The procedure specifies the need for a timer interfaced with two switchmat devices. In the absence of such equipment, careful timing with a stopwatch could provide a reasonable substitute with some concession for reduced accuracy.

The subject begins from a standing start 6 m in front of a staircase (Figure 8–2). Using his/her own discretion, the subject runs up the stairs as fast as possible, taking three stair steps at a time (the average stair step is approximately 174 mm high). A power output can be determined by recording the time (to the nearest 0.01 sec) required to climb from the 3rd step to the 9th step and applying the following formula, where power (P) is equal to the weight of the person (W) multiplied by the vertical height between the 3rd and 9th stair steps (D), the quantity divided by the time (t) from the 3rd to the 9th stair step.

$$[P = (W \times D) / t]$$

An example for a 190-lb (86.2 kg) athlete in which (D) equals 1.05 m and (t) equals 0.40 sec would be: P = (86.2 × 1.05) / 0.40 = 226.3 kg-m/sec. Power output norms for the Margaria-Kalamen test are listed in Table 8–1 for both men and women.

Caution must be exercised when administering any stair climbing test. Individuals who are out of shape or less experienced may have difficulty with foot placement, which might result in a fall and increased chance for injury. If predisposition for injury exists, another test should be selected.

Table 8–1. Norms for the Margaria-Kalamen test (18, 24, 25).

	Age, years		
Class	15–20	20–30	30–40
MEN			
Poor	<113 kg-m/sec	<106	<85
Fair	113–149	106–139	85–111
Average	150–187	140–175	112–140
Good	188–224	176–210	141–168
Excellent	>224	>210	>168
WOMEN			
Poor	<92 kg-m/sec	<85	<65
Fair	92–120	85–111	65–84
Average	121–151	112–140	85–105
Good	152–182	141–168	106–125
Excellent	>182	>168	>125

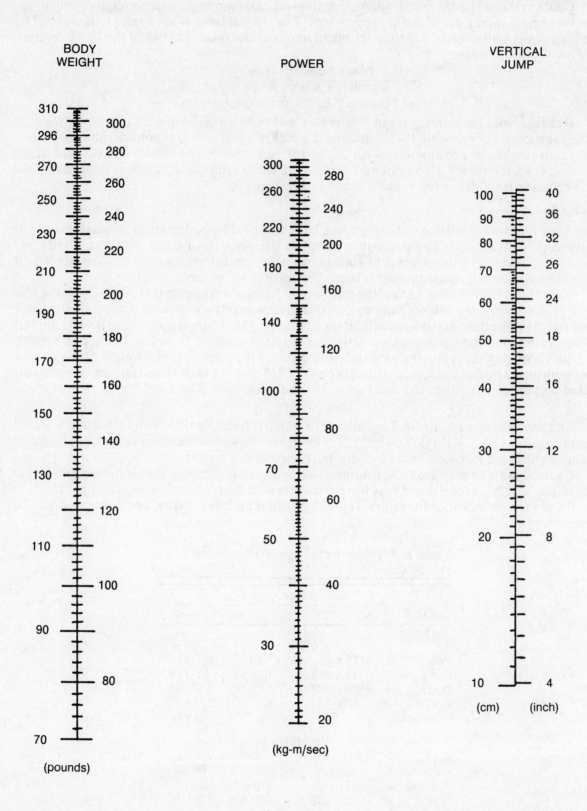

BODY
WEIGHT

POWER

VERTICAL
JUMP

(pounds)

(kg-m/sec)

(cm)   (inch)

Figure 8–1. Nomogram for Estimate of Leg and Hip Power from Vertical Jump and The Lewis Formula.

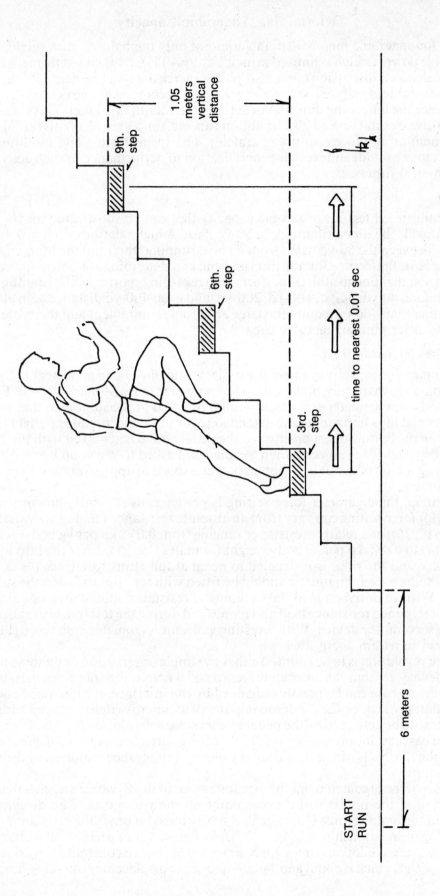

Figure 8–2. Margaria-Kalamen Procedure for Estimate of Power.

Determining Anaerobic Capacity

The capacity for anaerobic metabolism includes not only the ballistic movements described under anaerobic power (which is limited principally by ATP-CP bioenergetic mechanisms; see Chapter 2 for detailed discussion), but also places increasingly more demand on the energy pathways of anaerobic glycolysis. Anaerobic glycolysis becomes a prime determinant of maximal performance the longer the duration of activity (greater than 10 sec). This is the nature of many competitive events (basketball, the 800-m run, etc.) and may be of interest in the conditioning and monitoring process of many athletes. The sprint testing and modified Wingate ergometer test may provide indexes for generalization to performance in such activities if not for overall physical fitness.

Sprint Testing

An easily administered test for anaerobic capacity that can be substituted for the Margaria-Kalamen method is the timed running of a 50-yd dash. A high relationship (r = 0.97) has been found to exist between the 50-yd dash (from a 15-yd running start) and the Margaria-Kalamen test for power (23). Preference for a sprint run time as a determinant for power output can be supported if generalization to athletic performance regarding sport-specific running patterns is desired. Therefore, 40-yd, 60-yd, 100-yd, 200-yd, and even 400-yd distances can also be used. Distances farther than 400 yd require too large an aerobic component and therefore would not be suitable for determining anaerobic capacity.

Modified Wingate Ergometer Test

This test for anaerobic capacity requires the subject, who must be in good health, to perform a bicycle ride on a mechanically braked bicycle ergometer (e.g., Monark Bicycle Ergometer). Prior to the test, the ergometer seat height should be fitted to the subject so that while seated with shoulders and hips horizontal, the extended leg of the subject retains a slight bend in the knee joint when the bottom-most position of the pedal stroke is achieved with the heel resting squarely on the pedal. The subject is then weighed and asked to warm up by pedaling for 2–4 min against a light load of about 0.5 kilopon (kp) at a speed of approximately 50 pedal revolutions per minute (33).

After warmup, the ergometer force setting is predetermined while someone pedals fast. The protocol for force setting can vary from an absolute resistance ranging anywhere from 3–5 kp per person (7, 26), or a relative resistance ranging from 0.075 kp per kg body weight (2, 33) for females (19) to 0.085 kp per kg body weight for males (19, 21). After the initial setting the pedal is blocked and the rider is instructed to pedal at full effort for 20 sec (6). To facilitate maximal effort, the bicycle ergometer should be fitted with toe clips to fasten the subject's feet to the pedals. With an initial no-load start, ergometer resistance should then be quickly adjusted to the predetermined resistance load and monitored during the test by a testing assistant or a fast response servomotor device. With a testing assistant, ergometer resistance can be maintained constant to within about 2% (26).

Each pedal revolution is to be counted either by simple observation or by some mechanical or electrical device (26) that can accurately record pedal revolutions per 5-sec period. Data resolution and testing ease can be greatly enhanced by the interface of high speed counters and data manipulation devices (i.e., microcomputers) to microswitches placed either on the ergometer frame to be activated by the pedal arm with each revolution (yields anaerobic power per 6 m for an easy resolution of at least 0.01 sec (26), or attached every 90 degrees around the perimeter of the flywheel (with a potential of yielding 4 times the resolution of the previously mentioned setup).

The gearing of the ergometer and the circumference of the flywheel are such that one complete revolution of the pedals will move a point on the rim 6.0 m. The displacement per revolution and the braking force (1 kp equals 9.8 Newtons (N) times the resistance setting) are constant. Using the relationship of force and displacement, the experimental work/crank revolution is the number of kilopons times 9.8 N times 6.0 m times a constant for work done by the transmission (1.09), which is about another 9% above the displacement-braking function (26).

Example (for experimental work, no-load start):
If 6 kp is used as a resistance setting, the equation becomes
(6.0 kp) (9.8 N) (6.0 m) (1.09) = 385 joules (J)

Work remains constant per revolution and can be readily expressed as cumulative, varying only as a function of time (work versus time plot). Since, however, the time to complete one crank cycle will increase as the rider tires, work must be calculated by the following (26):

$$W_{(t)} = W_o [1 - \exp (- t / T_o)]$$
Where W_o and T_o are parameters dependent
on the rider's physical capabilities.

An approximation to instantaneous power in watts (W) can then be calculated by merely dividing the constant work (experimental)/revolution by the change in time. By differentiation of the above equation for calculated work and by taking the logarithm, power can be linearized (assuming exponential dependence) (26).

Whereas:
$$P_{(t)} = (W_o / T_o) \exp (- t / T_o)$$
and:
$$\ln P = \ln (W_o / T_o) - t / T_o$$

Power can be tabulated against time at the midpoint of each interval. The logarithm of power is then calculated and also plotted versus time. An example of the data for one crank revolution using the given values would be (26):

Crank revolution	= 1
Time (sec)	= 0.516
Experimental work (joules)	= 385
Calculated work (joules)	= 426
Midtime (sec)	= 0.258
Experimental power (Watts)	= 745
ln power (log power)	= 6.61

With the appropriate calculations, data from this test can yield indexes for: *peak power* (highest power output per unit of time), *time to peak power* (how quickly maximum power outputs were achieved), and *anaerobic capacity* (total work performed during the entire 20-sec period). Such information may provide the basis for individual as well as team status regarding relative level of initial conditioning, validation of training programs, and prediction of performance on related sport-specific tasks.

Determining Muscular Strength and Endurance

Muscular strength is the ability to exert force, or more specifically, the contractive force of muscle, as a result of a single maximal effort (9). Dynamic strength is commonly measured by the amount of weight that can be successfully lifted once (one repetition maximum; 1RM).

Muscular endurance is often regarded as the muscle's ability to perform work by holding a maximum contraction for a given length of time (static) or by continuing to move a submaximal load (dynamic) (9). For testing purposes, we limit our attention to dynamic muscular endurance and dynamic strength.

One Repetition Maximum Tests

A common method for assessing dynamic muscular strength is determination of a 1RM. The usual lifts used to monitor upper and lower body capabilities are the *supine bench press* and *parallel squat,* respectively (see Chapter 10 for illustrations and descriptions of technique). Some consider 1RM tests to be the preferred measure of dynamic strength (3, 28, 34, 38), particularly in the absence of isokinetic devices. Others have proposed variations in day-to-day measures of 10% to 20% (1), although some have reported smaller variation in both females (1.5% to 11.6%) and males (5.3% to 9.3%) (13). To minimize variation that could result from acute adaptations in the neuromuscular apparatus (1), the subject should perform a series of increasingly intense warmup lifts leading to the 1RM attempt as follows:

Step 1: The subject should warm up with one set of 5–10 reps with something light (40% – 60% of perceived maximum).

Step 2: After approximately a minute of rest and some light stretching, the subject should perform one set of 3–5 reps with something a little heavier (60% –80% of perceived maximum).

Step 3: After another minute of rest and some additional stretching, the subject should perform 3–4 1 rep attempts spaced by 30–60 sec rest with increments of increasingly heavier weights.

Step 4: The subject should attempt a 1RM. If this attempt is successful with specified technique (see Chapter 10), the subject should make additional 1RM attempts, spaced by brief rest pauses, with increased weight until he or she fails to complete the next lift.

Step 5: The last successfully executed lift weight is recorded as the individual's 1RM in that lift (parallel squat, supine bench press, etc.).

To maintain an adequate margin of safety, caution must be exercised. For heavy 1RM attempts, lifting racks (parallel squat, etc.) and double spotters should be used so that in the event of lifting failure, the lifter would not be injured during a fall. Furthermore, if 1RM procedures are to be performed by novice lifters or individuals who possess questionable technique, **subjects should be provided with instruction on proper mechanics and allowed adequate practice to acquire proficient technique well in advance of attempting initial strength measures.**

Once a 1RM has been recorded, this value can be divided by each individual's body weight and/or lean body weight to equate subjects in a group for differences in body composition. Another method that has sometimes been used in olympic lifting competition to achieve fairness between competitors of different body weights is the Hoffman formula (29). Table 8–2 gives the body weight (obtained prior to competition and rounded to nearest whole pound) and corresponding coefficient. A score is determined by multiplying the coefficient of the individual's body weight times her/his lifting total.

This approach can be particularly helpful in comparing the efforts of groups of individuals who are not matched in body weight or 1RM, and therefore may have application in the classroom or in athletic settings.

The Hoffman formula is based on some rather old data (1937) and is considered by some (30) to be biased against light lifters. Another, more recent method of comparing performances of olympic-style weightlifters of different body classifications is the *Sinclair formula* (30). This updated version of the Hoffman formula, first proposed in 1976, is based on the following:

1. The average for the world record in each weight class (excluding super heavy) was calculated for 1973 through 1975.

2. The common logs of this average total and of the body weights were plotted and fitted for a parabolic curve by least squares statistics.

3. All results were normalized about the 110-lb class.

A simplistic example of the relationship between body weight (X) in kilograms of a lifter and his lifts (Y) can be expressed by the formula:

$$Y = K (X)^{2/3}$$

This formula can be updated frequently to more accurately reflect current lifting records by revising the proportionality constant (K). Thus the formula can never become antiquated. Due to the ever-changing nature of the correction coefficients, the presently available data may be irrelevant soon after this book is published and therefore are omitted. Current coefficient value tables are available in the *United States Weightlifting Federation (USWF) Weightlifting Handbook.*

Table 8-2. Hoffman coefficients for men (modified from O'Shea, 1969) (29).

Body weight (pounds) and corresponding coefficient				
110—1.000	131—.885	151—.800	171—.736	191—.692
111—.994	132—.881	152—.797	172—.734	192—.691
112—.988	133—.876	153—.793	173—.731	193—.689
113—.982	134—.872	154—.790	174—.729	194—.688
114—.976	135—.867	155—.786	175—.726	195—.686
115—.970	136—.863	156—.783	176—.724	196—.685
116—.964	137—.858	157—.779	177—.721	197—.683
117—.958	138—.854	158—.776	178—.719	198—.682
118—.952	139—.849	159—.772	179—.716	199—.680
119—.946	140—.844	160—.769	180—.714	200—.679
120—.940	141—.840	161—.766	181—.712	201—.678
121—.935	142—.836	162—.763	182—.710	202—.677
122—.930	143—.832	163—.760	183—.708	203—.676
123—.925	144—.828	164—.757	184—.706	204—.675
124—.920	145—.824	165—.754	185—.704	205—.674
125—.915	146—.820	166—.751	186—.702	206—.673
126—.910	147—.816	167—.748	187—.700	207—.672
127—.905	148—.812	168—.745	188—.698	208—.671
128—.900	149—.808	169—.742	189—.696	209—.670
129—.895	150—.804	170—.739	190—.694	210—.669
130—.890				211—.668
				212—.667
				213—.666

Maximum Based on Repetitions

If, after due consideration of the previously mentioned safety factors, the regard for injury supersedes use of standard 1RM procedures, other alternatives may be explored. Although less accurate, estimates of 1RM may be determined from attempts using submaximal weight. Therefore, subjects would lift as much weight as possible in order to achieve a given number of repetitions. The resistances used in this procedure are lower and consequently may present less of a hazard for potential injury.

Table 8–3 illustrates how some have used this approach to approximate 1RM's based on a certain number of repetitions. For example, if you can lift 225 lb for 4 repetitions on the leg press, then your projected 1RM is 250 lb.

As the number of repetitions used in this procedure increases, the accuracy of prediction for 1RM may decrease. Also, some variation may exist in prediction from one person to another because of differences in muscle mass and total body weight. Other influences can include age, gender, the duration and nature of previous training, and a variety of biomechanical and anthropometric factors.

Percentage of Maximum Repetitions

Having previously determined 1RM values for each individual, a measure for relative local muscle endurance can be assessed by ascertaining the maximum number of repetitions performed with a percentage of 1RM during one set of a specified exercise. For example, endurance of the leg and hip extensor muscles can be evaluated by ascertaining the maximum number of repetitions performed during one set of parallel squats using a weight 80% of 1RM for each individual.

After an initial warmup and adequate rest, each subject would be asked to perform as many repetitions as possible with resistance set at a specified percentage (80% is a reasonable load) of previously established 1RM. To insure maximum effort, the performance of these maximum repetition tests should occur 1–3 days after 1RM procedures.

Table 8–3. Percentage of 1RM by repetitions (modified for Landers, 1985) (24).

100%/ 1 rep	94%/ 3 reps	88%/ 5 reps	75%/ 10 reps
100 lb.	94 lb.	88 lb.	75 lb.
125	117	110	94
150	140	132	113
175	163	154	131
200	187	176	150
225	210	198	169
250	233	220	188
275	257	242	206
300	280	264	225
325	303	286	244
350	327	308	263
375	350	330	281
400	373	352	300
425	396	374	319
450	420	396	338
475	443	418	356
500	466	440	375

See Appendix F for microcomputer program.

Practical Tests

It may not always be feasible to establish 1RM and therefore percentage of maximum repetitions. Such tests can often be impractical because of insufficient time to acquire technical lifting skills prior to testing. Furthermore, 1RM tests may slightly increase the potential for injury if spotting techniques, mechanics, or supervision is questionable.

Other methods can be used to evaluate general muscular strength and endurance and may have an application for courses oriented to *lifetime physical activity.* O'Shea (29) has outlined several such procedures, most notably *the practical test,* that can be administered in the absence of 1RM measures. The practical test consists of exercises performed with a set percentage of body weight for as many repetitions as possible. Presented in Table 8–4 are four exercises, their required percentage of body weight, and the proposed points awarded for repetitions executed.

Table 8–4. Practical test points (modified from O'Shea, 1969) (29).

Repetitions completed	Parallel squat (100%)	Sit-up (20%)	Bench press (80%)	Pull-up (body weight)
0	35	34	38	23
1–5	36–40	35–39	39–43	26–35
6–10	41–45	40–44	44–48	37–45
11–15	46–50	45–49	49–53	47–55
16–20	51–55	50–54	54–58	57–65
21–25	56–60	55–59	59–63	67–75
26–30	61–65	60–64	64–68	77–85
31–35	66–70	65–69	69–73	87–95
36–40	71–75	70–74	74–78	97–105
41–45	76–80	75–79	79–83	107–115
46–50	81–85	80–84	84–88	117–125
51–55	86–90	85–89	89–93	127–135
56–60	91–95	90–94	94–98	137–145
61–65	96–100	95–99	99–103	147–155

The resulting scores can be tallied and used as the basis for ranking each individual according to performance on the test. In a class setting, points can then be assigned for the practical test in reference to class rank and the maximum points of this test can be weighted toward the total grading scheme.

Absolute muscular endurance also can be evaluated by simply using a set submaximal weight and performing as many repetitions as possible. This method of testing for muscular endurance is strongly related to the 1RM (1, 18, 27).

Evaluating Skill

A composite score for both strength and technique can encourage student lifters to develop good technique while lifting reasonable amounts of weight, thus providing a challenge to extend the limits of their abilities. Point systems for lifting proficiency and technique checklists are presented here as two instruments for skill evaluation.

Lifting Proficiency

The practical test can be a helpful aid in classifying individuals according to their general level of muscular strength and endurance. A more specific tool may be needed for evaluating lifting proficiency in regard to a certain lift. O'Shea (29) proposed a point system for lifting proficiency similar to the one presented in Table 8–5. Such a classification system takes into account individual differences in body weight and provides point values for meeting a set criterion poundage on a specific lift.

Such a point value system can serve to motivate the student lifter and at the same time provide an objective standard for grade assignment. This proficiency grade would represent points achieved for strength and could be added to points awarded for technique evaluation, yielding a composite value for skill evaluation.

Technique Evaluation

As students are instructed on correct lifting technique (see chapter 10 for illustrations and descriptions) a mental, if not written, checklist can be helpful. A brief breakdown of items related to correct form and lifting mechanics can be assigned point values and therefore serve as a useful guide for performance expectations and subsequent skill evaluation. Some suggested guidelines are listed in Tables 8–6 through 8–9.

Evaluating Physique and Body Composition

In weight training, as in other vigorous physical activities, body composition changes can be a major concern and motivating force for the participant. Therefore, evaluating body composition should not be disregarded when assessing related performance variables.

Body composition is a function of body weight, which can be partitioned into the associated components of body fat and lean body weight by estimating fat from skinfolds (15, 32) or by hydrostatic weighing techniques (4, 37). Alterations in muscle hypertrophy and loss of body fat can produce changes in one's physique. These changes can be quantitatively expressed in girth measures of selected muscle sites and can, in some cases, demonstrate the positive effects of weight training more vividly than body composition.

Hydrostatic Weighing

Measurement of specific gravity is perhaps one of the most accurate but difficult methods for estimating fat content of the human body. One can determine specific gravity by applying Archimedes' principle, which states that an object immersed in water loses an amount of weight equal to the weight of the water that is displaced. Relative densities of fat and other body tissues can be calculated and partitioned into percentages of body fat and lean body mass.

A standard procedure commonly used for underwater weighing is a protocol previously described by Brozek, Grande, Anderson, and Keys (5) and later modified by Wilmore and Behnke (35). This procedure requires values for both *dry* (on land) body weight and *wet* (underwater) weight. Since buoyancy is affected by air in the lungs, the lungs must be as nearly

Table 8–5. Proficiency chart (modified from O'Shea, 1969) (29).

Body weight	Points*					
	30	**25**	**20**	**15**	**10**	**5**
SNATCH						
< 123	130	120	110	100	90	80
124–132	135	125	115	105	95	85
133–148	140	130	120	110	100	90
149–165	145	135	125	115	105	95
166–181	150	140	130	120	110	100
182–198	160	150	140	130	120	110
199–220	170	160	150	140	130	120
> 221	180	170	160	150	140	130
CLEAN AND JERK						
< 123	175	165	155	145	135	125
124–132	185	175	165	155	145	135
133–148	195	185	175	165	155	145
149–165	205	195	185	175	165	155
166–181	215	205	195	185	175	165
182–198	225	215	205	195	185	175
199–220	235	225	215	205	195	185
> 221	245	235	225	215	205	195
SUPINE BENCH PRESS						
< 123	180	170	160	150	140	130
124–132	195	185	175	165	155	145
133–148	210	200	190	180	170	160
149–165	225	215	205	195	185	175
166–181	240	230	220	210	200	190
182–198	255	245	235	225	215	205
199–220	270	260	250	240	230	220
> 221	285	275	265	255	245	235
PARALLEL SQUAT						
< 123	260	250	240	230	220	210
124–132	275	265	255	245	235	225
133–148	290	280	270	260	250	240
149–165	305	295	285	275	265	255
166–181	320	310	300	290	280	270
182–198	335	325	315	305	295	285
199–220	350	340	330	320	310	300
> 221	365	355	345	335	325	315

*An additional point is awarded for every 5 lb. over maximum lifted.
Note: Students who are repeating the course for additional credit, may choose to add the following to the criterion weight to be lifted; 10 lb. for snatch, 15lb. for clean and jerk, 15 lb. for bench press, and 15 lb. for squat.

Table 8-6. Snatch checklist.

	Technique description	Point value
A.	Starting position: head up, wide grip, back straight, shoulders slightly over bar.	0–3
B.	Pull: head up, double knee bend, bar close to body, high extension.	0–7
C.	Hop: quickness, balance, straight back, low squat, shoulder flexibility.	0–7
D.	Stand-up: lateral and forward stability, body alignment, elbows straight, bar horizontal.	0–3
	Total points:	0–20

Table 8-7. Clean and jerk checklist.

	Technique description	Point value
A.	Starting stance: head up, back straight, shoulders slightly over bar.	0–3
B.	Pull: head up, double knee bend, bar close to body, high extension.	0–5
C.	Clean: quickness, balance, straight back, low squat, elbows high in front, body alignment and balance on stand-up, bar horizontal.	0–5
D.	Jerk: high arm position, leg drive, split depth and quickness, body alignment and balance on stand-up, bar horizontal.	0–7
	Total points:	0–20

Table 8-8. Parallel squat checklist.

	Technique description	Point value
A.	Starting stance: body alignment and stability, lateral and forward balance.	0– 3
B.	Down phase: head up, back straight, feet flat, parallel position, no excess lean, controlled speed, bar horizontal.	0– 8
C.	Up phase: head up, back straight, feet flat, no excess lean, synchronous hip and shoulder raise, continuous even motion, bar horizontal, lateral alignment.	0– 7
D.	Ending position: body alignment and balance, complete knee and hip extension, bar horizontal.	0– 2
	Total points:	0–20

Table 8-9. Supine bench press checklist.

Technique description	Point value
A. Starting position: alignment under bar, no exaggerated back arch, feet flat.	0-5
B. Down phase: control speed, no exaggerated back arch, bar horizontal, lateral stability, bar touch chest, no bounce.	0-6
C. Up phase: stay in "groove," no exaggerated back arch, bar horizontal, lateral stability, full even elbow extension, continuous motion, feet flat on floor.	0-9
Total points:	0-20

deflated as possible (through maximal expiration) while submerged, with corrections made for residual volume. Residual volume (the amount of air you can never completely force out of the lungs) can be estimated from vital capacity (the most air exhaled after a maximal inhalation) as measured with a *spirometer* at standard barometric pressure and temperature. A constant for males (0.24) or females (0.28) can then be multiplied by the vital capacity (VC) to yield a residual volume (RV) estimate so that subsequent calculations can correct for lung buoyancy.

Body density can be computed with the following formula (see Appendix C):

When: BD = Body density
DW = Dry weight in kilograms
WD = Water density
WW = Underwater weight in kilograms
RV = Residual volume
TW = Tare weight in kilograms (extra weight belt)

$$BD = DW / \{ [DW - (WW - TW)] / WD \} - RV$$

Percentage fat can then be determined by the following calculations: (5)

$$\% \text{ fat} = [(4.570 / \text{body density}) - 4.142] \times 100$$

Lean body mass (LBM) also can be separated from total body weight with the following formula:

$$\text{Lean body mass (LBM)} =$$
$$\text{total body weight} - [(\% \text{ fat} / 100) \times \text{total body weight}]$$

See Appendix F for hydrostatic weighing microcomputer program.

Even though they are quite accurate, such hydrostatic procedures are time consuming, awkward to administer, and require special apparatus. A more practical approach may be to use percentage fat predictions from skinfolds.

Skinfold Measurements

A reasonable estimate of body fat can often be made by measuring the thickness of subcutaneous fat from selected skinfold sites on the body. Specific equations can then be used to predict total body fat from these weighted values. Determining percentage of fat in this manner can be quick and easy, but the experience and accuracy of the tester are of utmost importance.

Skinfold measurements obtained in this manner must be taken at very precise locations. Some frequently used sites are described below:

1. *Biceps:* This fold is to be taken longitudinally along the midline of the anterior aspect of the biceps brachii, approximately halfway between the shoulder and the elbow, measured in a relaxed, extended position (Figure 8–3).

2. *Triceps:* This fold is measured longitudinally on the back of the arm midway between the acromion and olecranon processes, with the elbow extended (Figure 8–4).

3. *Subscapular:* This skinfold runs downward and laterally in the natural fold of the skin from the inferior angle of the scapula (Figure 8–5).

4. *Suprailiac:* This fold lies vertically over the iliac crest in the midaxillary line (Figure 8–6).

5. *Thigh:* This fold is measured vertically along the anterior midline of the thigh, halfway between the inguinal ligament and the top of the patella, taken in a relaxed, extended position (Figure 8–7).

To avoid tester variation, the same individual should take all skinfold measurements. A fold of skin and subcutaneous tissue is picked up between the thumb and forefinger of the left hand and lifted firmly away from the underlying muscle. The fold should be held between the fingers throughout the duration of the measurement. The calipers are applied to the fold by slowly allowing the caliper faces to come together on either side of the fold at a point 1 cm below the fingers such that pressure on the fold at the point measured is exerted by the caliper and not the fingers. The value registered on the calipers sometimes decreases throughout the reading and can be stopped by taking a firmer pinch with the fingers of the left hand. If this problem continues, the reading should be taken immediately after application of caliper pressure. At least two measurements should be obtained at each site, read to the nearest millimeter; variations between duplicate trials should not be more than 5%.

A number of skinfold calipers are available commercially. Four of them are listed, along with suppliers and approximate cost, in Table 8–10.

Of the instruments presented, only the Lange caliper has a constant tension independent of skinfold thickness. In a recent comparison test on 800 subjects ranging from elementary to college age, no significant difference was found between the Lange, Fat-O-Meter, or Adipometer devices (20). The purpose of the study was to determine the relative variability of the four instruments with respect to all subjects, grade level, and a *wear factor.* Each instrument was manually compressed 10,000 times after an initial testing session and prior to a second test session to create a consistent and substantial wear factor. Only the Slim-Guide was found to have

Table 8–10. Skinfold test instruments (20).

Device	Supplier	Approximate cost
Lange	J. A. Preston Corporation 71 Fifth Avenue New York, NY 10011	$160
Slim-Guide	Slim-Guide/Creative Health Products 110 Saddle Ridge Rd. Plymouth, MI 48170	$ 20
Fat-O-Meter	Health and Education Services Division of Novel Products Inc. 80 Fairbanks St., Unit 12 Addison, IL 60101	$ 10
Adipometer	Ross Laboratories 625 Cleveland Avenue Columbus, OH 43216	$ 3

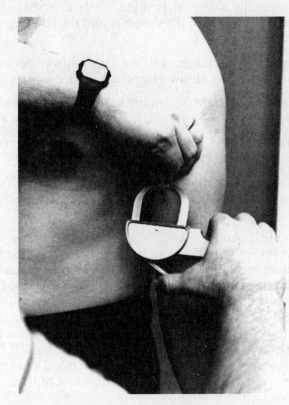 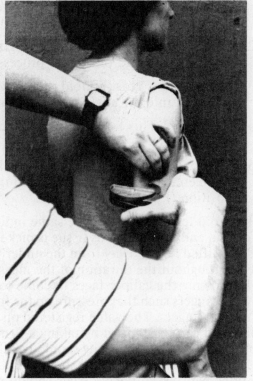

Figure 8–3. Site for Biceps Skinfold. **Figure 8–4.** Site for Triceps Skinfold.

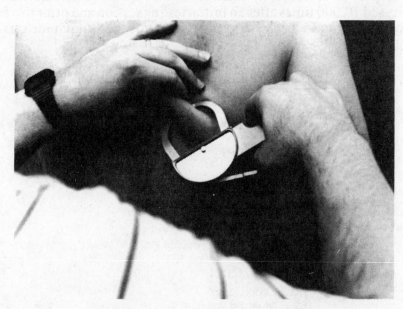

Figure 8–5. Site for Subscapular Skinfold.

Figure 8–6. Site for Suprailiac Skinfold.

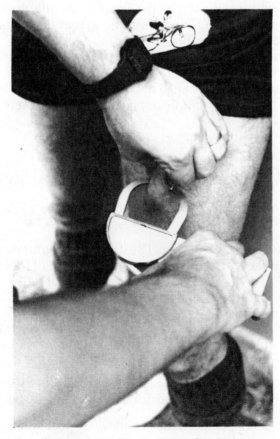

Figure 8–7. Site for Thigh Skinfold.

readings significantly different from the other devices. The results of this study are presented to aid in the selection of skinfold measuring devices based on the scope of application needed and financial support available.

Percentage of body fat can be determined by adding together the four skinfold (triceps, biceps, subscapula, and suprailiac) measurements (15) and using the chart presented in Appendix C. A shorter method requiring only two skinfolds for males aged 18–26 (thigh and subscapular) and two for females aged 17–25 years (tricep and suprailiac) uses prediction formulas for body density and percentage fat as follows (32):

$$\text{Body density} =$$
$$1.0764 - [.00081 \text{ (suprailiac)}] - [.00088 \text{ (triceps)}] \text{ for females}$$
$$1.1043 - [.00133 \text{ (thigh)}] - [.00131 \text{ (subscapular)}] \text{ for males}$$
$$\text{Percentage fat} =$$
$$100 [(4.570 / \text{body density}) - 4.142]$$

Nomograms derived from these calculations are presented in Figures 8–8 and 8–9 for easy estimation of percentage fat. (See Appendix F for more precise microcomputer programs). Note that predictions of body density from equations derived from skinfolds are specific to the population from which the equations were originally derived (29, 36). The skinfold predictions presented here, though widely used, are generalized equations for the specified age group. Furthermore, preliminary data and empirical evidence (27) suggest that due to weight-resistive training, tissue adaptation of certain sites may deem them inappropriate for use in skinfold procedures. For example, in females, the tricep skinfold appears to thicken in response to weight-resistive training of the upper body, even though body fat (determined hydrostatically) decreases (27). In men who weight train, the muscles of the upper leg (quadriceps) may hypertrophy and cause the skin and fascia to become so taut that obtaining accurate measurements at the thigh skinfold is impossible.

Based on a compilation of numerous studies, some typical values for percentage of body fat for various athletes are presented in Table 8–11. It may be desirable to calculate a target weight to facilitate long-term planning for a change in body composition. The following formulas are presented here for calculating *fat weight, lean body mass, target weight,* and *target weight loss* (17):

$$\text{Fat weight (FW)} =$$
$$(\% \text{ fat} / 100) \times \text{total body weight}$$
$$\text{Lean body mass (LBM)} = \text{total body weight} - \text{FW}$$
$$\text{Target weight (TW)} =$$
$$\text{LBM} / [1.00 - (\text{Target} \% \text{ fat} / 100)]$$
$$\text{Target weight loss} = \text{present weight} - \text{TW}$$

For example, if a person presently weighs 185 lb at 22% fat and wants to get his/her percentage of fat down to 16%, he/she would have a present fat weight of $[(22 / 100) \times 185] = 40.7$ lb, a lean body mass of $[185 - 40.7] = 144.3$ lb, a target weight of $\{144.3 / [1.00 = (16 / 100)]\} = 171.8$ lb, and consequently a target weight loss of $[185 - 171.8] = 13.2$ lb. (See Appendix F for simple microcomputer programs).

A person who attempts to achieve a *target weight* or *target percentage of fat* may also experience an undesirable loss of lean body mass, which indicates loss of muscle. To guard against such negative consequences, the following guidelines should be kept in mind (17, 18):

1. One pound of fat has a caloric equivalent of about 3500 to 3600 Kcal, so a deficit of at least 3500 Kcal must be established for every pound of fat weight lost.

2. A weight loss of 2 to 3 lb per week may be ideal. To lose weight at a rate faster than this, the person may sacrifice lean body mass and experience a significant decrease in work capacity.

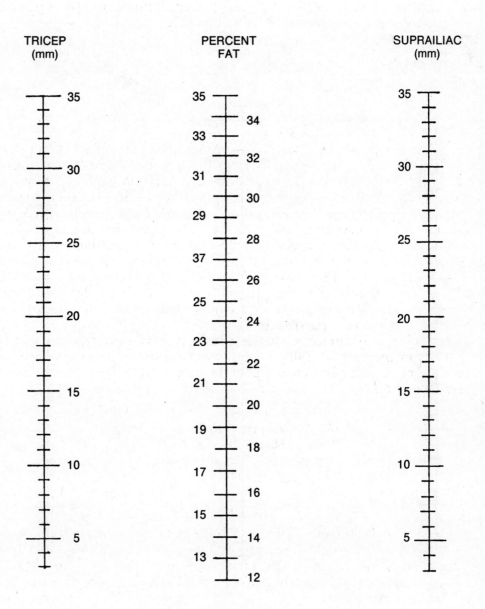

Figure 8-8. Nomogram for Estimate of Percent Fat in Females from Tricep and Suprailiac Skinfolds. (derived from Sloan and Weir formula) (26)

Note: See Appendix F for Simple Microcomputer Program.

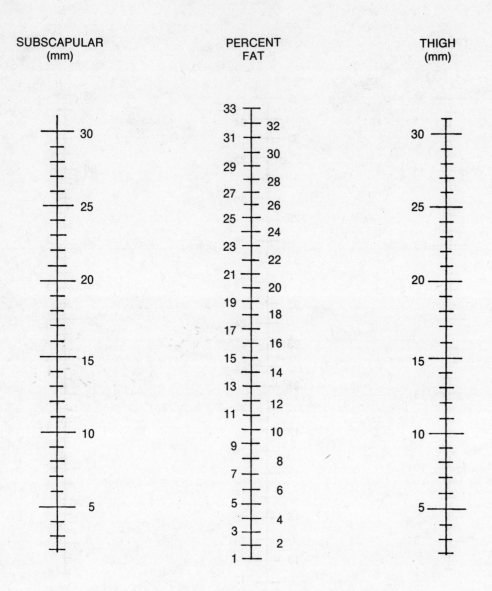

Figure 8–9. Nomogram for Estimate of Percent Fat in Males from Subscapular and Thigh Skinfolds. (derived from Sloan and Weir formula) (26)

Note: See Appendix F for Simple Microcomputer Program.

Table 8–11. Percentage of body fat among athletes (17, 18, 34).

Sport	Males	Females
Track and field athletes		
Runners	6.3–9.9	12.5–19.2
Discus and javelin throwers	13.9–19.6	24.9–25.0
Shotputters	16.5–19.6	20.0–28.0
Sprinters and hurdlers	8.4	13.4–19.3
Weight Lifters		
Powerlifters	15.0–15.6	—
Olympic lifters	8.0–12.2	—
Body builders	8.3– 8.4	—
Wrestlers	3.7–11.7	—
Swimmers		
Sprinters	5.0–9.5	14.6
Middle distance	5.0–11.8	24.1–26.3
Skiers		
Cross-country skiers	7.2–12.5	16.1–21.8
Alpine skiers	7.4–14.1	20.6
Baseball players	11.8–14.2	—
Football players		
Backs	9.4–12.4	—
Linebackers	13.4–14.0	—
Quarterbacks and kickers	14.4	—
Offensive linemen	15.6–18.5	—
Defensive linemen	18.2–18.5	—
Gymnasts	4.6–10.1	15.3–15.5
Jockeys	14.1	—
Hockey players	8.4–15.1	—
Basketball players	9.0–13.5	20.7–26.9
Volleyball players	12.0	17.9–25.3
Rowers	8.5–11.0	14.0
Cyclists	8.8–10.3	15.4
Tennis players	15.2	24.2
Canoeists	12.4	—
Nonathletes	16.0	25.5

3. The caloric deficit should represent both decreased caloric intake from the diet and increased metabolic demand from exercise.

4. The daily caloric deficit should not exceed 2000 Kcal.

5. Losing *fat weight* while gaining *lean body mass* (muscle) is not an easy task and requires careful selection of foods to maintain an adequate nitrogen balance (see Chapter 2) and proper planning of a superior training program.

6. An excess of about 2500 Kcal is needed to gain a pound of lean body mass.

7. To insure that weight gain is *lean body weight* and not extra fat, the gain in body weight should not exceed 2 to 3 lb per week.

Girth Measurements

Measurement of body girth and circumference alteration through training can provide a valuable supplement to if not a substitute for percentage of fat measures. Often adaptations in the physique offer vivid indications of positive changes in muscle hypertrophy and/or decrease in body fat. The procedure is simple and quick, and it can be conducted in the weight room, in a dressing facility, or at home. A *Gulick tape* is commonly used for girth measures, although any simple flexible tape can be used, with some concession for accuracy. The Gulick tape is equipped with a spring loaded attachment that permits a slight amount of constant tension on the tape and therefore more consistent measurements.

The procedure for girth measures does not require any special training or practice, but it does rely on precise landmarks and perpendicular tape orientation to the longitudinal axis of the segment for accurate comparisons between pretest and post-test data. The following sites and their descriptions are suggested for use in weight-training applications (Figure 8–10).

1. *Neckgirth:* The circumference immediately below the larynx.

2. *Chest:* Located at nipple level in males (Figure 8–10), and at the level of maximum circumference in females. Two measurements should be taken; one at the end of a normal expiration, and another at the end of a maximal inspiration.

3. *Bicep girth:* Two measures can be taken; one at the location of greatest circumference when flexed, and another when the arm is fully extended and the muscles are relaxed.

4. *Forearm girth:* Measured at the point of greatest circumference between the elbow and wrist in an extended, relaxed position.

5. *Waist girth:* Located at the level of the umbilicus and just above the iliac crests, to be taken after a normal expiration.

6. *Hip girth:* Measured at a level of maximal protrusion of the buttocks.

7. *Thigh girth:* Located at the point of maximal circumference midway between the hip and knee.

8. *Calf girth:* Located at the level of maximal calf circumference between the knee and ankle.

Girth measures are recommended at the onset of training to serve as base values for comparison and again at various intervals throughout the training cycle to reveal changes in physique. Improvements can be based on the relative change between test periods. Girth measures, as well as skinfolds, can be affected by the profusion of blood into muscular tissue, so all anthropometric data should be taken prior to the beginning of the exercise session.

Evaluating Cardiovascular Fitness

Cardiovascular efficiency involves the ability of the body to take in and utilize oxygen during recovery and during prolonged production of energy. Level of cardiovascular fitness is then a function of the ability of the vessels to transport blood and the capability of the heart to pump blood. In addition, maximal oxygen utilization relates to the rate of oxygen metabolism at the tissue level. The possible effects of weight-resistive training are discussed in Chapter 3. Presented here are two practical tests for work capacity and, therefore, predictive cardiovascular efficiency: the 12-minute walk/run (22) and the Harvard step test (4).

The 12-Minute Walk/Run

The performance objective of this test is to run or walk as far as possible in 12 minutes. A level running course of known distance, preferably a track, is required.

The runners assume a position behind a starting mark and begin upon an audible or visual signal. They run and/or walk as many laps as possible around the course within the 12 minutes allotted. Spotters are advised to maintain a count of each lap and any additional portion of a lap not completed before the signal to stop. Total yards completed can be determined by multiplying the number of completed laps by the distance of each lap, plus the number of additional yards. Comparisons can be made between participants on rank or total score in addition to pretest and post-test trials.

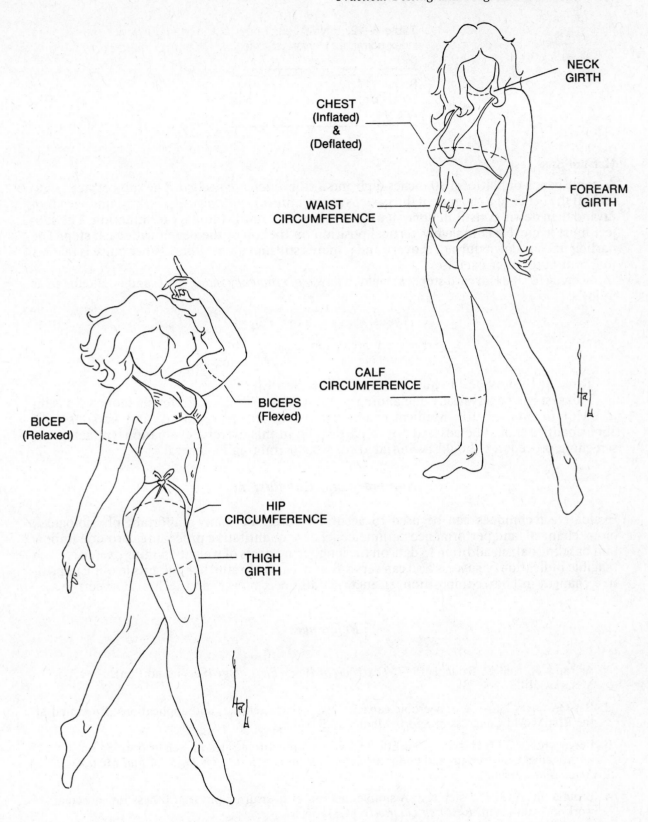

Figure 8–10. Sites for Selected Girth Measurements.

Table 8–12. Physical efficiency index norms for Harvard step test (22).

Below 50 . . . . Poor
50 to 80 . . . . Average
Above 80 . . . . Good

Harvard Step Test

A stable bench or platform 20 inches high and a stopwatch are needed. The subject steps onto and off the bench at a cadence of thirty steps per minute (*up, up, down, down;* bringing each foot up and then down, constitutes one step) for 5 minutes or until voluntary termination. The subject must achieve a completely vertical position on the top of the bench with each step. The participant sits down during recovery and remains still and quiet while his/her pulse is taken 1 to 1½ minutes after exercise.

Scoring for the Harvard step test yields a *physical efficiency index* (PEI) and is calculated as follows:

$$\text{Physical efficiency index (PEI)} = \frac{\text{duration of exercise in seconds} \times 100}{5.5 \times \text{pulse count for 1 to 1½ minutes recovery}}$$

Table 8–12 provides a scale for interpreting the PEI.

This test can be physically demanding and can constitute a hazard for someone who is injured or in poor health. Medical examinations should be required, and persons with abnormalities should be advised not to participate in this exercise evaluation. In fact, some screening procedures should be initiated for weight training in general.

Summary and Conclusions

Evaluative techniques can be used to accurately describe many important physiological, biomechanical, and performance parameters. These quantitative procedures provide important baseline data in addition to data on the long-term effects of weight-training exercise. Such tangible indication of success also can serve as motivation for further pursuits leading to positive changes in body composition, strength, endurance, power, and technical expertise.

References

1. Astrand, P., and K. Rodahl. 1977. *Textbook of Work Physiology* (Second edition). New York: McGraw-Hill.

2. Bar-Or, O. 1978. A new anaerobic capacity test—characteristics and applications. Presented at the 21st World Congress in Sports Medicine, Brasilia.

3. Berger, R., and M. Harris. 1966. Effect of various repetitive rates in weight training on improvement in strength and endurance. *Journal of Association for Physical and Mental Rehabilitation* 20:205.

4. Brouha, L. 1943. The step test: A simple method of measuring physical fitness for muscular work in young men. *Research Quarterly* 14:31–36.

5. Brozek, J., F. Grande, J. Anderson, and A. Keys. 1963. Densitometric analysis of body composition: Revision of some quantitative assumptions. *Annals of New York Academy of Science* 110:113–140.

6. Christian, V. 1983. Studies of anaerobic bikework power. Unpublished study, Appalachian State University, Boone, N.C.

7. Christian, V., and J. Seymour. 1985. Periodization: Specific power adaptations relative to strength-power training. *National Strength and Conditioning Association Journal* 6(6):32–34.

8. Clarke, H. 1971. *Physical and Motor Tests in the Medford Boy's Growth Study.* Englewood Cliffs, N. J.: Prentice-Hall, Inc.

9. Clarke, H. 1974. Strength development and motor-sports improvement. *Physical Fitness Research Digest* 4, serial No. 4.

10. Clarke, H. 1978. Muscular power of the legs. *Physical Fitness Research Digest* 8, serial No. 2.

11. Coaches Roundtable. 1984. Improving jumping ability. *National Strength and Conditioning Association Journal* 6(2):10–20.

12. Costill, D. 1974. Championship material. *Runner's World* 9:26–27.

13. DeVries, H. 1974. *Physiology of Exercise for Physical Education and Athletics* (Second edition). Dubuque: Wm. C. Brown Co.

14. DiGiovanna, V. 1943. The relationship of selected structural and functional measures in success in college athletes. *Research Quarterly* 14:199.

15. Durnin, J., and J. Womersley. 1974. Body fat assessed from total body density and its estimation from skinfold thickness. *British Journal of Nutrition* 32:95.

16. Everett, P. 1952. The prediction of baseball ability. *Research Quarterly* 23:15.

17. Fleck, S. 1983. Percent of body fat of various groups of athletes. *National Strength and Conditioning Association Journal* 5(2):46–50.

18. Fox, E., and D. Mathews. 1981. *The Physiological Basis of Physical Education and Athletics* (Third edition). Philadelphia: Saunders College Publishing.

19. Green, P., and H. O'Bryant. 1985. Effects of ammonia inhalation on muscular strength, anaerobic capacity, power, and performance. Unpublished masters thesis, Appalachian State University, Boone, N.C.

20. Hawkins, J. 1983. An analysis of selected skinfold measuring instruments. *Journal of Physical Education, Recreation, and Dance* (January):25–27.

21. Inbar, O. 1982. Unpublished description of the Wingate anaerobic test, Wingate Institute for Physical Education and Sport, Tel Aviv, Israel.

22. Johnson, B., and J. Nelson. 1979. *Practical Measurements for Evaluation in Physical Education* (Third edition) Minneapolis: Burgess Publishing Co.

23. Kalamen, J. 1968. *Measurement of Maximum Muscle Power in Man.* Doctoral dissertation, Ohio State University.

24. Landers, J. 1985. Maximum based on reps. *National Strength and Conditioning Association Journal* 6(6):60–61.

25. Margaria, R., I. Aghemo, and E. Rovelli. 1966. Measurement of muscular power (anaerobic) in man. *Journal of Applied Physiology* 21:1662–1664.

26. Nicklin, R. 1983. Bikework. *American Journal of Physics* 51(5):423–429.

27. O'Bryant, H. 1982. Unpublished data collected at HPERD Dept., Louisiana State University, Baton Rouge, La.

28. O'Shea, P. 1966. Effects of selected weight training programs on the development of strength and muscle hypertrophy. *Research Quarterly* 37:95–102.

29. O'Shea, P. 1969. *Scientific Principles and Methods of Strength Fitness.* Reading, Mass.: Addison-Wesley Publishing Co.

30. Sinclair, R., and K. Christensen. 1976. A modern Hoffman number. *Alberta Weight Lifter* June-July.

31. Sinning, W. 1978. Anthropometric estimation of body density, fat, and lean body weight in women gymnasts. *Medicine and Science in Sports* 10(4):243–249.

32. Sloan, A., and J. Weir. 1970. Nomograms for prediction of body density and total body fat from skinfold measurements. *Journal of Applied Physiology* 28(2):221–222.

33. Tharp, G., R. Newhouse, L. Uffelman, et al. 1985. Comparison of sprint and run times with performance on the Wingate anaerobic test. *Research Quarterly for Exercise and Sport* 56(1):73–76.

34. Wilmore, J. 1977. *Athletic Training and Physical Fitness: Physiological Principles and Practices of the Conditioning Process.* Boston: Allyn and Bacon, Inc.

35. Wilmore, J., and A. Behnke. 1968. Predictability of lean body weight through anthropometric assessment in college men. *Journal of Applied Physiology* 25:349–355.

36. Wilmore, J., and A. Behnke. 1970. An anthropometric estimation of body density and lean body weight in young women. *American Journal of Clinical Nutrition* 23:267–274.

37. Wilmore, J., C. Brown, and J. Davis. 1977. Body physique and composition of the female distance runner. *Annals of New York Academy of Science* 301:764–776.

38. Withers, R. 1970. Effect of varied weight-training loads on the strength of university freshmen. *Research Quarterly* 41:110.

Chapter 9

Ergogenic Aids: Difficult Problems and Different Perspectives

Ergogenic aids encompass a wide variety of substances and techniques thought to enhance performance. Most often, ergogenic aids are thought of only as drugs. In the broadest sense, however, all of the following are included in this same category: music, warmup, supplemental oxygen, vitamins and other nutritional substances such as carbohydrates and even water, a myriad of psychological phenomena including hypnosis and mental practice, and a variety of other motivational and suggestive techniques (13). Many ergogenic aids have been tried by athletes in the past. Table 9–1 lists some of these ergogenic compounds.

Table 9–1. Some ergogenic compounds (6, 13, 20, 46, 53).

1. Adrenaline	23. Lecithin
2. Alcohol	24. Liver
3. Alkalies	25. Marijuana
4. Amino acids	26. Nicotine
5. Ammonia	27. Nitroglycerin
6. Amphetamines	28. Noradrenalin
7. Anabolic steroids	29. Salicylates
8. Anti-estrogens	30. Spironolactone
9. Aspartates	31. Supplemental:
10. Barbiturates	Carbohydrates
11. Caffeine	Oxygen
12. Camphor	Protein
13. Cocaine	Vitamins
14. Cytomel	Minerals
15. Dimethyl sulfoxide	32. Strychnine
16. Digitalis	33. Sulfa drugs
17. Ephedrine	34. Wheat germ
18. Ethyl ether	35. Yeast
19. Gelatin	
20. Growth hormone (STH)	
21. Gonadotropin (HCG)	
22. Levidopa	

Much of the recent interest in ergogenic aids has been related to the effects of drugs on athletic performance. Drugs are substances that alter the normal physiology or structure of an organism. Their use in athletics is not a new idea. Throughout history, athletes have sought external chemical aids that would provide an advantage in competition. As early as the 3rd century B.C., Greek athletes ingested mushrooms to improve athletic performance (19). In the 19th century, athletes in several nations were known to use caffeine, alcohol, nitroglycerin, ethyl ether, opium, and even strychnine (6).

As early as 1954, European weightlifters were using synthetic testosterone to increase muscle size and strength (17). This practice quickly spread to the United States, where athletes, their physicians, and trainers welcomed this safer version of testosterone (17). By the early 1960s anabolic steroid use was widespread among athletes (17) and current trends suggest that its use has been increasing ever since. The International Olympic Committee (IOC) banned the use of anabolic steroids and began testing procedures, with punitive action, at the 1976 Montreal Olympic Games (17).

As is well known, the present use of drugs in sports and other athletic endeavors is widespread and increasing. The purpose of this chapter is to briefly discuss why athletes take drugs, possible positive and negative drug effects, and the pros and cons of drug testing.

Current Status of Drug Use

The following definitions are pertinent to the discussion of ergogenic aids (55):

1. *Drug Use:* When the sought after (and intended) effects are realized with minimal hazard.

2. *Drug Misuse:* When a drug is taken or administered under circumstances that significantly increase the hazard to the individual or others.

3. *Drug Abuse:* When a drug is taken sporadically, repeatedly, and/or compulsively to such a degree as to greatly increase the hazard or impair the ability of an individual to adequately function or cope with his/her environment.

Scientific development and the subsequent growth of the pharmaceutical industry have increased the availability of both legal and illegal substances that affect the mind and body in various ways. This phenomenon has been associated with concurrent changes in the attitude of large segments of society toward the use of such substances (55).

In 1978, Harris and associates (54) released the results of a U.S. survey indicating the projected number of users of various drugs (Table 9–2). These figures may also represent logical estimates of drug use for the 1980s.

In addition, about 100+ million use alcohol and about 55+ million use tobacco (45). To observe rather large amounts of alcohol and tobacco being consumed, all one has to do is simply look around while in attendance at the usual social and business gatherings (professional meetings, parties, political functions, etc.).

Prescription drugs make up a large portion of total drug use in the United States. Approximately 1.5 billion prescriptions are written per year (55), or about seven per capita per year. Drug use represents an estimated $90 billion industry in this country. We have the highest levels of illicit drug use of any nation in the industrialized world (10). The estimated economic loss associated with alcohol use in this country is $89.5 billion per year; drug abuse costs an additional $49.6 billion each year (10). Considering these data, it is logical to conclude that the United States is a drug-oriented society. And, since a large segment of the population believes that drug use (and even misuse and abuse) is acceptable, it is also logical to believe that this attitude would be reflected in the athletic setting. Current attitudes suggest that a *double standard* may exist. Many nonathletic drug abusers, particularly those who use alcohol and tobacco, are among the first to condemn athletes for their drug misuse and abuse.

Table 9–2. Perceived dangers and actual use of legal and illegal drugs (54)*.

Drug	Percentage feel dangerous to use	Projected number of users
Heroin	91	2,900,000
Pep pills	75	11,500,000
Cocaine	70	11,500,000
Diet pills	67	22,000,000
Sleeping pills	55	27,500,000
Birth control pills	55	29,500,000
Tranquilizers	52	51,000,000
Painkillers	44	52,000,000
Marijuana	37	33,500,000
Saccharine	22	65,000,000

*In 1978, Louis Harris and Associates released the findings of a nationwide poll on drug use. They found that most Americans perceive prescription drugs such as pep pills, tranquilizers, and painkillers as more dangerous than marijuana. Saccharine, which has been linked to cancer, is not considered as being particularly dangerous. Harris then projected the number of users based on 145,000,000 adults 18 years or older in the United States. He found that perceived danger had a limiting effect on the number of users but that temptation far exceeds education. People know what they like, and take it, regardless of the danger.

Incidence of Drug Use Among Athletes

The types of drugs banned by the IOC are shown in Table 9–3. The first three categories are the so-called *psyching-up* drugs. These drugs may allow the athlete to compete or train at higher levels of arousal than normal (33, 36). Some athletes think stimulants provide increased speed and endurance, which may explain the popularity of amphetamines among cyclists and football players (6). Athletes may take a drug for optimum arousal to produce a "best" performance, but too much of a drug can cause too much arousal and performance may decrease. Others, such as jockeys and wrestlers, may take advantage of the anorexic effects of these drugs to make competition weight (6). After years of competing, older athletes, often have problems psyching-up at competitions and so turn to arousal-producing drugs in hopes of bringing back the enthusiasm of earlier days. Relatively high percentages of caffeine and ephedrine use were reported in a survey of national class strength-power athletes from the southeastern United States (46) (Table 9–4). Ephedrine has been popular with swimmers because of its stimulatory effects on the central nervous system (CNS), coupled with its bronchial dilatory actions (6). Caffeine, which also is a CNS stimulant, has been attractive to cyclists and runners (6).

Ammonia inhalation to increase performance during competition has grown in popularity among powerlifters; its use among olympic weightlifters is somewhat less prevalent. Some athletes, coaches, and trainers believe this practice facilitates maximal effort toward strength performance due to an increased state of arousal. Due to a lack of appropriate research, the exact nature and mechanism involved are unknown.

In a recent study on this subject, significant improvements were noted in a 1RM supine bench press and in anaerobic leg power (measured by the vertical jump and the Lewis formula) when ammonia was inhaled prior to the measurements (16). Similar improvement could not be demonstrated during other strength and performance tasks of a greater technical nature. Results of this study suggest that ammonia inhalation may be an effective ergogenic aid in events requiring strength and anaerobic power if the events emphasize gross motor movements rather than technique (16).

Table 9–3. Substances banned by the International Olympic Committee at the 1984 Summer Olympic Games (49).

Psychomotor stimulants
Amphetamine
Benzphetamine
Chlorphentermine
Cocaine
Diethylpropion
Dimethylamphetamine
Ethylamphetamine
Fencamfamine
Meclofenoxate
Methylamphetamine
Methylphenidate
Norpseudoephedrine
Pemoline
Phendimetrazine
Phenmetrazine
Phentermine
Pipradol
Prolintane
(and related compounds)

Sympathominetics
Clorprenaline
Ephedrine
Etafedrine
Isoetharine
Isoproterenol
Methoxyphenamine
Methylephedrine
(and related compounds)

Miscellaneous central nervous system stimulants
Amiphenazole
Bemegride
Caffeine*
Doxapram
Ethamivan
Leptazol
Nikethamide
Picrotoxin
Strychnine
(and related compounds)

Narcotic analgesics
Anileridine
Codeine
Dextromoramide
Dihydrocodeine
Dipipanone
Ethylmorphine
Heroin
Hydrocodone
Hydromorphone
Levorphanol
Methadone
Morphine
Oxycodone
Oxymorphone
Pentazocine
Pethidine
Phenazocine
Thebacon
Trimeperidine
(and related compounds)

Anabolic steroids
Clostebol
Danazol
Dehydrochlormethyltestosterone
Fluoxymesterone
Mesterolone
Methenolone
Methandienone
Methyltestosterone
Nandrolone
Norethandrolone
Oxandrolone
Oxymesterone
Oxymetholone
Stanozolol
Testosterone†
(and related compounds)

*If the concentration in urine exceeds 12 micrograms/ml.
†If the ratio of total concentration of testosterone to epitestosterone in the urine exceeds 6.

In a survey of Canadian athletes (8) (33% return rate), data suggests that across all types of sports the use of various arousal drugs ranged from 2% to 6%. These data would suggest relatively wide use of arousal-type drugs by athletes.

Athletes commonly use local anesthetics to relieve the soreness and discomfort of injuries. They may use narcotic analgesics, including barbiturates, etc., to mask pain. Athletes usually avoid opioid analgesics (morphine, meperidine, etc.) during competition because they interfere with maximal performance. Instead, many athletes prefer *salicylates,* which relieve pain and also have anti-inflammatory properties (6) Salicylates have been shown to lower tolerance to heat and thus result in more susceptibility to heat stroke (15). Injured athletes often try to

Table 9–4. Admitted use of caffeine or ephedrine by strength-power athletes in the southeastern United States (46).

		Number who use	
Athletes		Caffeine	Ephedrine
Weightlifters			
Male	N=9	8	5
Female	N=7	6	
Powerlifters			
Male	N=8	8	7
Female	N=8	7	4
Shotputters			
Male	N=4	3	3
Female	N=2	2	1

compete, even when the injury is severe. Although masking pain may allow the athlete to compete, it increases the chances of sustaining a severe injury. One occasionally hears reports of long distance runners or cross-country skiers using low levels of narcotics to reduce the pain associated with this type of activity. Bodybuilders have been purported to use *Demerol* to reduce the pain associated with high volume weight training. *Catabolic steroids* (corticosteroids), not to be confused with *anabolic steroids,* are used frequently for the treatment of chronic injury and relief of inflammation (6).

Athletes have frequently used alcohol as an anti-anxiety drug. Acute alcohol ingestion does not improve strength; rather, it decreases strength, power, local muscle endurance, speed, and cardiovascular endurance. Acute ingestion of alcohol may decrease athletic performance most seriously in sports involving rapid reactions to changing stimuli because it has deleterious effects on many psychomotor skills such as reaction time, hand-eye coordination, accuracy, balance, and complex coordination (2).

Athletes use narcotic-analgesic-type drugs and bensodiazepine derivatives to reduce precompetition anxiety (6). Some athletes use these drugs or alcohol to decrease the arousal produced by stimulants. Evidence suggests that these substances are widely used by professional athletes (36).

Marijuana is now the most widely used illicit drug available in the United States. Sales in this country for 1983 were estimated at $25 billion (10). Besides producing various behavioral and psychological effects, marijuana seriously hinders psychomotor function (5). Damage of chromosomes may occur while causing irreversible brain changes after only 3 years of daily marijuana use (10). Marijuana smokers are 50% more susceptible to lung cancer than cigarette smokers (10). Use of marijuana decreases coordination, noticeably impairing mechanical skills, including perception and tracking ability. Decreased intellectual function alters the user's sense of time, resulting in a consistent overestimate of elapsed time (5). Other effects include altered pulmonary and cardiovascular function ranging from orthostatic hypotension to tachycardia and inappropriate alterations to heat stress (5).

In the opinion of American track athletes who were interviewed after the 1983 Pan-Am Games, 50% or more of America's world class track and field athletes were using drugs, the most popular being anabolic steroids (38). Anabolic steroids are synthetic derivatives of testosterone, which were originally developed in the 1950s to hasten tissue repair in severely debilitated patients (17). Although methods of administration vary, these drugs can be classified into two broad categories as oral (C_{17} derivatives) or injectable compounds. Table 9–5 lists some of the commonly available anabolic steroid compounds, their generic and popular drug names, and approximate costs.

Table 9–5. Some currently available anabolic steroids (4, 17, 48, 54).

Generic name	Popular drug name	Cost
	ORALS	
Oxandrolone	Anavar*	2.5mg tabs† @ $10.86/100
Oxymetholone	Anadrol-50*	50mg tabs† @ $34.56/100
Danazol	Danocrine	50mg caps† @ $42.24/100
Methandrostenolone	Dianabol*	5mg tabs† @ $16.34/100
Ethylestrenol	Maxibolin*	2mg tabs† @ $9.44/100
Stanozolol	Winstrol*	2mg tabs† @ $8.04/100
Fluroxymesterone	Halotestin	5mg tabs† @ $26.72/100
Methyl testosterone	Oreton Methyl	25mg tabs† @ $28.78/100
	INJECTABLES	
Nandrolone decanoate	Anabol* or Deca-Durabolin*	@ $7.33/2cc† 100mg/cc† @$16.20/2cc
Nandrolone phenpropionate	Durabolin*	@ $5.88/5cc†
Testosterone enanthate	Delatestryl	@ $12.44/5cc†
Testosterone cypionate	Depo-Testosterone*	@ $22.13/10cc†
Testosterone propionate	Oreton	@ $20–$25/10cc
Dromostanolone	Drolban	@ $9.10/10cc†

*Widely used.
†Approximate 1981 price per specified quantity. Black market prices may be three times this amount.

Like testosterone, these drugs stimulate an *anabolic* or building up process in the body and are associated with protein synthesis, which leads to enhanced muscle growth and tissue repair (17, 48, 52, 54). They are usually thought to be used by athletes who depend on muscle mass, strength, and power (shotputters and weightlifters, for example). As demonstrated in animal studies, anabolic effectiveness apparently is not maintained because enhanced nitrogen balance returns to normal even with continued steroid administration; this results in a *wearing off* phase (27). Conversely, cessation of steroid use generally produces a temporary *rebound,* negative nitrogen balance and subsequent loss of body weight (27). Both the dose and duration of steroid administration exert an influence on the anabolic response (55). Prolonging the period of steroid use and increasing the dose appear to result in a reduction of the relative effects on nitrogen retention and body weight while facilitating the reduction of body fat (30). Increasing the dose with continued administration delays the wearing off phase and may reduce the percentage of nitrogen lost in the rebound (29). Stress associated with intense training, particularly overtraining, can cause decreased levels of resting testosterone (18, 40) and a negative nitrogen balance (7, 32) with subsequent loss of lean body weight. Therefore, administering steroids may reduce the potential adverse side effects associated with overtraining-overstress. However, a negative nitrogen balance also can be decreased or reversed by using additional dietary protein (32, 42).

Testosterone is produced by the testes and adrenal glands in the male and, to a lesser extent, in the adrenals in the female. Normal daily adult testosterone secretion rates range from 5 mg to 10 mg in the male and from 0.04 to 0.12 mg in the female, with some normal variation (48, 55). Only about 1% (free form) of total testosterone transported by the blood is active, however (48). The rest is protein-bound and serves as a storage reservoir that is available if needed by the tissues (48). *Active* testosterone lasts only a short time before it is converted into water soluble compounds that are quickly excreted from the body into the urine (48). The concentration of these compounds can be detected in the urine and in general is the basis for the tests used in anabolic steroid detection. The *androgenic* or masculinizing effect, which is responsible for the secondary male sex characteristics of facial hair, deep voice, and aggressiveness, may be somewhat less pronounced with anabolic steroids than with testosterone (17). Perhaps the greatest effect of androgens on training is as a CNS stimulant that produces increased aggression, a feeling of well-being, and increased *training drive* (47, 55).

Results from the more than two dozen studies and reviews published in the past two decades indicate that total or lean body weight, strength, or anaerobic power are not likely to be influenced by administration of therapeutic doses of anabolic hormones in the absence of an exercise program that in itself promotes muscle anabolism and meaningful performance enhancement (55). Increases in performance or beneficial alterations in body composition are more likely to occur in athletes during hard training (21, 52, 53). Among studies using weight-trained subjects, the majority suggested that therapeutic doses of steroids can enable individuals to gain body weight and/or strength more rapidly than with training alone (55). However, results such as these must be regarded with caution, given the questionable methods of scientific procedure that were used (55).

Anabolic hormones have a stimulating effect on hemoglobin, hematocrit, and total blood volume and therefore could theoretically increase aerobic capacity and endurance performance (14, 22, 37). Some studies have shown increases in some endurance parameters (22, 26); others have not (11, 23).

Athletes have reported that androgens enhance recovery and mask pain. Anabolic steroids are used occasionally by gymnasts to deliberately stunt growth in children (6). Nevertheless, the greatest incidence of androgen use appears to be among strength-power athletes, although a wide variety of athletes, both men and women, are using them. Table 9–6 gives the incidence of use in various sports. These data were collected through questionnaires and through interviews with physicians, sport scientists, coaches, and athletes from all areas of the United States, Canada, and Great Britian.

At present it appears that androgens are likely the most widely used of the typical ergogenic aids (35). They are certainly the most controversial. As with other drugs, the incidence and extent of use increases with the level of competition. Many athletes use anabolic steroids in much higher doses and for much longer periods than the present studies have been able to evaluate. It is not uncommon for the dose level in a significant percentage of athletes to exceed 1 mg/kg of body weight per day, with a substantial number of those individuals using two or more times that quantity (55). Conclusions drawn from short-term, low dose studies may not accurately reflect what occurs in athletes who take androgens at higher doses, repeatedly, and/or for longer periods of time (55).

Some caution must be exercised in interpreting information concerning the incidence of drug use among athletes.

A major problem occurs with the use of surveys. Typically only one-third of those sent out are returned. Furthermore, drug users are likely to be the athletes who do **not** return surveys (8). Therefore, the incidence of drug use in many sports may be higher than is usually reported. The reluctance of athletes to admit drug use is in large part due to the fear of being reported and eventually banned from competition. Evidence of, and justification for, this attitude was borne out in the 1983 Pan American Games when 15 athletes (11 weightlifters, a bicyclist, a fencer, a sprinter, and a shotputter) representing several nations were disqualified and denied a total of 21 medals (38, 50).

The Controversy Surrounding the Use of Drugs in Sports

Currently, there is a scientific, ethical, and emotional controversy surrounding the use of drugs in sports, especially androgens. This controversy and current attitudes are depicted in Figure

Table 9–6. Estimated steroid drug use.*

Type of athlete	Usage among	
	Males (18 yr.+)†	Females (18 yr.+)‡
Strength-power athletes		
1. Weightlifers	95 plus%	15%
2. Powerlifters	99 plus%	25%
3. Shotputters, discus throwers, and javelin throwers	80%	20%
4. Football players	70%	—
5. Decathletes	60%	—
6. Sprinters	40%	1%
Endurance athletes		
1. Middle distance runners (1500,3000m)	10%	1%
2. Long distance runners	10%	1%
3. Long distance bicyclists	10%	—

*Based on interview with athletes and discussions with other scientists and coaches interested in this problem, the figures presented above appear to be reasonable estimates of anabolic steroid usage.
†Usage (percentage using) increases with the level of competition, as does the extent of usage (amounts and duration of use).
‡At some point during their career.

9–1. The perspectives and goals of the principal groups associated with this controversy are discussed briefly below (55).

Athletes, Coaches, Promoters, and Trainers. Members of this group are not typically trained in the scientific method. They do, however, conduct research based largely on empirical data, often using trial and error methods, but frequently producing sophisticated and productive methods of enhancing performance. The goal of this group is to promote spectator and athlete participation and to maximize performance so as to lead to victory in competition.

Members of Sports Federations and Athletic Governing Bodies. Members of these groups are generally not trained to interpret or apply the findings of research (medical committees of such groups may be the exception). Their primary goals are to promote friendship and brotherhood through sport, to promote equality and fair play, and to protect the future of their sport.

Members of the Medical Community. The academic and professional background and experience of the members in this group pertain to clinical diagnosis and treatment of patients in the general, nonathletic population and their restoration to normal health and function, rather than to the enhancement of performance. The major goal of this group is to protect health. Their guiding principle and philosophy is *primum non nocere* (first, do no harm). Therefore, they are to use drugs only in cases involving disease, deficiency, or injury.

Members of the Scientific Community. The members of this group are trained to design, conduct, and analyze the results of research using accepted scientific methods. Only with the recent growth in sports medicine and exercise physiology have scientists shown interest in assisting the other groups to achieve their goals. Even so, there exists a large schism between scientists as to the ethical legitimacy of such drug research and whether it should be carried out. Furthermore, there are considerable legal and financial constraints associated with addressing critical issues of this problem. The goal of this group is to carry out basic and applied research within the constraints mentioned above.

Because of the differing goals, perspectives, and experiences of these groups, and especially because of the constraints placed on scientists, there is a paucity of scientifically sound, athletically acceptable research. There is controversy over the existence and extent of both the beneficial and adverse effects of drugs. The results have included emotional polarization and the counterproductive alienation of groups (see Figure 9–1). This controversy is reflected in the emotional response, both pro and con, to drug testing in sports.

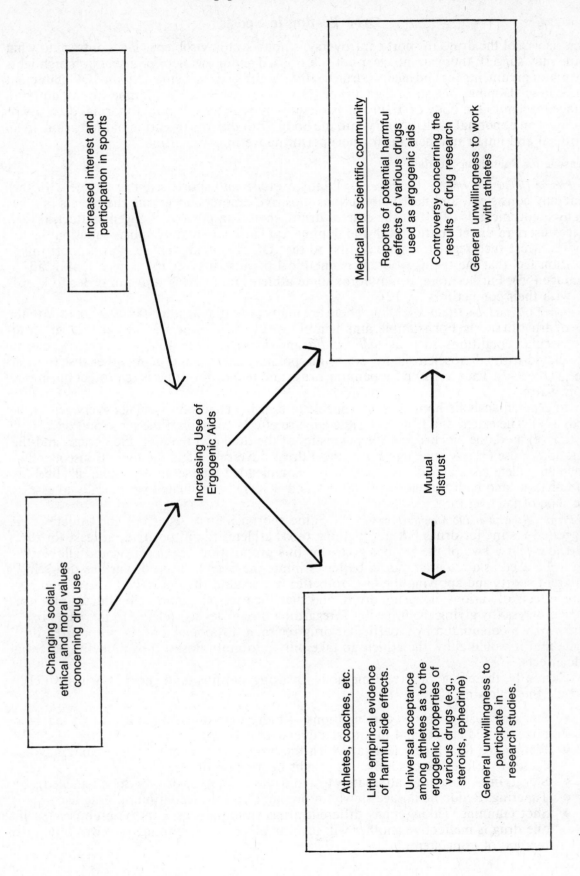

Figure 9–1. The Controversey of Drugs in Sport.

Drug Testing in Sports

This aspect of the drugs in sport controversy is not a simple problem, and, contrary to what some may suggest, there are no clear-cut solutions. The following brief discussion highlights the major arguments for and against drug testing. As preface, we being with the IOC statement on *doping*: "Doping consists of the administration of, or the use by a competitor of, any substance foreign to the body or of any physiological substances taken in abnormal quantity or taken by an abnormal route of entry into the body, with the sole intention of increasing, in an artificial and unfair manner, his (or her) performance in competition."

Reasons for Supporting Testing

To Prevent Unfair Performance Advantage.   Many exercise and sports scientists agree with the generally consistent, and nearly ubiquitous, positive reports concerning the effects of many ergogenic aids (9). If in the case of drugs, there is a positive ergogenic effect, this places users in direct conflict with the doping regulations issued by sports sanctioning bodies. Most such regulations are similar to the IOC statement. Those who support this position feel that the taking of drugs is unethical because it gives the user an unfair advantage (55). Furthermore, it may force some athletes into taking drugs in order to keep up with their competitors (9, 12).

To Protect Athletes From Health Risks.   There are many potential health risks associated with the use of drugs in sports. For example, amphetamines have been associated with pathological cardiovascular conditions such as *tachycardia* and *hypertension*. Anabolic steroids may be associated with atherosclerosis, hypertension, possibly cancer, and many other diseases (54) (see Table 9–7). Thus a reason for banning drugs and testing for drugs is to protect the athlete from harm.

In general, anabolic hormones are capable of exerting effects on virtually every cell in the body (28). The extent and nature of these adverse effects depend on the type (oral or injectable) used, the biochemical characteristics of the drug and the user, the dosage, and the duration of use (31). A large number of these drugs adversely affect the liver. Consequently, when an athlete takes anabolic steroids, it is recommended that serum bilirubin, alkaline phosphatase, and both transaminases (SGPT and SGOT) be evaluated periodically to assess the state of the liver (55).

To Permit Research and to Monitor Progress.   Some sport scientists, coaches, and athletes have suggested testing for drugs but not banning those athletes found positive, at least for the next few years. Two of the reasons given for this proposition are that it would allow testing to be used as a research tool to better estimate the extent of use of various drugs in different sports and applying the tests to better understand the potential positive and negative effects of various ergogenic drugs, and that such testing could help athletes monitor their progress (by giving them feedback regarding dosage levels) related to increases in performance potentiated by a particular drug regimen. Proponents of the second reason argue that it would allow the athlete to take only minimum doses, thus reducing potential side effects.

Currently, there is a variety of methods for using steroids (and general) drugs which include the following: (20)

- Stacking: Using various combinations of more than one drug at a time to maximize desired effects and minimize adverse effects.
- Plateauing: Reaching a level at which the drug is no longer working maximally and ceases to afford the desired gains sought in strength or size.
- Staggering: Using drugs alternately to avoid plateauing on a drug or drugs (stacked).
- Tapering: Reducing dosage slowly in preparation for discontinuing drug use.
- Shot Gunning: Taking many different drugs simultaneously on the premise that if one drug is ineffective another will take its place. Shot gunning once was a popular method of using steroids.

Table 9-7. Suggested diseases, abnormalities, and potential side effects associated with anabolic steroids (48, 52, 54).

Major forms

1. Liver dysfunction:
    Hepatocellular carcinoma (cancer)
    Peliosis hepatis (blood-filled sacs)
    Heptoma (tumor)
2. Leukemia

Minor forms (Postpubertal Reactions)

1. Hypertension
2. Chills, nausea, vomiting, diarrhea
3. Acne
4. Cancer conducive environment
5. Fluid retention
6. Hypercholesterolemic effects
7. Abnormal liver function
8. Psychological disturbances
9. Alterations in menstrual cycle (females)
10. Clitoral enlargement (females)
11. Menstrual irregularities (females)
12. Increased or decreased libido (sex drive)
13. Viral illness (after cessation of drugs)
14. Epistaxis (nose bleeding)
15. Changes in hair growth or distribution pattern
16. Alcopecia (baldness of some type)
17. Oily skin
18. Insomnia and nightmares
19. Increased appetite
20. Testicular atrophy (males)
21. Gynecomastia (breast tissue enlargement in males)
22. Impotence (males)
23. Reduction of breast tissue (females)
24. Deepening of voice
25. Abnormal blood clotting
26. Accelerated atherosclerosis
27. Hyperinsulinism
28. Increased blood pressure
29. Elevated serum triglycerides
30. Gastrointestinal disorders
31. Muscle cramps-spasms
32. Headache
33. Dizziness
34. Altered thyroid function

Minor Forms (Prepubertal Reactions)[†]

1. Penile enlargement (males)
2. Flushing of skin
3. Premature epiphyseal closure

*In general, conclusive evidence of the exact nature and extent of these health-related factors is lacking. Reasons why it is lacking including the following: clinical use of drugs by patients, use of untrained subjects, low drug doses, far less than adequate training programs, and the absence of long-term data.
[†]Not excluded from postpubertal reactions.

Some drug regimens (see Tables 9–8 and 9–9) involve large dosages that represent considerable personal expense and that allow little time to cycle off in order to normalize bodily functions.

Table 9–8. Hypothetical 6-week anabolic steroid regimen I (48).*

Drug	Dosage	Approximate cost
Winstrol	2mg/day	$ 60
Deca-Durabolin	200mg/week	$ 90

Yearly cost of four regimen cycles

Winstrol	$60 × four regimens	$240
Deca-Durabolin	$90 × four regimens	$360
Syringes, etc.—		$ 30
Physicians fees		$100
Laboratory fees		$ 60
Yearly total:		$790

*Cost estimates are based on Table 9–5. Costs based on black market prices could increase these expenses threefold or more.

Table 9–9. Hypothetical 22-week anabolic steroid regimen II (20).*

Weeks	Oral	Injectable	Cost
Off season			
	Anavar	Deca-Durabolin	
2	50mg/day	300mg/week	$ 79
2	25mg/day	200mg/week	$ 48
2	—	100mg/week	$ 16
2	—	2cc (HCG)	$ 20
			$160
		(Repeat again)	$160
Preseason			
1	20mg D-bol/day	100mg/week	$ 7
1	40mg D-bol/day	200mg/week	$ 13
1	20mg D-bol/day	300mg/week	$ 13
	50mg Androl/day		
1	100mg Androl/day	300mg/week	$ 11
1	50mg Androl/day	400mg/week	$ 14
	10mg Halotestin/day		
1	50mg Androl/day		$ 10
	20mg Halotestin/day		
			$ 68
		(Cost per cycle)	$388

Yearly cost of two regiment cycles

Drugs	$388 × two regimens	$776
Syringes, etc..		$ 30
Physicians fees		$100
Laboratory fees		$ 60
Yearly total:		$966

*Cost estimates are based on Table 9–5. Costs based on black market prices could increase these expenses threefold or more.

Reasons Against Testing

Not Taking Drugs Represents a Performance Disadvantage.   The notion exists that ergogenic aids work and that they are taken by large numbers of athletes. Therefore, some believe that not taking them places one at a disadvantage. Those who support this position argue that drugs are simply one more integral part of a vast array of training components (12, 20). Others argue that many differences, both congenital and acquired, already exist among athletes, and athletes can take neither the credit nor the blame for them (12). Many athletes seek advantages through special diets, better coaches, or better facilities. The question may then arise, do those taking drugs have an unfair advantage? A logical question might be whether we should object to athletes using superior training methods. A common goal for athletes is to become bigger, stronger, or faster. If using drugs to enhance performance is unfair, then should we not ban all other means to the same end (12)? Such a hypothetical dialogue illustrates the lack of easy answers to this issue.

There Is No Such Thing as an Ergogenic Aid.   Some argue that drugs do not and cannot aid performance. Research, they say, does not support the effects of drugs (43, 44). This argument has been extended to suggest that testing only fosters a false belief among athletes that drugs are useful in enhancing performance (43).

The Cost Is Too High.   Proper tests for banned drugs include gas chromatography/mass spectrometry (GS) and/or radio-immuno-assay (RIA). The costs of performing these tests are staggering. At the 1983 Pan-American Games the cost per athlete tested was about $150. Furthermore, considerable equipment and technical assistance must be acquired, which adds to the expense. For a major meet such as the Olympic Games, the expense would run into millions of dollars. Such an expense would be devastating to *minor sports.* Sanctioning and administrative bodies for sports (in the United States) such as judo, weightlifting, and archery have yearly budgets of only a few hundred thousand dollars. Drug testing at their national or olympic trials could consume as much as one-third of their annual budget which would greatly curtail their other activities. Furthermore, to truly "clean up" sports, testing would have to be performed not only at major meets, but periodically throughout the year, an expense that many sports simply could not afford (39).

Ethical and Practical Questions Related to Drug Testing.   These are questions that need answers! Although in some cases they represent arguments for completely stopping drug tests, in other cases they represent questions to which the answers may provide methods of enhancing the usefulness of the tests. In any case, it appears that the manner in which the tests have been administered to date has been inconsistent, ill-organized, and ineffective. The following represent some of these questions and problems.

1. Ethics: There are many ethical questions associated with taking drugs for sports, but two major issues are dealt with here. First, the IOC position clearly states that drugs are banned and taking them is against the rules. Therefore, taking banned substances is breaking the rules and is thus unethical. But, stepping back from the absolute rule and considering philosophical arguments, one can find a considerably different situation. Some different ethical approaches to drug use are presented in Hatfield's book on anabolic steroids (20). Hatfield argues that ethical and moral values are changing. Considering the apparent widespread use of ergogenic aids, this argument may to a large extent be a valid one.

   A second major ethical issue concerns a previously discussed question. Many people feel forced into taking drugs in order to keep up. Dr. Norman Fost (12) professor of pediatrics and director of the program in medical ethics at the University of Wisconsin School of Medicine, feels, as do others (20), that this concern is misplaced. He argues "that the ingestion of steroids (and other drugs) for competitive reasons can not be distinguished from the other tortures, deprivations, and risks to which athletes subject themselves to achieve success". No one is coerced into world class competition. Some feel athletes embark on such careers for their own inner needs and drives, cognizant of the hardships involved. If they find the costs excessive, they can withdraw. This argument may hold true for adults involved in sport, but a key phrase is "cognizant of the hardships involved". Many children are involved in sports. There is considerable anecdotal evidence of children taking drugs. It is unlikely that these children are cognizant of the hardships of sport, much less the effects of drugs. This raises the question of one's personal ethics. Children (and even other adults) often mimic adults and choose role models (many modern-day athletes are today's "heroes"). Therefore, athletes and others associated with sport can assume responsibility and set an example by not using drugs, including tobacco and alcohol.

2. Test Methodology: The current IOC testing rules, which most sanctioning bodies have now adopted, are complex. Interpreting these rules requires considerable patience and attention to details. The clinical nature of administering the test requires that the procedure be carried out under the direct supervision of appropriately trained medical and scientific personnel. The tests are also to be administered in an IOC-approved laboratory (for IOC sanctioned events). There are currently three in the world: one in Cologne, West Germany, one in Montreal, Canada, and one in Los Angeles, California, U.S.A. This in itself raises a serious question about how the Pan-Am athletes caught for drug use in 1983 could have been banned by the IOC since the Caracas, Venezuela laboratory apparently was not IOC-approved.

   The tests for drugs have been performed using gas chromatography/mass spectrometry (GS), and, with steroids, radio-immuno-assay (RIA) plus GS; currently only GS is used. It is debatable whether using GS alone is superior to using both RIA and GS. Duplicate urine samples must be found positive before the athlete can be banned from further competitions (9). The rules for collection of urine samples require a series of tasks that are time-consuming, tedious, and detailed. Minor infractions of the rules invalidate the test. Invalidation has occurred several times in the past during international contests. (After invalidation the samples are poured down a sink. Such tests are thus known among athletes as "sink tests".)

   Typically, these tests are only performed at major contests, which does nothing to stop use during training or at less important contests. American athletes and coaches often return from international contests with stories about how the Eastern Europeans were able to beat the tests. Stories about secret drugs that mask steroids, new nondetectable drugs, and urine transplants (introducing another person's biological fluid into the bladder via a catheter) abound. It does appear that the Eastern Europeans are beginning to dominate most of the strength-power sports at major international competitions. Are their superior athletic performances solely due to better coaching and/or superior genetic material?

3. Inconsistent Policy Among Sanctioning Bodies: Not all sport sanctioning bodies have adopted the IOC doping statement. Not until recently did the International Weightlifting Federation consider testosterone a banned substance (largely because it occurs naturally in the body). Testosterone as well as caffeine are now banned, but they were not at the 1980 Moscow Olympics. It has been only in the last few years that exogenous testosterone could be detected reliably (9). At the 1983 World Track and Field Championships in Helsinki, 30+ athletes were found positive for testosterone. This was reported in Scandinavian newspapers and became well known among coaches and athletes (41). Apparently the International Amateur Athletic Federation did not consider testosterone to be a banned substance at that time. This knowledge may have caused considerable confusion among athletes at the Pan-Am Games later that year. The Pan-Am Games used the IOC stance, which banned testosterone. As is well known, the Pan-Am Games were a fiasco for the Americans.

4. Sabotage: Consider the "win at all costs" philosophy and the following scenario. An athlete decides to rid himself/herself of his/her competition. He/she grinds up a Dianabol tablet and puts it in a ketchup bottle during lunch. Everyone who uses ketch-

up from that bottle is disqualified. Such a possibility might necessitate special food packaging, another expense.

5. Escalating Nonbanned Drug Use: In order to keep an edge and beat the tests, many athletes turn to nonbanned drugs or drugs that are not being tested for. At present, a list of drugs are required to be released at least 6 months in advance of the competition at which they are to be tested. This time lag may encourage experimentation. Testosterone was an early example of this approach. Some believe the drug of the future is human somatotropic hormone (STH), or growth hormone (25). Currently its use is limited because of its expense and its association with the onset of diabetes. But a synthetic form at affordable prices may soon be available (25). In addition, the molecular structure can now be synthetically produced without that portion of the molecule that has been linked to the onset of diabetes. Thus many deterrents will likely be absent.

Other "new" ergogenic drugs include: insulin, levodopa, and neostigmine. It is likely that these drugs and others will eventually be added to the ever-growing list of banned substances, further increasing the costs of the tests. Before that time, however, many athletes will have experimented with a variety of new drugs that have well-documented health risks. Thus, the tests, rather than decreasing drug use and potential health risks, may have the opposite effect.

6. Research (Performance–Health Risks): Although a look at the popular press might indicate otherwise, relatively little research has been directed at drugs as ergogenic aids. Consequently, little is known about potential (especially long-term) health risks (9, 54, 55). Much of the criticism leveled at past ergogenic drug research (especially that involving androgens) arose because most of the studies used untrained subjects, low drug doses (blood levels not checked), and far less than adequate training programs (55). Given the current state of paranoia concerning testing among athletes (and the legal constraints), there is little chance of conducting meaningful, athletically related research.

Although the potential harmful side effects of some drugs (e.g., amphetamines, narcotics) are well-documented (45), the health risks surrounding other drugs are not. Consider androgens as an example. Clinical human studies and short-term animal studies have suggested several potential harmful effects (see section on health risks). Not a single long-term study on the effects of androgens has been carried out. The long-term effects of androgens are largely unknown. Side effects increase with dosage and duration of use (55). On the other hand, many short-term and long-term studies have been carried out on birth control pills. There is considerable evidence to suggest they are associated with increased incidence of cancer (56) and cardiovascular disease (24). Birth control pills are generally made up of varying combinations of estrogens and progesterone (15), both of which naturally occur in women.

With this perspective in mind, consider the following: First, birth control pills are used by women as ergogenic aids (56). Estrogen is slightly anabolic (15) and menstruation can be controlled (9, 15), thus enhancing training and competition for many women. Taking birth control pills is not in keeping with the IOC statement because it places the women in an artificial (unnatural) condition, but as yet birth control pills are not banned. Second, a male contraceptive that contains androgens is currently being researched (1). MacDougall (34) suggests that anabolic steroids are no more dangerous to males than birth control pills are to women. Thus, a major question must arise with the advent of male birth control pills. Should males continue to be banned for essentially the same reasons the women are not banned?

Consider another example. The health risks associated with the use of nicotine are well known. Nicotine may be an ergogenic aid as it elevates heart rate, stimulates the CNS, and elevates growth hormone (15). But nicotine is not on the IOC banned substance list. Similarly, most diuretics are not currently tested for yet athletes use them regularly to make weight. Diuretics can cause dehydration and loss of electrolytes, particularly potassium (K+), resulting in a potentially harmful artificial state (15). If we are really concerned about the health risks associated with sports, then shouldn't similar attention be given to football, boxing, and other sports on the grounds that they are clearly frought with health risks?

As discussed previously, current drug testing is at least partially responsible for the use of new ergogenic drugs. These drugs, especially somatotropin, may have even more dangerous side effects. Somatotropin, for example, has been associated with diabetes, acromeglia, and the creation of an environment (physiological) conducive to cancer (15, 48). This seems counterproductive if the intent is to eliminate a potential health hazard. As stated previously, the health risks for some drugs have not been clearly delineated. Furthermore, the arguments for banning drugs contain inconsistent reasoning. Although there are potential dangers, empirical evidence suggests that they are few. Until more research delineates the health risks (especially long-term risks), physical educators, sport scientists, athletic trainers, and physicians should use caution in explaining health risks to athletes and coaches. Exaggerating what is known concerning drug use or health risks only serves to widen the gap between the medical-scientific community and athletes.

7. Second Rate Medical Care For Athletes: Many medicines contain banned substances. Unfortunately it is difficult to find adequate substitutes that produce equal results. For example, a commonly used drug for asthma is metaprel, a banned drug. We know of at least one case in which a swimmer who switched from metaprel to Intal, a nonbanned drug, was unable to control his asthma satisfactorily. Many of the banned substances represent drugs of first choice for many diseases. Should athletes receive second best medical treatment?

Summary and Conclusions

The ultimate potential and long-term hazards of ergogenic compounds are, at present, unknown. Reaching definitive conclusions about the health risks of androgens is difficult because of the lack of scientifically acceptable research and because the circumstances surrounding such research (low doses, short training durations, heterogeneous physiological status of subjects, etc.) are not generally applicable to the athletic community. The systems that appear to be at most risk are those involved in the transport and detoxification of fluids: the liver and the cardiovascular system. Oral anabolic steroids are associated with a variety of complications, some potentially fatal; the injectable compounds appear to be somewhat safer than the oral drugs (they bypass the portal vein that leads directly to the liver). A report from the American College of Sports Medicine concludes that although benefits may be obtained, they are not likely to be worth the health risks involved (3).

This discussion, we hope, has set forth objective (both pro and con) arguments concerning the problem of drug use, misuse, and abuse in sports. We have scratched only the surface of this complex problem. In actuality, the situation may be part of a much larger problem in sports.

Coaches are expected to win at all costs, and winning has become more important than playing the game. The reputations of universities are often based on winning or losing football teams rather than on academic excellence. Some athletes and coaches seem to be more concerned with a large paycheck than with the love of sport or the virtues of sportsmanship (an attribute that is now regarded by many as old-fashioned). Perhaps the current drug-in-sports problem simply reflects a changing world and the "new" ethics (12, 20). These attitudes and habits do not exclude the young, underscoring the importance of appropriate role models.

Some express the concern that athletic drug use will continue to proliferate and that drug testing will not solve the total problem. The use of "scare tactics" regarding health risks by opponents of this issue has yet to work (considered perhaps a weak argument in the absence of definitive data). Thus far, the preventive measures and punitive action seem to have been effective only at driving drug use further underground. There are, however, two actions that may eventually make a real difference:

1. Those who criticize the use of drugs in sports can set an example and clean up their own act in regard to drug use, including the use of tobacco and alcohol.

2. Athletes, coaches, trainers, sports federations, physicians, health personnel, and scientists can compromise and change their attitudes. Mutual condemnation must give way to a sincere effort at working together. This approach could lead to meaningful research and effective educational programs for everyone associated with sports and could allow all to work on mutual goals of improving performance with minimal health risks, protecting the future of sport, and promoting equality and fair play.

The final decision of whether or not to take drugs lies with the individual. Perhaps a return to the founding philosophy of the modern Olympic Games would be an axiom to live by: "the most important goal is to compete, and to compete honorably."

References

1. Aldercreutz, H. 1983. Ethical or medical problem? *They Physician and Sports Medicine* 11(8):135–136.

2. American College of Sports Medicine (ACSM). 1982. Position statement on the use of alcohol by sports participants. *Medicine and Science In Sports and Exercise* 14(6):ix–x.

3. American College of Sports Medicine (ACSM). 1984. Position stand on the use of anabolic-androgenic steroids in sports. *Sports Medicine Bulletin* 19:13–18.

4. Anonymous. Circa 1981. *The Underground Steroid Handbook: For Men and Women.* (An underground publication of unknown origin.)

5. Biron, S., and J. Wells. 1983. Summary of the effects of marijuana use on various body systems. *Athletic Training* 18:295–303.

6. Burks, T. F. 1981. Drug use in athletics: Introduction to symposium. *Federation Proceedings* 40(12):2680–2681.

7. Celajowa, I., and M. Homa. 1970. Food intake, nitrogen balance, and energy balance in Polish weightlifters during training camp. *Nutrition and Metabolism* 12:259–274.

8. Clement, D. B. 1983. Drug use survey: Results and conclusions. *The Physician and Sports Medicine* 11(9):64–65.

9. Coaches Roundtable, Steroids. 1983. *National Strength and Conditioning Association Journal* 5(4):12–72.

10. Conference on Drug Abuse in Athletics. 1985. Vanderbilt University, Nashville, Tenn.

11. Fahey, T. D., and C. D. Brown. 1973. The effects of an anabolic steroid on the strength, body composition, and endurance of college males when accompanied by a weight training program. *Medicine and Science in Sports* 5:272–276.

12. Fost, N. 1983. A second opinion, let them take steroids. *Medical World News* (psychiatry edition) October 13.

13. Fox, E. L., and D. K. Mathews. 1981. *The Physiological Basis of Physical Education and Athletics* (Third edition). Philadelphia: Saunders College Publishing.

14. Gardner, F. H., and J. C. Pringle. 1961. Androgens and erhthropoiesis. *Archives of Internal Medicine* 107:112–128.

15. Gilman, A. G., L. S. Goodman, and A. Gilman. 1980. *The Pharmacological Basis of Therapeutics* (Sixth edition). New York: MacMillian.

16. Green, P., and H. O'Bryant. 1985. The effects of ammonia inhalation on muscular strength, anaerobic capacity, power, and performance. Master's thesis, Appalachian State University, Boone, N.C.

17. Gregg, D. 1984. Anabolic steroids: the debate builds up. *Clinical Update: Sports Medicine* 1(1):3–5.

18. Guezennec, C. Y., P. Ferre, B. Serrurier, et al. 1984. Metabolic effects of testosterone during prolonged exercise and fasting. *European Journal of Applied Physiology* 52:300–304.

19. Hanley, D. F. 1979. Drug use and abuse. In Strauss, R. H. (Ed.). *Sports Medicine and Physiology.* Philadelphia: W. B. Saunders, pp. 396–404.

20. Hatfield, F. C. 1982. *Anabolic Steroids.* Los Angeles: Fitness Systems.

21. Haupt, H. A., and G. D. Rovere, 1984. Anabolic steroids—the facts. *Journal of Medical Technology* 1:553–557.

22. Holma, P. 1977. Effect of an anabolic steroid (Methandienone) on central and peripheral blood flow in well trained male athletes. *Annals of Clinical Research* 9:215–221.

23. Johnson, L. C., E. S. Roundy, P. E. Allison, et al. 1975. Effect of anabolic steroid treatment on endurance. *Medicine and Science in Sports* 7:287–289.

24. Kaplan, N. M. 1978. Cardiovascular complications of oral contraceptives. *Annual Reviews of Medicine* 29:3–10.

25. Kerr, R. 1982. *The Practical Use of Anabolic Steroids With Athletes.* R. B. Kerr, publisher, 316 East Las Tunas Dr., San Gabriel, Calif.

26. Keul, J., B. Deus, and W. Kindermann. 1976. Anabolic hormone: Schadigung, Leistungsfahigkeit and Stoffwechsel. *Medizinische Klinik* 71:497–503.

27. Kochakian, C. 1950. Comparison of protein anabolic property of various androgens in the castrated rat. *American Journal of Physiology* 160:53–61.

28. Kochakian, C., and N. Arimasa. 1976. The metabolism in vitro of anabolic-androgenic steroids by mammalian tissues. In C. D. Kochakian (Ed.). *Anabolic-Androgenic Steroids.* New York: Springer-Verlag.

29. Kochakian, C., J. Moe, and J. Dolphin. 1950. Protein anabolic effect of testosterone propionate in adrenalectomized and normal rates. *American Journal of Physiology* 163:332-346.

30. Kochakian, C., E. Robertson, and M. Barlett. 1950. Sites and nature of protein anabolism stimulated by testosterone propionate in rates. *American Journal of Physiology* 163:322–346.

31. Kruskemper, H. L. 1968. *Anabolic Steroids.* New York: Academic Press.

32. Laritcheva, K. A., N. I. Valovarya, V. I. Shubin, and S. A. Smirnov. 1978. Study of energy expenditure and protein needs of top weightlifters. In J. Parizkova and V. A. Rogozkin (Eds.). *Nutrition, Physical Fitness, and Health. International Services on Sport Sciences* (Vol. 7.). Baltimore: University Park Press.

33. Laties, V. G., and B. Weiss. 1981. The amphetamine margin in sports (Symposium). *Federation Proceedings* 40(12):2689–2692.

34. MacDougall, D. 1983. Anabolic steroids. *The Physician and Sports Medicine* 11(9):95–99.

35. Mandell, A. J. 1976. *The Nightmare Season.* New York: Random House.

36. Mandell, A. J., K. D. Stewart, and P. V. Russo. 1981. The Sunday syndrome: from kinetics to altered consciousness (Symposium). *Federation Proceedings* 40(12):2693–2698.

37. Moore, L. G., I. F. McMurtry, and J. T. Reeves. 1978. Effects of sex hormones on cardiovascular and hematologic responses to chronic hypoxia in rats. *Proceedings of the Society for Experimental Biology and Medicine* 158:658–662.

38. Neff, C. 1983. Caracas: A scandal and a warning. *Sports Illustrated.* 11(59):18–23.

39. Newton, H. 1983. United States national weightlifting coach (personal communication).

40. Pesquies, P. C., R. Morville, C. Y. Guezennec, and B. D. Serrarier. 1981. Effects of prolonged physical exercise on blood concentrations of adrenal and testicular androgens. In J. Poortmans and G. Niset (Eds.). *Biochemistry of Exercise IV-B.* Baltimore: University Park Press.

41. Rosen, M. 1983. Track coach, Auburn University; sprint coach for the 1984 Olympic Games (personal communication).

42. Rozenek, R., and M. H. Stone. 1984. Protein metabolism related to athletes. *National Strength and Conditioning Association Journal* 6(2):42–62.

43. Ryan, A. J. 1983. Drug testing in athletics: Is it worth the trouble. *Physician and Sports Medicine* 11(8):131–131.

44. Ryan, A. J. 1981. Anabolic steroids are fool's gold (Symposium). *Federation Proceedings* 40(12):2682–2688.

45. Schlaadt, R. G. 1982. *Drugs of Choice.* Englewood Cliffs: Prentice Hall.

46. Stone, M. H. 1983. Estimate of caffeine and ephedrine use among national class strength-power athletes from the southeastern United States (unpublished data from personal communication). NSRC, Auburn University.

47. Stone, M. H., and H. Lipner. 1978. Responses to intensive training and methandrostenelone administration, Vol. I, Contractile and performance variables. *Pflugers Archives* 375:141–146.

48. Taylor, N. 1982. *Anabolic Steroids and the Athlete.* Jefferson, N.C.: McFarland & Co., Inc.

49. U.S. Olympic Committee, Division of Sports Medicine and Science. 1985. In drug testing in sports: a roundtable. *The Physician and Sportsmedicine* 13(12):69–82.

50. Vecsey, C. August 28, 1983. Its not just "them" seeking athletic edge. *Winston-Salem Journal,* p. D9. August 28.

51. Vischi, T., K. R. Jones, E. L. Shank, and L. H. Lima. 1980. *National Data Book.* Rockville, Maryland: DHHS Publication No. (ADM), 80–938.

52. Wright, J. E. 1978. *Anabolic Steroids and Sports.* Natick, Mass.: Sports Science Consultants.

53. Wright, J. E. 1980. Anabolic steroids and athletics in R. S. Hutton and D. I. Miller (Eds.). *Exercise and Sports Science Reviews* 8:149–202.

54. Wright, J. E. 1982. *Anabolic Steroids and Sports* (Vol. 2). Natick, Mass.: Sports Science Consultants.

55. Wright, J. E., and M. H. Stone. 1985. NSCA statement on anabolic drug use: literature review. *National Strength and Conditioning Association Journal* 7(5):45–59.

56. Ziel, H. R., and W. D. Finkle. 1975. Increased risk of endometrial carcinoma among users of conjugated estrogens. *New England Journal of Medicine* 293:1167–1170.

Lifting Technique and Illustrations

Flexibility Drills and Exercises

Flexibility can be defined as the range of motion in a joint. This range of motion is specific to the joint and to the individual. In general, females are naturally more flexible than males. Regardless of gender, flexibility is important because it affects performance and helps prevent injury. Factors that limit flexibility are: shortness of ligaments, bone structure, occlusion of soft tissues (fat, muscle, etc.), and shortness of tendons and muscle. In most cases, fortunately, tendons and muscles can be conditioned to regain loss of flexibility resulting from neglected range of motion.

Flexibility and warmup exercises should precede any attempted weight workout. Running in place, jumping jacks, or a brief period of rope jumping should increase metabolism and blood flow prior to the majority of flexibility work and therefore facilitate stretching.

When stretching, the pace should begin slowly and progress from the general to the more specific areas of the body. As one becomes familiar with the exercises and moves swiftly from one exercise to another, the time required for the entire flexibility and general warmup segment should not be more than 5 or 10 minutes, and it will be time well spent. Movements through the joint range of motion should be slow and controlled without any sudden jerky movement or bouncing. The following figures (10-1 through 10-17) are provided to illustrate the body position, technique, and muscles involved in some suggested flexibility exercises.

Figure 10–1. Trunk rotations (intercostals, abdominals, and erector spinae).

Figure 10–2. Side lunge (hip adductors and hamstrings). Start with a side stance (1) and with hands on floor for balance. Move sideways to achieve a low stretched position (2).

Figure 10–3. Front lunge (hip flexors). Similar to Figure 10–2, but move forward with back leg extended (1) and then arch to bring upper body more erect.

Figure 10–4. Squat extension (hamstrings). Begin in squat position with palms on floor (1). Slowly straighten knees until locked, with palms kept flat on floor (2). Hold 3 seconds and repeat.

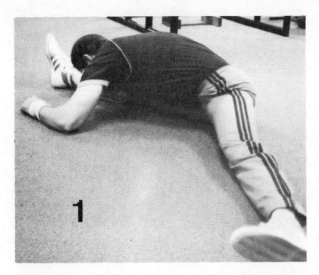 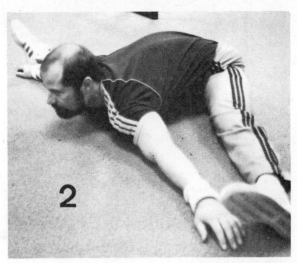

Figure 10–5. Straddle sit and reach (hamstrings and hip adductors). With legs straight, lay over one leg and then the other (1). Lay forward on floor between legs (2). Keep back as straight as possible.

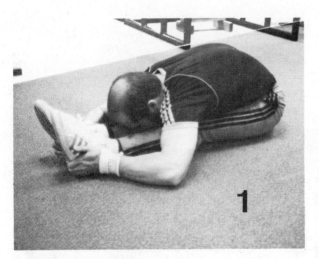 

Figure 10–6. Pike sit and reach (hamstrings, lower back, and gastrocnemius. With legs straight, lay as far as possible (1). Pull toes back (2).

Figure 10–7. Hurdler's stretch (hamstrings, sartorius, quadriceps, and hip adductors). Lay forward on the straight leg as in the straddle sit and reach (Figure 10–3). Next lay backward slowly into an intermediate position (1) and then work into a supine position with shoulders on the floor (2). (*Don't use this exercise if knee is damaged or weakened!*)

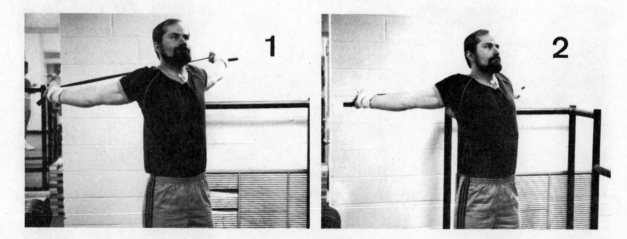

Figure 10–8. Shoulder dislocates (deltoids, pectoralis muscles, and biceps). Grasp a section of bicycle innertube with both hands spaced about shoulder width apart. Move both arms from in front of the body over the head and behind (1 and 2). The innertube should offer enough resistance to stretch tissues and yet lengthen enough at high stress positions to allow movement without undue chance of injury.

Figure 10–9. Shoulder hyperflexion (deltoids, pectoralis muscles, abdominals, and teres). Partner reaches through inside of subject's arms below elbows, hands on scapula. Chest and upper back is stretched as partners communicate where limits of movement occur. Partner moves slowly into and out of positions at subject's verbal signal.

Figure 10–10. Shoulder hyperextension (deltoids, pectoralis muscles, and biceps). Subject places hands on floor behind, shoulder width apart, and moves body forward increasing shoulder angle (1). Partner can assist for more concentrated work (2). Movements must occur on verbal cue from subject and proceed slowly into and out of positions.

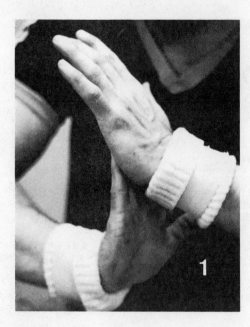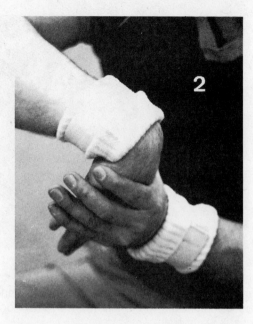

Figure 10–11. Wrist extension/flexion (1) illustrates pushing against underside of fingers to extend wrist. Gently push against anterior side of fingers and hand to flex wrist (2). Slow, careful movement is required during wrist flexion to avoid possible injury in this susceptible position.

Figure 10–12. Ankle flexion/extension (gastrocnemius and anterior tibialis). In a kneeling position, rock back on toes (1). Next, shift weight forward and raise hips so that toes and foot are forced into a full extension position (2).

Figure 10–13. Achilles stretch (Achilles tendon). Force acute angle on back ankle.

Figure 10–14. Squat stretch. To work deep squat position, partner stands on top of subject's thigh.

Figure 10–15. Ankle circumduction (peroneals, anterior tibialis, and gastrocnemius). Ankle is gently moved in a circular motion clockwise and again counterclockwise.

Figure 10–16. Arm pulls (lats, pectoralis muscles, teres, and intercostals). Reach behind head to grab arm below elbow (1). Pull to the side, stretching both arm and trunk.

Figure 10–17. Snatch squat stretch (specific to bottom position on snatch). Subject should strive for balance and proper body alignment as shoulders are stretched with a section of bicycle innertube, similar to exercise shown in Figure 10–8.

Multijoint/Large Muscle Mass Lifts

The *large muscle mass lifts* are those that typically involve several muscles simultaneously. These muscles usually span more than one joint and therefore control the movement of several body segments. Activating a large mass of muscle is often desirable to achieve high metabolic demands (as in programs for weight control). Multijoint movement also is characteristic of many sport-specific patterns and would be logical choices for the development of carryover strength for improved athletic performance. Because of the multijoint nature of these movements, which requires precise body alignment and sequential control of several body segments simultaneously, biomechanical faults are often more likely.

Figure 10–18. Parallel back squat, power lifting style (erector spinae, quadriceps, hamstrings, and gluteals). Picture sequence numbered frames 1 through 8 illustrates a technique typically used by powerlifters. Shown here is the down phase of the lift, in which the lifter bends the knees and lowers the body until the tops of the thighs are below parallel with the platform (see frame 8 for bottom position). The head should be kept up and the back should be straight throughout the exercise. Note the bar position far down on the back. A wider stance with toes pointed out can strengthen the adductors and may be used instead of a heel board for people with poor ankle flexibility (see Figure 10–19).

Figure 10–18. (continued). During the descent, bar velocity should be kept at a constant, slow, controlled rate. A common fault in less skilled lifters is to increase bar velocity during the initial phases of the descent (frames 1–5) and sharply reduce bar velocity during the final portion of the descent (frames 6–8) (6). Less skilled lifters are also likely to maintain greater trunk lean and exaggerate backward hip movement (6). The bar should be kept in a more or less vertical path (see Figure 10–21). The ascent portion of the lift should begin immediately after bottom position is achieved. It should be done with a relatively constant but rapid upward velocity of the bar and completed with a forward hip roll to a fully erect body stance.

Figure 10–19. Foot position during squat. Frame 1 illustrates the shoulder width position some lifters commonly use during a parallel squat. Others may use a wider stance (frame 2) with toes pointed slightly outward. Regardless of width, feet should remain flat throughout the entire lift.

 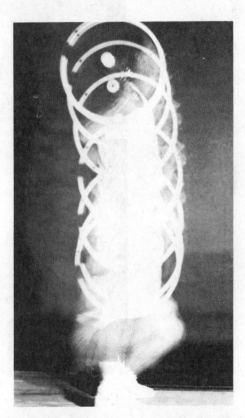

Figure 10–20. Bar position during olympic-style squat. Some athletes, including Olympic weightlifters, use a higher bar position for the performance of a squat.

Figure 10–21. Vertical path of bar during a parallel squat. This strobe photo illustrates that there is little horizontal deflection forward or backward.

Figure 10–22. Squat using step rack. (Photographs courtesy of Dr. Ralph Steben, L.S.U.) The lifter should always face into the step rack. Typically, two spotters are stationed, one on each end of the bar. Bar is lifted off the high portion of the rack. The lifter then relocates backward to be positioned directly over the low portion of rack (frame 1). Should the lifter be unable to complete the lift, the bar can simply be lowered to the rack without danger or injury to the spotters or the lifter.

Figure 10-23. Snatch squat (quadriceps, gluteals, hamstrings, deltoids, erector spinae, and trapezius). Using a wide grip with weight held overhead, perform the squatting movements as shown and described for Figure 10-18.

Figure 10–24. Overhead squat (erector spinae, quadriceps, hamstrings, gluteals, deltoids, and trapezius). Using a narrow grip with weight held overhead, perform the squatting movements as shown and described for Figure 10–18.

Figure 10–25. Quarter squat (gastrocnemius, hamstrings, and quadriceps). (Photographs courtesy of Dr. Ralph Steben, L.S.U.) This variation of the squat involves a shallow bottom position (frame 1) with the thigh only about 45 degrees to the horizontal. The upward thrust is executed swiftly with complete extension of the ankle and foot (frame 2).

Figure 10–26. Front full squat (quadriceps, gluteals, hamstrings, erector spinae, and anterior deltoids). This variation of the squat puts more stress on the lower end of the quadriceps just above the knee. This lift is sport-specific not only to Olympic weightlifting, but also to many sports in which leg drive strength is directed upward and forward, as in running and jumping movements. Note the high arm position and wrist flexibility, which positions the bar on the chest but off the sternoclavicular joint.

Figure 10–26. (continued). Note proper body alignment with head up, arms up, and back straight, even in the extreme bottom position (frame 6). Contrary to what some people have been taught, the full squat performed with a controlled descent does not cause knee joint injury (5). It can actually strengthen the knee at that position to help promote joint integrity.

Figure 10–27. Squat lunge (erector spinae, quadriceps, gluteals, and hamstrings). With weight resting on back (1) take a large step forward to a low position (2); then return back to an upright position (3) and (4). Repeat with the other leg.

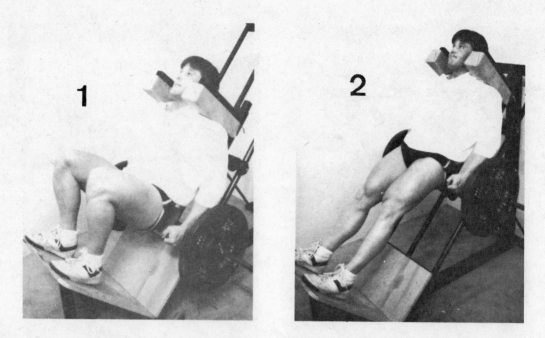

Figure 10–28. Hack squat machine. This version of the squat allows relatively heavy lifts with less stress on the lower back. More stress, however, may be placed on the lower portion of the quadriceps and knee joint.

Figure 10–29. Vertical leg press machine (quadriceps, hamstrings, and gluteals). This position, similar to the squat, is much like the hack squat machine shown in Figure 10–28. This movement does not put stress on the lower back, but the hamstrings may bear more stress during lifts, which are often very heavy. (Avoid hyperextension of the knee.)

Figure 10–30. Deadlift (erector spinae, trapezius, quadriceps, and hamstrings). This is a required lift among powerlifters and is performed with a mixed grip (one over, one under). Unlike the squat, the back is slightly rounded. This last point should not be taken lightly, for improper back position may constitute a susceptible body position for the unconditioned or less skilled lifter. Upward bar velocity is kept slow, continuous, and controlled, with the lower body primarily responsible for initiating movement (frames 1 and 2).

Figure 10–30. (continued). The bar is kept as close as possible throughout the lift. Latter phases of the lift require a vigorous straightening of the back and pulling through the shoulders (frames 3 and 4). The deadlift is completed with a slight rearward lean of the upper back and roll through the shoulders (frame 4).

Figure 10–31. Clean pull from floor, oblique view (quadriceps, hamstrings, trapezius, gluteals, erector spinae, and gastrocnemius). (Photographs courtesy of Dr. Ralph Steben, L.S.U.) Unlike the deadlift, the clean pull is done as fast as possible in one very powerful movement. The first part of the lift comes from the legs (frames 1–3). The bar starts and stays close to the body during the entire pull. The legs straighten as the bar clears the height of the knees.

Figure 10–31. (continued). The upper body comes into play during the last part of the lift (frames 3 and 4). A second knee bend in frame 4 is associated with a brief unweighting phase during which the hips roll in close to the bar, causing realignment of the body (2). This realignment permits an enhanced re-employment of the knee extensors as well as extension of the trunk, reducing undue stress on the back and trunk extensor muscles. The double knee bend and subsequent realignment provide for a very powerful, near vertical pull of the bar (3) ending in an upward shoulder shrug and complete extension through the ankle and toes (frame 5). Biomechanically, this lift is very similar to vertical jumping in both the muscles and movement dynamics (4). If performed correctly, this lift can be executed with relatively heavy weight without premature fatigue or overuse of the smaller muscle groups. Among the most common mistakes made by less skilled lifters are: rounded back during lift, premature pull of the upper body, lack of double knee bend, and bar pulled far in front of body. Note the width of the hand placement and use of wrist straps (see Figure 10–32).

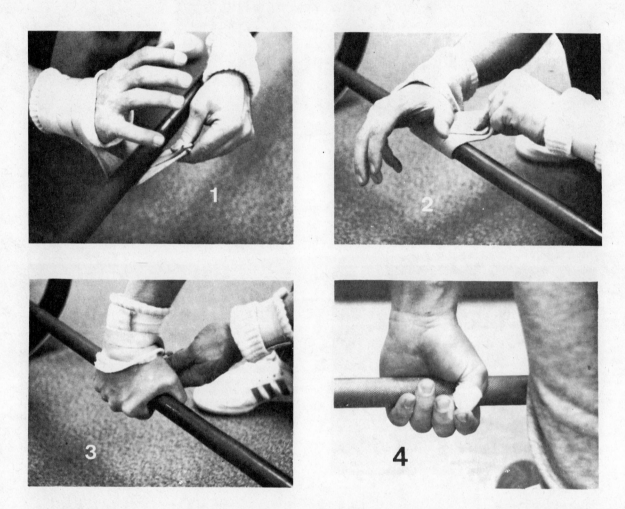

Figure10–32. Grip and use of straps. During training wrist straps are often used when executing pulls. These straps are pieces of 2–inch wide webbing cut in sections 20–22 inches long. The straps are wrapped under the bar in opposition to the fingers. Frame 1 illustrates the start of the wrap on the right hand, with frames 3 and 4 showing the completion of the wrap on the left hand. These straps help protect the hands from undue wear and tear as well as prevent premature fatigue of the forearm muscles necessary to grip the bar. Such straps are particularly helpful when executing high volume pull work. Frame 4 shows the *hook grip* often used in competition during the pull for the clean as well as the snatch. The hook grip provides a better grip on the bar by wrapping the thumb around the bar under the first two fingers, which apply opposing interlocking pressure over the thumb.

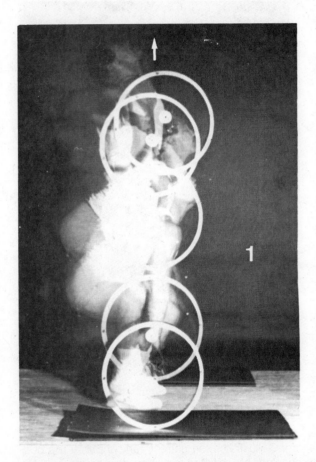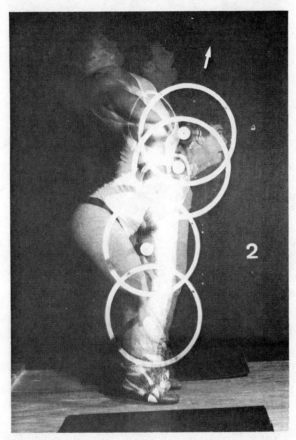

Figure 10–33. Path of bar during clean pull. Two strobe photos are provided here. Photo 1 shows the correct path of the bar during a clean pull. A slight *S* curve made by the path of the bar (as seen from the side) is characteristic of correct technique during the upward part of the lift. Photo 2 demonstrates a common mistake as the bar deviates horizontally in a forward direction while the body is being pulled backward through an exaggerated arch (see Figure 10–34).

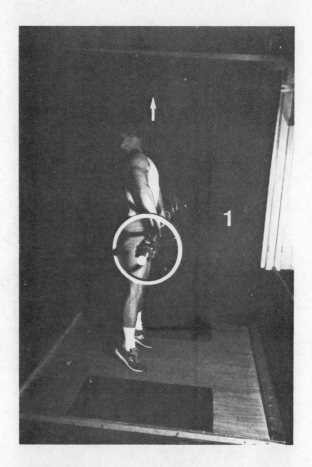 

Figure 10–34. Vertical versus nonvertical clean pull. Frame 1 illustrates the correct vertical pull at top position. The nonvertical pull shown in frame 2 results from shoulder pull initiated too soon during early phases of the lift, leaving the lifter to resort to a bouncing of the bar off the thigh and the subsequent exaggerated arch. The same mechanical faults are likely to occur during the performance of a *clean* or *snatch*.

Figure 10–35. Clean pull from mid-thigh. (Photographs courtesy of Dr. Ralph Steben, L.S.U.) The sequence presented here illustrates another version of a clean pull exercise concentrating on the second portion of the pull. Like the clean pull from the floor, the upward phase of this lift is also performed as fast as possible. This version of the pull does not require the force or range of motion from the hamstrings or gluteals as the former lift. But the hip and knee angles of this lift simulate those of many sport-specific movement patterns. This lift can often be easier to execute correctly than the clean pull from the floor. For this reason, the clean pull from mid-thigh is sometimes taught prior to the clean pull from the floor. Caution should be exercised when performing this lift from a hang as pictured here. Decelerating the bar on the latter portion of the lift can place undue stress on the muscles and connective tissues of the lower back (see frames 3 and 4). Boxes or a padded step rack should be used if high volume or high intensity lifts of this nature are to be done. When using boxes or a rack to achieve mid-thigh height, the bar can be lowered at the conclusion of each repetition without the lifter having to support the full braking force of the bar with his body.

Figure 10–36. Olympic-style clean. There are two clean styles. The olympic-style version shown here is used in competitive weightlifting. The pull portion (frames 1–4) is basically the same as described for figure 10–31. Note the bar orientation during the second pull (frames 3 and 4) as well as the second knee bend of the double knee bend technique (frame 3). The pull should be quick, vertical, and high (frame 4) to facilitate getting under the bar. A near vertical pull helps insure balance on the bottom.

Figure 10-36. (continued). After the pull, extreme quickness should be used to get under the bar to allow adequate time to set up the rack position (frame 5). A full squat with good wrist flexibility and a high arm rack is necessary for the correct bottom position. To complete the lift, a front squat is performed. In olympic-style competition, a jerk would follow, as discussed later.

Figure 10-37. Power clean. The power clean is used as a training exercise by many athletes. This lift is accomplished with less technique and therefore relies more on strength, particularly on the pull. Shown here in frames 1-3, the pull can be absent of any double knee bend. The greatest difference between the olympic-style clean and the power clean is demonstrated in frames 4-6.

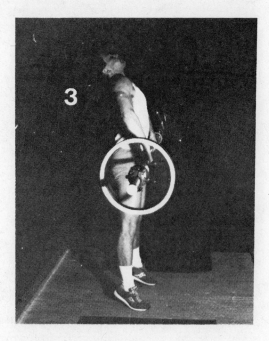

Figure 10–37. (continued). The hop under the bar during the last portion of the power clean does not usually require a deep squat position. In general, technique is not greatly emphasized to allow the less skilled lifter some immediate success. The power clean may not be a good choice as a primary exercise for conditioning the leg and hip extensors because of the limitations resulting from overuse of the wrist extensors. In other words, using enough weight to produce a sufficient training effect on the larger muscles of the lower body will likely cause the smaller muscles of the forearm and wrist to fatigue prematurely and eventually lead to symptoms of overuse (tendonitis, etc.). The clean pull may be a better choice. The clean pull can be mastered by progression from the mid-thigh position and does not compromise as much on correct technique as does the power clean, which can actually promote poor mechanics.

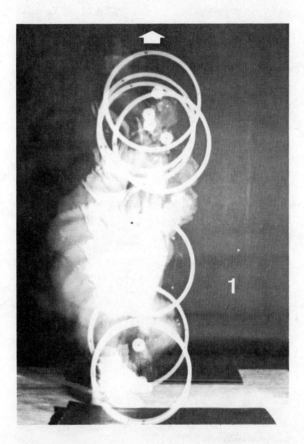 

Figure 10–38. Strobe sequence of olympic-style clean. Photo 1 illustrates a clean with correct technique (note slight *S* curve vertically and very little horizontal deviation occurring during the transition from the end of the pull to hop under the weight as seen at the top of the photo). Photo 2 demonstrates a pull with incorrect technique in which the bar is pulled too far backward at the top of the photo where the lifter is about to hop under the weight. This is a common mechanical flaw that can result from a nonvertical pull and poor head position (note head tilted far backward in photo 2). Many times such a fault can be traced to earlier problems such as poor starting stance, early pull of trunk, or bounce of bar off thighs causing a forward deviation and overcompensation with backward pull in an attempt to bring bar back in line with the vertical.

Figure 10–39. Split jerk, oblique view (quadriceps, hamstrings, gastrocnemius, erector spinae, and triceps). (Photographs courtesy of Dr. Ralph Steben, L.S.U.) Pictured here is a sequence demonstrating the last segment of the olympic clean and jerk. As seen here, the most common technique is the split style. Initiation of the movement is begun by a very vigorous upward leg drive (frames 2–4). Next there is a moment of unloading during which the lifter quickly moves under the weight and catches the bar with locked elbows.

Figure 10–39. (continued). The split is accomplished by the forward movement of one leg and the backward movement of the other so that the bar, which has been forced vertically, will be balanced as it is caught on the way down (see Figure 10–40 for side view). To complete the lift, the performer moves the back leg forward slightly to get balance, then again forward as the front leg comes back.

Figure 10–40. Split jerk, side view. Seen here from the side, the split jerk drive begins with the elbows well up so that a vertical thrust of the bar will occur from the chest (frames 1–4). Quickness getting underneath the bar will help ensure a strong bottom position in the split. Common mistakes are: elbows too far down, nonvertical thrust of bar, exaggerated forward or backward movement on split, and slow movement under bar resulting in bar caught with bent elbows.

Figure 10–41. Push jerk, oblique view. (Photographs by permission of Bruce Klemens.) This jerk style, which is used by a few lifters, requires superior leg strength. It is also a very good conditioning lift used to develop leg power. Pictured here is world champion Russian Olympic lifter Victor Sots at 100-kg (220-lb) weight class lifting 232.5 kg (512.7 lb) during the 1982 World Championships in Ljubljana, Yugoslavia. In this meet, he later set a new world record by lifting 242.5 kg (534.7 lb) in the clean and jerk.

Figure 10–41. (continued). Note the quickness getting under the weight between frames 4 and 5 in order to catch the weight with locked elbows.

Figure 10–42. Push jerk, side view. Provided here is a side view of the push jerk technique to illustrate body alignment and orientation of the bar to the body. Extreme quickness is exhibited between frames 3 and 4, with superior leg strength required to achieve the positions in frames 4 and 5. Note arm position and leg drive in frames 1–3.

Figure 10–43. Push press (triceps, quadriceps, hamstrings, gastrocnemius, erector spinae, and gluteals). This lift is frequently used in conditioning of strength-power athletes and is often confused with the push jerk. The major difference is illustrated in frame 4. A push jerk would have the knees bent and arms straight to allow the lifter to lock the elbows and lift the weight with the legs. The push press, on the other hand, is only initiated by the leg drive and depends on the press strength of the arms to finish.

Figure 10–43. (continued). The leg drive used to begin the push press should be very quick and powerful, as range of motion is short.

Figure 10–44. Olympic-style snatch, oblique view (gastrocnemius, trapezius, quadriceps, gluteals, hamstrings, deltoids, and erector spinae). The snatch is another lift performed in Olympic weightlifting competition. Pictured here is the full sequence, emphasizing the width of the grip.

Figure 10–44. (continued). The pull found in the snatch is not unlike that shown for the clean except that a weight belt is not usually used because it can hinder the path of the bar. A nonvertical pull can have even more of an effect on the success of the lift. A common mistake is to let the bar drift too far forward away from the body. In addition, less skilled lifters are likely to let the elbows drop at the top of the pull when transition for the hop under the weight is about to occur (frame 7). Shoulder and hip flexibility are a must for the correct technical execution of this lift (see flexibility and associative exercises).

Figure 10–44. (continued). Completion of the snatch is aided by squat strength developed in the hip and leg extensors and used to achieve the ending stance.

Figure 10–45. Olympic-style snatch, side view. The olympic-style snatch is shown from the side to emphasize the perspective between the bar and the body. Note the second knee bend and delayed upper body pull just as in the clean (frame 3).

Figure 10–45. (continued). Shown here is the high elbow pull (frames 4–6) just before the transition of the body underneath the bar. The pull should be kept continuous even though there is a tendency to let the bar rise only from its own momentum. Again, in order for there to be balance on the bottom position, the bar must be pulled somewhat vertical (note slight *S* curve) without undue deviation horizontally. The bar will be balanced and therefore easier to control if it is directly over the midline of the foot (frame 7). A common mistake, particularly with heavier weights, is to let the back round while standing up from the squat position. This may be largely due to lack of strength in the erector muscles of the lower back (see associative exercises).

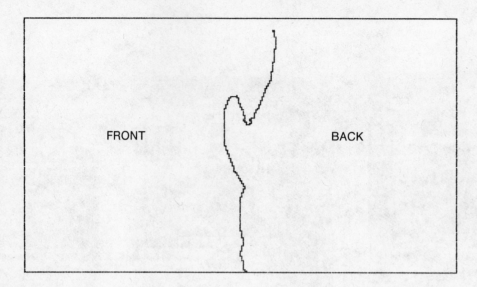

Figure 10–46. Bar plot during snatch. This computer-generated representation illustrates the correct path of the bar during a snatch, as pictured in Figure 10–45.

Figure 10–47. Bottom position during olympic-style snatch. (Photograph by permission of Bruce Klemens.) Pictured here is 100-kg (220-lb) Russian Olympic weightlifter Victor Sots lifting more than 400 lb (181.4 kg). Note how strength and flexibility go hand in hand.

Figure 10–48. Power snatch. A power snatch is to an olympic-style snatch as a power clean is to an olympic-style clean (see Figures 10–36 and 10–37). The analogy holds true for the technique in general as well as for the squat position. Frame 6 shows a shallower bottom position than that associated with the olympic style. Because of the shallow squat, the lifter must rely more on the amplitude and speed of the pull for execution of the lift, particularly if heavy weights are utilized.

Figure 10–48. (continued). Because of the great distance through which the weight is moved, large quantities of work can be done in a relatively short time (remember that work is a function of force and displacement). Therefore, this lift is a good choice for the person who is lifting for weight control and general fitness because of the large muscle mass involved and the high metabolic demands of the exercise.

Figure 10–49. Bench press grip. The bench press, even though it is not a large muscle mass lift, is a very popular multijoint exercise often used to develop upper body strength. Pictured here are two variations of the grip. In frame 1 the shoulder width commonly used is demonstrated. Frame 2 shows a wider grip, which is used to place more load on the muscles of the chest. The narrower grip pattern will put less load on the chest but more on the tricep of the arm.

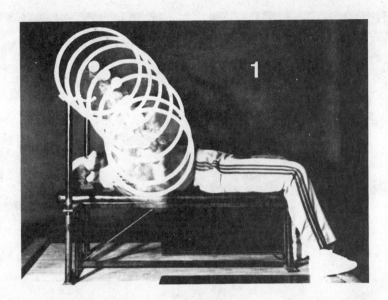

Figure 10–50. Supine bench press (triceps, pectoralis muscles, and deltoids). To place the triceps in the best position to assist the chest and shoulder muscles, the bar must follow a set path. Frame 1 illustrates the groove or arc path of the bar during the upward phase of the lift. This is the common technique used by powerlifters who keep the elbows pulled in close toward the body to take advantage of the passive resistance afforded by the latissimus dorsi muscles, which can aid in stability and upward movement from the lower position. Typical faults found among less skilled lifters are: raising the hips off the bench, an overly exaggerated arch of the lower back, and bouncing the bar off the chest (1). Many of these faults are committed in an attempt to change the arm/chest angle at the *sticking point* to result in a stronger position. Nevertheless, these are mechanical mistakes and substitute different muscles for those originally intended. Associative or assistive exercises would be a better alternative for the development of other muscles.

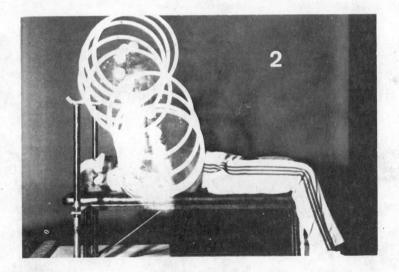

Figure 10–50. (continued). Frame 2 shows a different line of travel when the elbows are kept out, away from the body, during the upward lift of the supine bench press. This is a mechanical variation used in an attempt to maintain movement specificity by many athletes who condition to improve throwing ability (discus throwers, shotputters, football and baseball players, and others). Instead of an arc, the path of the bar follows more of an *S* configuration. This technique may also tend to utilize more arm adductors during execution past the *sticking point* while sparing stressful effort from those same muscles in the early portion of the upward movement of the press. Regardless of which technique variation is used, the bar should be brought low enough down on the chest to stretch the muscles of the chest and shoulder, therefore leading to a stronger contraction when those muscles must produce force to lift the weight (see Chapter 4).

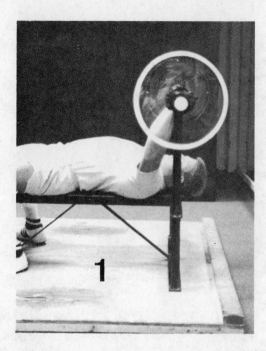 

Figure 10–51. Body position during bench press. Frame 1 indicates the body position for a supine bench press, during which the eyes are in line underneath the bar when lying in the rack of the uprights. This positions the lifter so that there is adequate room between the uprights and the bar for the correct line of travel during the upward press (frame 2).

Figure 10–52. Incline bench press. This is a variation of the supine bench press. Many athletes condition with this version because it closely approximates the shoulder angle used during execution of throwing and other sport-specific movements. The starting position is shown in frame 1 and the ending position in frame 2. Spotting assistance can be given from behind as shown and is important for this lift because the upward angle may be difficult for the less experienced lifter to stabilize.

Associative Lifts

The exercises presented in this section, which will be referred to as associative lifts, are considered movements that closely approximate a single phase or motion sequence of another major, multijoint/large muscle mass lift. Such supplemental exercises are intended to condition some of the same muscle groups used in the previously illustrated major lifts. Although not inclusive, the following lifts are examples of some of the associative lifts currently used in weight-resistive programs.

Figure 10–53. High pull. (Photograph by permission of Bruce Klemens.) Who is this Russian olympic weightlifter? Pictured here is a high pull with snatch grip being performed with approximately 500 lb (225 kg). This illustrates that even though associative lifts are not considered major lifts, they are certainly not to be taken lightly!

Figure 10–54. High pulls with different grip (trapezius and deltoids). The high pull is associated with the pull for both the clean (frame 1) and the snatch (frame 2). The exercise begins with the bar in the hang position and is vigorously pulled to the positions demonstrated in these photos. The elbows are to be kept turned out during the completion of the pull. The pull is intended to be performed only by muscles of the upper body.

Figure 10–55. Shoulder shrug (trapezius). The shrugging action demonstrated here comes strictly from the shoulder elevators without any upward lift contributed by the legs or hip extensors. This lift is associated with the olympic-style lifts as well as the deadlift.

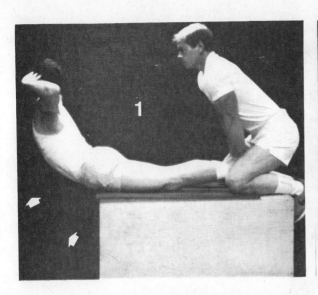

Figure 10–56. Back hyperextension (erector spinae, gluteals, and hamstrings). This is classified as an associative lift for the snatch, clean and jerk, squat, and deadlift, which can be done with (frame 2) or without (frame 1) weight. This is an excellent exercise to improve overall posture and a good choice for people with jobs that fatigue the muscles of the lower back (secretaries, businessmen, dock workers, etc.).

Figure 10–57. Good morning (erector spinae, hamstrings, and gluteals). The lower back is possibly one of the most neglected yet most important areas of the body for athletes and nonathletes alike. Along with the back hyperextension (Figure 10–56), the good morning is intended to strengthen this very vulnerable area. The exercise pictured here progresses from frames 1–3 and is shown with straight legs. The beginner or less conditioned person may want to first attempt this exercise with the legs slightly bent.

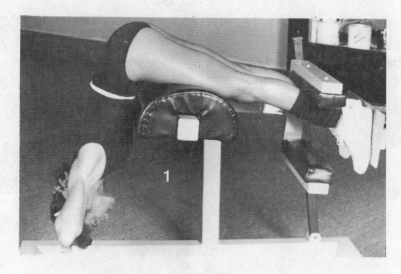

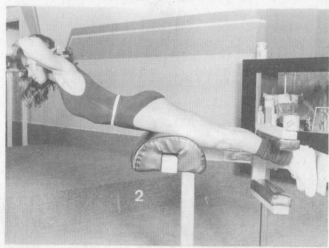

Figure 10–58. Glute-ham raise (gluteals, hamstrings, and erector spinae). (Photo courtesy of *Strength Training Magazine.*) Frames 1 and 2 show starting position similar to the back hyperextension exercise shown in Figure 10–56. Frame 3, however, indicates a transition of the stress, placing more emphasis on the gluteals and hamstrings.

Figure 10–59. Prone shoulder dislocates (deltoids and trapezius). The exercise pictured here is an associative lift for the snatch with a lesser degree of specificity to the clean. A wide grip is necessary for this exercise, which is intended to promote both strength and flexibility of the shoulder. The exercise starts with frame 1, slowly progressing to frame 4.

Figure 10–60. Narrow grip bench press (triceps, pectoralis muscles, and anterior deltoids). Using this narrow grip the stress is placed more upon the tricep than it is in the conventional bench press.

Figure 10–61. Incline dumbbell press (pectoralis muscles, triceps, and anterior deltoid). A good stretch can be achieved at the bottom position to stimulate a myototic reflex.

Figure 10–62. Seated overhead dumbbell press (deltoids, triceps, and trapezius). This variation on an overhead press reduces the stress placed on the lower back that can occur with a conventional straight barbell.

Figure 10–63. Supine dumbbell press (triceps, anterior deltoid, and pectoralis muscles). This variation on a supine press places more stretch on the active muscles at the bottom position when compared to a conventional supine barbell press.

Figure 10–64. Single dumbbell thrust (pectoralis muscles, triceps, abdominal oblique, and deltoid). Pictured here is an associative lift related to the bench press that is specifically used in the conditioning of throwers. The trunk torque demonstrated here is directly related to all overhead and sidearm throwing patterns. The one-arm movement from the shoulder is sport-specific to the shotput. A quick propulsive action progresses from frame 1 to frame 2.

Figure 10–65. Behind the neck press (deltoids, trapezius, and triceps). (Photographs courtesy of Dr. Ralph Steben, L.S.U.) This lift is associated with the snatch and the clean and jerk. It is done seated to reduce pressure on the lower back. This lift can be spotted from the side as pictured here, or from the back. The upward phase starts in frame 1 and ends in frame 2.

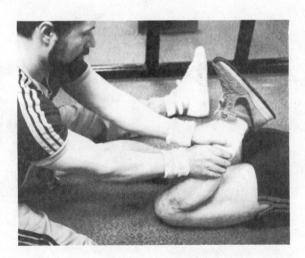

Figure 10–66. Leg extension (quadriceps). Partner resists as leg is slowly extended.

Figure 10–67. Seated machine leg extension (quadriceps). Presented here is an exercise that is associated with all the major lifts that require knee extension, particularly the squatting and leg drive movement patterns. The shearing forces may be greater in this variation, however, so this exercise is contraindicated for people with unstable knee joints.

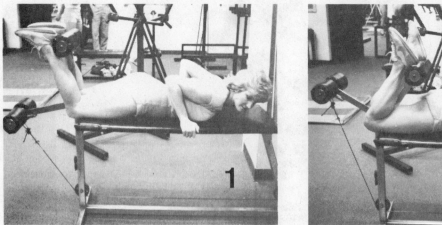

Figure 10–68. Prone machine leg curl (hamstrings, gluteals, and gastrocnemius). The leg curl movement is very important in conditioning the muscles used in extension of the hip during the leg drive of many lifts as well as in sport-specific jumping activities. A well-conditioned hamstring may also be much less prone to injury.

Figure 10–69. Single leg work. Frame 1 demonstrates a machine designed to allow single leg quadricep work. Frame 2 shows a machine for standing single leg hamstring conditioning.

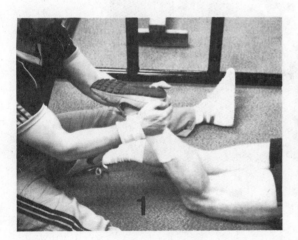 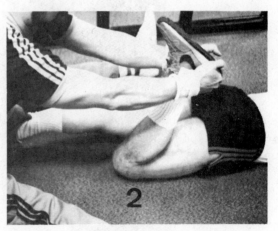

Figure 10–70. Partner-assisted prone leg curl (hamstrings, gluteals, and gastrocnemius). When leg curl machines are not available, a partner can resist during the movement of the leg and therefore provide the necessary resistance to produce a training effect.

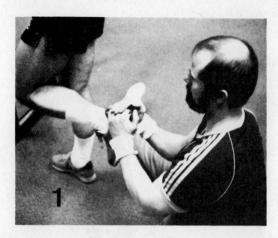
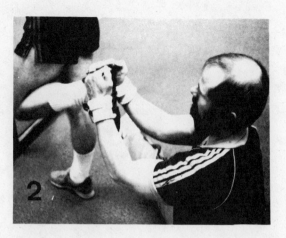

Figure 10–71. Partner-assisted standing leg curl. Similar to the exercise pictured in Figure 10–70, but it works the hamstrings at a slightly different angle and requires more work on the part of the hip stabilizers.

Figure 10–72. Hip extension with cable (gluteals, hamstrings, and erector spinae). (Photograph courtesy of *Strength Training Magazine.*) This exercise can be used as a variation for leg curls, glute-ham raises, and hyperextensions.

Assistive Lifts

The exercises in this section will be referred to as assistive lifts because although they can supplement the conditioning of the major movements discussed and illustrated earlier, they entail decidedly different muscle dynamics. Assistive lifts (sometimes called body building exercises) often limit action to single joint movement, characteristically isolate muscles, and typically involve a smaller muscle mass. Presented here are some of the common exercises that fall into this category, although there may be many more with numerous variations of each.

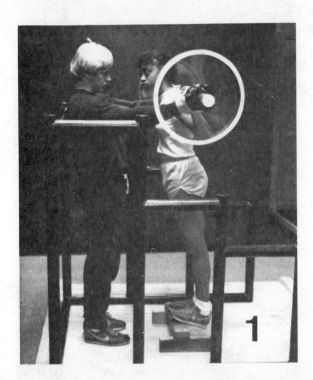 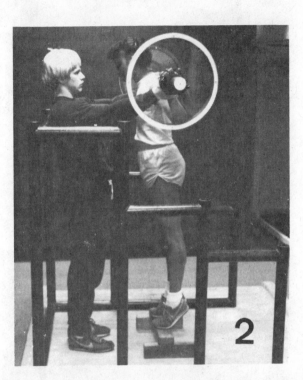

Figure 10–73. Heel rise (gastrocnemius and soleus). Frame 1 indicates the starting position with the heel below the support block. The movement is deliberate yet controlled to achieve the position in frame 2. This exercise can be an integral part of a workout session or done during warmup.

 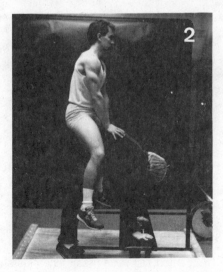

Figure 10–74. Donkey raise (gastrocnemius and soleus). A variation on the heel rise shown in Figure 10–73.

 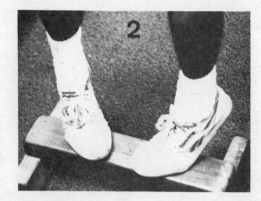

Figure 10–75. Heel rise foot placement. Here are two variations on foot placement to use while performing the heel rise (or donkey raise) that will condition the muscles and supporting tissues in slightly different ways.

 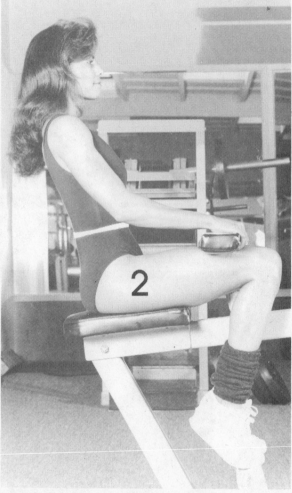

Figure 10–76. Seated calf raise (gastrocnemius and soleus). (Photograph courtesy of *Strength Training Magazine.*) A variation on Figures 10–73 and 10–74.

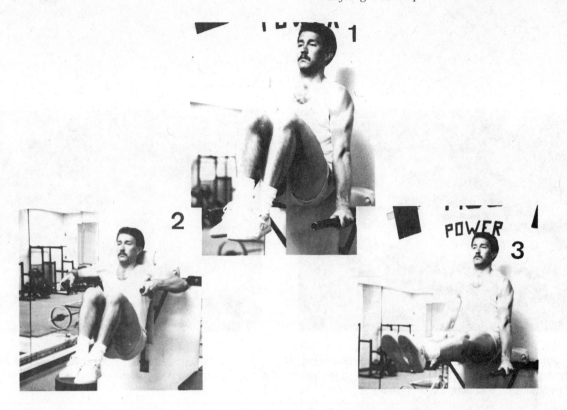

Figure 10–77. Knee raises (lower abdominals and hip flexors). Knee raises can be done either from a straight arm support (frame 1) or an underarm support (frame 2). The movement is begun from a straight leg hang and brought to the ending position shown here. Straight leg raises also can be done as pictured in frame 3.

Figure 10–78. Leg lifts from underarm support (abdominals and hip extensors). (Photograph courtesy of *Strength Training Magazine*.) A variation on knee raises (see Figure 10–77.)

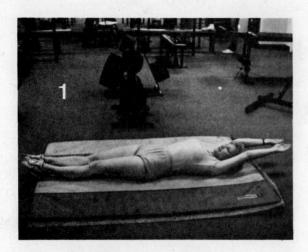 

Figure 10–79. V-ups (abdominals and hip flexors). A conditioning exercise for the midsection, with muscle dynamics somewhere between sit-ups and leg raises. Frame 1 demonstrates the beginning position with movement to end as shown in frame 2.

Figure 10–80. Cable leg pulls (abdominals and hip flexors). (Photograph courtesy of *Strength Training Magazine*.) A variation on the knee raises (see Figure 10–77.)

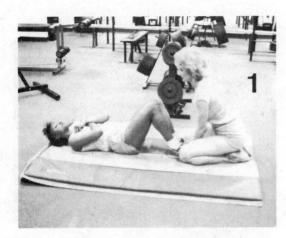 

Figure 10–81. Sit-ups (upper abdominals). Sit-ups done as pictured here with bent knees and with arms across chest will strengthen the midsection without placing undue stress on the lower back. This exercise can be done with or without weight and with or without a spotter.

 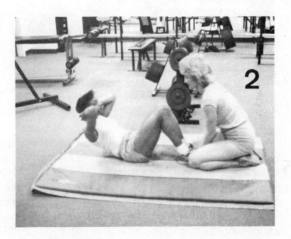

Figure 10–82. Sit-ups with hands on head. Some people place the hands behind the head as illustrated in frame 2, which may place unnecessary tension on the muscles and connective tissues of the cervical vertebra. If hands are placed on the head, they should be beside the head as in frame 1.

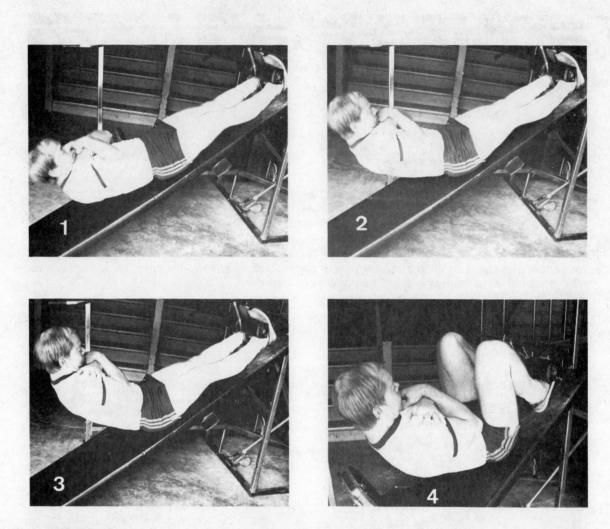

Figure 10–83. Incline board sit-ups. A variation of the sit-up for the well-conditioned is shown here. The purpose of the incline is not to increase the intensity so much as to increase the effective range of motion so that resistance is over a longer duration. When done straight legged (frames 1–3) caution should be taken to curl the body so the lower back area is the last to leave the board. Repetitions per set should be kept minimal because fatigue is more likely to cause an arch that will shift the stress from the abdominals to the hip flexors (psoas muscle) and, in turn, put undue stress on the lower back. If the exercise is done with knees bent (frame 4), this problem is not as likely to occur.

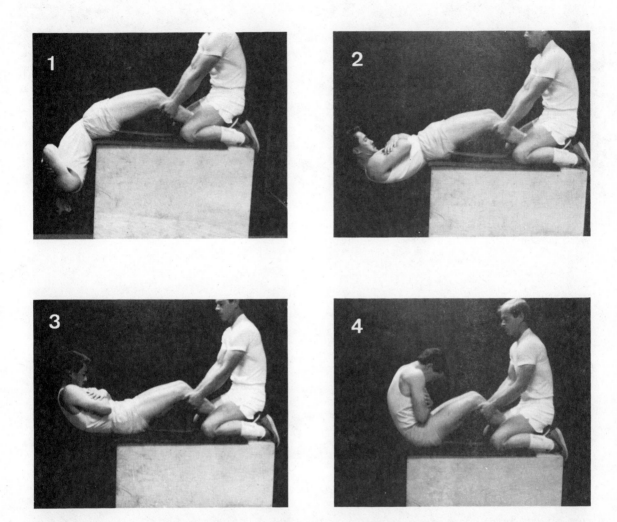

Figure 10–84. Roman chair sit-ups (sometimes known as super sit-ups). Another variation on the sit-up, this exercise can also increase the effective range of motion. This movement is also sport-specific to abdominal action during many throwing motions. It is important to curl the body upward to take stress off the lower back, as was discussed under Figure 10–83.

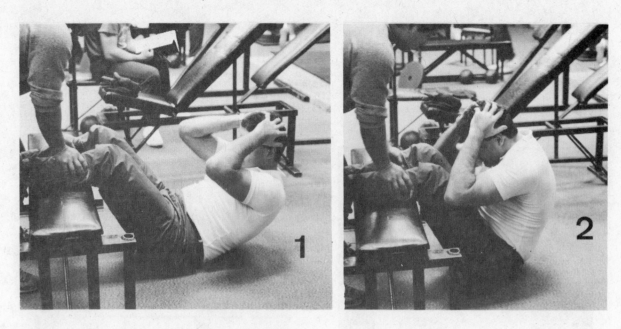

Figure 10–85. Crunches. This variation of a sit-up is done with the feet elevated.

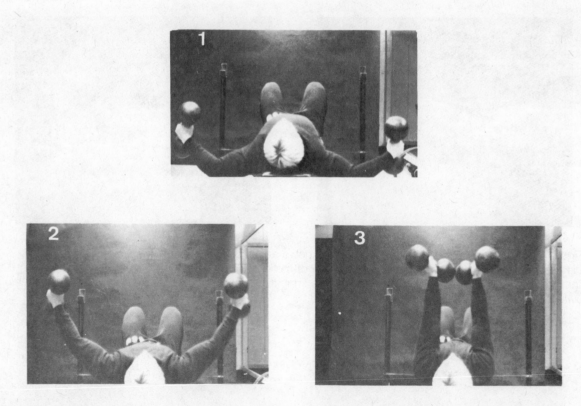

Figure 10–86. Butterflys (pectoralis muscles, biceps, and deltoids). Elbows are slightly bent. Upward phase of exercise progresses from frame 1 through 3.

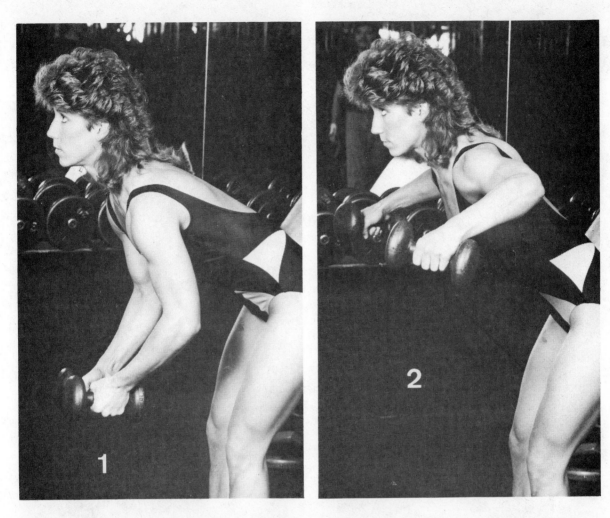

Figure 10–87. Bent over lateral raises (deltoids, latissimus dorsi, and trapezius). (Photograph courtesy of *Strength Training Magazine.*) This sequence demonstrates a variation in which the trunk is bent forward to place more stress on the latissimus dorsi and stabilizers of the scapula.

Figure 10–88. Seated lateral raise (trapezius and middle deltoid). This seated lateral raise incorporates a shoulder shrug at the end (frame 2) to condition the trapezius more.

Figure 10–89. Front raise (anterior deltoid and erector spinae). A swingbell is used to perform this good deltoid conditioner, which starts from a hang position and progresses through frames 1 and 2.

Figure 10–90. Lateral pulls (internal and external obliques and serratus). To correctly perform this exercise, one should not bend forward or backward at the waist but rather move only laterally.

Figure 10–91. Bent-over barbell rows (latissimus dorsi, trapezius, and posterior deltoid). This exercise works best when performed from a slightly raised platform in order to work through a greater range of motion. The knees are bent slightly to take stress off the lower back.

Figure 10–92. One arm dumbbell row (rhomboids, posterior deltoid and latissimus dorsi). (Photograph courtesy of *Strength Training Magazine*.) This variation on the bent-over row works one arm at a time so that the free arm can act as a support to take stress off the lower back and therefore concentrate on the pull itself. *Note: This exercise also can be done with the elbow rotated outward.*

Figure 10–93. Seated pulls (latissimus dorsi, erector spinae, and biceps). This is another rowing type movement for the back and arms.

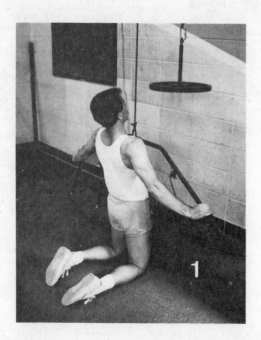
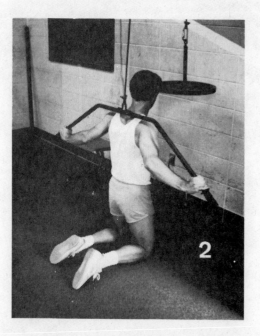

Figure 10–94. Lat pull (latissimus dorsi and pectoralis muscles). There are two variations of this movement. Both are usually done during a single set by alternating a front pull (frame 1) with a back pull (frame 2). The front position works the pectoralis, whereas the back pull works the latissimus dorsi more.

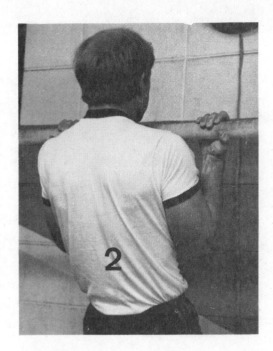
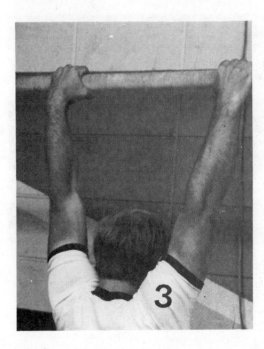

Figure 10–95. Pull-ups (latissimus dorsi, biceps, brachioradialis, and pectoralis muscles). Frames 1–2 show a narrow undergrip version that works the biceps more, along with the latissimus dorsi. This can also be done with an overgrip (frame 3), which will work more brachioradialis. A wide grip works nicely to work latissimus dorsi and pectoralis muscles more, as shown in frame 4.

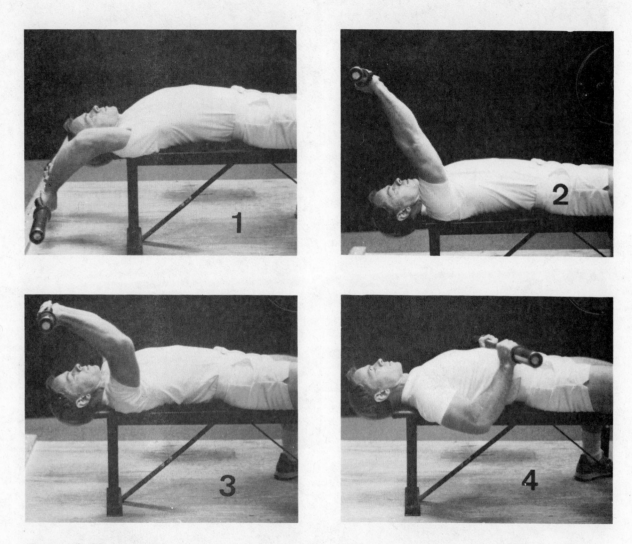

Figure 10–96. Bent arm pull-over (pectoralis muscles, serratus, and latissimus). This exercise is usually done with a slight elbow bend as shown here (frames 1–4). Sometimes a straight arm pull-over is attempted, but this technique puts much pressure on the *rotator cuff* of the shoulder and can easily cause tendonitis or irritate bursitis problems in or around the shoulder joint.

Figure 10–97. Roman chair pull-over. This is a variation on the pull-over presented in Figure 10–96. It expands the rib cage and places more stretch on the muscles and connective tissue involved. This is a popular exercise among bodybuilders to develop the musculature of the chest.

Figure 10–98. Cross-over chest pulls (pectoralis muscles, anterior deltoid, and biceps). This is another popular exercise of the bodybuilder for developing the chest to define the pectoralis muscles.

Figure 10–99. Forward arm curl (biceps and anterior deltoid). Traditionally this exercise is performed with both hands in an undergrip and is executed without dipping the shoulders. Much volume with this straight bar can cause some irritation at the elbow joint because this places tension at unnatural angles.

Figure 10–100. Reverse arm curl. This variation of the arm curl places more stress on the brachioradialis and may be a good supplemental exercise for athletes who need extra strength for wrist control.

Figure 10–101. Concentration curls (bicep and anterior deltoid). This exercise is a good choice for isolation of the biceps. The free arm is used as a support to take pressure off the back.

Figure 10–102. E-Z curl. This variation of the arm curl uses a bent bar to place tension on the elbow at more natural angles.

Figure 10–103. Preacher curl. Using this bench, the biceps can be isolated. Frame 1 shows use of dumbbell, and frame 2 (photo courtesy of *Strength Training Magazine*) shows the use of cables.

Figure 10–104. Zottman curl (brachioradialis, biceps, and anterior deltoid). This unusual variation of the arm curl incorporates both the reverse and forward curl into one sequence, as pictured in frames 1–4.

Figure 10–105. Wrist curl (wrist flexors). This is a conditioner of the wrist flexors and is particularly good for athletes who need wrist and hand strength.

Figure 10–106. Forward and reverse wrist roll (wrist flexors and extensors). A simple homemade device is used here. Frame 1 demonstrates how a reverse wrist roll can be performed against resistance. Frame 2 illustrates the forward wrist roll, also against resistance. These movements can be done concentrically and eccentrically.

Figure 10–107. Wrist abduction (wrist abductors). This exercise is good for strength needed to control sport implements such as in tennis, racketball, golf, baseball, etc.

Figure 10–108. Wrist adduction (wrist adductors). This is a companion exercise for the wrist abduction shown in Figure 10–107.

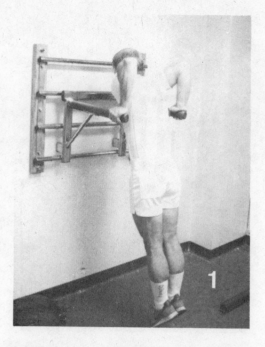
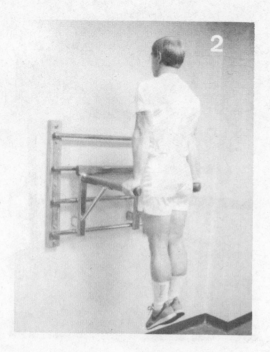

Figure 10–109. Bar dips (triceps, anterior deltoid, and pectoralis muscles). The sequence pictured in frames 1 and 2 shows the sequence for the movement. The exercise can be done against one's own body weight or with additional resistance. This is an excellent exercise for athletes to improve support strength of the arm and shoulder girdle (for gymnasts, pole vaulters, and others).

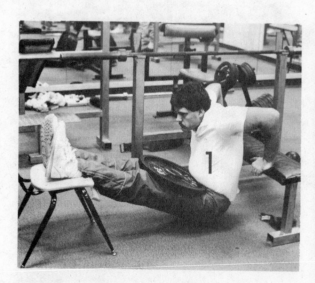

Figure 10–110. Bench dips (triceps, anterior deltoid, and pectoralis muscles). This is a variation on bar dips that may be desirable in the absence of parallel bars or if multiple stations are needed for group workouts.

Figure 10–111. Two-arm tricep extension (tricep). (Photograph courtesy of *Strength Training Magazine*.) Elbows must be kept high throughout the movement for correct lifting technique and stress on the intended muscles.

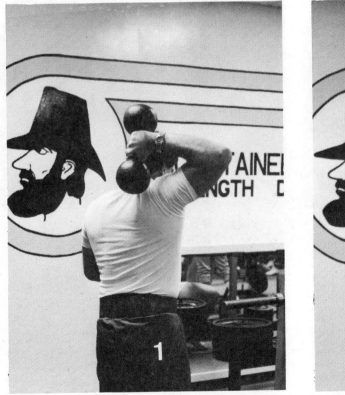

Figure 10–112. One-arm tricep extension. This is a variation of the tricep extension shown in Figure 10–111.

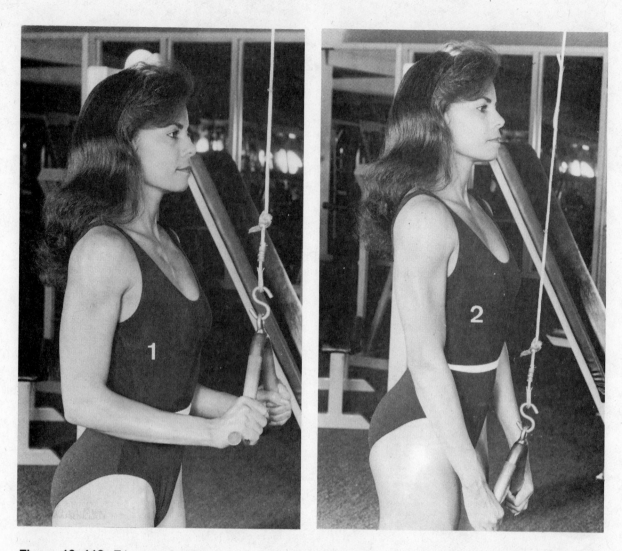

Figure 10–113. Tricep push-down (tricep). (Photograph courtesy of *Strength Training Magazine*.) This is a machine-assisted exercise variation of the tricep extensions shown in Figures 10–111 and 10–112.

Jump Drills

This section includes jumping exercises that involve a combination of eccentric and concentric movements using both counter-type and static starting positions. Before any of these drills are attempted one should be familiar with the discussion on plyometrics in Chapter 4. The figures provided here are presented in order of suggested progression, which relates directly to prerequisite factors leading to successful implementation.

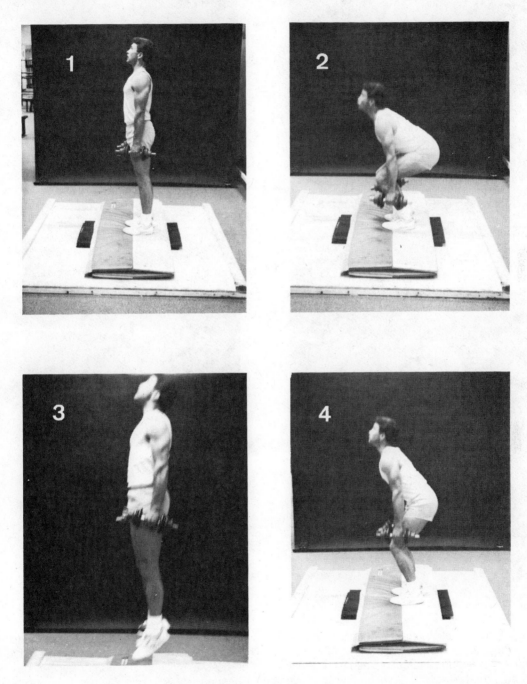

Figure 10–114. Counter-type dumbbell jumps. From a stand, quickly lower to a preparatory crouch and immediately jump straight up as high as possible. Start with light weight and progress to heavier as strength is improved. Each jump should be maximal.

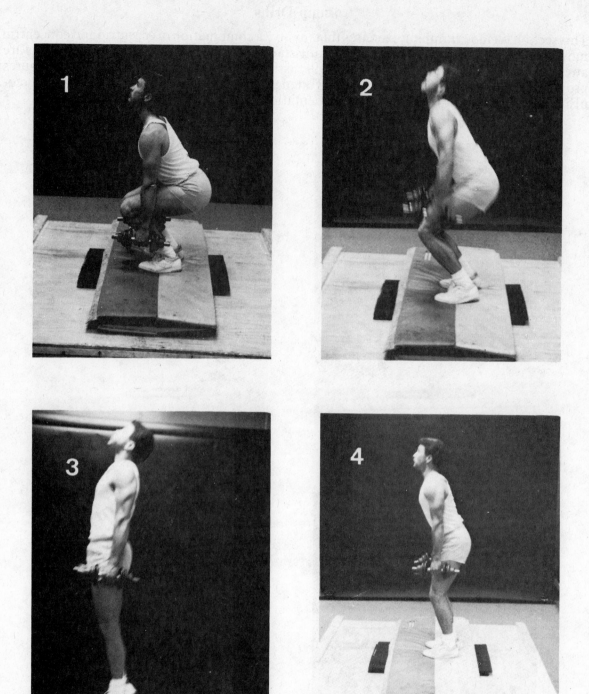

Figure 10–115. Static dumbbell jumps. This exercise is performed just like the one shown in Figure 10–114, but from a static squat position held for a 3-second count before jumping. This takes advantage of maximum cross-bridge interaction, as discussed in Chapter 4. As a variation, the dumbbells can be released after the hold at the moment upward movement is begun.

Figure 10–116. Counter-type dumbbell release jumps. This is similar to the exercise shown in Figure 10–114, but with some variation. The weight is released as the person begins the upward movement for the jump. The person should expect to jump much higher as the weights are released in this manner.

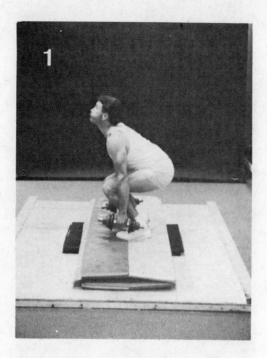
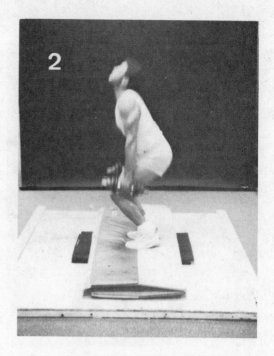
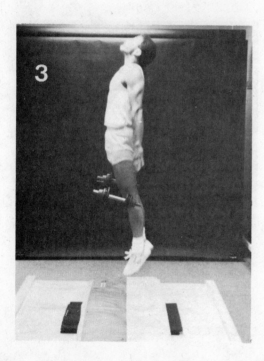
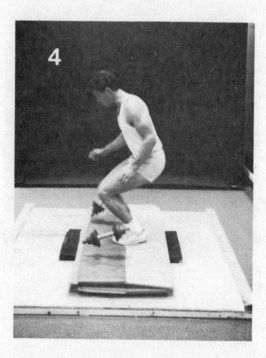

Figure 10–117. Static dumbbell release jumps. This is similar to the movement shown in Figure 10–116, but it is executed from a static squat position held for a 3-second count before jumping. The dumbbells are to be released at full leg extension, just before take-off from the floor. In all release dumbbell jumps the mat should be higher in the middle than at the edges so the dumbbells will bounce or roll away from the person to eliminate the possibility of landing on one or both and causing injury such as an ankle sprain.

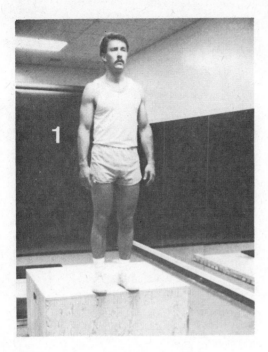

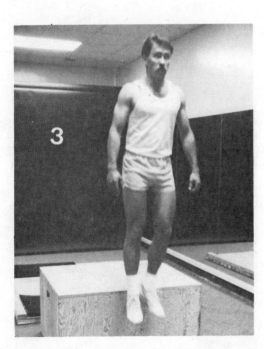

Figure 10–118. Depth jumps. This is sometimes known as a box drill. The person steps (not jumps) off a box about 18–22 inches high. Upon contact with the floor an immediate rebound jump is performed as quickly and as high as possible (after frame 4), and the person finishes with a landing on the floor in front of the box.

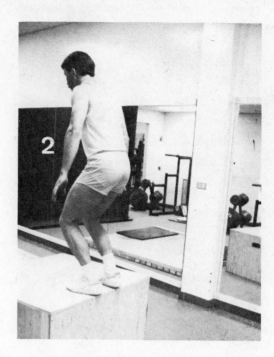

Figure 10–119. Low box jumps. From a standing position on the floor, jump up onto a box 18–22 inches high and back down to the floor again.

Figure 10–120. High box jumps. Performed the same as the low box jumps but onto and from a box 36–48 inches high.

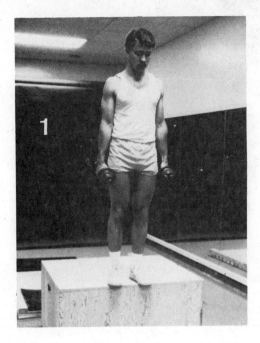

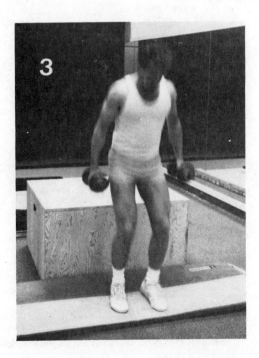
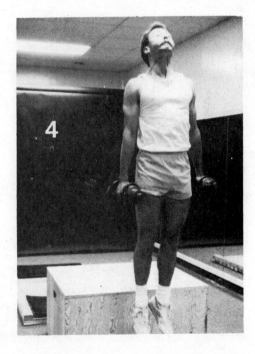

Figure 10–121. Depth jumps with dumbbells. This jump is performed the same as the one shown in Figure 10–118, but with dumbbells. Weight can be increased as evidence of a training effect appears. A dumbbell release could also be incorporated into this drill.

Figure 10–122. Box jumps with dumbbells. Frame 1 illustrates a low box jump with dumbbells; frame 2 illustrates the same jump but with a high box (see Figures 10–119 and 10–120).

Figure 10–123. Vertical dumbbell swing (deltoids, trapezius, quadriceps, and gastrocnemius). A series of vertical jumps is executed while swinging a dumbbell or swingbell. Jumping action should integrate an effective arm swing for maximum vertical height.

Figure 10–124. Horizontal dumbbell swing (abdominal obliques, transverse abdominals, and deltoids). This exercise is designed as a torso drill for trunk torque. The dumbbell is swung sideways with a twisting action of the upper body.

Figure 10–125. Push-up from single bench (abdominal obliques, triceps, pectoralis muscles, and transverse and rectus abdominis). An explosive push-up action with one arm vigorous enough so the upper hand clears the bench. Deceleration occurs on the following drop. Successive repetitions rapidly follow each other, with a quick transition from the drop to the next push-up.

Figure 10–126. Push-up drop from benches (rectus abdominis, triceps, and pectoralis muscles). Start with a push-up position on top of benches or chairs (1). Drop to a push-up position on the floor (2) and immediately execute an explosive push-up to achieve a position on top (3 and 4).

References

1. Algra, B. 1982. An in-depth analysis of the bench press. *National Strength and Conditioning Association Journal* pp. 6–11;70–72.

2. Enoka, R. 1979. The pull in Olympic weightlifting. *Medicine and Science In Sports* 11(2):131–137.

3. Garhammer, J. 1978. Biomechanical analysis of selected snatch lifts at the U.S. Senior National Weightlifting Championships. In *Biomechanics of Sport and Kinanthropometry* F. Landry and W. Orban (Eds.). Miami Florida: Symposia Specialists, pp. 475–484.

4. Garhammer, J., and R. Gregor. 1979. Force plate evaluations of weightlifting and vertical jumping (Abstract). *Medicine and Science In Sports* 11(1):106.

5. Kulund, D., J. Dewey, C. Brubaker, and J. Roberts. 1978. Olympic weightlifting injuries. *The Physician and Sports Medicine* pp. 111–119, Nov.

6. McLaughlin, T., C. Dillman, and T. Lardner. 1977. A kinematic model of performance in the parallel squat by champion powerlifters. *Medicine and Science in Sports* 9(2):128–133.

Setting Up the Program

Setting up a weight-training program requires considerable forethought and attention to detail. This chapter contains information that can help the strength coach or instructor in carrying out simple weight-training programs and classes.

Program and Course Outlines

For any program to be successful, participants must understand the basic principles of training, how these principles can be adapted to weight-training, and what the specifics of the training program are (exercises, safety procedures, etc.).

A key to achieving these objectives is to develop a reasonable program (or course) outline. Examples of a program outline for an athletic team and for a weight-training class are shown in Appendixes A and B. These outlines should stress the objectives and purpose of the program, what information the program will cover, sources of reference material, how progress through the program will be evaluated, the training routine (see Appendixes A and B), time constraints, and proper training attire. Remember that the previous achievements (skill level) of the participants are an important consideration.

Purpose and Objectives

Weight training should reflect the purpose of the program or course. The purpose of a program of weight-training for athletics should be to improve athletic performance, the primary objective being the improvement of specific physical factors (strength, power, etc.) as a result of training.

The purpose of a weight-training course should be to provide information concerning training principles, appropriate practical aspects of training, and the physiological, psychological, and biomechanical adaptations that accompany weight training. The primary objectives of a weight-training course should be to have the students learn information and techniques that will allow them to use weight-training as a lifelong physical activity. A secondary objective is to improve the physical fitness of the student during the training program. (The objectives of a weightlifting or powerlifting class would include learning the rules of the sport as well as increasing student proficiency as a competitive lifter.)

Information Content

Information can be presented through lectures and assigned readings. In the athletic setting, an initial presentation should include a description of the training program, expected progress, progress evaluation methods and times, and organizational information (i.e., group divisions, training times, etc.). Considerable time should be spent using motivational techniques. Several classroom lectures can be used to discuss the biomechanical, physiological, and psychological adaptations to various types of weight-training. By placing these content lectures at the beginning of the course the students will have a better understanding of subsequent demonstrations and the training program. Additional lectures and demonstrations of lifting and spotting techniques can be scheduled during the course of the weight-training class. Specific readings (textbook, research papers, or handouts) should be assigned to coincide with the lectures.

Evaluations

Various performance tests are described in Chapter 8. The evaluation of weight training for sports must include a variety of performance tests. As pointed out in Chapters 6 and 8, specificity of training must be recognized (a 12-minute run for a shotputter is not appropriate). Typical tests for sports such as football may include one repetition maximum (1RM) lifts such as the squat or bench press, maximum anaerobic power tests such as the vertical jump or stair climbing tests, and anaerobic capacity tests such as the 400-m run.

Students in a weight-training course can be evaluated through written tests or performance evaluations. If lectures are given at the beginning of the course, a written test may be appropriate soon after lectures have been completed. Additional information imparted during the remainder of the course (as well as review of content material) can be evaluated with a final written test (see Appendix B).

Strength evaluations can be accomplished by using 1RM lifts, 1RM/kg of BW, 1RM/kg of LBM, a combination of absolute and relative strength, or by using maximum repetitions with a percentage of 1RM or of body weight. The Sinclair formula also can be used to account for differences in body weight (see Chapter 8). O'Shea (5) has outlined several excellent methods of evaluating strength gains that take experience and body weight into account. Power increases can be evaluated using the vertical jump and the Lewis formula (2).

When using the maximum effort method, several testing periods may be necessary. Tables 11–1 through 11–3 give estimated mean values for the measurement of squat, bench press, vertical jump, and vertical jump power after 10 weeks (3 days/week) training comparing periodized training to 3×6 RM using college-aged men and women. These means are based on several studies (4, 6, 7) as well as observation.

A more useful method of evaluating strength gains may be to keep track of the volume, intensity, and load of day-to-day training. Figures 11–1 through 11–3 represent the expected volume intensity and load for the *squat* during a 10-week program using the exercises and training variations shown in Table 11–1. Using the volumes, intensities, and loads shown in

Table 11–1. Program example.

Group	4 wks.	4 wks.	2 wks.
(G_1) Periodized	5×10	3×5 $(1 \times 10)^*$	3×2 $(1 \times 10)^\dagger$
(G_2) 3×6 RM	3×6	3×6	3×6
T_1	T_2	T_3	T_4

Monday and Friday	Wednesday
1. Parallel squat	1. Clean pulls (floor)
2. Bench press	2. Clean pulls (thigh)
3. Hyperextensions	3. Shoulder shrugs
4. Sit-ups	4. Behind neck press
	5. Sit-ups

*Followup set with 70% of original 1 RM
†Followup set with 75% of original 1 RM

Table 11–2. Estimated means for 10 weeks of training for males based on using untrained and moderately trained subjects (4, 6, 7).

	Group	T_1	T_2	T_3	T_4
1RM squat	G_1	100.0	118.0	130.0	141.0
(kg)	G_2	100.0	118.5	122.0	132.0
1RM bench	G_1	80.0	84.5	89.0	92.0
(kg)	G_2	80.0	84.5	89.0	90.5
Vertical jump	G_1	52.0	52.8	53.8	57.0
(cm)	G_2	52.0	52.5	53.0	53.3
Vertical jump power	G_1	120.0	120.0	122.5	126.5
(kg-m/sec)	G_2	120.0	120.0	121.0	123.0

the three figures will result in the gains for men shown in Table 11–2. The corresponding figures (intensity and load) for women would be about 30%–50% lower (Table 11–3).

Although the 1RM and related methods are essential to strength-oriented programs, other methods can be used in a Lifetime physical activity course. The 1RM method of evaluation may not be useful in health-oriented courses because:

1. Testing 1RM for several exercises with large groups is time consuming (the testing of the 1RM squat alone can take a complete class period if there are large numbers of students.)

2. Although injuries are rare in well-supervised programs (see Chapter 7), the 1RM test may raise the potential for injury slightly, especially for the spotters.

3. Gains in 1RM strength through resistive training are well documented. There is no reason to believe 1RM strength increases would not occur in any well-planned strength training program of reasonable length. It is more useful to keep track of volume, intensity, and load.

By using this alternate method, the student will become familiar with keeping a log as well as with calculating volume, intensity, and load (Chapter 7). Furthermore, the effect of physical variation of training and the calculation of volume, intensity, and load can be graphically related by having the student (or coach) plot these variables across the period of the course (as with Figures 11–1 through 11–3). This procedure is most useful in helping the student understand the training principle of variation.

Table 11–3. Estimated means for 10 weeks of training females based on using untrained subjects (4, 6, 7).

	Group	T_1	T_2	T_3	T_4
1RM squat	G_1	45.0	54.0	59.0	64.0
(kg)	G_2	45.0	54.0	57.5	60.0
1RM bench	G_1	27.0	33.5	37.5	40.0
(kg)	G_2	27.0	33.0	36.0	38.5
Vertical jump	G_1	34.5	35.5	37.5	39.0
(cm)	G_2	34.5	35.0	37.0	37.5
Vertical jump power	G_1	74.0	76.0	77.5	79.0
(kg-m/sec)	G_2	74.0	76.0	76.5	77.0

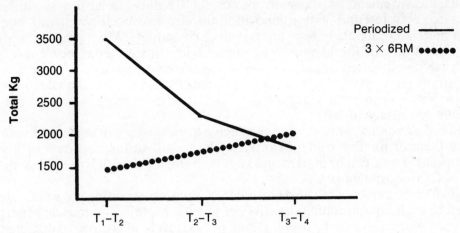

Figure 11-1. Means for daily squat load (reps × weight) over 10 weeks.

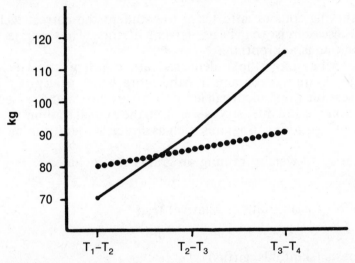

Figure 11-2. Means for daily squat intensity (mean weight) over 10 weeks.

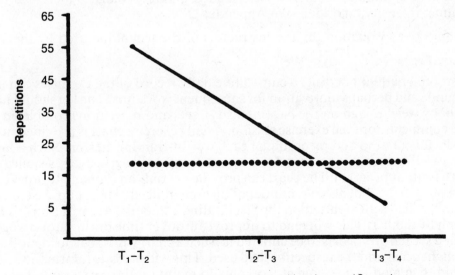

Figure 11-3. Means for daily squat volume (repetitions) over 10 weeks.

Additional measurements of fitness are also useful. Cardiovascular fitness can be evaluated through a max $\dot{V}O_2$ test and body composition through hydrostatic weighing (see Chapter 8). Although more accurate, these tests are *very* time consuming. More practical tests for cardiovascular fitness include the 12-minute run or a variety of step tests (see Chapter 8). Body composition can be estimated by anthropometric tests (see Appendix C). Typical changes in body composition expected for the training program in Table 11–1 are shown in Figures 11–4 through 11–6. *Notice the effect of variation of volume (and decreasing load) on body composition (especially percentage of fat).*

Note that higher volume work is more conducive to causing positive changes in body composition (see Chapter 6). The student can easily be taught to take his own or his training partner's skinfolds. These can be plotted and kept in the log book, either as total skinfolds or as percentage of fat (see Appendix C).

Simple girth measurements can also be used in evaluating a training program. These measurements can be useful in estimating the effect of specific exercises on muscle hypertrophy in specific muscles. They also may be useful (along with skinfold measures) in demonstrating to women that typically they will not gain large amounts of muscle or make large gains in girth (see (3) and Chapter 2).

A purpose of weight-training courses is to teach the student the correct techniques of weight-training exercises. These exercises can be used over a lifetime. Thus a subjective evaluation of the student's technique is appropriate.

By using the methods described above the student can learn useful, practical techniques for evaluating physical fitness and training programs. Furthermore, when using programs similar to the example used in this section, the student can learn to relate performance and physiological changes to variations in volume and intensity as well as to the overall training program. The benefits of other types of weight-training programs such as circuit weight training also can be evaluated.

In summary, the evaluation of weight-training programs can include:

1. Written tests

2. Maximum lifting effort (or absolute or relative) tests

3. Cardiovascular tests

4. Body composition tests (skinfolds, girths)

5. A log book containing results of performance, and physiological measures and plots of volume, intensity, and load (see Appendix D).

6. A subjective evaluation (by the instructor) of the technique used by the students.

Daily Exercise Log

In the classroom or athletic setting, a cumulative daily record of the exercises can provide an important guide and perhaps motivation for subsequent workouts. The log should include: the date, total body weight, load on the bar (intensity), sets and repetitions completed (volume), and general comments for each exercise session. A daily exercise chart is provided in Appendix E for easy documentation and recording of each weight-training session. Such a log can help chart the course for an individual workout as one employs progressive resistance principles throughout a training program. The chart can provide not only an immediate order of exercises for the workout session, but also a reminder of the weight needed to set up the bar in preparation for an individual's lifting attempt, thus facilitating a smooth and swift transition from one lifting station to another. This will tend to improve turnover time during group workouts and, if a prescribed set-rep protocol is to be adhered to, such a chart will also help identify any deviations that might occur and the respective load used. This will provide information upon which to reflect and then modify subsequent workouts to maintain the correct number of sets and repetitions. This servo-mechanism will act as a type of self-monitoring system for the control

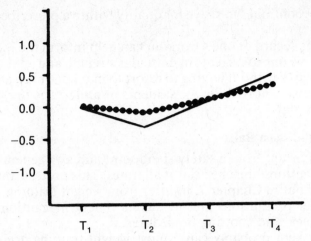

Figure 11-4. Change in body weight over 10 weeks.

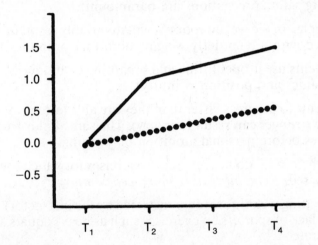

Figure 11-5. Change in lean body mass over 10 weeks.

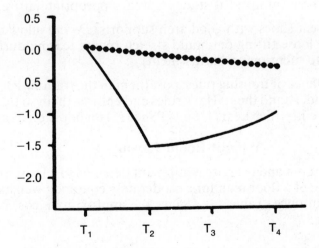

Figure 11-6. Change in % fat over 10 weeks.

of workout intensity as one continues to strive for quality within a prescribed repetition maximum protocol.

In addition, the ongoing record of one's workout can help inform the individual as well as the supervisor of quantitative improvements in muscular strength and endurance, allowing for day-to-day monitoring of gains without having to resort to maximal 1 rep attempts. This in itself can be a source of intrinsic motivation for students or athletes as they see their workout loads increase from day to day.

Safety Precautions and Weight Room Rules

Weight room rules are important from a safety standpoint and as a general courtesy. Proper and reasonable safety precautions must be used at all times. This protects the athlete, student, and instructor. As pointed out in Chapter 7, injuries from weight training are rare, but accidents can happen if proper precautions are not taken. Safety precautions must extend to facilities, exercise techniques, and spotting procedures.

Facilities not properly kept probably cause most weight-training accidents. Disorderly weight rooms can result in accidents and cause increased wear and tear on equipment. All equipment should be inspected regularly and kept in working order. Frayed cables and barbells that do not revolve correctly are accidents waiting to happen. Cleanliness of facilities is also important. *Weight-training* safety precautions are paramount:

1. Do not allow horseplay in the weight room; it will invariably result in an accident (especially when coupled with a disorderly weight room that promotes tripping, etc.).

2. Insure that all students use proper lifting and breathing techniques. (Too much weight = bad body mechanics and position = injury).

3. Do not allow students to progress faster than they are able (attempting to keep up with others who may be stronger can result in injury). The same holds true for athletic programs; safety comes before personal ambition or winning.

4. In conjunction with point 3, do not introduce exercises for which the students (or athletes) are not prepared. *Remember, fatigue precedes injury.*

5. Insist on proper spotting techniques (demonstrated by the instructor). Few exercises require spotters, but lack of spotters on exercises such as heavy squats and bench presses should not be tolerated.

6. Make an effort to keep the weight room at a reasonable temperature. Research suggests that cool temperatures allow the greatest work output. The effects of cold or hot room temperatures can be minimized if students wear appropriate attire.

7. Be sure trainees wear shoes with good arch supports. *Do not* allow barefoot training. Clothes should be loose fitting or should stretch (pants tearing during squatting can cause injury, not to mention embarrassment).

Remember the importance of training rules; post them in the training room and make sure those who use the room understand them. Have rules and enforce them so the weight room can be a productive training facility. (See Lear (1) and O'Shea (5) for additional safety advice.)

Weight Room Layout

The quality of the weight room and exercise equipment depends to a large extent on finances. Figure 11–7 is a schematic of a floor plan for a moderately equipped weight room capable of handling 20–25 trainees at once. Table 11–4 gives the approximate cost breakdown.

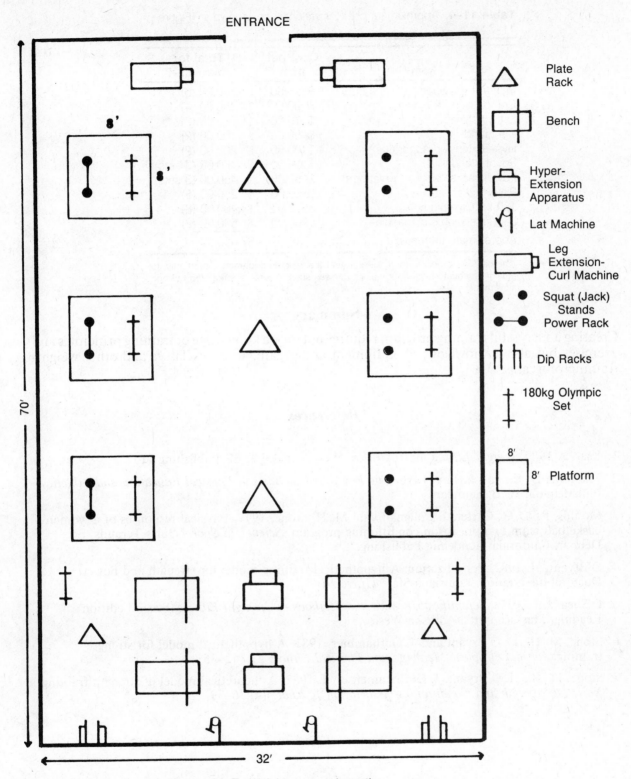

Figure 11–7. Weight room schematic.

Table 11–4. Approximate cost for weight room shown in (Figure 11–7.)

Item	Cost per item	Total for figure 11–7
Platform (plywood, 2 × 4's etc.)*	$125.00	$ 750.00 (6)
Competition style bench	$100.00	$ 400.00 (4)
Lat machine	$ 75.00	$ 150.00 (2)
Dip stands	$ 50.00	$ 100.00 (2)
Hyperextension apparatus	$100.00	$ 200.00 (2)
Squat stands	$150.00	$ 450.00 (3 sets)
Power racks (bolted to platform)	$150.00	$ 450.00 (3 sets)
Plate racks	$ 50.00	$ 250.00 (5)
180 kg Olympic set	$550.00	$4,400.00 (8)
Leg extension-curl machine	$250.00	$ 500.00 (2)
Approximate total cost		$7,650.00

*The platform is necessary to help protect the weights and, more importantly, to provide adequate footing for major exercises such as squats, jerks, and pulling movements.

Summary

Creating a successful training program requires not only a knowledge of training principles and exercises but also a knowledge of equipment and organization of classes and other weight-training programs.

References

1. Lear, J. 1980. *Weight Lifting.* East Ardsley, West Yorkshire: EP Publishing Ltd.

2. Mathews, D. K., and E. Fox. 1976. *The Physiological Basis of Physical Education and Athletics.* Philadelphia: W. B. Saunders.

3. Moulds, B., D. R. Carter, J. Coleman, and M. H. Stone. 1979. Physical responses of a women's basketball team to a preseason conditioning program. *Science in Sports* (Juris Terauds, Ed.). Delmar, California: Academic Publishing.

4. O'Bryant, H. 1982. Periodization: A hypothetical training model for strength and power. Doctoral dissertation, Louisiana State University.

5. O'Shea, J. P. 1976. *Scientific Principles and Methods of Strength Fitness* (Second edition). Reading, Massachusetts: Addison-Wesley.

6. Stone, M. H., H. O'Bryant and J. Garhammer. 1981. A hypothetical model for strength training. *Journal of Sports Medicine and Physical Fitness* 21:342–351.

7. Stone, M. H., H. O'Bryant, J. Garhammer, et al. 1982. A theoretical model of strength training. *National Strength and Conditioning Association Journal* 4(4):36–39.

Glossary of Terms

Aerobic: Use of the oxidative energy-producing systems; with oxygen.

Anabolic: Biochemical reactions dealing with building up or synthesis of molecules; requiring energy.

Anaerobic: Use of the nonoxidative energy-producing systems; without oxygen.

Anaerobic capacity: The ability of the anaerobic energy-producing systems to endure. Strongly related to muscular endurance.

Anaerobic power: The rate of work performed using primarily anaerobic (nonoxidative) energy systems (i.e., ATP-CP and Fast Glycolysis). Strongly related to explosive movements.

Androgen: Related to the male hormone testosterone; male creating.

Anthropometry: Measurement of the physical dimensions of humans; the measurement of man.

Bioenergetic: Energy production in living systems.

Biomechanics: The application of mechanics to human movement.

Capillization: Addition of capillaries or the opening of latent capillaries.

Catabolic: Biochemical reactions dealing with tearing down or destroying molecules; release energy.

Countermovement: Eccentric contraction (negative work) preceding a concentric contraction (positive work).

Densitometry: The measurement of the specific gravity of an object. Used in calculating the body composition of humans.

Drug: Any chemical substance used to alter the biochemistry, physiology, or biological functioning of an organism.

Ergogenic: Work-creating. Any mechanism (drug, etc.) used to enhance performance is an ergogenic aid.

Ergometry: The process of measuring work output using physical exercise. Typical ergometers are stationary cycles and treadmills.

Estrogen: The female hormone; female creating.

Exercise: A single bout or a short series of bouts of the same movement. (Example: running 800 meter or doing 3×10 RM squats.)

Exercise physiology: The study and description of performance, physical, and physiological adaptations to exercise and training.

Fascia: The connective tissue in and around organs, especially muscles, that lend shape, support, and protection.

Food: Large molecules with considerable energy stored in their chemical bonds. These molecules consist of proteins, carbohydrates, and fats.

Histochemistry: Method of identifying various tissues using microscopic techniques.

Hormone: Substances released by endocrine glands that travel in the blood and affect biochemical changes in specific target tissues.

Hydrostatic weighing: Method of estimating body composition using Archemides' and densitometry principles; underwater weighing.

Hyperplasia: An increase in cell number.

Hypertrophy: Enlargement of the cell.

Inhibitory: Stimulus producing a decrease in function or a negative result.

Intensity of training: The power output during training per exercise, session, etc. The intensity of work can be estimated by the average weight being used.

Kinesiology: The study of movement, especially as it pertains to humans.

Krebs cycle: Also called the citric acid cycle or tricarboxylic acid cycle. It is made up of a sequence of reactions by which acetyl groups are oxidized. These reactions function as a unit to remove electrons from acetyl groups and to *feed* the electrons to the electron transport system (oxidative phosphorylation pathway).

Mass spectrometry: The measurement of the distribution of particles in a magnetically resolved beam.

Maximum oxygen uptake: The maximum amount of oxygen (max $\dot{V}O_2$) that can be taken up and used in aerobic energy production; aerobic power.

Metabolism: Sum total of all the anabolic and catabolic biochemical reactions in the body.

Multijoint: Pertaining to large muscle mass exercises (snatch, clean and jerk, squats, etc.) in which several body parts are used; more than one joint.

Myototic: Pertaining to the muscle and to the stretch reflex.

Neuromuscular: An integrated system composed of nervous and muscle tissue.

Nomogram: A graph consisting of three lines, each graduated for a specific variable. (A line intersecting all of the three variables can be used to predict an unknown from the two known values.)

Overload: A stimulus requiring an organism to adapt. The amount of resistance needed to increase maximum strength.

Overtraining: A plateauing or loss in performance with accompanying nonbeneficial psychological, physical, or physiological symptoms. Overtraining is related to monotonous programs and to overstress and overwork.

Platform: A slightly raised structure, usually made of wood, that is typically used with Olympic barbells. It may be of various dimensions (competition platforms are 4 meters by 4 meters). The platform gives protection for the weights and lifter by providing appropriate resiliency and footing.

Power: Work per unit of time or force (strength) times velocity.

Postpubertal: Past the point of sexual maturation (about 13 years).

Prepubertal: Before the point of sexual maturation.

Prestretching: An eccentric contraction (or start from an elongated position of the muscle) preceding a concentric contraction.

Psychomotor: Relating to the integration of the central nervous system and the muscle organ system. A psychological stimulus resulting in movement.

Repetitions maximum (RM): The maximum weight (mass) that can be used for a specified number of repetitions or group (sets) of repetitions. (Example: 3×10 RM = the maximum weight used for three sets of ten repetitions.)

Stimulatory: Excitatory action producing an increased function or a positive result.

Strength: The ability of a muscle to produce force varying from 0% to 100%.

Training: Regular exercise over an extended period (months, years, etc.).

Training load: The intensity (weight) times the volume (repetitions) per exercise, session, month, etc. Training load is an estimate of total work performed.

Training principles: Defined guidelines that give direction to the planning of physical training programs.

Ultrastructure: The smallest anatomical and functional units of tissue. The whole comprises the parts; parts make up the whole.

Underload: A stimulus that does not require an organism to adapt. A resistance less than the overload value.

Volume of training: The total work performed during training per session, week, month, etc. The volume of work can be estimated by the load or by total repetitions.

Work: Force times vertical displacement.

Example of Conditioning Program for Football

Football requires an athlete to be highly motivated, aggressive, and mentally disciplined. These attributes are necessary to produce superior performances not only under game conditions, but also during the conditioning program.

Physiologically, football players require above average endurance, but most importantly they need great explosive power. Therefore, the training program must be designed to bring the athlete up to maximum strength-power levels and to maintain these levels through the season. This can be best accomplished by dividing the training year into specific phases:

1. *Off-season strength program* (end of season $\rightarrow$ spring training). Designed to increase LBM and the strength of the large muscle groups of the torso and limbs.

2. *Spring training.* Designed to maintain the strength of the athlete, which has been built up during the off-season program. Somewhat more rigorous than the in-season program.

3. *Early summer program.* Similar to the off-season program.

4. *Late summer strength-power program.* Emphasizes explosiveness and becomes more skill-specific. The intensity (FXV) is increased but the volume and load are decreased to bring power to a peak and to make a smooth transition into the in-season program.

5. *In-season program.* Volume, intensity, and load are reduced. The emphasis is on *maintaining* the strength-power capabilities of the athlete. Efforts at increasing strength during the football season may increase the possibility of injury due to chronic fatigue. Furthermore, a strenuous strength training program during the season reduces the capabilities of the athlete on the field, again due to the fatigue factor. (Because of a reduced on-the-field load, redshirts and some freshmen can use a somewhat more strenuous strength training regimen during the season).

The Program

For the strength training program to produce optimal results, it must be properly integrated with a running program. The concept of specificity of training indicates that the running program for football should be of a primarily anaerobic nature. Research and coaches' observations indicate that long distance running induces biochemical and other changes in physiology that are detrimental to the development of explosive power. Therefore, a program of interval training, not normally exceeding a distance of 400 m will produce optimal cardiovascular conditioning and help to increase endurance without compromising strength and power.

Always warm up - Do jumping jacks for 30 seconds, follow this with flexibility exercises, paying particular attention to the Achilles tendon, hamstrings, and quadriceps. After stretching, do 3 sets of power snatches using no more than 40 kg. Each major exercise is to be preceded by light and moderate warmup sets. (*Employ a similar flexibility program following each workout.*)

Injuries or specific weaknesses should be reported to the coaches and trainers *before* training.

Use rest periods of about 1½ to 2½ minutes during the off-season and summer programs and about 2–3 minutes during the spring training and in-season programs.

Example of Summer Training for Football
Leading up to Fall Training

I. *Hypertrophy Phase* (3 weeks)

Monday and Friday
1. Squats—3 × 10
2. Leg extensions—1 × 10
3. Leg curls—3 × 10
4. Bench press—3 × 10
5. Lateral raises—3 × 10*
6. Waistwork—3 × 10

Tuesday
1. 3 × 10—Standing vertical or long jump
2. 5 × 400m—3 to 4 minute intervals

Thursday
1. 3 × 10—Standing vertical or long jump
2. 3 × 300m—3-minute intervals
3. 3 × 200m—2-minute intervals

Wednesday
1. Pulls from mid-thigh—3 × 10
2. Pulls from floor—3 × 10
3. Shoulder shrugs—3 × 10
4. Inclines—3 × 10
5. Behind neck press—3 × 10
6. Waistwork—3 × 10

Saturday
1. Pulls from knee—3 × 10
2. Shoulder shrugs—3 × 10
3. Leisure games of racketball

*Add neck work following lateral raises as needed.

I. *Basic Strength* (2 weeks)

Monday and Friday
1. Squats—3 × 5 (1 × 10)
2. Leg extensions—1 × 5
3. Leg curls—3 × 10
4. Incline press—3 × 5 (1 × 10)
5. Lateral raises—3 × 5
6. Waistwork—3 × 5 (1 × 10)

Tuesday
1. 3 × 5—Weighted vertical long jump
2. 5 × 300m—3-minutes intervals

Thursday
1. 3 × 5—Plyometrics
2. 5 × 200m—2-minute intervals

Wednesday
1. Pulls from mid-thigh—3 × 5
2. Pulls from floor—3 × 5 (1 × 10)
3. Shoulder shrugs—3 × 5
4. Hyperextensions—3 × 5
5. Behind neck press—3 × 5
6. Waistwork—3 × 5 (1 × 10)

Saturday
1. Pulls from knee—3 × 5
2. Shoulder shrugs (snatch grip)— 3 × 5
3. Volleyball or basketball

II. *Hypertrophy* (3 weeks)

Monday and Friday
1. Squats—5 × 10
2. Straight-legged deadlifts
   —3 × 10 *light*
3. Leg curls—1 × 10
4. Dumbbell bench press—5 × 10
5. Seated dumbbell press—3 × 10
6. Lateral raises—5 × 10
7. Waistwork—5 × 10

Tuesday and Thursday
1. Same as under Basic Strength.

Wednesday
1. Pulls from floor—3 × 10
2. ¼ Squats in power rack
   —5 × 10
3. Hyperextensions—3 × 10
4. Dumbbell incline press—5 × 10
5. Lateral raises—5 × 10
6. Waistwork—5 × 10

Saturday
1. Pulls from mid-thigh—3 × 10
2. Shoulder shrugs—3 × 10
3. Volleyball or basketball

II. *Basic Strength* (4 weeks)

Monday
1. Squats—3 × 5 (1 × 5)
2. Front quarter squats in rack—3 × 5
3. Vertical jumps—3 × 5
4. Inclines—3 × 5 (1 × 5)
5. Lateral raises—3 × 5
6. Waistwork—3 × 5 (1 × 10)

Wednesday
1. Strides—5 × 50m—2-minutes
   intervals
2. 3 × 200m—2-minute intervals

Saturday
1. Power snatch—3 × 5
2. Shoulder shrugs—3 × 5
3. Strides—5 × 50m—2-minute intervals

Tuesday
1. Power snatch—3 × 5
2. Pulls mid-thigh—3 × 5
3. Weighted jumps—3 × 5
4. Shoulder shrugs—3 × 5
5. Seated press—3 × 5
6. Waistwork—3 × 5 (1 × 10)

Thursday
1. Deadstop squats (Rack)—3 × 5
   (1 × 5)
2. Vertical jumps—3 × 5
3. Inclines—3 × 5 (1 × 5)
4. Waistwork—3 × 5 (1 × 10)

Strength-Power (2 weeks)

Monday and Friday
1. Squats—3 × 3 (1 × 5)
2. Vertical jumps—3 × 5
3. Inclines—3 × 3 (1 × 5)
4. Waistwork—3 × 5 (1 × 10)

Tuesday and Thursday
1. Standing vertical or
   long jumps—3 × 5
2. 3 × 50m strides—1-minute
   intervals

Wednesday
1. Power snatch—3 × 3 (1 × 5)
2. Shoulder shrugs—3 × 5
3. Behind neck press—3 × 5
4. Waistwork—3 × 5 (1 × 10)

Saturday
1. Pulls from mid-thigh—3 × 3
2. Bounding—3 × 20m
3. 3 × 20m strides—1-minute
   intervals

Maintenance (3–4 hours before practice is preferable)

Monday
1. Quarter squats in rack—3 × 3
   (1 × 5)
2. Power snatch—3 × 3
3. Inclines—3 × 3 (1 × 5)
4. Waistwork—3 × 5 (1 × 10)

Wednesday
1. Power snatch—3 × 3
2. Weighted jumping—3 × 3
3. Inclines—3 × 3
4. Waistwork—3 × 5 (1 × 10)

The following is an example of a 3/1 intensity cycle. This basic idea should be incorporated into the various phases outlined (see Chapter 7).

Week	M	T	W	Th	F	S
1	MH	M	H	M	ML	M
2	H	L	M	H	L	M
3	VH	VL	L	M	L	ML
4	L	VL	M	L	L	ML

Intensity for Sets and Reps

VH – 90% – 10%
H – 85% – 90%
MH – 80% – 85%
M – 75% – 80%
ML – 70% – 75%
L – 65% – 70%
VL – 60% – 65%

Lift: MWFS
Run: T Th S—Rest intervals after longer sprints should include slow walking and/or stretching.
Example of using projected goals for set
and repetition intensities

Intensity table

Intensity (sets & reps)		Goals (kg)
VH	95–100	— 190–200
H	90–95	— 180–190
MH	85–90	— 170–180
M	80–85	— 160–170
ML	75–80	— 150–160
L	70–75	— 140–150
VL	65–70	— 130–140

Variation table

Week	M	T	W	TH	F	S		Week	M	T	W	TH	F	S
1	MH				M			1	180				170	
2	H				M			2	190				170	
3	VH				ML			3	200				160	
4	L				L			4	150				140	

In this example the athlete sets a goal of 200 kg for 3×10RM in the squat during a hypertrophy subphase. All other intensities (weights) are selected according to the pre-established variation table based on the goal of 200 kg. (For clarity, only squatting days are shown on the variation table.)

Example of Course Overview and Outlines

Course Overview

HPRE 1146
Weight Lifting

Instructor_____
Credit, 1 semester hour

Purpose of the Course

Olympic weightlifting is a specialized individual sport. The underlying principles that produce the most efficient training programs are often misunderstood and misapplied. Furthermore, these principles can be applied to other athletic endeavors or to weight-training programs used for general conditioning. Thus, a sound understanding of these principles will aid the student in preparing individualized and specialized weight-training programs.

Objectives

1. To understand and apply basic scientific principles that will produce the most effective programs.

2. To develop a minimal understanding of the physiological changes that accompany weight-training programs.

3. To learn methods of evaluating training programs.

4. To elicit positive changes in body composition.

5. To develop a knowledge of the rules and regulations of Olympic weightlifting.

6. To become proficient in Olympic weightlifting (snatch and clean and jerk).

Course Requirements

1. Suitable, clean uniform and footwear.

2. Regular, prompt attendance.

3. Satisfactory participation.

4. Satisfactory response to exams.

5. Observance of safety and lifting etiquette.

6. Satisfactory maintenance of weight-training facility (RETURN ALL EQUIPMENT TO ITS PROPER PLACE).

Evaluation Procedures

1. Written examinations—40%
   Midterm—15%
   Final—25%

2. Notebook (or recordkeeping forms)—10%

3. Skill—35% (subjective rating of the student's ability to perform the required exercises with proper technique)

4. Performance—10% (snatch and clean and jerk, based on AAU standards)

5. Attitude—5% (subjective rating of the student's cooperativeness, attendance, etc.*)

   *In accordance with the HPRE department policy statement, a student who misses six sessions at any time in order will be advised to drop the course.

Course Outline

I. General Description of Course (handouts 1, 2, and 3)
   A. Relationship of Olympic weightlifting to other facets of weight training.
   B. Course requirements, etc.

II. Benefits of weight training
   A. Body Composition
      1. percentage fat (underwater weighing, skinfolds measurement, etc.)
      2. lean body weight
      3. relationship to total energy output
   B. Acquisition of strength-power
      1. all or none law
      2. learning effect
         a. recruitment-facilitation
         b. stimulus frequency (increase firing frequency)
         c. synchronization
      3. relationship to fiber type and cross-sectional area
         a. slow and fast twitch fibers
         b. hypertrophy
   C. Muscular endurance
   D. Flexibility

III. Principles of training
   A. Quantity (volume) and quality (intensity)
      1. work = force $\times$ distance (displacement)
      2. power = work/time
      3. variation of volume and intensity and avoidance of overtraining
   B. Year-round training program
      1. macrocycle (year-long)
         a. preparation (hypertrophy-basic strength)
         b. transition 1 (strength-power)
         c. competition (peaking for a meet)
         d. transition 2 (active rest)
      2. mesocycle (between meets)
         3 to 1 or 2 to 1 variation in intensity
      3. microcycle (week to week)
         variation of intensity within a week
      4. running

IV. Mechanics of lifting
   A. Double knee bend pulling technique for the clean and snatch lifts
   B. Squat style snatch and clean
   C. Rotary jerk drive

V. Machines versus free weights

Weight Training Rules

1. Completely unload the bar when finished.

2. Return weights to rack they were taken from.

3. Any equipment (benches, belts, etc.) must be returned to proper place after use.

4. Kilo plates and pound plates are kept separate.

5. No metal plates to be used on the large platform (metal should not touch the wood).

6. Gym bags are to be checked in at the door with attendant or strength coaches, along with I.D.

HPR, Weight Training 1, 2 Credits
Instructor_____

Purpose-Objectives

The ability to properly execute a variety of weight-lifting exercises is a prerequisite for successful participation in a weight-training program. In addition to learning such basic skills, the students are introduced to underlying physiological and biomechanical principles, the application of which results in more efficient and productive training programs. Students are taught the types of physical changes the body can undergo during a weight-lifting program and how minor changes in the structure of the program can emphasize one or another of these changes. Methods for objectively evaluating lifting programs and for measuring strength and power are discussed.

Course outline

I. Course introduction
   A. Definition of terms
   B. Course requirements, student evaluation methods

II. Benefits of weight training
   A. Body composition
      1. percentage fat (underwater weighing, skinfolds measurement, etc.)
      2. lean body weight
      3. relationship to total energy output
   B. Acquisition of strength-power
      1. all or none law
      2. learning effect
         a. recruitment-facilitation
         b. stimulus frequency (increase firing frequency)
         c. synchronization

      3. relationship to fiber type and cross-sectional area
        a. slow and fast twitch fibers
        b. hypertrophy
   C. Muscular endurance
   D. Flexibility
   E. Cardiovascular changes

III. Principles of training
   A. Quantity (volume) and quality (intensity)
      1. work = force × distance (displacement)
      2. power = work /time
      3. variation of volume and intensity and avoidance of overtraining
   B. Year-round training program
      1. macrocycle (year-long)
        a. preparation (hypertrophy-basic strength)
        b. transition 1 (strength-power)
        c. competition (peaking for a meet)
        d. transition 2 (active rest)
      2. Mesocycles
      3. Microcycles
   C. Running and weight training

IV. Mechanics of the lifts
   A. Double knee bend pulling technique for the clean and snatch lifts
   B. Pushing movements
   C. Overhead movements—jerks
   D. Squatting technique
   E. Associated and assistance exercises

V. Machines versus freeweights
   A. Mechanics
   B. Training philosophy

Evaluation Procedures

1. Written examinations—50 points
   Midterm—25%
   Final—25%

2. Notebook (volume, intensity, load, etc.)—25 points

3. Performances (subjective rating of ability to perform lifts with proper techniques, use correct spotting and safety precautions, etc.)—20 points.

4. Attitude (proper attire, attendance, etc.)—5 points

The maximum number of possible points is 100. The student with the most points becomes 100%. All other students are based on that student's score.

$$A = 90\%–100\%$$
$$B = 80\%–89\%$$
$$C = 70\%–79\%$$
$$D = 60\%–69\%$$
$$F = < 60\%$$

Course Schedule 3 days per week (10 weeks)

Week	Day	Objective
1	1	Lecture—Definitions, explanation of expectations
	2	Lecture—Benefits of weight training
	3	Lecture—Benefits of weight training; principles of training
2	1	Lecture—Principles of training, biomechanics
	2	Lecture and demonstration—Lifts, spotting and safety procedures
	3	Students begin training (1 set only)
3	1	*Physical evaluation*
	2	Training (2 sets)
	3	Training (complete workout)
4	1	
	2	
	3	
5	1	Midterm (written)
	2	Training
	3	
6	1	
	2	
	3	
7	1	*Physical evaluation*
	2	Training
	3	
8	1	
	2	
	3	Lecture—weight-training programs for health
9	1	
	2	
	3	
10	1	*Physical evaluation*
	2	REVIEW
	3	Final (written)

Example of a weight-training program for a 10-week course (3 days/week) (8 training weeks):

2 weeks	3 weeks	1 week	1 week	1 week
5×10	3×5	3×5	3×3	3×2
$(1 \times 10)^*$	$(1 \times 5)^*$	$(1 \times 5)^*$	$(1 \times 5)^*$	

Monday and Friday
1. Squats
2. Straight-legged deadlifts (light)
3. Bench press
4. Behind neck press
5. Sit-ups

Wednesday
1. Quarter squat (power rack)
2. Pulls from mid-thigh
3. Shoulder shrugs
4. Lat work
5. Behind neck press
6. Waistwork

Example of a weight-training program for a 20-week course (3 days/week) (8 training weeks):

3 weeks	*3 weeks*	*1 week*	*2 weeks*	*1 week*	*4 weeks*	*4 weeks*
5 × 10	3 × 5	3 × 5	3 × 3	3 × 2	C†	A‡
	(1 × 5)*	(1 × 5)*	(1 × 5)*	(1 × 5)*		

*Warmdown set.
†C—circuit training and/or high energy cost priority system.
‡A—advanced exercise such as snatch and clean and jerk.

Example of an advanced weight-training program for a 10-week course (3 days/week) (4 training weeks):

(1) 2 weeks	(2) 2 weeks	(3) 3 weeks
Sets of 1–3	Sets of 1–3	Various

(1) Powerlifting techniques

(2) Weightlifting techniques

(3) Advanced training (high energy cost → peaking methods, plyometrics, etc.).

Important: All training sessions should be preceded by:

1. Stretching

2. Power snatch

3. Light and moderate warmup sets for the major exercises

Appendix
C

Methods of Estimating
Body Composition

Determination of percentage of body fat from sum of skinfolds

(modified from Durnin and Womersley, 1974).

To determine percentage of body fat, match sum of skinfolds (tricep, bicep, suprailiac, subscapula) row to percentage of fat/age column.

Percentage of body fat, males.[*]

Sum of skinfolds (mm)	Age(years) 17–29	30–39	40–49
15	4.8%	——	——
20	8.1	12.2%	12.2%
25	10.5	14.2	15.0
30	12.9	16.2	17.7
35	14.7	17.7	19.6
40	16.4	19.2	21.4
45	17.7	20.4	23.0
50	19.0	21.5	24.6
55	20.1	22.5	25.9
60	21.2	23.5	27.1
65	22.2	24.3	28.2
70	23.1	25.1	29.3
75	24.0	25.9	30.3
80	24.8	26.6	32.2
85	25.5	27.2	32.1
90	26.2	27.8	33.0
95	26.9	28.4	33.7
100	27.6	29.0	34.4
105	28.2	29.6	35.1
110	28.8	30.1	35.8
115	29.4	30.6	36.4
120	30.0	31.1	37.0
125	30.5	31.5	37.6
130	31.0	31.9	38.2
135	31.5	32.3	38.7
140	32.0	32.7	39.2
145	32.5	33.1	39.7
150	32.9	33.5	40.2
155	33.3	33.9	40.7
160	33.7	34.3	41.2
165	34.1	34.6	41.6
170	34.5	34.8	42.0
175	34.9	——	——
180	35.3	——	——
185	35.6	——	——
190	35.9	——	——

[*]In 66% of males sampled, error for percentage of fat was 5%.

Percentage of body fat, females[*].

Sum of skinfolds (mm)	Age (years) 16–29	30–39	40–49
15	10.5	——	——
20	14.1	17.0	19.8
25	16.8	19.4	22.2
30	19.5	21.8	24.5
35	21.5	23.7	26.4
40	23.4	25.5	28.2
45	25.0	26.9	29.6
50	26.5	28.2	31.0
55	27.8	29.4	32.1
60	29.1	30.6	33.2
65	30.2	31.6	34.1
70	32.1	32.5	35.0
75	32.2	33.4	35.9
80	33.1	34.3	36.7
85	34.0	35.1	37.5
90	34.8	35.8	38.3
95	35.6	36.5	39.0
100	36.4	37.2	39.7
105	37.1	37.9	40.4
110	37.8	38.6	41.0
115	38.4	39.1	41.5
120	39.0	39.6	42.0
125	39.6	40.1	42.5
130	40.2	40.6	43.0
135	40.8	41.1	43.5
140	41.3	41.6	44.0
145	41.8	42.1	44.5
150	42.3	42.6	45.0
155	42.8	43.1	45.1
160	43.3	43.6	45.8
165	43.7	44.0	46.2
170	44.1	44.4	46.6
175	——	44.8	47.0
180	——	45.2	47.4
185	——	45.6	47.8
190	——	45.9	48.2
195	——	46.2	48.5
200	——	46.5	48.8
205	——	——	49.1
210	——	——	49.4

[*]In 66% of females sampled, error for percentage of fat was 3.5%.

Underwater Weighing Procedures

1. Determine **dry weight** in air (on land). Subject should be wearing only what will be worn under water. Stomach, bladder, etc., should be empty.

2. Measure or estimate **residual volume (RV).**

    RV (for adult males) = vital capacity (0.24)
    RV (for adult females) = vital capacity (0.28)
    [or]
    Estimated residual volume (cubic centimeters)*

Age in years	Female	Male
6–10	600	900
11–15	800	1100
16–20	1000	1300
21–25	1200	1500
26–30	1400	1700

*D. R. Lamb. *Physiology of Exercise.* 1984, p. 118.

Note: Some people add 100 ml to residual volume to account for air trapped in the gut.

3. Measure water temperature to determine water density.

4. Correct for water density at different temperatures (V. Christian and R. Johnson. 1984. *Laboratory Experiences in Exercise Physiology.* Bauer Publishers.)

5. Calibrate underwater weighing scale; weigh chair underwater; weigh weight belt under water.

6. Position subject in chair, wet subject completely to remove any air bubbles in clothing and hair.

7. Take measurements: be certain subject is relaxed and completely expires air while under water. Subject should stay under water for 5–10 seconds and remain completely still. If subject does not become completely submersed, add weight around subject's waist.

8. Take 6–10 measurements. Generally measurements taken later will be more accurate as subject learns to relax and to expire maximally.

9. Record to nearest 0.5 kilo.

10. Perform calculations to determine percentage of body fat.

Underwater Weighing (hydrostatic weighing)

Note: See Appendix F for microcomputer program.

Subject information: Sport:_____   Date:_____

Name:_____   Gender:_____   Age:_____

Vital capacity:_____(liters)   Residual volume:_____

Dry weight:_____(lb.)   /   2.205 = _____(kg)

Water temperature:_____(C)

Weight of chair under water:_____(kg)

Weight of weight belt under water:_____(kg)

Subject measurements:

1. ___   2. ___   3. ___   4. ___   5. ___

6. ___   7. ___   8. ___   9. ___   10. ___

Calculations:

DW = Dry weight in kilogram. . ._____

WD = Water density. . ._____

WW = Underwater weight in kilograms. . ._____

RV = Residual volume in liters. . ._____

BD = Body density. . ._____

TW = Tare weight (chair + belt) in kilograms. . ._____

PF = Percentage of fat. . ._____

FW = Fat weight in pounds. . ._____

LBW = Lean body weight in pounds. . ._____

$BD = DW / \{ [DW - (WW - TW)] / DW \} - RV$

$PF = [(4.57 / BD) - 4.142] (100)$

$FW = [(PF / 100) DW] (2.205)$

$LBW = [(DW) (2.205)] - FW$

Log Book Example
of Calculation
# of Volume, Intensity, and Load

Date_____   VJ _____
                          Sum of skinfolds _____
                          Percentage of fat _____
                                   BW _____

Exercise	Sets	Reps/Set	Reps × Sets	Average (kg)	Load (kg)
1. Squats	1	10	10	60	600
	1	10	10	80	800
	3	10	30	100	3,000
Total squats	5	10	50	88	4,400
2. Bench press	1	10	10	60	600
	1	10	10	70	700
	3	10	30	75	2,250
Total bench press	5	10	50	71	3,550

Example of
Weight-Training
Daily Exercise Chart

Student: ALAN O'BRYANT

Group: "A"

Instructor: M. STONE

Time: 2:00 - 3:00 MWF

Note: 20-kg bar = 44 lb.
45-lb. bar = 20.5 kg

Date: 5-18-86   Body weight: 175

| | load / repetitions | | | | |
Exercises	set #1	set #2	set #3	set #4	set #5
PARALLEL SQUATS	295 / 10	295 / 10	295 / 10	295 / 10	295 / 10
CLEAN PULLS (FLOOR)	305 / 10	305 / 10	305 / 8	290 / 10	290 / 10
SIT-UPS	BWT / 30	BWT / 30	BWT / 30	BWT / 30	BWT / 30
BENCH PRESS	205 / 10	205 / 10	205 / 10	205 / 10	205 / 10
HYPEREXTENSIONS	25 / 10	25 / 10	25 / 10		
LEG CURLS	100 / 10	100 / 10	100 / 10		
Comments	"MUSCLES SORE" — "LACK OF SLEEP"				

Weight-Training Daily Exercise Chart

Student: _____

Group: _____

Instructor: _____

Time: _____

Note: 20-kg bar = 44 lb.
45-lb. bar = 20.5 kg

Date: _____ Body weight: _____

Exercises	Load / Repetitions				
	set #1	set #2	set #3	set #4	set #5
Comments					

Date: _____ Body weight: _____

Exercises	Load / Repetitions				
	set #1	set #2	set #3	set #4	set #5
Comments					

Date: _____ Body weight: _____

Exercises	Load / Repetitions				
	set #1	set #2	set #3	set #4	set #5
Comments					

Date: _____ Body weight: _____

Exercises	Load / Repetitions				
	set #1	set #2	set #3	set #4	set #5
Comments					

Weight-Training Daily Exercise Chart

Student: _____

Group: _____

Instructor: _____

Time: _____

Note: 20-kg bar = 44 lb.
45-lb. bar = 20.5 kg

Exercises	Date: _____ Body weight: _____					Date: _____ Body weight: _____				
	Load / Repetitions					Load / Repetitions				
	set #1	set #2	set #3	set #4	set #5	set #1	set #2	set #3	set #4	set #5
Comments										

Exercises	Date: _____ Body weight: _____					Date: _____ Body weight: _____				
	Load / Repetitions					Load / Repetitions				
	set #1	set #2	set #3	set #4	set #5	set #1	set #2	set #3	set #4	set #5
Comments										

Weight-Training Daily Exercise Chart

Student: _____

Group: _____

Instructor: _____

Time: _____

Note: 20-kg bar = 44 lb.
45-lb. bar = 20.5 kg

Exercises	Date: _____ Body weight: _____					Date: _____ Body weight: _____				
	Load / Repetitions					Load / Repetitions				
	set #1	set #2	set #3	set #4	set #5	set #1	set #2	set #3	set #4	set #5
Comments										

Exercises	Date: _____ Body weight: _____					Date: _____ Body weight: _____				
	Load / Repetitions					Load / Repetitions				
	set #1	set #2	set #3	set #4	set #5	set #1	set #2	set #3	set #4	set #5
Comments										

Weight-Training Daily Exercise Chart

Student: _____

Group: _____

Instructor: _____

Time: _____

Note: 20-kg bar = 44 lb.
45-lb. bar = 20.5 kg

Date: _____   Body weight: _____

Exercises	Load / Repetitions				
	set #1	set #2	set #3	set #4	set #5
Comments					

Date: _____   Body weight: _____

Exercises	Load / Repetitions				
	set #1	set #2	set #3	set #4	set #5
Comments					

Date: _____   Body weight: _____

Exercises	Load / Repetitions				
	set #1	set #2	set #3	set #4	set #5
Comments					

Date: _____   Body weight: _____

Exercises	Load / Repetitions				
	set #1	set #2	set #3	set #4	set #5
Comments					

Weight-Training Daily Exercise Chart

Student: _____

Group: _____

Instructor: _____

Time: _____

Note: 20-kg bar = 44 lb.
45-lb. bar = 20.5 kg

Exercises	Date: _____ Body weight: _____					
		Load / Repetitions				
		set #1	set #2	set #3	set #4	set #5
Comments						

Exercises	Date: _____ Body weight: _____					
		Load / Repetitions				
		set #1	set #2	set #3	set #4	set #5
Comments						

Exercises	Date: _____ Body weight: _____					
		Load / Repetitions				
		set #1	set #2	set #3	set #4	set #5
Comments						

Exercises	Date: _____ Body weight: _____					
		Load / Repetitions				
		set #1	set #2	set #3	set #4	set #5
Comments						

Weight-Training Daily Exercise Chart

Student: _____

Group: _____

Instructor: _____

Time: _____

Note: 20-kg bar = 44 lb.
45-lb. bar = 20.5 kg

Date: _____   Body weight: _____

Exercises	Load / Repetitions				
	set #1	set #2	set #3	set #4	set #5
Comments					

Date: _____   Body weight: _____

Exercises	Load / Repetitions				
	set #1	set #2	set #3	set #4	set #5
Comments					

Date: _____   Body weight: _____

Exercises	Load / Repetitions				
	set #1	set #2	set #3	set #4	set #5
Comments					

Date: _____   Body weight: _____

Exercises	Load / Repetitions				
	set #1	set #2	set #3	set #4	set #5
Comments					

Weight-Training Daily Exercise Chart

Student: _____

Group: _____

Instructor: _____

Time: _____

Note: 20-kg bar = 44 lb.
45-lb. bar = 20.5 kg

Exercises	Date: _____ Body weight: _____					Date: _____ Body weight: _____				
	Load / Repetitions					Load / Repetitions				
	set #1	set #2	set #3	set #4	set #5	set #1	set #2	set #3	set #4	set #5
Comments										

Exercises	Date: _____ Body weight: _____					Date: _____ Body weight: _____				
	Load / Repetitions					Load / Repetitions				
	set #1	set #2	set #3	set #4	set #5	set #1	set #2	set #3	set #4	set #5
Comments										

Weight-Training Daily Exercise Chart

Student: _____

Group: _____

Instructor: _____

Time: _____

Note: 20-kg bar = 44 lb.
45-lb. bar = 20.5 kg

Date: _____ Body weight: _____

Exercises	Load / Repetitions						Load / Repetitions				
	set #1	set #2	set #3	set #4	set #5		set #1	set #2	set #3	set #4	set #5

Comments

Date: _____ Body weight: _____

Exercises	Load / Repetitions						Load / Repetitions				
	set #1	set #2	set #3	set #4	set #5		set #1	set #2	set #3	set #4	set #5

Comments

Weight-Training Daily Exercise Chart

Student: _____

Group: _____

Instructor: _____

Time: _____

Note: 20-kg bar = 44 lb.
45-lb. bar = 20.5 kg

Date: _____

Body weight: _____

Exercises	Load / Repetitions				
	set #1	set #2	set #3	set #4	set #5
Comments					

Date: _____

Body weight: _____

Exercises	Load / Repetitions				
	set #1	set #2	set #3	set #4	set #5
Comments					

Date: _____

Body weight: _____

Exercises	Load / Repetitions				
	set #1	set #2	set #3	set #4	set #5
Comments					

Date: _____

Body weight: _____

Exercises	Load / Repetitions				
	set #1	set #2	set #3	set #4	set #5
Comments					

Weight-Training Daily Exercise Chart

Student: _____

Group: _____

Instructor: _____

Time: _____

Note: 20-kg bar = 44 lb.
45-lb. bar = 20.5 kg

Date: _____						Date: _____				
		Body weight: _____						Body weight: _____		
		Load / Repetitions						Load / Repetitions		
Exercises	set #1	set #2	set #3	set #4	set #5	Exercises	set #1	set #2	set #3	set #4	set #5
Comments						Comments					

Date: _____						Date: _____				
		Body weight: _____						Body weight: _____		
		Load / Repetitions						Load / Repetitions		
Exercises	set #1	set #2	set #3	set #4	set #5	Exercises	set #1	set #2	set #3	set #4	set #5
Comments						Comments					

Weight-Training Daily Exercise Chart

Student: _____

Group: _____

Instructor: _____

Time: _____

Note: 20-kg bar = 44 lb.
45-lb. bar = 20.5 kg

Chart 1 (left):

Date: _____   Body weight: _____

Exercises	Load / Repetitions				
	set #1	set #2	set #3	set #4	set #5

Comments

Date: _____   Body weight: _____

Exercises	Load / Repetitions				
	set #1	set #2	set #3	set #4	set #5

Comments

Chart 2 (right):

Date: _____   Body weight: _____

Exercises	Load / Repetitions				
	set #1	set #2	set #3	set #4	set #5

Comments

Date: _____   Body weight: _____

Exercises	Load / Repetitions				
	set #1	set #2	set #3	set #4	set #5

Comments

Weight-Training Daily Exercise Chart

Student: _____

Group: _____

Instructor: _____

Time: _____

Note: 20-kg bar = 44 lb.
45-lb. bar = 20.5 kg

Date: _____   Body weight: _____

Exercises	Load / Repetitions				
	set #1	set #2	set #3	set #4	set #5
Comments					

Date: _____   Body weight: _____

Exercises	Load / Repetitions				
	set #1	set #2	set #3	set #4	set #5
Comments					

Date: _____   Body weight: _____

Exercises	Load / Repetitions				
	set #1	set #2	set #3	set #4	set #5
Comments					

Date: _____   Body weight: _____

Exercises	Load / Repetitions				
	set #1	set #2	set #3	set #4	set #5
Comments					

Weight-Training Daily Exercise Chart

Student: _____

Group: _____

Instructor: _____

Time: _____

Note: 20-kg bar = 44 lb.
45-lb. bar = 20.5 kg

Date: _____

Body weight: _____

Exercises	Load / Repetitions					Body weight:				
	set #1	set #2	set #3	set #4	set #5	set #1	set #2	set #3	set #4	set #5

Comments

Date: _____

Body weight: _____

Exercises	Load / Repetitions					Body weight:				
	set #1	set #2	set #3	set #4	set #5	set #1	set #2	set #3	set #4	set #5

Comments

Weight-Training Daily Exercise Chart

Student: _____

Group: _____

Instructor: _____

Time: _____

Note: 20-kg bar = 44 lb.
45-lb. bar = 20.5 kg

Exercises	Date: _____ Body weight: _____					Date: _____ Body weight: _____				
	Load / Repetitions					Load / Repetitions				
	set #1	set #2	set #3	set #4	set #5	set #1	set #2	set #3	set #4	set #5
Comments										

Exercises	Date: _____ Body weight: _____					Date: _____ Body weight: _____				
	Load / Repetitions					Load / Repetitions				
	set #1	set #2	set #3	set #4	set #5	set #1	set #2	set #3	set #4	set #5
Comments										

Microcomputer Programs

Maximum Based on Reps Program

(Apple II or IIe required)

```
40   HOME
45   HTAB (7)
50   INVERSE : PRINT "MAXIMUM BASE
     D ON REPS PROGRAM"
55   NORMAL : VTAB (3)
60   REM :WRITTEN BY H.S. O'BRYAN
     T 1-1-86; MODIFIED FROM : La
     nders, J. "maximum based on
     reps". NSCA Journal 6(6):60-
     61, 1985.
65   HTAB (14): PRINT "BY H.S. O'B
     RYANT"
70   VTAB (5): HTAB (16): PRINT "(
     JAN 1, 1986)"
80   PRINT
90   PRINT "MODIFIED FROM: Landers
     , J. Maximum basedon reps. N
     SCA Journal 6(6):60-61, 1985
     .
95   PRINT
100  PRINT "CAUTION: Some varianc
     e in prediction of maxs from
     reps may exist from one
        person to another regardi
     ng differences in muscle mas
     s and total body weight.
110  PRINT "Other influences may
     also occur from:   age, gend
     er, the duration and nature
     of previous training, and va
     rious bio-     mechanical an
     d anthropometric factors.
115  PRINT
120  PRINT "IN ADDITION: Accuracy
      in prediction of 1RM is li
     kely reduced as the number o
     f reps used are increased.
130  PRINT : PRINT : HTAB (8): INPUT
     "HOW MANY REPS WERE USED ? "
     ;R
```

```
135  HOME
140  INPUT "WHAT WAS THE MAXIMUM
     WEIGHT (lbs) LIFTEDDURING TH
     E EXECUTION OF THE PREVIOUSL
     Y  STATED REPS ? ";WT
150  Y = 101.30137 + ( - 2.6712328
     9 * R)
160  MAX = WT / (Y / 100)
163  MAX =  INT (MAX * 10) / 10
165  VTAB (12): HTAB (8)
170  PRINT "PREDICTED 1RM (lbs) =
     ";MAX
180  GOSUB 300
190  VTAB (22): HTAB (11)
200  INPUT "ANOTHER CALCULATION ?
                             Y
     /N ";A$
220  IF A$ = "N" THEN  GOTO 240
225  HOME
230  IF A$ = "Y" THEN  GOTO 130
240  HOME
250  END
300  VTAB (20): PRINT "_____

     _____"
310  RETURN
```

Volume-Intensity-Load Program*

(Apple II or IIe required)

```
10   REM  :VOL-INT-LOAD WEIGHT PRO
     GRAM (12-NOV-85) by Jeff Lan
     ders
20   GOTO 40
30   VTAB 4: FOR I = 1 TO 20: PRINT
     SPC( 70): PRINT : NEXT I: RETURN

40   D$ = CHR$ (4)
50   DIM A(73,9,1): REM [exercise,
     set,values](74,10,2)
60   DIM NM$(4),EX$(73),VL(73),V2(
     4),IN(73),I2(4),LO(73),L2(4)
     ,F(4),L(4),LI(73)
70   F(0) = 0:F(1) = 17:F(2) = 41:F
     (3) = 51:F(4) = 60
80   L(0) = 16:L(1) = 40:L(2) = 50:
     L(3) = 59:L(4) = 73
90   FOR I = 0 TO 4: READ NM$(I): NEXT
     I
100  FOR I = 0 TO 73: READ EX$(I)
     : NEXT I
110  HOME : INVERSE : PRINT TAB(
     34): PRINT : PRINT "***** WE
     IGHT RECORD PROGRAM *****": PRINT
     TAB( 34): PRINT : NORMAL
120  PRINT "
                   1. BEGIN New Workout
     File"
130  PRINT "
                   2. READ Old Workout F
     ile from Disk"
140  PRINT "
                   3. CHANGE Workout Fil
     e"
150  PRINT "
                   4. PRINT Workout File
     "
160  PRINT "
                   5. CALCULATE Volume,
     Intensity, Load,": PRINT SPC(
     5)"and K-Factor"
170  PRINT "
                   6. STORE Workout Data
     (if you didn't already)"
180  PRINT "
                   7. STORE SUMMARY Data
     (if you didn't already)"
190  PRINT "
                   8. CATALOG"
200  INPUT "
                   Enter Choice: ";CH
210  ON CH GOSUB 280,860,1010,122
     0,1550,680,1360,240
220  GOTO 110
230  END
240  :
250  HOME : VTAB 10: INPUT "Enter
     Drive # (1 or 2): ";G$
260  PRINT D$;"CATALOG,D";G$
270  INPUT "Press 'RETURN' for Me
     nu: ";G$: RETURN
280  :
290  HOME : INVERSE : PRINT "* B
     EGIN NEW DATA FILE *": NORMAL
295  PRINT "(PLEASE WAIT 20 SECON
     DS!)"
300  FOR I = 0 TO 73: FOR J = 0 TO
     9: FOR K = 0 TO 1:A(I,J,K) =
     0: NEXT K: NEXT J: NEXT I
310  FOR I = 0 TO 73:LI(I) = 0: NEXT
     I
320  VTAB 3: INPUT "Enter Workout
     # (ex. 01): ";W$:W = VAL (
     W$)
330  VTAB 5
340  FOR I = 0 TO 4: PRINT NM$(I)
     : NEXT I
350  PRINT "
                   Enter Exercise Type:
     ";: GET ET$: PRINT ET$
360  IF ET$ = CHR$ (13) THEN 330

370  ET = VAL (ET$)
380  GOSUB 30
390  VTAB 3: HTAB 25: PRINT "Exer
     cise Type is ";NM$(ET)
400  VTAB 5
410  FOR I = F(ET) TO L(ET) STEP
     2
420  PRINT EX$(I);
430  IF I + 1 ) L(ET) THEN 450
440  PRINT TAB( 35);EX$(I + 1)
450  NEXT I
460  INPUT "
                   Enter Exercise #: ";E
     N
470  EV = F(ET) + EN
480  VTAB 16: HTAB 25: PRINT "Exe
     rcise is ";EX$(EV)
490  PRINT
500  VTAB 19: INPUT "Enter # of S
     ETS: ";S1
505  IF S1 ( .5 THEN 600
510  FOR I = 0 TO S1 - 1
520  REM ONERR GOTO 510
530  VTAB 19: PRINT "Enter Set #
     ";I + 1;" REPS:";: INPUT " "
     ;A(EV,I,0)
540  REM POKE 216,0
550  REM ONERR GOTO 540
560  VTAB 19: HTAB 25: PRINT "WEI
     GHT:";: INPUT " ";A(EV,I,1)
570  PRINT
580  REM POKE 216,0
590  NEXT I
600  LI(EV) = S1
610  FOR J = S1 TO 9: FOR K = 0 TO
     1:A(EV,J,K) = 0: NEXT K: NEXT
     J
620  PRINT "Another 1-Workout, 2-
     Ex.Type, 3-Ex., 4-Menu, ";
630  PRINT "5-STORE Data to Disk
     ?";: GET G$:G = VAL (G$): PRINT
     : IF G = 4 THEN RETURN
640  IF G = 5 THEN GOSUB 680: RETURN

650  IF G ( 1 OR G ) 5 THEN 620
660  GOSUB 30
670  ON G GOTO 320,330,400
680  :
690  HOME : INVERSE : PRINT "* S
     TORE DATA TO DISK *": NORMAL

700  PRINT "
                   Current filename is "
     ;F$
710  PRINT "
                   Current Workout # is
     ";W$
720  INPUT "
                   Press (RET) or New Wo
     rkout #: ";G$: IF G$ = "" THEN
     740
730  W$ = G$
740  INPUT "
                   Enter Lifter's Initia
     ls (ex. JEL): ";F$
750  F$ = F$ + "." + W$
760  PRINT D$;"OPEN";F$;",D2": PRINT
     D$;"WRITE";F$
770  PRINT F$
780  FOR I = 0 TO 73: PRINT LI(I)
     : NEXT I
790  FOR I = 0 TO 73: IF LI(I) (
     .5 THEN 810
800  FOR J = 0 TO LI(I) - 1: FOR
     K = 0 TO 1: PRINT A(I,J,K): NEXT
     K: NEXT J
810  NEXT I
820  PRINT D$;"CLOSE";F$
830  PRINT "
                   Data File [ ";F$;" ]
     Stored on Disk"
840  INPUT "
                   Press 'RETURN' for Me
     nu: ";G$
850  RETURN
860  :
870  HOME : INVERSE : PRINT "* R
     EAD DATA FROM DISK *": NORMAL

880  INPUT "
```

---

*The authors extend special thanks to Jeff Lander for his volume-intensity-load program.

Volume-Intensity-Load Program (continued)

```
            Enter Filename (ex. J
EL.01): ";F$
890  PRINT D$;"OPEN";F$;",D2": PRINT
     D$;"READ";F$
900  INPUT F$: PRINT "F$ is ";F$
910  FOR I = 0 TO 73: INPUT LI(I)
     : NEXT I
920  FOR I = 0 TO 73: IF LI(I) (
     .5 THEN 950
930  PRINT EX$(I)
940  FOR J = 0 TO LI(I) - 1: FOR
     K = 0 TO 1: INPUT A(I,J,K): NEXT
     K: NEXT J
950  NEXT I
960  PRINT D$;"CLOSE";F$
970  PRINT "
            Data File [ ";F$;" ]
in Memory"
980  INPUT "
            Press 'RETURN' for Me
nu: ";G$
990  W$ = RIGHT$ (F$,2)
1000 RETURN
1010 :
1020 HOME : INVERSE : PRINT "*
     CHANGE DATA FILE *": NORMAL

1030 PRINT "
            You Must READ Data f
rom Disk First"
1040 PRINT "
            Press (R) to READ Da
ta Now: ";: GET G$: PRINT G$

1050 IF G$ = "R" OR G$ = "r" THEN
     GOSUB 880
1060 PRINT "
            Press (V) to View Fi
le Data: ";: GET G$: PRINT G
$
1070 IF G$ = "V" OR G$ = "v" THEN
     1090
1080 GOTO 1160
1085 PRINT "SET #","REPS","WEIGH
T": PRINT "____","____","__
     "
1090 FOR I = 0 TO 73: IF LI(I) (
     .5 THEN 1140
1100 PRINT EX$(I)
1110 FOR J = 0 TO LI(I) - 1
1120 PRINT J + 1,A(I,J,0),A(I,J,
     1)
1130 NEXT J: PRINT
1140 NEXT I
1150 GOTO 1060
1160 :
1170 INPUT "
            Press 'RETURN' to UP
DATE Data File: ";G$
1180 HOME : GOSUB 330
1190 PRINT "
            DATA UPDATED"
1200 INPUT "
            Press 'RETURN' for M
enu: ";G$
1210 RETURN
1220 :
1230 HOME : INVERSE : PRINT "*
     PRINT DATA FILE *": NORMAL

1240 PRINT "
            Press (P) to Line-Pr
int: ";: GET G$: PRINT G$
1250 IF G$ = "P" OR G$ = "p" THEN
     PR# 1
1260 PRINT F$,"Workout # ";W$
1265 PRINT "SET #","REPS","WEIGH
T": PRINT "____","____","__
     "
1270 FOR I = 0 TO 73: IF LI(I) (
     .5 THEN 1320
1280 PRINT EX$(I)
1290 FOR J = 0 TO LI(I) - 1
1300 PRINT J + 1,A(I,J,0),A(I,J,
     1)
1310 NEXT J: PRINT
1320 NEXT I
1330 IF G$ = "P" OR G$ = "p" THEN
     PR# 0
1340 INPUT "Press 'RETURN' for M
enu: ";G$
1350 RETURN
1360 :
1370 HOME : INVERSE : PRINT "*
     STORE SUMMARY DATA TO DISK
*": NORMAL
1380 PRINT "
            Current Filename is
";F$
1390 PRINT "
            Program will add [.S
UMMARY] to name you enter"
1400 PRINT "Enter New Filename (
     ex. JEL.01)"
1410 INPUT "
            or (RET) for Old:
";G$
1420 IF G$ = "" THEN 1440
1430 F$ = G$
1440 F$ = F$ + ".SUMMARY"
1450 D$ = CHR$ (4)
1460 PRINT "
            Storing ";F$
1470 PRINT D$;"OPEN";F$;",D2": PRINT
     D$;"WRITE";F$
1480 PRINT F$
1490 FOR I = 0 TO 73: PRINT VL(I
     ): PRINT LO(I): NEXT I
1500 FOR I = 0 TO 4: PRINT V2(I)
     : PRINT L2(I): NEXT I
1510 PRINT D$;"CLOSE";F$
1520 PRINT "
            Data File [ ";F$;" ]
Stored on Disk"
1530 INPUT "
            Press 'RETURN' for M
enu: ";G$
1540 RETURN
1550 :
1560 HOME : INVERSE : PRINT "*
     CALC VOL, INT, LOAD & K-FACT
OR *": NORMAL
1570 PRINT "
            Calculating Volume,
Intensity and Load"
1580 PRINT "by individual exerci
se"
1590 FOR I = 0 TO 73:VL(I) = 0:I
     N(I) = 0:LO(I) = 0: NEXT I
1600 FOR I = 0 TO 73: IF A(I,0,0
     ) ( .5 THEN 1650
1610 FOR J = 0 TO 9: IF A(I,J,0)
     ( .5 THEN 1650
1620 VL(I) = VL(I) + A(I,J,0)
1630 LO(I) = LO(I) + A(I,J,0) * A
     (I,J,1)
1640 NEXT J
1650 NEXT I
1660 FOR I = 0 TO 73: IF VL(I) (
     .5 THEN 1680
1670 IN(I) = LO(I) / VL(I)
1680 NEXT I
1690 PRINT "
            Calculating Volume,
Intensity and Load"
1700 PRINT "by Exercise Category
"
1710 FOR I = 0 TO 4:V2(I) = 0:L2
     (I) = 0:I2(I) = 0: NEXT I
1720 FOR G = 0 TO 4: FOR I = F(G
     ) TO L(G):V2(G) = V2(G) + VL
     (I):L2(G) = L2(G) + LO(I): NEXT
     I: NEXT G
1730 FOR I = 0 TO 4: IF V2(I) (
     .5 THEN 1750
1740 I2(I) = L2(I) / V2(I)
1750 NEXT I
1760 PRINT "
            Print Vol, Int & Loa
d by Exercise"
```

Volume-Intensity-Load Program (continued)

```
1770  PRINT "Press (P) to Line-Pr
      int: ";: GET G$: PRINT G$
1780  IF G$ = "P" OR G$ = "p" THEN
      PR# 1
1790  PRINT F$,"Workout # ";W$
1800  PRINT "Exercise"; TAB( 35);
      "Volume","Intensity","Load"
1810  FOR I = 0 TO 73: IF VL(I) <
      .5 THEN 1830
1820  PRINT EX$(I); TAB( 35);VL(I
      ),IN(I),LO(I)
1830  NEXT I
1840  PR# 0
1850  PRINT "
              Print Vol, Int & Loa
      d by Category"
1860  PRINT "Press (P) to Line-Pr
      int: ";: GET G$: PRINT G$
1870  IF G$ = "P" OR G$ = "p" THEN
      PR# 1
1880  PRINT F$,"Workout # ";W$
1890  PRINT "Exercise"; TAB( 35);
      "Volume","Intensity","Load"
1900  FOR I = 0 TO 4: PRINT NM$(I
      ); TAB( 35);V2(I),I2(I),L2(I
      ): NEXT I
1910  PR# 0
1920  PRINT "
              Press (K) to calcula
      te K-Factor: ";: GET G$: PRINT
      G$
1930  IF G$ = "K" OR G$ = "k" THEN
      1950
1940  GOTO 2200
1950  HOME : INVERSE : PRINT "*
      CALCULATE K-FACTOR *": NORMAL

1960  VTAB 5
1970  FOR I = 0 TO 4: PRINT NM$(I
      ): NEXT I
1980  PRINT "
              Enter Exercise Type:
      ";: GET ET$: PRINT ET$
1990  IF ET$ = CHR$ (13) THEN 33
      0
2000  ET = VAL (ET$)
2010  GOSUB 30
2020  VTAB 3: HTAB 25: PRINT "Exe
      rcise Type is ";NM$(ET)
2030  VTAB 5
2040  FOR I = F(ET) TO L(ET) STEP
      2
2050  PRINT EX$(I);
2060  IF I + 1 ) L(ET) THEN 2080
2070  PRINT  TAB( 35);EX$(I + 1)
2080  NEXT I
2090  INPUT "
              Enter Exercise #: ";
      EN
```

```
2100  IF EN$ = CHR$ (13) THEN 20
      30
2110  EV = F(ET) + EN
2120  VTAB 16: HTAB 25: PRINT "Ex
      ercise is ";EX$(EV)
2130  PRINT
2140  PRINT "
              Intensity is ";IN(EV
      )
2150  INPUT "
              Projected Maximum fo
      r this Lift: ";PM
2160  PRINT "
              K-Factor is ";IN(EV)
      / PM
2170  PRINT "
              Press (RET) or (A) f
      or Another: ";: GET G$: PRINT
      G$
2180  IF G$ = "A" OR G$ = "a" THEN
      1950
2190  RETURN
2200  :
2210  PRINT "
              Press (S) to Store S
      ummary Data: ";: GET G$: PRINT
      G$
2220  IF G$ = "S" OR G$ = "s" THEN
      2240
2230  GOTO 2260
2240  INVERSE : PRINT "
              * STORE S
      UMMARY DATA TO DISK *": NORMAL

2250  GOSUB 1380
2260  RETURN
2270  DATA "0- Squats","1- Pulls"
      ,"2- Presses","3- Jerks","4-
      Assistance"
2280  DATA " 0- Full Squat (para.
      or below)"," 1- Front Squat"
      ," 2- Narrowstance Squat","
      3- 1/4 Squat (rack)"," 4- 1/
      4 Squat (free)"," 5- 1/3 Squ
      at (rack)"
2290  DATA " 6- 1/4 Fr.Squat (rac
      k)"," 7- 1/4 Fr.Squat (free)
      "," 8- Dead Stop (bottom)","
      9- Dead Stop (pull pos.)","
      10- Overhead Squat","11- Dro
      p Snatch"
2300  DATA "12- VJ's (regular)","
      13- VJ's (pause)","14- VJ's
      (dumb.)","15- VJ's (dumb./pa
      use)","16- VJ's (dumb./pause
      /drop)"
2310  DATA " 0- C.G.Pulls (floor)
      "," 1- C.G.Pulls (knee)"," 2
```

```
      - C.G.Pulls (thigh)"," 3- C.
      G.Pulls (hang)"," 4- C.G.S.S
      ."," 5- S.G.Pulls (floor)"
2320  DATA " 6- S.G.Pulls (knee)"
      ," 7- S.G.Pulls (thigh)"," 8
      - S.G.Pulls (hang)"," 9- S.G
      .S.S.","10- Cleans","11- C &
      J"
2330  DATA "12- Snatch","13- S.S.
      Clean","14- S.S.Snatch","15-
      Power Snatch","16- Power Cl
      ean","17- Clean (hang)","18-
      Snatch (hang)"
2335  DATA "19- Snatch (knee)","2
      0- Snatch (thigh)","21- Clea
      n (knee)","22- Clean (thigh)
      ","23- Good Morning"
2340  DATA " 0- Bench Press"," 1-
      B.P.(dumb.)"," 2- Inclines"
      ," 3- I.P.(dumb.)"," 4- B.N.
      P.(seated)"
2350  DATA " 5- B.N.P.(standing)"
      ," 6- Dumb.Press (seated)","
      7- Dumb.Press (standing)","
      8- Recovery Press (partial)
      "," 9- B.N.P.(wide)"
2360  DATA " 0- Push Press"," 1-
      Push Jerk"," 2- Push Press (
      behind)"," 3- Push Jerk (beh
      ind)"," 4- Jerk"
2370  DATA " 5- Jerk (behind)","
      6- Split Press"," 7- Split R
      ecovery"," 8- Squat Recovery
      "
2380  DATA " 0- Leg Extension","
      1- Leg Curl"," 2- S.L.D.L.",
      " 3- Lat"," 4- Cable Row","
      5- Upright Row"
2390  DATA " 6- Upright Row (wide
      )"," 7- Bent-Over-Row"," 8-
      Bent-Over-Row (dumb.)"," 9-
      Lying Fr.Raise (snatch)","10
      - Lateral Raise","11- Waist
      Work","12- Back Hypers","13-
      Tricep Work"
```

Hydrostatic Calculations

(Apple II or IIe required)

```
40   HOME
60   INVERSE : PRINT "HYDROSTATIC
     WEIGHING CALCULATION PROGRAM
     "
65   REM : WRITTEN BY H.S. O'BRYAN
     T 1-1-86
70   NORMAL
75   VTAB (4): HTAB (14)
80   PRINT "BY H.S. O'BRYANT"
90   VTAB (6): HTAB (16): PRINT "(
     JAN 1, 1986)"
100  VTAB (9): HTAB (6)
105  INPUT "DRY WEIGHT IN POUNDS
     ?   ";DW
110  DW = DW / 2.205
120  VTAB (11): HTAB (6)
125  INPUT "VITAL CAPACITY IN LIT
     ERS ? ";VC
130  VTAB (14): HTAB (14)
140  HTAB (9)
150  INPUT "MALE = 'M' FEMALE = '
     F'
     ";SEX$
160  IF SEX$ = "F" THEN B = .28
170  IF SEX$ = "M" THEN B = .24
185  RV = VC * B
190  REM  : WATER TEMP CORRECTIO
     N              ]    RO
     UTINE - LINES            25
     0 TO 900
200  HOME
210  INPUT "TRUE UNDERWATER WEIGH
     T IN (kg) ?    ";WW
220  PRINT
250  INPUT "WATER TEMPERATURE ?
     ";A
252  PRINT
253  INPUT "IS WATER TEMPERATURE
     IN CENTIGRADE (C)  OR FAHREN
     HEIT (F) ? ";A$
255  IF A$ = "F" THEN  GOTO 257
256  IF A$ = "C" THEN  GOTO 260
257  A = (5 / 9) * (A - 32)
258  A =  INT (A * 1) / 1
260  IF A = 20 THEN 500
270  IF A = 21 THEN 520
280  IF A = 22 THEN 540
290  IF A = 23 THEN 560
300  IF A = 24 THEN 580
310  IF A = 25 THEN 600
320  IF A = 26 THEN 620
330  IF A = 27 THEN 640
340  IF A = 28 THEN 660
350  IF A = 29 THEN 680
360  IF A = 30 THEN 700
370  IF A = 31 THEN 720
380  IF A = 32 THEN 740
390  IF A = 33 THEN 760
400  IF A = 34 THEN 780
410  IF A = 35 THEN 800
420  IF A = 36 THEN 820
430  IF A = 37 THEN 840
440  IF A = 38 THEN 860
450  IF A = 39 THEN 880
460  IF A = 40 THEN 900
500  WD = .99823: GOTO 1000
520  WD = .99802: GOTO 1000
540  WD = .99780: GOTO 1000
560  WD = .99756: GOTO 1000
580  WD = .99732: GOTO 1000
600  WD = .99707: GOTO 1000
620  WD = .99681: GOTO 1000
640  WD = .99654: GOTO 1000
660  WD = .99626: GOTO 1000
680  WD = .99597: GOTO 1000
700  WD = .99567: GOTO 1000
720  WD = .99537: GOTO 1000
740  WD = .99505: GOTO 1000
760  WD = .99473: GOTO 1000
780  WD = .99440: GOTO 1000
800  WD = .99406: GOTO 1000
820  WD = .99371: GOTO 1000
840  WD = .99336: GOTO 1000
860  WD = .99299: GOTO 1000
880  WD = .99262: GOTO 1000
900  WD = .99224
1000 BD = DW / (((DW - WW) / WD) -
     RV)
1010 PF = ((4.57 / BD) - 4.142) *
     100
1015 PF =  INT (PF * 10) / 10.0
1020 PRINT
1030 PRINT "PERCENT FAT = ";PF
1035 DW = DW * 2.205
1040 FW = DW * (PF / 100)
1050 PRINT
1060 PRINT "FAT WEIGHT (lbs) = "
     ;FW
1070 LBM = DW - FW
1080 PRINT
1090 PRINT "LEAN BODY MASS (lbs)
     = ";LBM
1100 PRINT
1110 PRINT "_____
     _____"
1120 PRINT
1130 INPUT "TARGET WEIGHT CALCUL
     ATIONS ?    Y/N   ";TGC$
1140  IF TGC$ = "Y" THEN  GOTO 13
     00
1150  INPUT "ANOTHER % FAT CALCUL
     ATION ? Y/N     ";CAL$
1160 HOME
1170  IF CAL$ = "Y" THEN  GOTO 40
1180  IF CAL$ = "N" THEN  GOTO 11
     90
1190 END
1300 HOME
1310 INPUT "WHAT % FAT DO YOU WI
     SH TO ACHIEVE ?    ";TF
1320 HOME
1330 PC = 1.00 - (TF / 100)
1340 TW = LBM / PC
1350 TW =  INT (TW * 10) / 10.0
1360 WL = DW - TW
1370 WL =  INT (WL * 10) / 10.0
1380 TCD = WL * 3500
1390 TCD =  INT (TCD * 10) / 10.0
1400 DA = TCD / 2000
1410 DA =  INT (DA * 10) / 10
1420 DB = DA * 2
1430 PRINT "AT THE SAME LEAN BOD
     Y MASS. THE TARGET  BODY WEI
     GHT (lbs) = ";TW
1440 PRINT
1450 PRINT "WEIGHT LOSS (lbs) WO
     ULD BE = ";WL
1460 PRINT
1470 PRINT "(ONE POUND OF FAT LO
     SS REPRESENTS A 3500 KCAL DE
     FICIT.)"
1480 PRINT
1490 PRINT
1500 PRINT "TOTAL CALORIC DEFICI
     T NECESSARY TO      ACHIEVE
     TARGET WEIGHT (kcal) = ";TCD
1510 PRINT
1520 PRINT
1530 PRINT "THE CALORIC DEFICIT
     PER DAY SHOULD NOT  EXCEED 1
     000 TO 2000 KCAL."
1540 PRINT
1550 PRINT
1560 PRINT "THE NUMBER OF DAYS T
     O LOSE TO THE TARGETWEIGHT S
     HOULD BE BETWEEN ";DA" AND "
     ;DB
1570 PRINT "_____
     ____"
1580 PRINT
1590 INPUT "ANOTHER % FAT CALCUL
     ATION ? Y/N       ";CAL$
1600 HOME
1610 IF CAL$ = "Y" THEN  GOTO 40
1620 IF CAL$ = "N" THEN  GOTO 11
     90
```

Skinfold Calculations

(Apple II or IIe required)

```
40   HOME
60   INVERSE : PRINT "BODY COMPOSI
     TION PROGRAM USING SKINFOLDS
     "
65   REM  : WRITTEN BY H.S. O'BRYA
     NT 1-1-86
70   NORMAL
75   VTAB (4): HTAB (14)
77   PRINT "BY H.S. O'BRYANT"
78   VTAB (6): HTAB (16): PRINT "(
     JAN 1, 1986)"
80   VTAB (9): HTAB (14)
90   PRINT "MALE OR FEMALE ?": VTAB
     (14)
95   HTAB (9)
100  INPUT "MALE = 'M'   FEMALE =
     'F'             QUIT = 'Q
     '   ";SEX$
110  IF SEX$ = "Q" THEN  GOTO 635

120  IF SEX$ = "F" THEN  GOTO 390

130  HOME
140  PRINT "(BODY COMPOSITION FOR
     MALES AGES 18-26  YEARS)"
150  PRINT
160  PRINT
164  PRINT
165  PRINT
170  INPUT "WHAT IS THE PERSON'S
     BODY WEIGHT IN LBS  ?    ";B
     WT
180  PRINT
190  IF BWT = 0 GOTO 170
200  PRINT
210  INPUT "WHAT IS THE PERSON'S
     THIGH SKINFOLD IN  (MM) ?
     ";THIGH
215  PRINT
220  IF THIGH = 0 GOTO 210
230  INPUT "WHAT IS THE PERSON'S
     SUBSCAPULAR       SKINFOLD
     IN (MM) ?       ";SUB
240  PRINT
250  IF SUB = 0 GOTO 230
260  D = 1.1043 - 0.00133 * THIGH -
     0.00131 * SUB
270  CENT = 100 * (4.570 / D - 4.1
     42)
280  CENT =  INT (CENT * 10) / 10.
     0
290  PF = BWT * (CENT / 100)
300  LBW = BWT - PF
305  HOME
310  PRINT "THE PERCENT OF BODY F
     AT IS                  ";C
     ENT
320  PRINT

330  PRINT "THE FAT WEIGHT IN POU
     NDS IS                  ";P
     F
340  PRINT
350  PRINT "THE LEAN BODY MASS IN
     POUNDS IS              ";L
     BW
352  PRINT
353  PRINT "  _____"
354  PRINT
355  INPUT "TARGET WEIGHT CALCULA
     TIONS    ?        Y/N   ";TGC$

356  IF TGC$ = "Y" THEN  GOTO 800

360  INPUT "ANOTHER % FAT CALCULA
     TION ?   Y/N    ";CAL$
370  IF CAL$ = "N" THEN  GOTO 635

380  IF CAL$ = "Y" THEN  GOTO 90
390  HOME
400  PRINT "BODY COMPOSITION FOR
     FEMALES AGES 17-25 YRS"
410  PRINT
420  PRINT
430  INPUT "WHAT IS THE PERSON'S
     BODY WEIGHT IN LBS ?      ";B
     WT
440  PRINT
450  IF BWT = 0 GOTO 430
460  PRINT
470  INPUT "WHAT IS THE PERSON'S
     SUPRAILIAC SKINFOLD IN (MM)
     ?        ";SUP
480  PRINT
490  IF SUP = 0 GOTO 470
500  INPUT "WHAT IS THE PERSON'S
     TRICEPS SKINFOLD IN (MM) ?
     ";TRI
505  HOME
510  IF TRI = 0 GOTO 500
520  D = 1.0764 - 0.00081 * SUP -
     0.00088 * TRI
525  CENT = 100 * (4.570 / D - 4.1
     42)
527  CENT =  INT (CENT * 10) / 10.
     0
530  PF = BWT * (CENT / 100)
540  LBW = BWT - PF
550  PRINT "THE PERCENT OF BODY F
     AT IS       ";CENT
560  PRINT
570  PRINT "THE FAT WEIGHT IN POU
     NDS IS      ";PF
580  PRINT
590  PRINT "THE LEAN BODY MASS IN
     POUNDS IS     ";LBW

600  PRINT
610  PRINT "  _____"

620  PRINT
623  INPUT "TARGET WEIGHT CALCULA
     TIONS ?    Y/N    ";TGC$
625  IF TGC$ = "Y" THEN  GOTO 800

630  INPUT "ANOTHER % FAT CALCULA
     TION ? Y/N        ";CAL$
635  HOME
640  IF CAL$ = "Y" THEN  GOTO 80
650  IF CAL$ = "N" THEN  GOTO 660

660  END
800  HOME
810  INPUT "WHAT % FAT DO YOU WIS
     H TO ACHIEVE ?      ";TF
813  HOME
814  PC = 1.00 - (TF / 100)
820  TW = LBW / PC
823  TW =  INT (TW * 10) / 10.0
835  WL = BWT - TW
837  WL =  INT (WL * 10) / 10.0
840  TCD = WL * 3500
845  TCD =  INT (TCD * 10) / 10.0
850  DA = TCD / 2000
855  DA =  INT (DA * 10) / 10
856  DB = DA * 2
860  PRINT "AT THE SAME LEAN BODY
     MASS. THE TARGET  BODY WEIG
     HT (lbs) = ";TW
870  PRINT
880  PRINT "WEIGHT LOSS IN (lbs)
     WOULD = ";WL
881  PRINT
882  PRINT "(ONE POUND OF FAT LOS
     S REPRESENTS A 3500 KCAL DEF
     ICIT.)"
885  PRINT
890  PRINT
895  PRINT "THE TOTAL CALORIC DEF
     ICIT NECESSARY TO  ACHIEVE T
     ARGET WEIGHT (kcal) = ";TCD
897  PRINT
898  PRINT
900  PRINT "THE CALORIC DEFICIT P
     ER CAY SHOULD NOT  EXCEED 10
     00 TO 2000 KCAL."
910  PRINT
920  PRINT
1000 PRINT "THE NUMBER OF DAYS T
     O LOSE TO THE TARGETWEIGHT S
     HOULD BE BETWEEN ";DA" AND "
     ;DB
1010 PRINT "  _____"

1017 PRINT
1020 INPUT "ANOTHER % FAT CALCUL
     ATION ? Y/N        ";CAL$
1026 HOME
1030 IF CAL$ = "Y" THEN  GOTO 80

1040 IF CAL$ = "N" THEN  GOTO 66
     0
```

Power Index Program (From Vertical Jump)

(Apple II or IIe required)

```
40   HOME
45   HTAB (3)
50   INVERSE : PRINT "POWER INDEX
     PROGRAM FOR VERTICAL JUMP"
55   NORMAL : VTAB (3)
60   REM :WRITTEN BY H.S. O'BRYANT
     1-1-86
65   HTAB (14): PRINT "BY H.S. O'B
     RYANT"
70   VTAB (5): HTAB (16): PRINT "(
     JAN 1, 1986)"
100  A = BWT
110  B = VJ
115  VTAB (10): HTAB (3)
120  INPUT "WHAT IS THE PERSON'S
     BODY WEIGHT IN      POUNDS ?
     ";BWT
130  VTAB (13): HTAB (3): INPUT "
     WHAT IS THE PERSON'S VERTICA
     L JUMP ?               ";VJ

131  VTAB (16): HTAB (3): INPUT "
     IS THE VERTICAL JUMP MEASURE
     D IN         CENTIMETERS (CM)
     OR INCHES (IN) ?";V$
132  IF V$ = "CM" THEN  GOTO 134
133  VJ = VJ * 2.54
134  PWR = SQR (4.9) *  SQR (VJ /
     100) * BWT / 2.205
135  VTAB (19): HTAB (3): PRINT "
     POWER INDEX = ";PWR" (kg-m/s
     ec)"
140  GOSUB 300
145  X = X
147  VTAB (22): HTAB (11)
155  INPUT "ANOTHER CALCULATION ?
                              Y/
     N ";A$
160  IF A$ = "N" THEN  GOTO 170
165  IF A$ = "Y" THEN  GOTO 40
170  END
300  VTAB (20): PRINT "_____
     _____
     _"
310  RETURN
```

Weightlifting and Powerlifting Rules

The following are the basic rules for weightlifting and powerlifting. Rule changes are made frequently; therefore, interested readers should contact the U.S. Weightlifting Federation or the U.S. Powerlifting Federation for details.

Weightlifting

Weightlifting currently consists of two lifts, the snatch and the clean and jerk. The snatch is the first lift in competition. Only three attempts are allowed for each lift. Each lift is judged by three referees. Each referee has control of two lights, one signifying a good lift (usually white) and the other signifying an unacceptable lift (usually red). Thus, a good lift is signified by 2 or 3 white lights. The head referee sits directly in front of the platform (4 m × 4 m) and is responsible for giving the lifter the down signal (completion of the lift). Causes for disqualification are:

1. Unacceptable dress; national meets require a one-piece suit.

2. Unacceptable bandaging or wraps, or a support belt wider than 10 cm.

3. Making more than one motion in the snatch (the snatch is brought from the floor to full arm extension overhead in one motion).

4. Not racking the bar correctly (catching the bar low on the chest and pushing the bar up to the shoulders during the clean portion of the clean and jerk.) During the clean and jerk, the bar is first brought to the shoulders, then, using the legs, it is jerked overhead.

5. Press out (arms bending or not locked bending during the lift).

6. Walking off the platform during the execution of a lift.

7. Not having the feet parallel at the completion of a lift.

8. Not waiting for the *down* signal before returning the bar to the floor.

9. Dropping the bar from an excessive height.

10. Allowing any part of the lifter (including wraps) to touch the platform.

Powerlifting

The platform and referee setup is similar to that of weightlifting. As with weightlifting, the head referee signifies the completion of a lift with a down signal. The three lifts contested and the order of events are the squat, bench press, and dead lift. In the squat and bench press, the head referee gives a start signal. Causes for disqualification are:

1. Inappropriate attire; a one-piece suit is required.

2. Unacceptable bandaging or wraps or a support belt wider than 10cm.

Squat

1. Not waiting for the start (squat) signal. Lifter must be stable and standing erect before the referee will signal squat.

2. Replacing the bar in the squat racks before the down (rack) signal.

3. Not going low enough. The top of the thighs must break parallel with the floor.

4. Carrying the bar too low on the shoulders (back).

Bench Press

1. Beginning the lift before the appropriate signal. (The lifter can lower the bar to the chest, but it must become stationary before the head referee will give the start signal (a hand clap).

2. Replacing the bar in the racks before the down (rack) signal.

3. Uneven arm extension.

4. Raising the hips off the bench during the lift.

5. Using too wide a grip.

Deadlift

1. Replacing the bar on the floor before the down signal (lifter initiates lift).

2. Excessive bouncing or hitching on the thighs during the lift.

3. Stopping the bar during the lift.

4. Not standing fully erect with shoulders back.

Weightlifting and powerlifting are divided into body weight classes. These body weight classes are different for the two sports and for men and women within the same sport.

References for Additional Information

The following references are not cited in the text.

Textbooks, Manuals, and Yearbooks

1. Fleck, S. and W. Kraemer. A weight-training text to be published by Human Kinetics, Urbana, Ill.

2. Garhammer, J. J. Strength training *Sports Illustrated.* Time/Life Publications, New York.

3. Miller, C. Olympic Lifting Training Manual. *Iron Man,* 808 W. Fifth St., Alliance, NE 69301.

4. Roman, R. A., and M. S. Shakirzynow. *The Snatch and Clean and Jerk* (Translation by Andrew Charniga). 11024 Denne, LiVonia, MI 48150.

5. Russian Weightlifting Yearbooks (Translation by Andrew Charniga). 11024 Denne, LiVonia, MI 48150.

6. Star, B. *The Strongest Shall Survive.* Fitness Products Ltd., 129 Seven Ave. Annapolis, MD 21403.

Sports Journals, Periodicals, Newsletters, Etc.

1. *International Weightlifter,* Box 65835, Los Angeles, CA 90054

2. *Iron Man,* 808 W. Fifth St., Alliance, NE 69301

3. *National Strength and Conditioning Association Journal,* 251 Capital Beach Blvd., Lincoln, NE 68528

4. National Strength Research Center Newsletter, *Strength-Power Update,* 2050 Memorial Coliseum, Auburn University, AL 36849-3501

5. *Sport Fitness,* 21100 Erwin Street, Woodland Hills, CA 91367

6. *Strength and Health,* P.O. Box 1707, York, PA 17405

7. *Strength Training for Beauty,* 1400 Stierlin Road, Mountview, CA 94043

8. *Track and Field Quarterly Report,* 1705 Evanston Street, Kalamazoo, MI 49008

9. *Track Technique,* Box 296, Los Altos, CA 94022

10. *Weightlifters Newsletter,* 30 Combria Road, W. Newton, MA 02165

11. *World Weightlifting,* IWF Secretariat, 1374 Budapest, pf 614, Hungary

Resource/Professional Organizations

1. American College of Sports Medicine
   P.O. Box 1440
   Indianapolis, IN 46206

2. National Strength and Conditioning Association
   P.O. Box 81410
   Lincoln, NE 68501

3. National Strength Research Center
   Department of HPER
   2050 Memorial Coliseum
   Auburn University, AL 36849

GUIDELINES FOR USING THIS TEXT

The following table suggests the appropriate reading level for beginning, intermediate, and advanced (including academic) classes.

	Beginner	Intermediate	Advanced
Introduction	X	X	X
1 Muscle Physiology			
Muscle Structure		X	
Dynamics of Contraction		X	
Muscle Fiber Types		X	X
2 Bioenergetics			
The Biological Energy Systems			X
The Metabolic Costs of Weight Training		X	
Nutrition and Athletic Performance		X	X
Protein Metabolism			X
Carbohydrate Metabolism			X
Lipid Metabolism			X
Hormonal Control of Energy Metabolism			X
3 The Importance of Weight Training as a Lifetime Physical Activity			
Cardiovascular Fitness	X		
Effects of Weight Training on Cardiovascular Factors		X	
Strength	X		
Flexibility	X		
Body Composition	X		
Volume and Intensity Considerations	X		
Psychological Considerations	X		
4 The Biomechanics of Lifting			
Movement Terminology	X		
Muscle Dynamics			X
Body Mechanics		X	
Plyometrics		X	
5 Considerations for Gaining a Strength-Power Training Effect: Training Principles and Modes and Methods			
Basic Principles	X	X	
Strength-Power Gains		X	
Mechanical Specificity		X	
Research: Comparisons of Modes and Methods			X
6 Training Theory and Its Adaptation to Resistance Training			
Basic Principles and Concepts	X		
Results of Research		X	
Additional Considerations		X	
Combination Training		X	
Special Considerations for the Preparation of Strength-Power Athletes		X	
Basic Concepts Concerning Anaerobic Capacity			X
7 Practical Considerations for Weight Training			
Estimation of Workload	X		
Methods of Varying Intensity, Volume, and Load	X		
Frequency of Training	X		
Workout Length	X		
Exercise Order	X		
Exercise Selection	X		
Exercise Speed		X	
Effective Resistance (Overload)	X	X	
Methods of Strength Training	X		
Repetitions per Set	X		
Isometric Training		X	
Eccentric Training		X	
Warmup	X		
Breathing During Weight-Training Exercise	X		
Factors That Affect Strength, Power and Muscular Endurance		X	
Injuries	X		

8 Practical Testing and Progress Evaluation		
Determining Anaerobic Power		X
Determining Anaerobic Capacity		X
Determining Muscular Strength and Endurance		X
Evaluating Skill		X
Evaluating Physique and Body Composition		X
Evaluating Cardiovascular Fitness		X
9 Ergogenic Aids: Difficult Problems and Different Perspectives		
Current Status of Drug Use	X	
Drug Testing in Sports	X	
10 Lifting Technique and Illustrations		
Flexibility Drills and Exercises	X	
Multijoint/Large Muscle Mass Exercises	X	X
Associative Lifts	X	X
Assisstive Lifts	X	
Jump Drills		X
11 Setting Up the Program		
Program and Course Outline		X
Weight Room Layout	X	
Glossary of Terms	X	